THE ROAD TO VICTORY

EDITOR
ROBERT O'NEILL
WITH A FOREWORD BY
DALE DYE

THE ROAD TO VICTORY

FROM PEARL HARBOR TO OKINAWA

OSPREY
PUBLISHING

First published in Great Britain in 2011 by Osprey Publishing,
Midland House, West Way, Botley, Oxford, OX2 0PH, UK
44-02 23rd Street, Suite 219, Long Island City, NY 11101, USA
E-mail: info@ospreypublishing.com
Osprey Publishing is part of the Osprey Group

Previously published as Campaign 18, *Guadalcanal 1942*, Joseph Mueller, 1992; Campaign 62, *Pearl Harbor 1941*, Carl Smith, 1999; Campaign 77, *Tarawa 1943*, Derrick Wright, 2000; Campaign 81, *Iwo Jima 1945*, Derrick Wright, 2001; Campaign 96, *Okinawa 1945*, Gordon Rottman, 2002; Campaign 110, *Peleliu 1944*, Jim Moran and Gordon Rottman, 2002; Campaign 146, *Marshall Islands 1944*, Gordon Rottman, 2004; Campaign 163, *Leyte Gulf 1944*, Bernard Ireland, 2006; Campaign 214, *Coral Sea 1942*, Mark Stille, 2009; Campaign 226, *Midway 1942*, Mark Stille, 2010.

A CIP catalogue record for this book is available from the British Library
ISBN: 978 1 84908 716 2
ePub EBOOK ISBN: 978 1 84908 887 9
PDF EBOOK ISBN: 978 1 84908 917 3

Page layout by Josh Beatman, Brainchild Studios
Index by Sandra Shotter
Typeset in Gotham Book and MetaSerif
Originated by Blenheim Colour, UK
Printed in China through Bookbuilders

11 12 13 14 15 10 9 8 7 6 5 4 3 2 1

Osprey Publishing is supporting the Woodland Trust, the UK's leading woodland conservation charity, by funding the dedication of trees.

www.ospreypublishing.com

Front Cover: USMC via Tom Laemlein
Back Cover: NARA
Title Page: USMC via Tom Laemlein
Contents Page: NARA

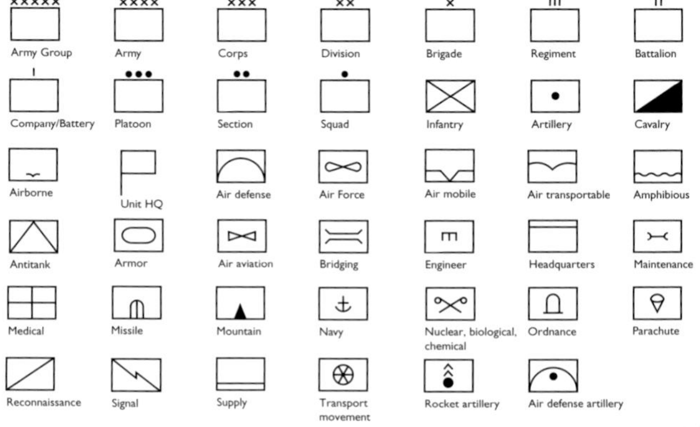

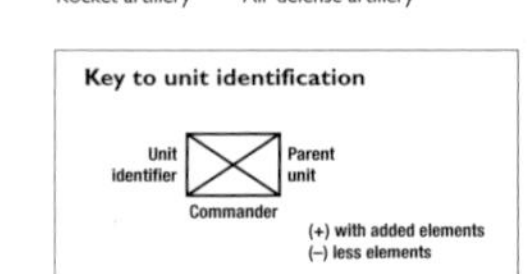

CONTENTS

FOREWORD 7

INTRODUCTION 11

PEARL HARBOR *by Carl Smith* 15

CORAL SEA *by Mark Stille* 43

MIDWAY *by Mark Stille* 65

GUADALCANAL *by Joseph Mueller* 91

TARAWA *by Derrick Wright* 117

MARSHALL ISLANDS *by Gordon L. Rottman* 141

PELELIU *by Jim Moran and Gordon L. Rottman* 167

LEYTE GULF *by Bernard Ireland* 191

IWO JIMA *by Derrick Wright* 217

OKINAWA *by Gordon L. Rottman* 245

INDEX 268

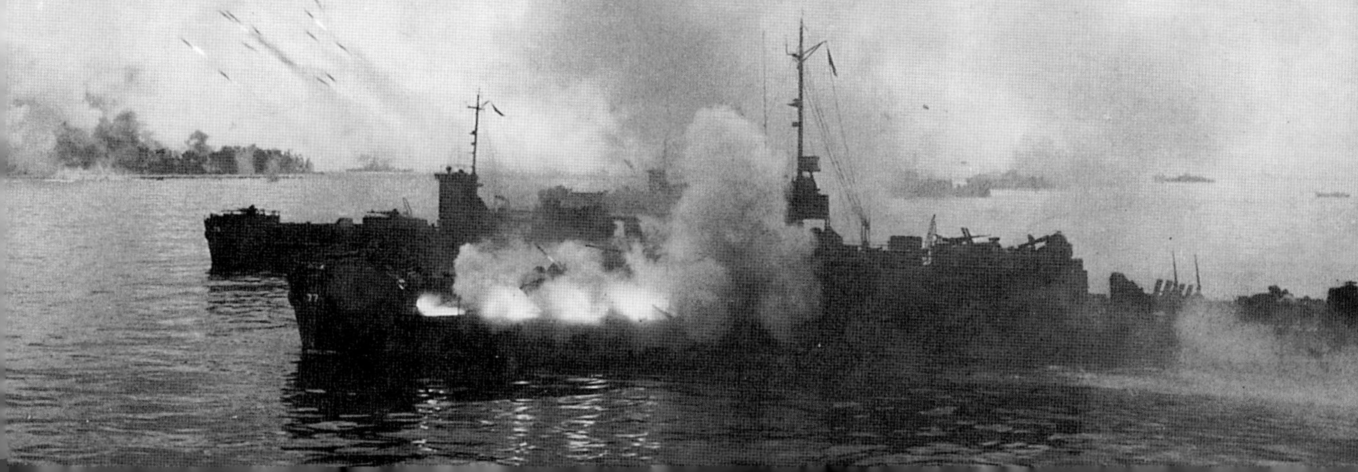

FOREWORD

ON A HOT, MUGGY SUMMER day I strolled through the Punchbowl Cemetery on Oahu looking for a little shade to help preserve the creases melting out of my uniform. An old-timer leaning on a cane spotted me and patted a spot next to him on a marble bench. He was in his seventh or eighth decade of hard living and wearing an overseas cap that attested to his service as a Marine in the Pacific during World War II. "Hell of a thing," he said sweeping an arthritic hand across the ranks of sparkling headstones. "It was a dollar job on a dime budget all the way from Pearl Harbor to Okinawa. Everybody was worrying about Hitler and the Nazis."

His complaint was overstated but entirely understandable. In 1940 when American leadership was contemplating involvement in a world war for the second time in the 20th century, there was a tacit agreement that the initial effort would be against Axis powers in Europe. As most Americans at the time claimed some ancestry or familial descent from European nations, it was perhaps a natural reaction among war planners. And then the infamous Japanese attack on American forces and facilities in Hawaii on December 7, 1941, made a two-front war a reality. Pearl Harbor threw the American planners into a frenzy of shifting priorities. There were angry voices in Congress and across the country calling for an immediate counterstrike against the Japanese Empire but the leadership fell back on the default setting when the US declared war on Germany three days later.

There were practical as well as philosophical reasons for this: America's striking power for what would clearly be a naval campaign against the Japanese in the Pacific had been badly damaged at Pearl Harbor. It would take time, money, and manpower to get those forces ready to begin a long and bloody struggle across vast expanses of ocean to stem the Japanese tide of victories in the Pacific and save Allied nations such as Australia and New Zealand from conquest. In the meantime, embattled American commanders such as General Douglas MacArthur in the Philippines and Admiral Chester Nimitz in Hawaii were forced to focus on survival as opposed to counterattack.

The tide began to turn in 1942 with the battle of the Coral Sea, the first naval engagement between opposing aircraft carrier task forces operating over the horizon from each other, and with the first American ground

OPPOSITE
Blazing Japanese installations send up huge puffs of white smoke as Roi Island, the Japanese airbase on Kwajalein Atoll in the Marshall Islands, rocks under the shattering impact of American bombs. Carrier-based US planes raided the island stronghold in preparation for landings by US Marine assault troops in early 1944. American forces captured Kwajalein during the continuing offensive in the Central Pacific. (Topfoto)

OPPOSITE
Japanese Navy Type 99 carrier bombers ("Val") prepare to take off from an aircraft carrier during the morning of December 7, 1941. The ship in the background is the carrier *Soryu*. (US Navy)

offensive at Guadalcanal in the Solomon Islands. Both battles were won on very tight margins and quickly demonstrated to Allied planners that war in the Pacific would be a brutal island-hopping affair focused on wrenching vital airfields from Japanese control. To support and supply the soldiers, sailors, and Marines fighting and dying on battlefields with often unpronounceable names, America and her Allies had to rely on a logistical tail that stretched across thousands of miles of ocean patrolled and controlled early in the war by marauding Japanese air and naval armadas.

Sailors aboard surface combatants and submarines and operating off aircraft carriers through the South and Central Pacific learned hard and costly lessons when they came up against a Japanese Navy schooled and experienced in night-time engagements. Infantry forces slugging it out with fanatical defenders on Pacific flyspecks like Tarawa, Saipan, and Peleliu mostly had to make do with whatever was at hand. Resupply was a long way off and requisitions often took months to fill. It was brutal in the extreme; and different in many respects from combat in the European Theater of Operations. Marines and soldiers in Pacific combat encountered an enemy that fought with an obsessive, no-quarter psychology that differed shockingly from Western approaches to warfare.

They got it done minus much of the fanfare and publicity that attended Allied advances and victories in other theaters of World War II. Among fighting men in the Pacific a sort of perverse pride often developed as they read newspaper clippings or heard radio broadcasts celebrating Allied campaigns in Europe following D-Day in 1944. Marines in the Pacific claimed to be Uncle Sam's Misguided Children (USMC) and American Army survivors of the Japanese steamroller in the Philippines called themselves the "Battling Bastards of Bataan, no mama, no papa, no Uncle Sam." Of course, none of them did what they did in the Pacific for glory or acclaim. That was the farthest thing from their minds as they battled through Leyte Gulf, over the bloody black sands of Iwo Jima and into the agonizing meat-grinder of combat on Okinawa and right up to the end of the war.

They just wanted to get the job done, to survive, to go home, and pick up where they left off when war interrupted their lives. Those of us who live free today have had 70 years to contemplate their service and sacrifice and we've not done enough to let the aging survivors know how vital it was to our way of life. Books like this one are dedicated to help correct that. It's the least we can do.

Captain Dale Dye USMC (Ret)
May 2011

FOR

INTRODUCTION

ON THE EVENING OF December 8, 1941, I sat huddled with my parents in front of our radio, listening to the first reports coming in of the Japanese attack on Pearl Harbor. I was five at the time but the impact of the news was so great that I can still recall it clearly. Although we were in Melbourne, Australia, and a long way from the scene of the American disaster, there were only meagre British, Dutch, and Australian forces between ourselves and the oncoming Imperial Japanese forces. Two days later we were shaken by news of the sinking off the coast of Malaya of the only British capital ships in regional waters, the *Prince of Wales* and the *Repulse*. We began building air raid shelters in our back-gardens and thinking about evacuation to the countryside. My father patrolled the streets at night as an Air Raid Precautions warden, enforcing the blackout of house and external lighting to deny any Japanese bombers an aiming mark.

How had this disaster for the United States and its friends and Allies happened in so short a time? Could the advance of the Japanese armed forces be halted? What would it take to hurl them back onto their home soil and force them to surrender? This very timely volume offers in depth answers to the second and third of these questions, but let me address some thoughts by way of reply to the first, with gratitude to my paternal grandfather who fought against the Boxer Rebellion in China, 1900–01, and in World War I, on each occasion with Japanese as allies. He had 40 years of naval experience between 1888 and 1928, and was a keen observer of strategic matters in the Pacific. In turn, he helped to develop my interest in these issues while I was in my teens.

Japan discovered the potential of modern seapower in the 1880s and through British naval tutelage and the purchase of British warships, it soon had a powerful fleet led by competent officers. The Japanese sank the Chinese Navy in two major battles of 1894 (the Yalu River) and 1895 (Wei Haiwei), and proved themselves as the top naval power of north-east Asia. Japan had been fostering the expertise of the remarkable man who was to be known as "the Nelson of the East," Admiral Heihachiro Togo, by sending him to Britain for seven years of training and experience. In 1902 the British went so far as to conclude a formal alliance with Japan – which was particularly helpful for Britain, Australia, and New Zealand in resisting German pressures during

OPPOSITE
Marines on Mount Suribachi, Iwo Jima, wiring the US flag onto a pole for the first flag raising at that site. It was later deemed "not impressive enough" and they found a better, larger flag and flag pole and that became the most famous picture to come out of the Pacific. (Tom Laemlein)

World War I. The combination of even more powerful British-made warships and Togo's leadership enabled the Japanese to defeat the strong fleet that Russia sent to the Far East at the battle of Tsushima in 1905. As a result, Japan was fully established as a major Pacific naval power.

It took remarkably little time for the Japanese to develop naval airpower. In September 1914 they made the first successful attack by naval aircraft in the history of warfare when they struck the Germans in the battle of Tsingtao, China. Having removed the German Navy from western Pacific waters, the only potential rival that the bold, thrusting Japanese naval leadership then faced was the United States Navy. The Americans had been keeping a close eye on the Japanese since their victory over the Russians in 1905, and in 1906 the US moved ahead to develop a war plan to defeat any future Japanese naval threat to US interests in the Pacific. American authorities formally adopted the final version of this plan, Plan Orange, in 1924, although it had its origins in the thinking of Rear Admiral Raymond P. Rodgers from as early as 1911. It assumed that, in the event of hostilities, the initial Japanese pressure would be applied to the Philippines and the small Pacific island bases of the US. The American response, after a period of mobilization and force concentration, would be to re-take their own island bases, and remove the Japanese from theirs, while US naval forces were en route to relieve the Philippines. The US fleet would then confront the Imperial Japanese Navy in a fight to the finish. Japan was then to be brought to her knees by a naval blockade.

The Japanese, for their part, correctly assessed the nature of the US war plan and made their own which would allow a US fleet to reach the Philippines, while suffering losses from Japanese naval air and submarine attacks along the way. This weakened fleet would then be annihilated by the Japanese in a great naval battle, similar to the one that the US Plan Orange envisaged.

The development of the striking power of the respective fleets in the 1920s and 30s was thus crucial to the course of the war in the Pacific. Another factor strengthening the Japanese hand was its acquisition of mandates from the League of Nations to govern the former German islands of the northern and central Pacific: the Carolines, the Marianas, and the Marshalls. These mandates placed the islands virtually under Japanese law but, like all mandate holders, they were not permitted to fortify them. Nonetheless, that is what the Japanese did, creating a strategic barrier through which US forces intending to relieve the Philippines in a future war would have to fight their way.

The Japanese became the object of US diplomatic pressure soon after World War I. The Americans wanted to end the Anglo-Japanese alliance and to constrain the further growth of Japanese naval power. Both objectives were secured at the Washington Naval Conference of 1921–22. The Japanese were both humiliated and angry at this outcome, and this in turn fed the tensions that caused the war in the Pacific. Severe limitations on Japanese migration to the US, pressure to withdraw from former German territory in China, and trade restrictions aggravated the Japanese further during the 1920s and 30s. All of this played into the hands of military and political leaders who wanted to exploit Japan's naval strength in the Pacific to create a new international order there and in China.

In the meantime both the US and Japan had gone ahead with the planning and development of through-deck aircraft carriers, so that by the 1930s both navies had formidable airpower capabilities. Despite their differences and enmity, the Japanese and the Americans made sporadic efforts to settle their differences peacefully. These initiatives proved unsuccessful and the Japanese finally decided in 1941 to use force. In turn, the British, having alienated the Japanese by commencing construction of a great naval base at Singapore, had scaled down their presence, and were no longer a great naval power in the Pacific. By 1941 Britain had little power to spare as it was heavily engaged in action in Europe, North Africa, and the Middle East. When the Japanese decided to strike they had only the United States to focus on, enabling the execution of the bold and complex plan for striking the US Navy in its base at Pearl Harbor.

This book examines the complex series of events leading up to the attack of December 7, 1941, the attack itself, and the bloody consequences which were to follow. I invite the reader to study and evaluate the expert views set forth in the following chapters, and to think about the question of whether so great a catastrophe could befall a major power in the Pacific in the 21st century.

Professor Robert O'Neill

June 2011

FOREWORD • INTROD

PEARL HARBOR

ORIGINS OF THE CAMPAIGN

Below, thick fluffy clouds blanketed the blue sky. Shoving the stick forward, Lieutenant Mitsuo Matsuzaki dropped his Nakajima B5N2 Type 97 "Kate" into more blue sky, the horizon broken by the low land mass he was approaching. His observer, Commander Mitsuo Fuchida, the mission commander, was watchful. Hawaii looked green and oddly peaceful. He scanned the horizon. It looked too good to be true; other than his fliers, no aircraft were visible.

It was 0730hrs Hawaii time; the date, December 7, 1941. Fuchida's destination was the home of the US Pacific Fleet – Pearl Harbor. The fleet and three aircraft carriers berthed there were the key targets. A statement notifying the US that war had been declared had been scheduled for delivery to Washington an hour earlier. This air strike would be the first act of war between Imperial Japan and the United States.

OPPOSING COMMANDERS

THE US COMMANDERS

Admiral Husband (Hubby) E. Kimmel was the naval commander at Pearl Harbor. In February, 1941, he was promoted to Commander-in-Chief Pacific (CINCPAC), becoming the navy's senior admiral. As CINCPAC, Kimmel moved to Pearl Harbor, home of the Pacific Fleet. He was unhappy with the defense arrangements in Hawaii and Pearl Harbor. At the time responsibility for them was split: the Army was responsible for land and air defense and the Navy for the Navy Yard itself. The Navy was responsible for reconnaissance but the Army controlled the radar stations and both air and shore defenses in case of invasion. In addition, each service had to compete for allocation of supplies and material. Kimmel let his strong feelings about this tangled web of responsibilities be known. Still, he was a career officer, and having stated his objections, he followed orders.

Lieutenant-General Walter C. Short was the Army commander at Pearl Harbor. His men were well drilled but, under his command, unit commanders carefully watched the use of expendable ammunition and materiel. Short followed his orders to the letter, but failed to read between the lines and was surprised when the Japanese attacked Pearl Harbor. Ten days after the attack, he was recalled to Washington and replaced by General Delos Emmons.

Admiral Harold (Betty) R. Stark became Chief of Naval Operations (CNO) in 1939 and

OPPOSITE
The magazine of USS *Shaw* exploded after being attacked on Decmber 7, 1941. (US Navy/Topfoto)

> "Yesterday, December 7, 1941 – a date which will live in infamy – the United States of America was suddenly and deliberately attacked by naval and air forces of the Empire of Japan... As Commander-in-Chief of the Army and Navy, I have directed that all measures be taken for our defense... With confidence in our armed forces – with the unbounded determination of our people – we will gain the inevitable triumph – so help us God."
>
> — **PRESIDENT F. D. ROOSEVELT**, DECEMBER 8, 1941

overcame strong isolationist sentiment to start construction of modern naval vessels and bases. He beefed up the Pacific Fleet at Pearl, and, aided by information from the MAGIC code, knew that Japanese–American relations were dramatically declining and approaching a state of war. He gave commanders warnings, but because of the prevailing belief that Pearl Harbor was so strong, he felt the Japanese would attack elsewhere. When Ambassador Nomura's message declaring war was translated by MAGIC on December 7, 1941, he started to send a message to Pearl Harbor, but General George C. Marshall assured him that Army communications could get it there just as fast. In fact, it arrived after the air raid had begun. Stark was relieved as CNO on March 7, 1942, although Marshall retained his position.

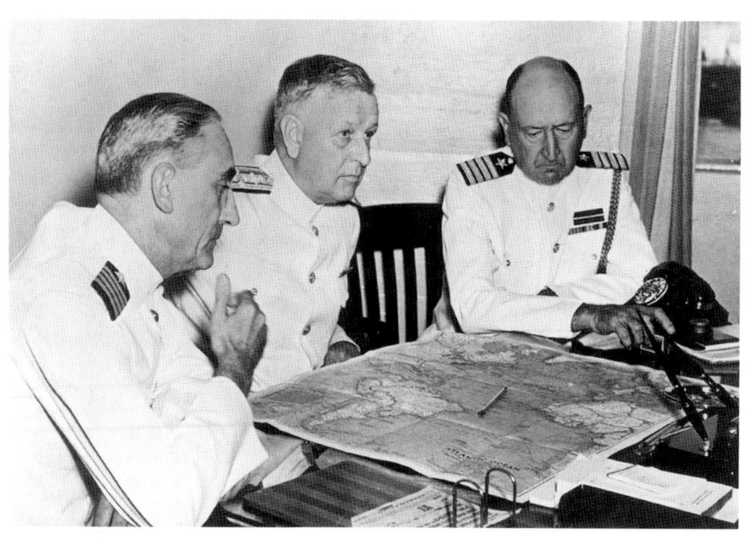

Admiral Kimmel (center) photographed with his operations officer Captain Delaney (left) and his assistant chief of staff Captain Smith (right). Although aggressive and vigilant, Kimmel shared responsibility for Pearl Harbor with Lieutenant-General Short. Both were surprised by the audacious Japanese thrust at an island almost everyone thought too well defended to be a target. (US Navy)

President Franklin D. Roosevelt appointed General George C. Marshall as Chief of Staff on September 1, 1939, and gave him his fourth star. Despite his position, unlike many others, no stigma for the debacle was attached to him. Marshall fully supported the "defeat Germany first" concept, and many would later blame the length of the Pacific War on his cautious approach to planning and implementation of war plans.

THE JAPANESE COMMANDERS

As a mere captain Isoroku Yamamoto had successfully negotiated an increase in Japan's naval allowance at the London Naval Conference in 1923. He returned to Japan a diplomatic hero and became Vice-Minister of

A photograph of a Japanese model of Pearl Harbor, showing ships located as they were during the attack. The model was constructed after the attack for use in making a motion picture. (US Naval Historical Center)

the Navy. Yamamoto favored air power, and he relegated the steel navy to a secondary position, opposing the building of the battleships *Yamato* and *Musashi* as antiquated technology, stating: “These … will be as useful … as a samurai sword.” He championed new aircraft carriers and acknowledged that he had no confidence whatsoever in Japan’s ability to win a protracted naval war.

In mid-August, 1939, he was promoted to full admiral and became Commander-in-Chief of the Combined Fleet. He became a Rommel-like figure to the men of his command, inspiring them to greater efforts by his confidence, and improved the combat readiness and seaworthiness of the Imperial Japanese Navy (IJN) by making it practice in good and bad weather, day and night. Yamamoto did not wish to go to war with the US, but once the government had decided, he devoted himself to the task of giving Japan the decisive edge. It was he who decided that Pearl Harbor would be won with air power, not battleships, and the final attack plan was his.

Commander Mitsuo Fuchida entered the Naval Academy and befriended Commander Minoru Genda when they discovered a shared love for flying. Their friendship and mutual respect was to last for years, and in many ways it helped shape the concept of air war and the attack on Pearl Harbor. While in China, Fuchida learned the art of torpedo bombing, and he was recognized throughout the IJN as a torpedo ace.

Rear-Admiral Takijiro Onishi had Commander Minoru Genda write a feasibility study for a proposed Japanese attack on Pearl Harbor. Commander Genda wrote the study and constructed a strategy with ten main points, most of which were incorporated into the final plan. He developed the First Air Group’s torpedo program, and proposed a second attack on Pearl Harbor several days after the first, wanting to annihilate the US fleet. He remained aboard the carrier *Akagi* as Vice-Admiral Chuichi Nagumo’s air advisor, and was on deck to welcome Fuchida’s flight back.

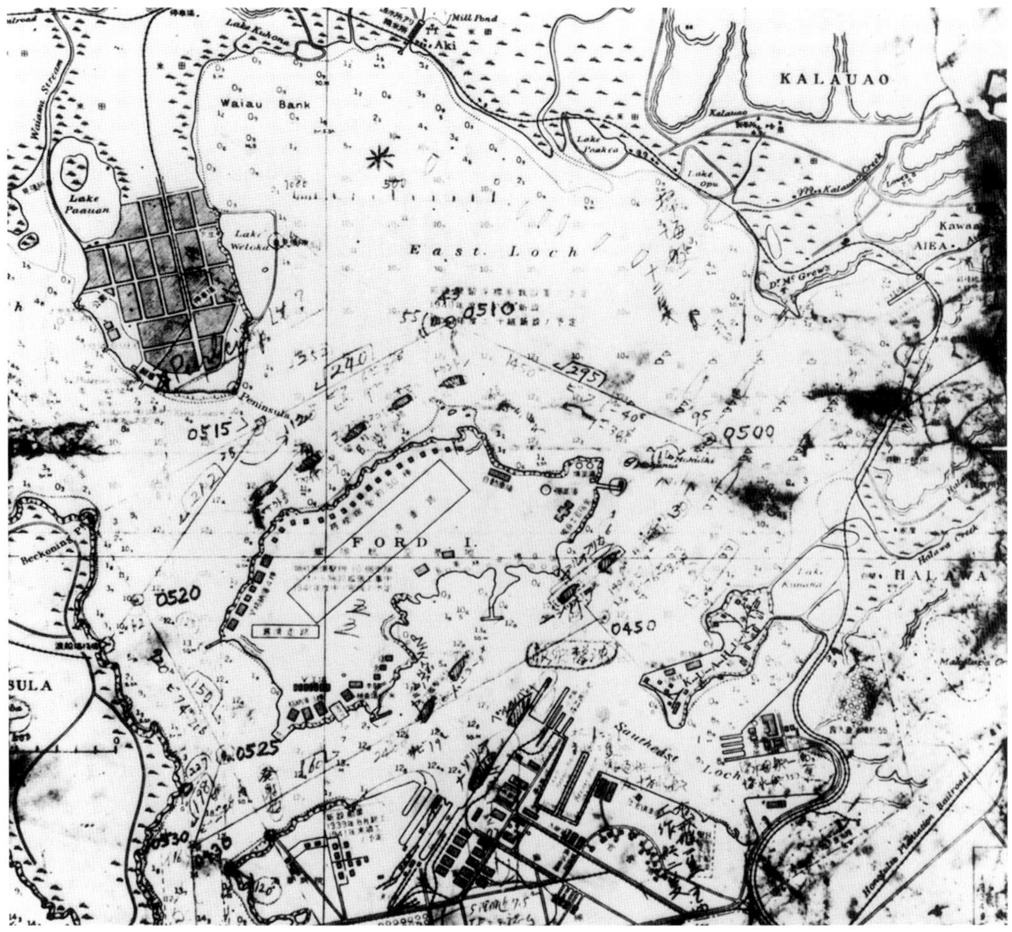

The Japanese attack was well planned and the targets plotted. This contemporary map was captured from a Japanese midget submarine, *HA-19*, commanded by Lieutenant Kazuo Sakamaki. Note the chart is in English, the notations Japanese. (NARA)

Vice-Admiral Chuichi Nagumo was a career naval officer and an expert in torpedo warfare. He was appointed commander of the Kido Butai, the 1st Air Fleet, despite his lack of familiarity and experience in naval aviation. He commanded the 1st Air Fleet at Pearl Harbor from the deck of his flagship, *Akagi*.

Admiral Kichisaburo Nomura was the Japanese ambassador to Washington at the time of Pearl Harbor, and was cast unwittingly in the role of villain. Both Emperor Hirohito and Yamamoto insisted that at least 30 minutes notice be given the to US prior to the outbreak of hostilities at Pearl Harbor. A message was sent to Nomura: he was to give it to Secretary of State Cordell Hull at 1300hrs Washington time. The message was sent in 14 parts and decoded as it arrived. Because of the security on this message, Nomura did not have a competent typist with sufficient clearance. The person selected was slow and Nomura postponed his appointment until 1400hrs. Nomura saw Hull at 1420 and delivered the message. Hull was infuriated and terse during the meeting. Nomura soon discovered the reason for Hull's reception: Pearl Harbor had already been attacked by Japan. Hull declared to the press immediately afterward that he had never seen a message so full of "falsehoods and distortions ... on a scale so huge that I never imagined ... any government ... was capable of uttering them."

THE JAPANESE PLAN

The Japanese had watched the expansion of Pearl Harbor with considerable interest and concern. It was clearly the strongest US Navy base and the first way-station from the mainland to the Far East. Due to their experiences during the Russo-Japanese War (1904–05) and the victories at Port Arthur and Tsushima, many in the Japanese High Command believed in a "Great All-Out War" with the US Navy. Japanese warships had been thoughtfully designed to better their American counterparts with an extra gun, extra speed, more torpedo tubes, or by any other means.

Within the IJN, there was a rift between the battleship admirals and the younger air power admirals: the former held true to the Great All-Out War theory, while the latter realized that British success at Taranto in 1940 when British aircraft sunk the pride of the Italian fleet presaged the future of naval warfare. As a result, Yamamoto trained young officers for air war.

In early 1941, Yamamoto began preparation for the Southern Operation, the Japanese plan to conquer the resource-rich areas of Asia. One of the operation's components, the Hawaii Operation, comprised the thrust on Pearl Harbor. Plans were clear: if negotiations had not succeeded by November 23, 1941, a military solution would commence.

The IJN had clear details on Pearl Harbor. As the harbor was in plain view of the city, and visitors could take aerial sight-seeing trips over the naval basin and near most military posts, espionage was relatively simple. Within a few months the IJN had a complete record of all vessels stationed at Pearl, their schedules, which ships were under repair, which had left for sea duty, and the disposition of aircraft.

The US Navy and Army commands did take some preventative measures. Lieutenant-General Short, concerned about sabotage, ordered all Army aircraft to be bunched together so they could be better guarded: however, this also made them sitting ducks for an air assault. He ordered munitions secured, coastal artillery put on alert, and radar stations shut down at 0700hrs. Admiral Kimmel started rotating carriers in and out of the harbor and set up ship and naval aircraft patrols. Vessels were alert for submarine threats to shipping. Nonetheless, the aircraft carrier *Lexington* was ordered to take aircraft, which Kimmel felt were sorely needed at Pearl, to Midway.

Despite precautions, no one really dreamed of an air attack. Warships, yes; sabotage and possibly an invasion force, yes; but air attack? No one gave it much credence.

Throughout the months leading up to the attack, US government cryptographers carefully monitored Japanese transmissions. Washington, while still neutral, agreed with London that the Allies would concentrate on defeating Germany first. As a result, London was given three of the ultra-secret MAGIC decoders, but Pearl Harbor did not receive any. Moreover, because of the "defeat Germany first" mentality, men and materiel which could have bolstered the Pacific operations were diverted to the Atlantic.

THE ATTACK ON PEARL HARBOR

OPENING MOVES

Although he did not know the significance of the date, Nomura was told to complete negotiations by November 22, although this deadline was later extended by seven days.

Nomura could not know that the deadline coincided with the sailing of the Southern Operation task force.

Japanese naval vessels slipped out of anchorage in twos and threes to rendezvous at Hitokappu Bay in the Kurile Islands on November 22, 1941. They would sail on November 26, following a northerly route to avoid accidental sightings by US vessels and aircraft, which operated on a more southerly route. Once under way, the fleet would maintain radio silence, and dummy transmissions from near the Japanese mainland would maintain the illusion for Allied listening posts that the task force was still in Japanese waters.

OPPOSITE
The commanding officer of the Japanese aircraft carrier *Shokaku* watches as planes take off to attack Pearl Harbor during the morning of December 7, 1941. The Kanji inscription at left is an exhortation to pilots to do their duty. (US Navy)

THE HAWAII OPERATION

The Japanese military plan had three phases. Phase I was to surprise Pearl Harbor, neutralize the American fleet, and extend the perimeter to include Wake Island, the Gilberts, the northern Solomons, most of New Guinea, Java, Sumatra, Malaya, Burma (east to the Indian border), Thailand, the Philippines, and Borneo. Phase II was to strengthen the military presence on the new perimeter. Phase III was defensive: to protect the perimeter and destroy any incursions from the outside. Simultaneous Army and Navy attacks were to batter Pearl Harbor, the Philippines, and Malaya. The Imperial Japanese Army (IJA) would land on the latter two and thrust toward Java. Wake Island, Thailand, Guam, and Hong Kong would also be occupied by the Army. Two destroyers, *Ushio* and *Sazanami*, would shell Midway, and carriers returning from Pearl Harbor would complete the reduction of any defenders on Wake. Although there was no overall commander, Army and Navy attacks would be simultaneous: one swift thrust and the ripe fruits of the Pacific would fall into Japanese hands.

BELOW
In late October Ford Island (center), the tank farm on the South-East loch (center left, opposite Ford Island), and Hickam Field (top left) were business-as-usual bases. War was in Europe or China and was not expected to impact on the well-guarded Pearl Harbor. (US Navy)

Preparations

The planned attack on Pearl Harbor called for a concentrated assault using dive-bombers, high-altitude bombing, and torpedo attacks. Bombers began practice runs, both high-altitude and dive-bombing. The pilots' scores constantly improved and their hit ratios soared. Torpedo bombers also began practicing, but their scores were less impressive, and although Genda did everything within his power, there was a barrier his men could not break, no matter how much they practiced. The harbor was simply too shallow for the conventional torpedoes then in use, and the Japanese Type 91 Model 1 torpedoes would penetrate too deeply into the water and would stick in the mud of the shallow harbor.

Despite the success of the British torpedo attack at Taranto, the US did not put out torpedo nets in Pearl Harbor: they were extremely time-consuming to erect and it was generally accepted that the harbor was

司令長官

too shallow for conventional torpedoes to function. This false sense of security was heightened by Pearl's seemingly impregnable defenses, which rendered sea bombardment an unlikely eventuality.

Based on the action at Taranto, Japan had correctly identified bombing and torpedo runs as the most effective way to destroy the ships of the US fleet. The major problem remained, however, the shallowness of the harbor.

Fuchida, Genda, and Lieutenant-Commander Shigeharu Murata insisted that torpedo attacks in waters up to 33ft deep must improve. Generally the attackers dropped torpedoes which followed a depth of approximately 65ft. With practice, the pilots improved, but they could not achieve the 33ft requirement. Almost despairing, they studied the situation, and eventually devised an innovative solution; the use of torpedoes with added wooden fins to provide additional stability and buoyancy. Scores for kills in maneuvers rose dramatically to 70 percent, and higher on stationary vessels.

For identification purposes, the Japanese had broken Pearl Harbor into district areas: A (between Ford Island and the Navy Yard); B (the northwest area of Ford Island); C (East Loch); D (Middle Loch); and E (West Loch). District A was subdivided into five areas: the docks northwest of the Navy Yard; the mooring pillars; the Navy Yard repair dock; the docks; and the remaining area.

As of December 3, the Japanese knew *Oklahoma*, *Nevada*, *Enterprise*, two heavy cruisers, and 12 destroyers had left Pearl Harbor, and five battleships, three heavy cruisers, three light cruisers, 12 destroyers, and a seaplane tender had arrived. There seemed to be no unusual activity to suggest that the US was preparing for an attack, and shore leaves were being granted as usual. On December 4, the disposition of ships was the same, and no undue air traffic was noted. As of December 5, *Oklahoma* and *Nevada* arrived in the harbor and *Lexington* and five cruisers departed: the total ships reported in harbor were eight battleships, three light cruisers, 16 destroyers and four *Honolulu*-class light cruisers, as well as five destroyers. *Utah* and a seaplane tender reentered the harbor although the carrier *Enterprise* remained at sea on maneuvers. Furthermore, the

The Japanese hoped to catch the US carriers *Lexington, Saratoga,* and *Enterprise* at Pearl Harbor. *Saratoga* was at San Diego and *Enterprise* was delivering planes to Wake while *Lexington* was on its way to Midway when the Japanese struck. (US Navy)

report showed that no defensive balloons were up, no blackout was enforced, no anti-torpedo nets had been deployed, and there were no evident patrol flights.

Each part of the Pearl Harbor task force had responsibility for specific areas and certain targets: Air Attack Force (the carriers *Akagi*, *Kaga*, *Hiryu*, *Soryu*, *Shokaku*, and *Zuikaku*), 1st Air Fleet, air attacks; 1st Destroyer Squadron (17th Destroyer Division, *Nagara* flagship and 18th Destroyer Division, *Akiguma* flagship), screening and escort; 3rd Battleship Division and 8th Cruiser Division, screening and support; 2nd Submarine Division (*I-17* flagship, *I-21*, and *I-23*), patrol; 7th Destroyer Division, the attack on Midway air base; 1st Supply Unit (*Kyokuto Maru* flagship, *Kenyo Maru*, *Kokuyo Maru*, and *Shikoku Maru*) and 2nd Supply Unit (*Tohu Maru* flagship, *Toei Maru*, and *Nippon Maru*), daily refueling.

"Climb Mount Niitaka"

The Pearl Harbor task force sailed on November 26 toward Pearl Harbor, radio operators listening while maintaining radio silence. Yamamoto sent Chuichi Nagumo a coded message: "*Niitaka yama nobore*" ("Climb Mount Niitaka") meaning that the attacks would go forward as planned. Admiral Nagumo subsequently received a telegram on December 2, 1941, at 1700hrs telling him to open a top-secret envelope. Inside, he found the fateful message: "Our Empire has decided to go to war against the United States, Britain and Holland in early December." The message set the date for December 8 (December 7, Pearl Harbor time). The attack was on.

THE FIRST WAVE

With dawn over an hour away the minesweepers USS *Crossbill* and USS *Condor* patrolled nearly two miles south of the Pearl Harbor entrance buoys. On watch aboard the *Condor* at 0342hrs, Ensign R. C. McCloy sighted a white wake and asked Quartermaster Uttrick what he thought the object was. Through glasses, Uttrick identified it as a periscope, and at 0357hrs contacted USS *Ward*, on entrance patrol, to investigate. Uttrick's blinker message read: "Sighted submerged submarine on westerly course, speed 9 knots."

Lieutenant William Outerbridge commanded *Ward* while she patrolled the harbor entrance. A new officer on his first command, he was aware of degenerating relations between the US and Japan, and decided that what Uttrick had seen was most likely a Japanese submarine. He requested a status report from *Condor* and was told that their last sighting was at 0350hrs and that the object was moving toward the harbor entrance. "Sound general quarters," Outerbridge ordered.

For the next hour, the USS *Ward* conducted a fruitless sonar sweep of the area. At 0435hrs, Outerbridge had *Ward* stepped down from general quarters. The protective net to Pearl Harbor was scheduled to swing open at 0458hrs to admit the minelayers, and would remain open until 0840hrs. Although they did not know it, the sub probably intended to shadow the minesweeper into the safety of the harbor, a wolf sliding in among the sheep.

The sighting, although not an everyday occurrence, was not unheard of, and was duly logged. *Ward* continued her rounds. Entering the harbor after a standard tour of duty at 0458hrs, *Crossbill* and *Condor* returned to their berths. However, the harbor's anti-submarine net did not close.

At 0530hrs, the Japanese task force turned northeast, heading into a 28-knot wind. The first wave prepared for take-off at 0615hrs. About 250 miles north of Oahu, the first

NEXT SPREAD
Aboard either the *Zuikaku* or *Shokaku*, crewmen cheer as an IJN Type 97 carrier attack plane takes off as part of the second wave attack on December 7. (US Naval Historical Center)

"Our Empire has decided to go to war against the United States, Britain and Holland in early December."

— JAPANESE TELEGRAM ANNOUNCING WAR AGAINST THE UNITED STATES

planes steadily took off from the six Japanese carriers and circled, waiting for all 183 of the aircraft in the first wave to join them. At 0630hrs, they took up V-formation and headed south-southwest toward their target.

West of Pearl Harbor at 0620hrs, 18 SBDs took off from the USS *Enterprise* on a routine scouting mission to fly ahead and land at Ford Island. Although their crew were aware of uneasy Japanese–US relations, this seemed a routine training mission and they planned to arrive in time for breakfast, around 0800hrs. At this stage the *Enterprise* lay 200 miles west of Oahu and was heading home.

The crew of the USS *Antares*, a supply ship, also sighted what they thought was a sub and notified *Ward* at 0630hrs. A PBY also sighted the sub and dropped a smoke marker on it just as *Ward* arrived on the scene. Lieutenant Outerbridge saw what appeared to be a submarine's conning tower breaking the surface. Though it could have been friendly, the vessel did not surface or attempt to communicate. Following standing orders that unidentified vessels were considered hostile, Outerbridge opened fire at 0645hrs. One round penetrated the sub's conning tower while *Ward* covered the projected course of the unknown submarine with depth charges. The PBY completed two circles, and dropped a depth charge on each pass. Without knowing it, the Americans had fired the first shots in the battle for Pearl Harbor.

The sub did not resurface, and Outerbridge thought they had hit her. At 0653hrs, he sent coded signals to 14th Naval District headquarters, saying: "Attacked, fired upon, and dropped depth charges upon a submarine operating in a defensive area." The PBY reported to Patrol Wing 2 headquarters as well.

Hawaiian radio stations often broadcast music throughout the night when flights of incoming aircraft were expected from the mainland United States. As a result, the station's signal was loud and clear to the approaching Japanese, and at 0700hrs Commander Fuchida ordered his men to use it as a directional locator. Less than five minutes later, privates Lockard and Elliott, manning the mobile US Army radar post on Opana Ridge, saw a blip on their screen, a sizable force of unidentified aircraft, 132 miles north of Oahu and closing. They wondered where the aircraft were from and if the radar station's equipment was defective. If the blip was accurate, its size indicated a group of more than 50 aircraft.

At 0710hrs Elliott notified headquarters at Fort Shafter but the Signal Corps telephone operator responded that all Signal Corps personnel had left for breakfast. By this time the blip was 100 miles north and closing.

The duty officers of the 14th Naval District received Outerbridge's message, which had been delayed in decoding, at 0715hrs. Meanwhile about 260 miles north the second wave of the Japanese attack – 168 aircraft – took off.

At 0720hrs, the operator called Opana Ridge radar back. He had found an Air Corps officer, Lieutenant Kermit Tyler, who had observed the morning activities at the plotting boards. On listening to Lockard explain about an incoming blip, he remembered the radio had played all night and thus knew that some planes from the mainland were due to arrive. Lockard did not mention the size of the blip, and Tyler would not have known any different had the size been revealed.

Meanwhile, in Washington DC, the final installment of the decoded Japanese 14-part message was received. It read: "The Japanese Government regrets ... it is impossible to reach an agreement through further negotiations."

A Japanese Val seen here overhead at Pearl during the fateful attacks. (Tom Laemlein)

Although the language of the message clearly indicated that war was a distinct possibility the decision was made not to send any warning to Pearl Harbor.

At 0738hrs, an Aichi E13IA Type 11 ("Jake") reconnaissance float plane gave a visual confirmation that the main US fleet was in Pearl Harbor: "Enemy ... at anchor, nine battleships, one heavy cruiser, six light cruisers." The pilot relayed prevailing conditions to the approaching first wave: "Wind direction from 80 degrees, speed 14m, clearance over enemy fleet 1,700m, cloud density seven." The second recon aircraft reported that there were no enemy vessels at the deep-water anchorage at Lahaina which would have made the attack considerably easier and the attack would have to focus on the shallow Pearl Harbor anchorage. Their new torpedo modifications would get their baptism of fire. Having reported, the pilot swept wide to the south, trying to find the carriers; but he did not fly west, and *Enterprise* remained undiscovered.

By 0739hrs at Opana Ridge, Elliott and Lockard had lost the incoming blip because of the ground clutter pattern caused by the hills behind Opana Ridge. At 0749hrs, Fuchida ordered his pilots to deploy into attack formation by firing a single shot from his flare gun, signifying "torpedo planes to attack." His radioman tapped out the signal "To-To-To" (the first syllable of *tosugekiseyo*, meaning "to charge"). Believing that Lieutenant-Commander

Itaya might have missed his signal, Fuchida fired a second shot. Lieutenant-Commander Takahashi saw both shots and misunderstood, thinking that dive-bombers were now ordered to strike. Lieutenant-Commander Murata realized there had been a misunderstanding, but it could not be rectified, so he led his torpedo group into its attack pattern. Aircraft reduced altitude and flight leaders singled out the designated target.

Wheeler Field, an airfield and base eight miles from Pearl Harbor, was a primary target in the Japanese attack plan to prevent any American retaliation. There were no trenches and no anti-aircraft guns, with aircraft neatly grouped on runways. Quite simply, Wheeler Field was a sitting duck. The Zeros banked and came in low, guns blazing, shredding everything in their wake. They were followed by a devastating bombing raid from *Zuikaku* Vals at 0751hrs.

Kaneohe and Ewa Mooring Mast Field then came under attack at 0753hrs, and Fuchida radioed the task force on a broad band: "*Tora, Tora, Tora*" ("Attack-Destroy"), indicating that so far their approach had been a complete success and the US Naval and Army installations had been caught unaware. The Japanese strike force roared away, leaving Wildcats and scout bombers blazing, and utility aircraft destroyed. Their losses? Just one Zero.

Smoke from the Navy Yard (left) and Ford Island (center) rises while anti-aircraft bursts dot the skies during the attack. Although surprised, naval vessels reacted as quickly as possible, so that when the second wave arrived, it was severely challenged. (US Navy)

The Japanese first-wave attack aircraft then descended on Ford Island and Hickam airfields as torpedo bombers began their runs on Battleship Row. Pearl Harbor itself was now under attack. On this particular Sunday morning all was SOP – standard operating procedure – in the Pacific Fleet. Chapel services were planned, mess halls and galleys were laying out breakfast, launches to and from shore were readying, and men on duty rosters were preparing for their watch. Japanese aircraft swooped out of the morning sky, lining their sights on capital ships. At 0755hrs, Lieutenant-Commander Logan Ramsey stood at the window of Ford Island Command Center watching the color guard hoist the flag. A plane buzzed by and he snapped, "Get that fellow's number!" Then he recalled, "I saw something ... fall out of that plane..." An explosion from the hangar area cut his words short. Racing across the hallway, Ramsey ordered the radioman to send out the following message: "Air raid, Pearl Harbor. This is NO drill." The message went out on the local frequencies at 0758hrs.

Just as the battle alert call went out torpedo planes nosed down, leveling and dropping their deadly loads into the water. The training ship *Utah* and the light cruiser *Raleigh* both reeled under torpedo explosions. Sailors immediately manned *Raleigh*'s 3in guns while she began listing to port.

South of Ford Island, 1010 Dock experienced a slashing attack while at 0757hrs, on Battleship Row, Lieutenant Goto flew straight at *Oklahoma*, released his torpedo and climbed. Aboard the repair ship *Vestal*, outboard of the battleship *Arizona* – a key Japanese target – the general quarters was sounded. Men poured from below decks and the mess area, and within ten minutes *Vestal*'s guns were firing at the invaders. About 0800hrs, crewmen Huffman and De Jong of PT 23, a patrol torpedo boat, opened fire on the attacking aircraft with twin .50cal machine guns. One attacking aircraft went down, possibly the first blood the American anti-aircraft fire had drawn.

The USS *Oklahoma* was staggered by torpedo hits. Men rushed to ammunition lockers, only to find them secured. But even once the lockers had been forced open, there was no compressed air to power the guns, and the ship had begun to list markedly when more torpedoes knifed home. Rescue parties began pulling sailors from below, up shell hoists and to the deck, while her executive officer, Commander J. L. Kenworthy, realized she was in danger of capsizing. As the eighth torpedo hit, he gave the order to abandon ship by the starboard side and to climb over the side onto the bottom as it rolled over.

Lieutenant-Commander F. J. Thomas was the ranking officer aboard *Nevada* and Ensign J. K. Taussig Jr was officer of the deck and acting air defense officer when general quarters sounded. Taussig ran to the nearest gun. At 0805hrs, *Nevada* blasted a torpedo plane that was approaching on its port beam beginning a torpedo run. *Nevada*'s 5in guns and .50cal machine guns poured fire into the aircraft. But the burning torpedo plane managed to release its torpedo. The explosion punched a hole in *Nevada*'s port bow: compartments flooded and she began to list to port. Thomas ordered counter-flooding but burning fuel oil from the *Arizona* drifted toward her, and Thomas ordered her underway to avoid it. Meanwhile, Taussig was hit in the thigh and refused aid while he commanded a gun crew. Smoking and listing, *Nevada* struggled toward the harbor entrance.

At 0805hrs, a bomb hit the *Arizona* aft of No. 4 turret and one hit *Vestal*. Until now, outboard vessels had suffered the majority of the torpedo damage, but high above the harbor the drone of bombers closed. Then bombs began falling on all inboard ships at Battleship Row from high above. As *Oklahoma* capsized, *Arizona* and *Vestal* were struck again at 0806hrs. The bomb pierced the *Arizona*'s forward magazine, and the explosion was so powerful that damage control parties aboard nearby *Vestal* were blown overboard as a fireball erupted. Immediately, *Arizona* began settling. A total of 1,177 died with her in that devastating moment, including Admiral Isaac Kidd.

All across the harbor, shipboard intercoms and PAs blasted out general quarters. Aircraft were ordered up to seek out the enemy. Sluggishly, vessels began to respond, smoke pouring at first slowly and then steadily from their stacks, and their sporadic anti-aircraft fire dotted the skies, which were filled with aircraft displaying the Rising Sun. The target ship *Utah* began to settle, turning over, while a shuddering *Oklahoma* had already capsized. Damage control parties aboard *Raleigh* fought to keep her afloat and upright while the first wisps of oily smoke from a score of vessels rose into the morning sky.

At 0800hrs, 12 stripped-down, unarmed B-17s flying singly from the mainland (which had been originally misidentified as the radar blip) sighted Oahu and began their descent. Meanwhile, the 18 recon SBDs from the USS *Enterprise* commenced their approach to Ford Island. Some were caught by enemy aircraft, and desperate American anti-aircraft fire.

Admiral Kimmel had observed the beginning of the attack from his home. He summoned his

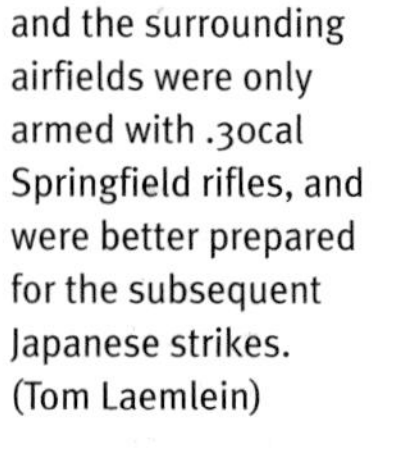

The defenders at Pearl and the surrounding airfields were only armed with .30cal Springfield rifles, and were better prepared for the subsequent Japanese strikes. (Tom Laemlein)

driver and rushed to headquarters. Kimmel arrived at CINCPAC headquarters and watched helplessly as plane after plane dived, wheeled, and circled like vultures above the now-smoking ships in the anchorage. He later said: "My main thought was the fate of my ships." In the midst of the fighting, one SBD from *Enterprise* successfully landed. Desperate American anti-aircraft fire knocked one SBD into the sea, but its crew was rescued, while Japanese aircraft accounted for a further five. The remainder reached Ford Island Naval Air Station (NAS) or Ewa Field later in the day: they would be refitted and sent hunting for the Japanese fleet.

The B-17s from the mainland were due to land at Hickam just as the Japanese aircraft attacked the base. Bombs splintered the Hawaiian Air Depot, a B-24 on the transit line, and two more hangars. Some Japanese aircraft ignored the grounded planes and, guns blazing, made straight for the incoming B-17s. The latter headed off in all directions to escape their attackers. When the smoke cleared, more than half the aircraft at Hickam were burning or shattered hulks.

Meanwhile local radio station KGMB interrupted its broadcast and transmitted: "All Army, Navy and Marine personnel, report to duty!" Back in the harbor, USS *West Virginia* began to list strongly to port when she was struck twice, the bombs coming so close together that one felt almost like the aftershock of the other, setting her No. 3 turret aflame. Before the end of the day, *West Virginia* was to take nine torpedoes and two bomb hits.

At 0812hrs, Kimmel sent a message to the Pacific Fleet and Washington, DC: "Hostilities with Japan commenced with air raid on Pearl Harbor." However, through the smoke and flame came a sight to give hope to all the sailors and personnel witnessing the devastation: a destroyer had fought its way clear of the smoke and was heading toward the mouth of the harbor – the USS *Helm* was making her run to the open sea and exited Pearl Harbor at 0817hrs.

Admiral Kimmel was watching the battle when a spent bullet shattered his office window, hitting him in the chest and knocking him backward a few steps. Men standing nearby were astounded to see Kimmel slowly bend over and pick up the spent round. He studied it for a while and then pronounced: "It would have been merciful had it killed me."

ABOVE
A .30cal anti-aircraft gun at the Naval Air Station near the American base of Pearl Harbor is photographed after the devastating attack. (Tom Laemlein)

BELOW
USS *Nevada* moves away from the carnage of Pearl Harbor during the Japanese raid. (Tom Laemlein)

THE SECOND WAVE

There was no real break between the first and the second waves of attack, just a momentary pause in the battering before the rain of death resumed. If the first wave was smooth and took little damage, the second wave bore the brunt of the US resistance. Although initially surprised and mauled, the remaining US air defenses were determined to even the score. Two American pilots, 2nd lieutenants George Welch and Kenneth Taylor, had heard the first crackle of gunfire and thumps of nearby bombs at 0751hrs and had immediately ordered their P-40s readied. They took off just after 0900hrs. A few other P-36 and P-40 aircraft also managed to get airborne.

In the harbor, USS *Alwyn* started seaward. Bombs splashed around her and she slowly surged forward, ordered to sortie. A bomb fell just short of her fantail, slamming her stern into an anchor buoy and damaging one of her screws. Aboard, only ensigns commanded *Alwyn*, all other officers being ashore. She made the open sea at 0932hrs.

At the same time, the battered battleship *Nevada* moved sluggishly away from her berth northeast of Ford Island. Smoke partly obscured visibility as her screws clawed their way toward the sea. The wind blew through her shattered bow, which sported a large gouge.

Lieutenant-Commander Shimazaki's second wave arrived near Kaneohe at 0855hrs, with 54 high-level bombers, 78 dive-bombers, and 36 fighters. Eighteen *Shokaku* high-level bombers struck Kaneohe at 0855, escorted by Zeros. The high-level bombers made strikes down the tarmac and on the hangars. Aircraft in the hangars exploded and burned in place. After one pass, Lieutenant Nono took his eight Zeros farther south to Bellows Field for a strafing run against some of the planes trying to get airborne.

Gordon Jones and his brother Earl had been stationed at Kaneohe on December 2, 1941, and yet only five days later they were to have their baptism of fire. Between the first and second waves, they were kept busy trying to extinguish fires and move less-damaged planes to safer locations. When the attack began, they had no reason to suspect that the second wave would be any different to the first, as Gordon recalls: "When this new wave of fighters attacked, we were ordered to run and take shelter. Most of us ran to our nearest steel hangar ... this bomb attack made us aware that the hangar was not a safe place to be ... several of us ran north to an abandoned Officer's Club and hid under it until it too was machine gunned. I managed to crawl out and took off my white uniform, because I was told that men in whites were targets. I then climbed under a large thorny bush ... for some reason I felt much safer at this point than I had during the entire attack." For most of the men at Kaneohe, there was little else they could do but take cover until the devastating assault had passed.

Chief Ordnanceman John William Finn, a Navy veteran of 15 years service, was in charge of looking after the squadron's machine guns at Kaneohe, but Sunday, December 7, was his rest day. The sound of machine gun fire awoke him rudely though, and he rapidly drove from his quarters to the hangars and his ordnance shop to see what was happening. Maddened by the scene of chaos and devastation that he saw, he set up and manned both a .30cal and a .50cal machine gun in a completely exposed section of the parking ramp, despite the attention of heavy enemy strafing fire. He later recalled: "I was so mad I wasn't scared." Finn was hit several times by bomb shrapnel as he valiantly returned the Japanese fire, but he continued to man the guns, as other sailors supplied him

The USS *Arizona* explodes during the fight for Pearl. (Tom Laemlein)

with ammunition. He was later awarded the Congressional Medal of Honor for his valor and courage beyond the call of duty in this action. One Japanese Zero, commanded by Lieutenant Fusata Iida, did crash but despite this loss the attack on Kaneohe achieved its aims. Three PBYs were out on patrol, but of those remaining, 33 were destroyed. Iida's fellow fighters began to re-form to fly to Wheeler when holes opened in their aircraft – they were under attack! US fighters with blazing machine guns were coming after them. Four pilots from the 46th Pursuit Squadron had managed to get airborne in their P-36s from Wheeler and were vectored to Kaneohe. Iyozo Fujita, Iida's second-in-command, shot down one P-36, but left the battle heavily damaged with two other damaged Zeros. On the north shore two more P-36s attacked and he could not come to the aid of his men who were shot down. Fujita himself was barely able to make it back.

Pearl Harbor was filled with burning oil, its smudgy plumes darkening the skies above the twisted metal hulks of American warships. Stragglers and survivors were taken to aid centers or headquarters. A dive-bombing raid on Battleship Row commenced at 0905hrs with hits on USS *New Orleans*, *Cassin*, and *Downes*. Both of the latter were soon in flames and had to be abandoned. Another dive-bomber put a hit on *Pennsylvania*'s starboard side at 0907hrs, doing a relatively small amount of structural damage but killing 18 and wounding 30 officers and men.

Aerial view of Battleship Row, beside Ford Island, during the early part of the horizontal bombing attack on the ships moored there. Ships seen are (from left to right): USS *Nevada*; USS *Arizona* with USS *Vestal* moored outboard; USS *Tennessee* with USS *West Virginia* moored outboard; and USS *Maryland* with USS *Oklahoma* moored outboard. (US Naval Historical Center)

USS *Blue* started for the mouth of the harbor. Two Japanese Vals buzzed the destroyer and were met with .50cal fire. One went down off the channel entrance as *Blue* broke through to the open sea and began patrolling. There was a sound on sonar, and *Blue* responded with depth charges. A pattern of bubbles and an oily patina colored the waters for 200ft, suggesting a hit.

At the same time dive-bombers singled out larger ships. *Raleigh* had survived the first wave, but now was wracked by a hit and a near miss aft. One bomb passed through the deck and missed *Raleigh*'s aviation fuel tanks by less than four yards. *Raleigh* reeled and threatened to capsize. Only by sheer hard work did her commander keep her upright and afloat.

Welch and Taylor made their presence known at Ewa Mooring Mast Field. Taylor got two when he dropped into groups of strafing *Hiryu* and *Akagi* dive-bombers, first firing at the one ahead, and taking fire from one behind him. Welch also claimed two. They landed at Wheeler to refuel and rearm.

Through the oily smoke poked a battered bow: the battleship *Nevada* was making her run south. Minutes earlier she had picked up a few floating survivors from the *Arizona* as she was gaining momentum. Twenty-three Vals homed in on *Nevada*. She took a dozen bomb hits as the *Kaga* unit singled her out for destruction. Eight bombs fell near her, their explosions sending splinters into her side and geysers of water sluicing over her decks. It appeared that she would escape without further damage when one last bomb exploded in front of her forecastle.

Lieutenant-Commander Thomas knew the peril. *Nevada* was responding with difficulty, and he realized she was taking on water. If she went down here, she would partially block the harbor and make undamaged vessels still in the harbor sitting targets. He gave orders to turn to port and sluggishly she reacted, her bow plowing into shore at Hospital Point, knocking sailors sprawling, and grounding *Nevada*. Her bow looked as if it had been gnawed off, and her superstructure was partly buckled – but she had not sunk! It was a minor victory, but every vessel denied the enemy was one more vessel which could later take the fight to them.

Meanwhile, chaos ruled the basin. Burning oil floated toward *California*; *Maryland* struggled to free herself from inboard of *Oklahoma*, which had capsized; *Arizona* smoldered.

St. Louis' commander, Captain Rood, had her make way and at 0940hrs, with her engines full astern, she sped down the channel, disregarding the normal 8-knot speed limit in harbor and certain that at any moment Japanese aircraft could sight her and attack. *St. Louis*' speed crept up to 22 knots and she cleared the harbor at 1004hrs. No doubt Rood thought *St. Louis* was clear, but then the watch saw two torpedo wakes closing with her stern. He ordered her on an immediate evasion course, and an explosion rattled her when the torpedoes hit a coral reef. A midget submarine surfaced and *St. Louis*' gun crews opened fire, but the sub's conning tower had disappeared. *St. Louis* was the last ship to leave Pearl Harbor during the attack. After bombing the harbor, the Vals flew toward Hickam, Wheeler, and Ewa

USS *Cassin* photographed here in a dry dock after the Japanese attackers had left and the dust had finally settled over Pearl Harbor. (Tom Laemlein)

to strafe the airfields and buildings. At Wheeler, Welch and Taylor had their fuel tanks filled and almost had the cowlings buttoned up when the *Kaga* Vals began strafing. Both got in the air and shot down two enemy planes just outside the base. They chased the others to claim two more. Welch then flew on to Ewa and secured another victory.

Lieutenant-Commander Shimazaki's Kates hit Hickam and were joined by dive-bombers that helped strafe hangars and aircraft on the runway. The B-17s absorbed a great deal of damage, but showed once more why they were called "Flying Fortresses" due to their resilience. Having little more to do and needing to reach the rendezvous, Shimazaki's men headed away from the airfield. At 1100hrs, Commander Fuchida began his recon and assessment flight over Oahu. Carefully, he noted which ship positions were burning, which had capsized or were now low in the water, and which appeared unharmed. Fuchida stayed over the harbor, observing and rounding up stragglers. When the last aircraft of the latest wave turned west, Fuchida looked at the sun overhead and headed toward *Akagi*.

At 1000hrs, aircraft of the first wave returned to the task force and began landing on *Akagi*,

Looking down the dry dock at 1010 Pier, *Cassin* and *Downes* (center rear) are smoldering. *Helena* sits beside the pier, and the dry docked *Pennsylvania* is visible in the background. In the center, the minelayer *Oglala* has capsized. (US Navy)

Kaga, and other carriers positioned 260 miles north of Oahu. Back on the island, Governor Poindexter issued a state of emergency for the entire Hawaiian territory, first to newspapers, and 15 minutes later via a radio broadcast. Reports of civilian casualties started coming in from hospitals, and by 1042hrs all radio stations had shut off their transmitters to prevent them being used as homing beacons by attacking aircraft. Meanwhile, Lieutenant-General Short conferred with Poindexter about placing the entire territory under martial law while the first false reports of invading enemy troops began circulating. All schools were ordered closed. That night, and every night in the near future, there would be a blackout in Hawaii.

Surviving American aircraft took off from damaged fields and immediately began the search for their attackers. They flew 360 degrees, but did not sight the Japanese task force. At 1230hrs, the Honolulu police, aided by the FBI, descended on the Japanese embassy, where they found consular personnel near wastepaper baskets full of ashes and still-burning documents.

Commander Fuchida touched down at 1300hrs aboard the *Akagi*. He discussed launching a third wave with Admiral Nagumo, but Nagumo believed they had done well enough and decided not to launch another attack. At 1630hrs, Nagumo turned the taskforce to withdraw. Tadao Fuchikami delivered the message from Washington to Lieutenant-General Short's headquarters at 1145hrs. It still had to be decoded and would not be seen by Short for another three hours. Almost seven hours after the attack had started, and easily seven and a half hours too late to be of any use, word of the now-past danger reached Short.

AFTERMATH

Japanese losses were minimal – indeed negligible – in view of the victory they had won: just 64 killed (it is not known how many were wounded). American losses were staggering: 2,390 casualties (2,108 Navy/Marines, 233 Army, and 49 civilians) and 1,178 were wounded (779 Navy/Marines, 364 Army, and 35 civilians).

The *Arizona* saw the greatest loss of life, accounting for half the naval casualties. As a result of Pearl Harbor, 16 Congressional Medals of Honor, 51 Navy Crosses, 53 Silver Crosses, four Navy and Marine Corps Medals, one Distinguished Flying Cross, four Distinguished Service Crosses, one Distinguished Service Medal, and three Bronze Stars were awarded for the 110 minutes of combat.

A tally of vessels shows 21 sunk or damaged, testifying to the accuracy of Japanese attacks; five battleships, one minelayer, three destroyers, two service craft, and one auxiliary sunk; one cruiser and one auxiliary severely damaged; three battleships, two cruisers, one destroyer, and one auxiliary moderately damaged. The US lost 171 aircraft (97 Navy and 74 Army) and 159 were damaged.

The results for the Japanese commanders were not clear-cut. Confusion, because of multiple and overlapping attack responsibilities, had commanders duplicate results given by other commanders but the success of the attack was still unquestionable.

Actual damage to the fleet and the subsequent fate of the ships was as follows:

US ship losses

Arizona BB39, two bomb hits, sunk; now the final resting place for the fallen crew of the ship.

NEXT SPREAD
Sailors in a motor launch rescue a survivor from the water alongside the sunken USS *West Virginia* during or shortly after the Japanese air raid on Pearl Harbor. USS *Tennessee* is inboard of the sunken battleship. Note extensive distortion of *West Virginia*'s lower midships superstructure, caused by torpedoes that exploded below that location. (US Navy)

Although the Japanese suffered few casualties, not all pilots made it home safely. This Mitsubishi A6M2 Type 00, Zero-Sen, was shot down next to the ordnance machine shop, adjacent to Hickam Field, during the attack. The pilot and three soldiers died. (NARA)

California BB44, two torpedo hits, one large bomb hit, one or more bomb near misses, sunk; later raised and repaired.

Maryland BB46, two bomb hits, damaged; repaired and modernized.

Nevada BB36, one torpedo hit, five or more bomb hits, two bomb near misses, heavily damaged; beached, repaired, and modernized.

Oklahoma BB37, five or more torpedo hits, capsized and sunk.

Pennsylvania BB38, one bomb hit, damaged; repaired.

Tennessee BB43, two bomb hits, damaged; repaired.

West Virginia BB48, two bomb hits, five to seven torpedo hits, sunk; raised, repaired, and modernized.

Helena CL50, one torpedo hit, heavily damaged; repaired.

Honolulu CL48, one bomb near miss with moderate damage; repaired.

Raleigh CL7, one torpedo and one bomb hit, heavily damaged; repaired and refitted.

Cassin DD372, one bomb hit, secondary

explosions caused by depth charges; damaged beyond repair.

Downes DD375, two bomb hits, secondary explosions caused by depth charges and torpedoes; damaged beyond repair.

Helm DD388, one bomb near miss, moderate damage; repaired.

Shaw DD373, three bomb hits, bow blown off in explosion; repaired.

Oglala CM4, one torpedo that passed under the ship, sunk; salvaged and repaired.

Curtiss AV4, one bomb hit, damaged; repaired.

Sotoyomo YT9, sunk; raised and repaired.

Utah AG16, two or three torpedo hits, capsized; sunk.

Vestal AR4, two bomb hits, heavily damaged; grounded, refloated, and repaired.

YFD-2 sunk; raised and repaired.

US aircraft losses

Bellows Field: three planes.

Ewa Marine Corps Air Station: 33 planes.

Ford Island Naval Air Station: 26 planes.

Hickam Field: 18 planes.

Kaneohe Naval Air Station: 28 planes.

Wheeler Field: 53 planes.

USS *Enterprise*: ten planes.

Japanese losses

Aircraft: nine fighters, 15 dive-bombers, five torpedo planes.

Submarines: five midget subs.

Casualties: 55 airmen, nine midget submarine crewmen.

Japanese midget (two-man) submarines were ferried to Pearl aboard larger Japanese submarines. This one was dimpled by depth charges, rammed by *Monaghan* and consequently beached. (NARA)

Before the oily smoke had drifted away, the United States was no longer neutral. After two hours of air strikes, the day of the battleship had passed as decisively as the day of horse cavalry. Air power, which had been tolerated and given lip service by many, became the branch of service of the hour.

Yamamoto was correct in stating that the Japanese attack on Pearl Harbor awakened a sleeping giant, because it unified the American people against a common enemy. Americans rallied around the icon of Pearl Harbor the way earlier generations had heeded the nationalistic imperative of "Remember the Alamo." The war with Japan would end on the deck of the USS *Missouri* at 0903hrs on September 2, 1945, in Tokyo Bay, but it all began at 0645hrs, December 7, 1941, at Pearl Harbor.

HARBOR • CORAL SEA

ORIGINS OF THE CAMPAIGN

Fortunately for the Americans, none of the Pacific Fleet's aircraft carriers were present at Pearl Harbor. With these ships, and an entirely new doctrine, the US Navy pondered how to reverse the tide of Japanese expansion. Even the Imperial Japanese Navy (IJN) was caught unaware by its success at Pearl Harbor. The concept of massing all of the fleet's large carriers into a single cohesive unit, combined with the excellent aircraft and superb aircrews of the carriers themselves, had created a revolution in naval warfare. The destruction of the American battlefleet had clearly demonstrated that air power was now the dominant factor in naval warfare. As with the Americans, this development rendered the IJN's pre-war calculations irrelevant. The IJN was also built for a decisive clash of dreadnoughts for mastery of the Pacific, but this clash would never occur. However, with its decided edge in aircraft carriers, the IJN could now conduct a war of expansion with the hopes that it could construct an unassailable position in the Pacific.

As part of the agreed expansion plan of both the Japanese Army and Navy the first operational stage of the war called for the occupation of the Philippines, Malaya, the Dutch East Indies, Burma, and Rabaul. One of the hallmarks of the early campaigns was the virtually uncontested success of the IJN's carrier force or Kido Butai. Following the Pearl Harbor operation, the Kido Butai was used to cover the capture of Rabaul in January 1942 and the Dutch East Indies in February. In April, Japanese carriers moved into the Indian Ocean to conduct a rampage against British naval forces and shipping.

Allied naval forces were unable to stop the Japanese advance. The US did conduct some offensive operations, such as the carrier strikes against Japanese forces on the Marshall and Gilbert islands, as well as a raid on Tokyo itself. Whatever the psychological results were for American morale or for Japanese fears of further raids on their homeland, the commitment of half of the Pacific Fleet's carriers to this operation meant that the US could not respond to the next Japanese offensive move in the South Pacific in early May. During the second operational stage, the Japanese envisioned further expansion into eastern New Guinea, New Britain, the Fijis, and Samoa in the South Pacific. With the Japanese now ready to execute these plans, the unavailability of *Enterprise* and *Hornet*, the two US carriers assigned to

OPPOSITE
A Japanese strike is prepared from the deck of the carrier *Shokaku*. (US Navy)

OPPOSITE
It remains unclear why Yamamoto was so highly regarded by his peers as he engineered the attack on Pearl Harbor, the most politically disastrous naval operation in modern history; the invasion of Midway, a stunning and avoidable setback; and the catastrophic air war of attrition against US forces in the South Pacific. (US Naval Institute)

the action against Tokyo, meant that the commander of the Pacific Fleet could deploy only two carriers to the South Pacific by the time the Japanese offensive was predicted to begin in early May. With part of the Kido Butai committed to support the South Pacific operation, the scene was set for history's first carrier battle.

OPPOSING COMMANDERS

THE JAPANESE COMMANDERS

By early 1942, following the success of the Pearl Harbor attacks, Admiral Isoroku Yamamoto's primacy in shaping Japanese naval strategy was assured. Despite his opposition to further operations in the South Pacific, which he viewed as contrary to his preferred Central Pacific drive in order to bring the US Pacific Fleet to a decisive battle, Yamamoto grudgingly gave his approval to the attack on Port Moresby (designated Operation *MO*) and even contributed a significant proportion of the Kido Butai. This act was to have massive consequences not only for the Coral Sea battle, but also for the subsequent battle of Midway.

BELOW
Vice-Admiral Takagi Takeo was charged with the most important role in the *MO* Operation as commander of the Carrier Striking Force. He squandered several chances to deal a devastating blow to the American carriers and ultimately failed either to protect the Invasion Force or to destroy the American carriers. (US Naval Institute)

Vice-Admiral Inoue Shigeyoshi was commander of the 4th Fleet, also known as the South Sea Force. He was the former chief of the Aeronautical Department and was therefore fully aware of the role aircraft now played in naval warfare. He aggressively pushed to expand Japan's operations in the South Pacific and he was the designer of the Japanese operations into the Coral Sea.

Rear-Admiral Takagi Takeo was commander of the *MO* Carrier Striking Force, the attack on Port Moresby, and had previously enjoyed success with the 5th Cruiser Division during the battle of Java Sea. Because Takeo's cruisers were never assigned to work with the IJN's carrier force during the early part of the war, Takeo had no experience with carriers. The unfamiliarity of Takeo and his staff with carrier operations led him to delegate full authority for carrier operations to Hara, the commander of the 5th Carrier Division.

Rear-Admiral Chuichi Hara was given command of the 5th Carrier Division consisting of the IJN's two newest and most modern carriers. This division had taken part in the Pearl Harbor attack and the Indian Ocean raid. Thus by May 1942, Hara had accumulated a wealth of carrier experience in a short time.

THE US COMMANDERS

The paramount figure behind all US naval strategy during World War II was Ernest J. King. In the command shake-up after Pearl Harbor, King was promoted to Commander-in-Chief US Fleet. In March, he was also appointed as Chief of Naval Operations, giving him ultimate authority over all US naval strategy and operations. With this sweeping authority, he quickly sought to expand the Navy's freedom of action in the Pacific, which under the "Germany First" strategy was clearly defined as a secondary theater. He was determined to fight for the South Pacific and to begin offensive operations as soon as possible.

The commander of the US Pacific Fleet, effective December 31, 1941, was Admiral Chester W. Nimitz. His calm, determined demeanor saw him selected over many more senior admirals to assume the role of Pacific Fleet commander in the aftermath of the Pearl

Harbor disaster. On April 3, Nimitz was appointed as Commander-in-Chief of the Pacific Ocean Areas (including the North Pacific, Central, and South Pacific Areas) in addition to his duties as commander of the Pacific Fleet. This meant that Nimitz was responsible for the execution of King's plans to launch offensive operations as soon as possible.

The most important American naval command personality in the battle was Rear-Admiral Frank Jack Fletcher. Despite his lack of aviation experience, by the time of Coral Sea he was one of the US Navy's most seasoned carrier commanders. During the actual carrier battle phase, Fletcher gave tactical control of the carrier task force over to Rear-Admiral Aubrey Fitch. At the time, Fitch commanded one of the two carrier divisions in the Pacific Fleet. (The other was commanded by the US Navy's senior naval aviator, Vice-Admiral William F. Halsey.) Fitch was junior to Fletcher but had considerable carrier experience. He qualified as a pilot in 1930 at age 47, and thus became known as a "Johnny Come Lately" to officers who had spent their entire career as aviators.

The captains of the two American carriers at Coral Sea were both naval aviators, as were all carrier skippers per US Navy regulation. The captain of USS *Yorktown* was Elliott Buckmaster, known for his excellent seamanship and his willingness to let his aviators experiment. *Yorktown*'s air group had become one of the best in the fleet. Captain Frederick "Ted" Sherman had been commanding officer of *Lexington* for two years and had worked the ship into a high state of efficiency. He was one of the first US naval officers to realize the value of concentrating multiple carriers into a single task force and these principles were used during the Coral Sea battle even though this strategy was against prevailing US Navy doctrine of the day.

OPPOSING FLEETS

THE IJN CARRIER FORCE

In early 1942, the IJN's carrier force was at its zenith. The Kido Butai (literally "mobile force" but better understood as "striking force") had

LEFT TO RIGHT Admiral Chester Nimitz (left) receiving the Distinguished Service Medal from Admiral King aboard USS *Pennsylvania* on June 30, 1942. The award was given for his leadership of the Pacific Fleet during the battles of the Coral Sea and Midway. (US Naval Historical Center); Admiral Frank Fletcher in September 1942. Despite criticism from many quarters, he was the victor at the battle of the Coral Sea and the first Allied naval commander to inflict a strategic defeat on the IJN during the Pacific War. (US Naval Historical Center); Captain Frederick Sherman in 1938 before assuming command of the *Lexington*. His career was not affected by the loss of his ship at Coral Sea and he went on to command carrier task forces. (US Naval Historical Center)

accomplished every mission it had been assigned and had smashed all Allied opposition before it without the loss of a single carrier. However, it had yet to meet the US Navy's carrier force. In May 1942, the IJN's carrier force held both a numerical and qualitative edge over its American counterpart. Had the force remained massed as it had been during the first part of the war, it would have retained a numerical edge in any battle with the US Navy's carrier force. However, for the Coral Sea operation only three carriers would be committed.

The heart of the *MO* Operation was the two ships of the *Shokaku* class, the *Shokaku* and the *Zuikaku*, which made up the Kido Butai's 5th Carrier Division. They were the epitome of Japanese carrier design and the most powerful and best-balanced carrier design in the Pacific at the time. Huge, yet incredibly fast, they also carried a heavy defensive armament with eight Type 89 twin 5in guns fitted in pairs, each with its own fire-control director. They were supported by *Shoho* – originally a high-speed oiler converted very successfully into a light carrier. She was capable of adequate speed but lacked sufficient defensive armament.

Unlike the Americans, no Japanese carrier began the war fitted with radar. This situation persisted until after the battle of Midway. This made the task of controlling defending fighters very difficult. In the early-war period, half of the 18-aircraft fighter squadron was dedicated for defense. With no radar, air defense was accomplished by conducting standing patrols. However, only a few aircraft (usually a section of three) would be airborne at any time with the remaining aircraft standing by to be scrambled if adequate warning was gained. Adding further difficulty to the fighter defense problem was the inferior quality of Japanese aircraft radios, which made it virtually impossible to control aircraft already airborne.

A close-up shot of the cockpit and the Type 91 air-launched torpedo carried aboard a Type 97 carrier attack plane. The combination of this relatively fast torpedo plane and an excellent torpedo provided the IJN with a superb ship-killing capability. (US Naval Historical Center)

The primary defense against air attack was mounted by fighters or by the ability of a carrier's captain to maneuver skillfully under attack. When exposed to air attack, Japanese carrier escorts maneuvered independently to give the carrier maximum room for maneuver. In contrast, American carrier escorts also gave the carrier room for radical maneuvers, but were still expected to stay close enough to the carrier to provide anti-aircraft support.

One important advantage exercised by the Japanese at the start of the war was their ability to mass carrier air power. In April 1941, the Japanese brought all their fleet carriers into a single formation, the 1st Air Fleet. The Kido Butai was the operational component of the 1st Air Fleet. Three carrier divisions made up the Kido Butai, including the 5th with the newly completed *Shokaku* and *Zuikaku*. Throughout 1942, including at Coral Sea, the IJN was able to integrate operations from different carriers far better than the US Navy and routinely achieved a higher level of coordination.

Each Japanese carrier had its own air group. This air group was named after its parent ship and was permanently assigned to the ship. The aviators of the air group as well as all of the personnel required to support the aircraft were assigned to the ship's company.

Shokaku-class carriers had air groups made up of three different types of flying units: fighter, dive-bombers, and torpedo bombers. Even with relatively light aircraft losses, by May 1942 the IJN was unable to provide the two ships of 5th Carrier Division with approximately 63 aircraft. As a light carrier, *Shoho* embarked only two types of squadrons, fighter and carrier attack and only embarked 18 aircraft in total due to previous losses.

THE US NAVY CARRIER FORCE

The carrier force was untouched in the Pearl Harbor attack. *Enterprise* and *Lexington* were both in the area of Pearl Harbor, but were not actually in the harbor on December 7. Numerically, the US Navy had a fleet carrier force equal to the Japanese in 1942, but in terms of employment, aircraft capabilities, and personnel training, the two opposing carrier forces were very different.

The *Lexington* was the first true US Navy fleet carrier. Converted from a battlecruiser, she displaced over 36,000 tons. Her most salient feature (shared with her sister ship the *Saratoga*) was the huge smokestack on the starboard side located just behind the separate island. *Lexington* was fast but not very maneuverable due to her length. However, in 1940 a CXAM air search radar was installed on the forward part of *Lexington*'s stack. For anti-aircraft protection there were 5in/25 gun mounts and a large battery of automatic weapons including .50cal machine guns.

Yorktown, alongside her two sister ships, was the first of the truly modern US Navy fleet carriers. These 20,000-ton ships were large enough to permit the incorporation of protection against torpedo attack. A 4in side armor belt was fitted over the machinery spaces, magazines, and gasoline storage tanks. Vertical protection was limited to 1.5in of armor over the machinery spaces. The main deck was the hangar deck with the unarmored flight deck being built of light steel. The primary design focus of the class was to provide adequate space to operate a large air group. The *Yorktown* class also received a heavy defensive battery to counter enemy air attack including the new 5in/38 dual-purpose guns, which proved to be the best long-range anti-aircraft weapon of the war in any navy. Another important improvement was the addition of radar. *Yorktown* was one of the ships to receive one of the first CXAM air search radar sets.

As the Americans believed their carriers to be extremely vulnerable to air attack, prewar doctrine dictated that carriers should be separated so as to avoid potential simultaneous detection and destruction. But radar did provide a huge advantage, although its inability to give reliable altitudes, combined with a general lack of experience and wider

Lexington in February 1933 pictured off the Hawaiian Islands. The ship's battlecruiser lineage and the large stack aft of the small bridge are evident. The US Navy's emphasis on embarking a large air group can be seen by the large numbers of aircraft spotted forward and aft on the flight deck. (US Naval Historical Center)

Dauntless dive-bombers of *Yorktown*'s Bombing Squadron Five shown on deck in April 1942. The Dauntless dive-bomber was the primary offensive weapon of US Navy carrier air groups, as events during the battle of the Coral Sea would demonstrate. (US Naval Historical Center)

communication problems, would greatly complicate fighter direction.

Typically, half of a carrier's fighters would be retained for fleet air defense. These were used to mount standing combat air patrols (CAP) of two to three hours' duration during daylight hours above the carrier. The remaining fighters would be fueled and armed on deck ready for launch to augment the existing patrols.

Early 1942 American carrier strike doctrine was less mature than that practiced by the IJN. Typically, in the morning, a number of dive-bombers would be launched to perform reconnaissance. If a target was located, a strike was launched as soon as possible with every available dive-bomber and torpedo plane. The fighter squadron was usually divided, with half providing strike escort and the other half providing CAP. The problem with US Navy strike doctrine was that it remained focused on the operations of a single air group from a single carrier, while the Japanese had made the mental leap to mass all their fleet carriers into a single unit and could operate aircraft from multiple carriers as a single entity in combat. The ranges of US aircraft were also inferior to those of the Japanese.

OPPOSING PLANS

THE JAPANESE PLAN – THE NAVAL GENERAL STAFF VS. THE COMBINED FLEET

The first part of the second operational stage went smoothly when Lae and Salamaua in Papua New Guinea were captured on March 8.

ABOVE
The heavy cruiser *Myoko* was the lead ship of a four-ship class. Two of these powerful ships were assigned as the primary screening units for the *MO* Carrier Striking Force. With ten 8in guns and 16 24in torpedoes, they were more heavily armed than any Allied cruiser in 1942. (Yamato Museum)

However, the Japanese illusion of a continued run of unchallenged successes was shattered on March 10 when American carrier-based aircraft struck the Japanese invasion force, preventing additional advances until Japanese forces in the region were reinforced to deal with potential future intervention by American carriers.

The continued expansion in the South Pacific therefore depended on the willingness of Yamamoto to contribute some of the Combined Fleet's carriers to the effort. But Yamamoto preferred to put off any South Pacific expedition until his decisive clash at Midway could be finished. During the first week of April, the issue of future strategy was decided in Yamamoto's favor and his plan to attack Midway approved. However, in a move to placate the Naval General Staff, it was also agreed that the Kido Butai's 5th Carrier Division would be made available to support the Port Moresby operation before it was used in the Midway operation.

The attack on Port Moresby, the largest town in Papua New Guinea, was codenamed the *MO* Operation. The primary job of the two fleet carriers assigned to the *MO* Striking Force was to take out the Allied air bases in Australia, not to engage US carriers. After their

RIGHT
Aircraft on an IJN carrier prepare for attack. (akg-images)

surprise attack on Townsville, the carriers would refuel and move into position in the center of the Coral Sea to intercept Allied naval forces, which were only then expected to respond to the invasion. Additional air raids could be conducted on other air bases as required. The carriers (including *Shoho*) would eventually return to Japan to be incorporated into the huge force being gathered for the *MI* Operation – the invasion of Midway.

The whole *MO* Operation featured a force of some 60 ships assigned to Vice-Admiral Shigeyoshi's South Seas Force. This included two large carriers, one light carrier, six heavy cruisers, three light cruisers, and 15 destroyers. The balance of the force was composed of a variety of auxiliaries. Altogether, some 250 aircraft were assigned to the operation (not including floatplanes) and of these, some 140 were aboard the three carriers.

As was typical in Japanese operational planning, the *MO* Operation's plan depended on close coordination of widely separated forces. Any delay in any aspect of the plan had the potential to throw the entire operation into jeopardy. This was amply demonstrated by the example of the *MO* Carrier Striking Force's mission of ferrying nine Type Zero fighters from Truk to Rabaul. The delay in executing this seemingly simple mission in turn delayed the arrival of the carriers into the Coral Sea, imperiling the entire operation. Even before its execution, the *MO* plan had met severe resistance from the admirals expected to execute it, who had a growing suspicion that American carriers could be present in the area. This prompted Lieutenant-Commander Shigeharu Murata to authorize Takeo on April 29 to cancel the Townsville raid if surprise could not be achieved. The same day, Yamamoto weighed in and ordered that all strikes from the carriers against targets in Australia be cancelled and that the *MO* Carrier Striking Force be prepared instead to engage enemy carriers. This effectively meant that there would no longer be adequate air cover for the *MO* invasion fleet despite the overwhelming Allied land-based aircraft which were in range.

The standard 5in gun aboard all US heavy cruisers at the battle of the Coral Sea was the 5in gun. This is the No. 3 mount aboard heavy cruiser *Astoria*. (US Naval Historical Center)

The most damning aspect of the plans for the *MO* Operation was its utter disregard for the actions of the enemy. By committing only a portion of the Kido Butai, Yamamoto not only jeopardized the success of the *MO* Operation, but exposed those units to defeat in detail. If those carriers, the decisive edge the IJN held over the US Navy's carrier force, were lost or damaged, they would be unable to participate in Yamamoto's decisive assault on Midway.

THE US PLAN

King's first orders to the commander of the Pacific Fleet were to hold the key Central Pacific positions at Hawaii and Midway, but also to protect the sea-lines of communications from the US to Australia. King was determined that the "Germany first" strategy would not prevent him from local offensive operations. Japanese expansion into the South Pacific virtually ensured that King would get his way. The Japanese seizure of Rabaul on January 23 heightened fears that the Fijis or New Caledonia would be next.

On April 22, Nimitz sent his orders to Fletcher. He warned Fletcher about the impending Japanese offensive and gave him an idea of the size of the enemy force (three or four carriers). The heart of the directive was contained in this phrase: "Your task is to assist in checking further advance by enemy in above areas [New Guinea–Solomons] by seizing favorable opportunities to destroy ships shipping and aircraft." The order is noteworthy in that Nimitz did not tell Fletcher how to accomplish the mission. This was totally up to Fletcher.

Nimitz issued detailed instructions to commanders on April 29. By this time, additional intelligence was also provided to Fletcher. It now seemed all but certain that the enemy intended to strike at both Port Moresby and Tulagi. To take on the Japanese, Fletcher had the carrier *Yorktown*, which with her escorts of three cruisers and four destroyers comprised Task Force 17 (TF-17). After a short stop in Pearl Harbor beginning on March 26, the carrier *Lexington* (with her escorting two cruisers and five destroyers making up TF-11) was ordered to rendezvous with Fletcher in the eastern Coral Sea on May 1. Fletcher would assume command of the combined carrier force. With his two carriers, Fletcher had the basic mission of covering Port Moresby and the Solomons. After meeting with TF-11 on May 1, 300 miles northwest of New Caledonia, Fletcher decided to move to a point 325 miles south of Guadalcanal to be prepared to react to any Japanese movement. Supporting Fletcher was General Douglas MacArthur's Southwest Pacific Area Naval Forces organized into TF-44. This force would rendezvous on May 4, 350 miles southwest of Guadalcanal, and come under Fletcher's overall control. Four US Navy submarines were also provided by MacArthur and assigned patrols in Japanese areas.

Overall, Fletcher's plan was simple and showed flexibility. With half of the Pacific Fleet's operational carriers entrusted to him, he displayed a prudent combination of caution mixed with opportunistic aggressiveness. His focus was on protecting Port Moresby as it was here that the greatest threat seemed to be. He was hamstrung by inadequate air reconnaissance and logistical resources, but both were beyond his control. If there was a fault with his planning, it was the focus on the Coral Sea and the approaches to Port Moresby. No air searches were focused on the area east of the Solomons where, unknown to Fletcher, the greatest danger lay.

Both Nimitz and King were overconfident regarding the capability of US carriers, and were willing to accept battle on inferior terms. Even when it appeared that the Japanese force would contain as many as four carriers, Nimitz was determined to bring the Japanese carrier forces in the Coral Sea to battle. If he could reduce their strength, the offensive power of the entire IJN would be blunted.

THE BATTLE OF THE CORAL SEA

OPENING MOVES

The first blow of the battle was delivered on the morning of May 3 when the 3rd Kure Special Naval Landing Force landed unopposed on the

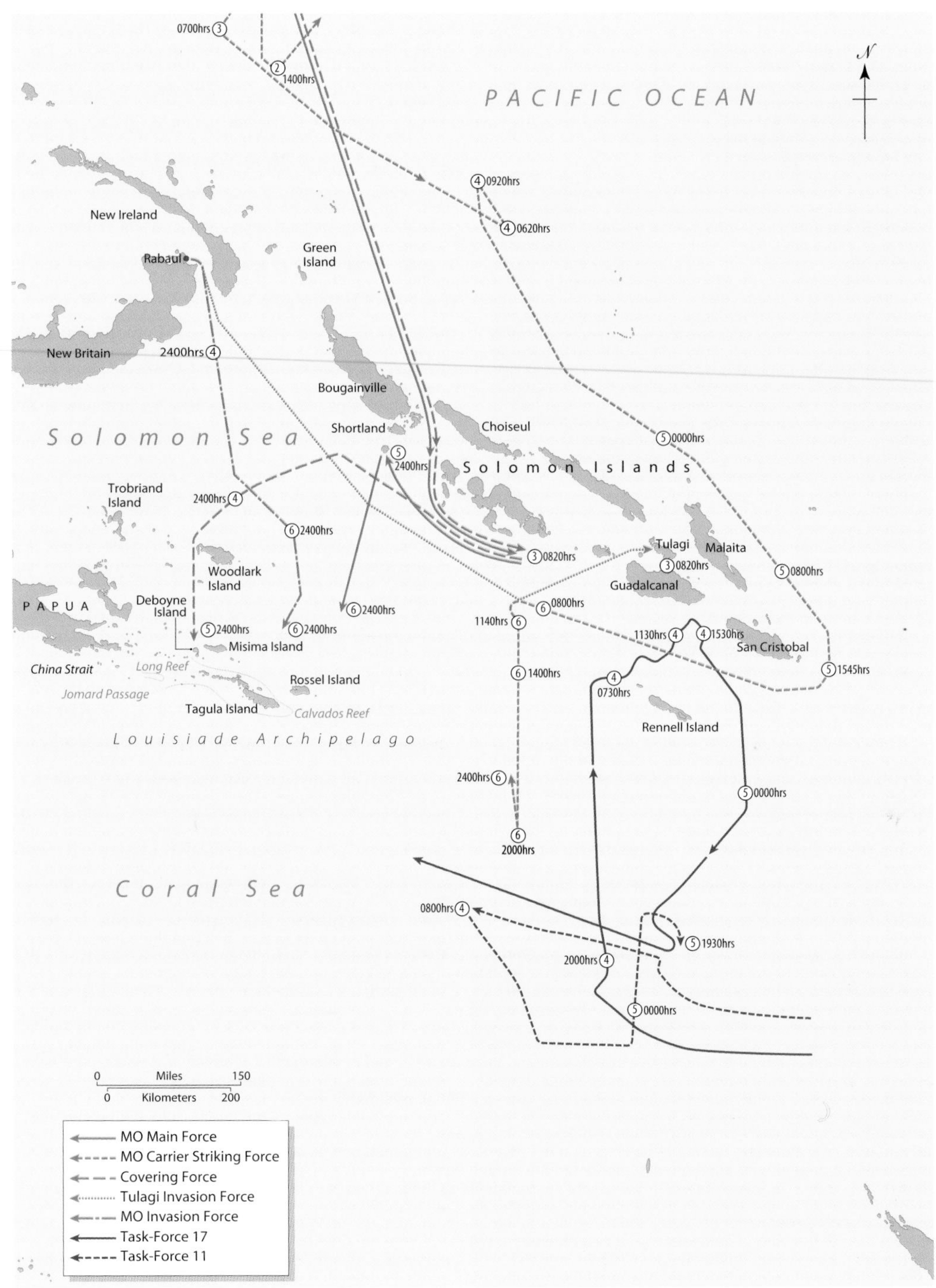

A map showing the movement of US and Japanese forces between May 2 and 6. (Osprey Publishing Ltd.)

islands of Tulagi and Gavutu. However, by the end of May 3, the tightly synchronized *MO* plan was already running into trouble. The Carrier Striking Force was tasked with the seemingly simple mission of ferrying nine Zero fighters from Truk to Rabaul to increase their chances

> "We have awakened a sleeping giant and instilled in it a terrible resolve."
>
> **— ADMIRAL YAMAMOTO**

were severely let down by the efforts of their reconnaissance aircraft and crews and these series of mistakes would shape the battle. Allied Air Forces' aircraft continued to focus their efforts on the area north of the Louisiades and into the Solomon Sea, augmented with flights of Dauntlesses from *Yorktown*. The Japanese also made a large-scale scouting effort using land and carrier based aircraft. The first side to receive solid contact reports would probably be the first to launch its strike, thus grabbing victory.

Also at dawn on May 7, Fletcher decided to detach TG-17.3 under the command of British Rear-Admiral J. G. Crace. Under his command Crace had three cruisers and three destroyers. Crace's mission was to prevent the *MO* Invasion Force from passing south of the Louisiades. This was a controversial move as it removed one third of Fletcher's already weak carrier screen and placed a force with no air cover within range of Japanese land-based aircraft. But Fletcher's rationale was that if the carrier battle neutralized both forces, as often happened in US Navy prewar exercises, then Crace would be positioned to contest the Japanese advance into the Coral Sea. Under the circumstances, this seemed a good insurance move by Fletcher.

Given the relatively small area of operations and the numbers of ships and aircraft in motion, contact reports quickly filtered up to the respective commanders. At 0722hrs, two Type 97 carrier attack planes from *Shokaku* reported an American force of one carrier, one cruiser, and three destroyers only 163 miles south of the Japanese carriers and Hara made preparations to launch a full strike. By 0815hrs, a total of 78 aircraft (18 fighters, 24 torpedo bombers, and 26 dive-bombers) were on their way to destroy the carrier under the command of Lieutenant-Commander Takahashi Kakuichi.

What appeared to be a promising situation for the Japanese quickly turned into a potential disaster. Upon arriving at the reported contact just after 0900hrs, Kakuichi found only an oiler and its escort. An enlarged search of the area found nothing. Things got worse when Hara received reports that American carriers southeast of Rossel Island had been spotted. The force consisted of a *Saratoga*-class carrier and a second carrier, and at 1008hrs they were in the process of launching a strike. Faced with this alarming turn of events, Hara recalled his strike at 1100hrs but not before Kakuichi's dive-bombers had successfully sunk the destroyer and badly damaged the oiler.

The Japanese had squandered an opportunity to ambush the Americans and had sunk only two minor ships in return. The last of the strike had not returned until after 1500hrs, so the prospects of launching another strike that day on the real American carriers looked doubtful. Fortunately for Chuichi Hara, the strike on the oiler group did not fatally compromise his position. Later in the day, Fletcher was aware that the oiler had been attacked, but neither ship had radioed a distress signal before it was sunk or put out of action.

As the Japanese struggled to clarify their situation, an almost identical situation developed for the Americans but more favorably. As early as 0735hrs, Fletcher received word from his scouts of Japanese activity. The first sighting was of two cruisers northwest of Rossel Island. The location of the force was 225 miles northwest of TF-17, which put it beyond the range of the fighters and torpedo planes. However, with the Japanese force reported moving south and Fletcher moving north, a full attack was judged to be possible. Fletcher waited over an hour to launch, but beginning at 0926hrs *Lexington* began to put her strike of ten fighters, 28 dive-bombers, and 12 torpedo bombers into the air. At 0944hrs, *Yorktown* began the first of two launches, committing eight fighters, 25 dive-bombers, and ten torpedo bombers to the attack.

However, as soon as the planes were headed north, things began to go wrong. The return of the scout plane that had reported the two carriers revealed that the actual report had meant to report the spotting of four light cruisers and two destroyers. Confronted with the same dilemma that Hara had faced, Fletcher declined to recall his strike. He knew from Allied Air Forces' reporting that there was heavy Japanese activity in the planned strike area. The situation brightened when Fletcher received a report at 1022hrs from Port Moresby that two hours earlier a B-17 had reported a large force including a carrier just south of the false carrier report. Fletcher passed this new information to the airborne strikes and let them proceed to the target area in the hope that they would find suitable targets.

DEATH OF A CARRIER

Located in clear weather, and with a total of 93 American aircraft headed her way, *Shoho*'s first and last battle was destined to be a quick one. *Lexington*'s aircraft spotted her around 1040hrs about 40 miles to the north. *Shoho* had just landed her four-plane CAP and a carrier attack plane and just three other aircraft were airborne while several others

The light carrier *Shoho* was attacked on the morning of May 7 by a total of 93 aircraft from two American carriers. Within 15 minutes, the carrier was ripped apart by some 13 bombs and at least seven torpedo hits. *Shoho* quickly sank with heavy loss of life. (US Naval Historical Center)

were being readied on deck. *Lexington*'s air group was the first to attack and at 1118hrs, two hits with 1,000lb bombs were scored. These caused massive fires on the hangar deck that were fed by the fueled aircraft on deck. Simultaneously with the dive-bomber attack, a torpedo attack was launched at 1119hrs. Five hits were gained, enough to cause fatal damage.

The *Yorktown*'s aircraft then arrived to begin their attack on the listing *Shoho*. Fifteen hits were claimed against the non-maneuvering target and Japanese sources confirm as many as 11 hits. This brought *Shoho* dead in the water. *Shoho* had been literally torn apart by a barrage of bombs and torpedoes. Of her crew of 834, only 203 survived. US losses were just three aircraft.

By 1450hrs, both American air groups had recovered and were spotted on their carriers for additional strikes. Fletcher's aviators had done a good day's work, sinking the first Japanese carrier of the war. Given the impossibility of launching and recovering a strike before dark, and the bad weather in the area, Fletcher decided not to launch a second. While Fletcher escaped a Japanese air attack, TG-17.3 did not as it was within range of land-based aircraft. But Crace's skillful maneuvering and heavy anti-aircraft fire avoided disaster, although the Japanese were still confident they had scored heavily.

With the loss of *Shoho*, Shigeyoshi delayed the Port Moresby landings by two days and moved the invasion convoy out of range. The attack on *Shoho* did succeed in putting a greater sense of urgency into Takeo and Hara. Given the number of aircraft involved in the attack on *Shoho*, it was clear that two American carriers were on the loose. With the *MO* Operation in shambles, everything depended on the ability of the Carrier Striking

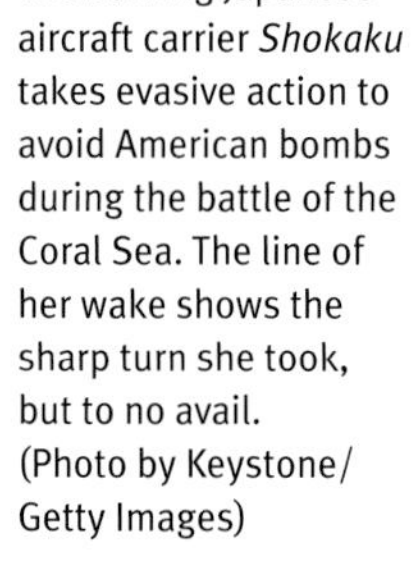

The burning Japanese aircraft carrier *Shokaku* takes evasive action to avoid American bombs during the battle of the Coral Sea. The line of her wake shows the sharp turn she took, but to no avail. (Photo by Keystone/ Getty Images)

Force to sweep the American carriers from the scene and get the operation back on schedule. Accordingly, Hara was now inclined to take a risk with a dangerous dusk strike. From *Zuikaku*, nine carrier attack aircraft and six carrier bomber crews were selected to participate, joined by six more carrier attack aircraft and six carrier bombers from *Shokaku*. The fact that there was more than a small degree of desperation involved in this venture was obvious. Some of the crews had just returned from a seven-hour strike earlier in the day and now these crews were expected to take off again in increasingly terrible weather conditions against an unlocated target.

Predictably, the operation did not go well. Unknown to the Japanese, the American carriers were only some 150 miles away but hidden under heavy clouds. When the Japanese strike arrived at its designated area, nothing was there. After an incomplete reconnaissance of the area, the three groups headed home after jettisoning their ordnance. On their return, the Japanese ran afoul of the US carriers. Wildcats directed by radar intercepted the first group, and six carrier attack planes and one carrier bomber were shot down for the loss of three Wildcats. The second and third group arrived over the American carriers in the dark and, certain they were their own ships, attempted to land. Anti-aircraft fire from the Americans accounted for another attack plane. Of the 27 aircraft launched, 18 eventually returned, a remarkable achievement. However, the loss of nine precious carrier attack planes would be felt the next day. Once debriefed, the Japanese aviators reported that TF-17 was a mere 40–60 miles to the west. Both sides now knew the other was close. The next day would certainly bring the deciding clash of the battle.

PRE-BATTLE PREPARATIONS – MAY 8

Both sides knew that quick and accurate reconnaissance was the key to deciding events on May 8. During the night, both sides attempted to place themselves in a favorable position for the forthcoming battle. Crace ordered his force to head west in order to remain southeast of Port Moresby in position to intercept any Japanese forces advancing on Port Moresby in the wake of the carrier battle. On the morning of May 8, TF-17 possessed 117 operational aircraft (31 fighters, 65 dive-bombers, and 21 torpedo bombers). A full 360-degree search was required which would take 18 SBDs. The northern part of the search pattern was carried out to 200 miles while the southern part was limited to 125 miles. Each carrier allocated eight fighters for CAP missions during the day and *Yorktown* dedicated eight SBDs for anti-torpedo bomber patrols. On both carriers, the remaining aircraft were ready to conduct the strike when locating information was received.

Compared with TF-17, the *MO* Carrier Striking Force could muster 21 fewer aircraft, with the primary difference being the marked American edge in dive-bombers. By 0600hrs, the *MO* Carrier Striking Force was located some 220 miles northeast of TF-17 under heavy weather. Weather played an important role in the events of May 8. The edge of the weather front had moved 30–50 miles to the north and northeast. This brought TF-17 out from under the heavy weather that offered a degree of protection from enemy reconnaissance and placed it in an area of light haze with greatly increased visibility. Conversely, the Japanese carriers now operated in an area of heavy weather with thick clouds and squalls. This would make the job of the American aviators more difficult.

THE AMERICANS STRIKE THE *MO* CARRIER FORCE

Japanese search aircraft were in the air by 0615hrs, followed by the 18 TF-17 SBDs at 0635hrs. It did not take long for each side to find what they were looking for. The Japanese were the first to have success. At 0802hrs, *Yorktown*'s radar reported a contact 18 miles to the northeast, but TF-17's CAP was unable to find or intercept the snooper. At 0822hrs, a report was issued by the Japanese search plane that two American carriers had been spotted and reported at 235 miles from the *MO* Striking Force on a bearing of 205 degrees. Radio intelligence units on *Lexington* and *Yorktown* both confirmed the fact that the Japanese aircraft had spotted TF-17 and had issued a report.

The first report received by Fletcher and Fitch was at 0820hrs when a SBD spotted the *MO* Carrier Striking Force in bad weather. When plotted out, the contact was 175 miles from TF-17 on a bearing of 28 degrees and was headed away from the American carriers. At 175 miles, the Japanese carriers were at the edge of the striking range of the TBDs; nevertheless, it was decided to launch a full strike and head TF-17 toward the contact to reduce the distance the strike would have to fly back to their home carriers.

The Americans were the first to get their strikes in the air. At 0900hrs, the *Yorktown* began launching her strike of 39 aircraft (six fighters, 24 dive-bombers, and nine torpedo bombers), followed at 0907hrs with a 36-aircraft strike from the *Lexington* (nine fighters, 15 dive-bombers, and 12 torpedo bombers). With the air battle now beginning, at 0908hrs Fletcher gave Fitch tactical control of TF-17. Per American doctrine, the two air groups were widely separated with no single strike commander. Additional reports placed the Japanese carriers 191 miles from TF-17 at 0934hrs. Immediately after recovering his morning reconnaissance aircraft, Fitch planned to head to the northeast to reduce the distance to the Japanese carriers.

When the *Yorktown* strike arrived in the area of the *MO* Carrier Striking Force, the Japanese force was separated into two sections. *Zuikaku*, escorted by two heavy cruisers and three destroyers, was some 11,000 yards ahead of the *Shokaku* with her two cruisers. As the dive-bombers maneuvered into position for attack, the *Zuikaku* group disappeared into a squall. *Shokaku*, remaining in an area of clear visibility, took the brunt of *Yorktown*'s attack. The 24 SBDs scored two hits with 1,000lb bombs although the torpedo attack completely failed. Some 30 minutes later, *Lexington*'s attack commenced. Storms had scattered *Lexington*'s strike force, and the overall results were even more disappointing than *Yorktown*'s. Most of the aircraft missed their target altogether in the bad weather, although another 1,000lb bomb did hit *Shokaku*.

Damage to *Shokaku*, in the form of three 1,000lb bomb hits, was severe, but she was in no danger of sinking. Casualties totaled 109 dead and another 114 wounded. While the fires aboard *Shokaku* were quickly extinguished, the damage left her unable to operate aircraft. She was ordered to depart the area at 30 knots under the escort of two destroyers. But *Zuikaku* had escaped.

THE JAPANESE STRIKE TF-17

As the American strike neared, on board *Shokaku* and *Zuikaku* 18 Type Zero fighters, 33 Type 99 carrier bombers, and 18 Type 97 carrier attack planes equipped with torpedoes

ABOVE
A somewhat indistinct but compelling photo of *Lexington* as seen from one of the attacking Japanese aircraft. *Lexington* is already burning and the number of splashes around the ship suggests this shot was taken during the dive-bombing attack. (US Naval Historical Center)

LEFT
Survivors of the sinking of *Lexington* climb aboard another ship following the battle of the Coral Sea. (Photo by Time Life Pictures/Getty Images)

were spotted in readiness. Unlike American doctrine, the entire force departed at 0930hrs and proceeded in a single group under the control of Kakuichi. Takeo followed his strike group south at 30 knots. Had he maintained his position, it would have been unlikely that any of the short-ranged American TBDs would have been able even to reach the area of the Japanese carrier force.

Fully expecting a Japanese morning attack, Fitch had done his best to mount a robust CAP. Eight Wildcats were already aloft supported by 18 SBDs on anti-torpedo plane duty. At 1055hrs, radars on *Lexington* and *Yorktown* reported a large group of aircraft. Immediately, nine more Wildcats and five additional SBDs were launched. The nine new Wildcats were ordered to proceed down the line of bearing to intercept the Japanese aircraft as far as possible from TF-17. But the aircraft failed to intercept the Japanese dive-bombers.

Of the 18 Type 97 carrier attack planes, 14 were assigned to attack *Lexington* with only four remaining to attack *Yorktown*. Despite the efforts of the defending CAP, 15 of the 18 Type 97s survived to launch attacks. The four allocated to attack *Yorktown* all missed for the loss of two aircraft. With 14 Type 97s available to attack *Lexington*, and the limited maneuverability of the huge ship, the Japanese achieved much better results. Two scored hits on the port side. The first, at 1120hrs, buckled the port aviation fuel tank and caused small cracks. In turn, this caused gasoline vapors to spread. The second hit was scored under the island near the firerooms.

Kakuichi's orders for the dive-bombers to take a position upwind placed them several minutes behind the torpedo attack. He ordered 19 dive-bombers from *Shokaku* to deal with *Lexington* with the balance of the dive-bombers from *Zuikaku* to attack *Yorktown*. Despite bravely pressing their attacks against increasingly heavy anti-aircraft fire, the results were very disappointing for the Japanese. Both American carriers were deluged in a series of near misses, but only a total of three bombs hit their targets. Against *Yorktown*, a combination of attacks by two defending Wildcats, good ship handling by Captain Buckmaster, and a crosswind drop meant the 14 *Zuikaku* dive-bombers scored only a single hit. The Japanese strike had not been as devastating as the Americans had expected. *Yorktown*'s crew had quickly put out the fires and the firerooms were re-manned bringing her speed up to 28 knots. Even *Lexington*, recipient of much greater damage, seemed to be battleworthy and in no danger of sinking. After the strike, Kakuichi radioed back at 1125hrs that a *Saratoga*-class carrier had sunk as a result of nine torpedo hits and ten bomb hits. Despite the best efforts of the American CAP, Japanese losses were relatively light although the strike leader Kakuichi himself was lost.

AFTER THE STRIKES

Both the Japanese and American air groups had been shattered by events of May 8. Neither was in a position to resume the battle immediately. Concerned about the damage to *Lexington* and the fuel status, Fletcher proposed at 1315hrs that TF-17 retire to the south. At this point, the battle of the Coral Sea was effectively over, but the reckoning for the US Navy was not done. The torpedo damage to *Lexington* proved mortal. The escaping vapors caused further explosions and fires. Eventually it had to be abandoned and finally sunk at 1952hrs.

However, the failure of the Carrier Striking Force to crush the American carriers meant the end of the *MO* Operation. When Yamamoto heard of the progress of the battle he took immediate action. At 2200hrs, he ordered Shigeyoshi to continue to pursue the American forces and to complete their destruction. The *MO* Carrier Striking Force spent May 9 refueling, then re-entered the Coral Sea on May 10 to reopen the battle with additional aircraft provided. By dawn on May 10, Takeo was some 340 miles southwest of Tulagi. From this position, he conducted a search but gained no contact. On May 11, the futility of continuing operations was obvious and the Carrier Striking Force headed north.

MacArthur's aircraft had already reported the northerly movement of the invasion convoy, so Fletcher could safely assume that the threat of invasion at Port Moresby was over. For the remainder of May 8, he moved south into the Coral Sea and continued to retire at high speed.

AFTERMATH

Both sides paid a high price in the first carrier battle of the Pacific War. The invasion of Port Moresby had been turned away, but the Japanese did add Tulagi to their list of conquests. Losses to the IJN had been high, in fact more severe than any battle to date in the war. The light carrier *Shoho* was sunk, the largest ship lost thus far in the war. In addition, a destroyer and several minor ships were lost in the American carrier raid on Tulagi. Most importantly, the bomb hits on *Shokaku* kept her in the shipyard until July 1942. Carrier

An explosion rocks the burning USS *Lexington* with a force that pitches a plane from her deck. (Corbis)

aircraft losses were also very severe. US losses were highlighted by the loss of *Lexington*, constituting 25 percent of the Pacific Fleet's operational carrier strength. *Yorktown* suffered minor damage, but her survival allowed the Americans to rightfully claim a strategic victory.

It has become commonly accepted that the battle of the Coral Sea, while an American strategic victory, was also an American tactical defeat. This might be true if the battle is considered in isolation. While sinking only a light carrier and damaging a fleet carrier, the US Navy lost one of its four operational Pacific Fleet carriers. However, this view lacks credibility as the battle cannot be examined in isolation. For the Japanese it may have been a subsidiary operation, but its impact was decidedly strategic. Yamamoto's main goal in early 1942 was to attack what he considered to be the American center of gravity in the Pacific – the US Navy, and more specifically its carriers. This was not the aim of the *MO* Operation, but it was the principal objective of the *MI* Operation (the codename for the attack on Midway), which was scheduled for less than a month after the intended Port Moresby invasion. To conduct the *MI* Operation successfully, Yamamoto's plan depended on maintaining superiority in fleet carriers. Violating the principle of mass, Yamamoto committed one-third of the Kido Butai's carriers to the *MO* Operation. Though neither was sunk in the operation, both were removed from his order of battle for the *MI* Operation. Down to only four carriers, Yamamoto had lost his decisive edge in carriers so necessary to guarantee success for the coming decisive clash with the US Navy. The turning of the Japanese tide begun at Coral Sea led eventually to Japan's surrender in August 1945.

ORIGINS OF THE CAMPAIGN

As planned by the Japanese, the operation to invade Midway and engage the remaining strength of the US Pacific Fleet would be the ultimate effort of the Imperial Japanese Navy (IJN). All eight of its operational carriers were committed, as well as the fleet's 11 battleships. Of 18 heavy cruisers, 14 were assigned roles in the operation, as were the bulk of the navy's light cruisers and destroyers. This force was under the command of 28 admirals. Such a force was certainly guaranteed success. Once the Pacific Fleet had been crippled, the Japanese would again turn south to cut off the sea-lines of communications between the US and Australia. Hawaii itself, devoid of protection from the US Navy, was also a potential target.

For his part, Nimitz had the invaluable advantage of superior intelligence regarding his enemy's strength and intentions. This intelligence was far from omniscient, but, combined with Nimitz's innate aggressiveness and strategic insight, it guaranteed that America's remaining naval strength was placed in the best position to do the most potential damage to the Japanese. Nimitz committed all his remaining strength to defending Midway, including all three of his carriers. Pearl Harbor had not eliminated the US Navy's battleship strength in the Pacific, despite popular myth, and by June 1942 seven battleships were operational in the Pacific. Mindful of the lessons taught to him at Pearl Harbor, Nimitz resisted repeated demands that he aggressively employ his battleships and instead moved them to the West Coast out of the way. Unlike Yamamoto's, Nimitz's plan for the upcoming battle was almost totally dependent upon the carriers of the Pacific Fleet. With Yamamoto throwing the entire strength of the IJN at Midway, and Nimitz prepared to defend it with his entire remaining strength, the scene was set for the single most dramatic and important battle of the Pacific War.

OPPOSING COMMANDERS

THE JAPANESE COMMANDERS

The driving figure behind the Midway battle was the commander of the Combined Fleet,

OPPOSITE
Group photo of the pilots in a US Navy torpedo bomber squadron prior to the battle of Midway in which all but one of them would be killed. (Photo by Time Life Pictures/Getty Images)

LEFT
Vice-Admiral Chuichi Nagumo, commander of the First Air Fleet at Pearl Harbor and Midway. A man out of place in naval aviation, which he knew virtually nothing about, he has been castigated for command failures in both operations. After Midway he continued to command carriers, but was dismissed after the battle of Santa Cruz in October 1942. As commander of the forces on Saipan he committed suicide when the island was overrun by US forces in 1944. (NARA)

RIGHT
Rear-Admiral Tamon Yamaguchi was one of the most air-minded of Japanese admirals. Like Yamamoto, Yamaguchi had served as naval attaché in Washington and had attended Princeton University. Highly regarded by the fleet commander he took command of the 2nd Carrier Division in November 1940 and led it in the attacks on Pearl Harbor and at Midway where he chose to go down with his flagship, the carrier *Hiryu*, on June 5.

Admiral Isoroku Yamamoto. His reputation for brilliance and for being a gambler had been forged in the prewar years and at Pearl Harbor. But the battle of the Coral Sea in May had resulted in a tactical and strategic defeat. At Midway, despite his reputation as an advocate of air-power, he planned a battle more reminiscent of prewar Japanese plans for a decisive battleship clash in the Western Pacific, a crucial error.

The admiral charged to carry out Yamamoto's strategic design was once again 55-year-old Vice-Admiral Chuichi Nagumo, by then the most experienced carrier commander in the world. Since Nagumo demonstrated little concern for learning the intricacies of carrier warfare, he relied heavily on his staff. His chief of staff was Rear-Admiral Ryunosuke Kusaka. Though involved in naval aviation since 1926, he was not an aviator and did not possess a deep knowledge of air warfare. The most important figure on Nagumo's staff was the air officer, Commander Minoru Genda, the driving force behind the creation of 1st Air Fleet, and he enjoyed the complete trust of Nagumo.

The commander of the 2nd Carrier Division, comprising half of Nagumo's carrier force, was 50-year-old Rear-Admiral Tamon Yamaguchi, who was held in high esteem within the IJN.

THE US COMMANDERS

The battle of Midway was Admiral W. Chester Nimitz's battle. Nimitz had an uncanny ability to pick good leaders and then give them the room they needed to get their jobs done.

The most combat-experienced American carrier commander in June 1942 was Rear-Admiral Fletcher. He had been commended by Nimitz for his performance during the battle of the Coral Sea. When he returned to Pearl Harbor in the damaged *Yorktown*, Nimitz placed him in overall charge of the entire American carrier force operating off Midway. He would play an important role in executing the initial strikes but his subordinate, Spruance, was in actual charge of the carrier force for the majority of the battle. Rear-Admiral Raymond A. Spruance was a surface line officer with no aviation experience. He did have some knowledge of carrier warfare, as he had been commanding Vice-Admiral William Halsey's cruiser screen since the start of the war, and upon assuming command following Halsey's compulsory shore leave (as the result of a debilitating skin illness) Spruance kept Halsey's entire staff. Spruance emerged from the battle with the lion's share of the credit for the victory and a reputation as a cool, calculating thinker.

OPPOSING FORCES

THE JAPANESE FLEET

Three carrier divisions made up the Kido Butai, each with two carriers. For the Midway operation, 1st and 2nd Carrier Divisions were committed. 1st Carrier Division possessed the IJN's largest carriers, while 2nd Carrier Division possessed the smaller but more nimble *Soryu* class. The flagship of the 1st Kido Butai was *Akagi*. She was a converted battlecruiser, so possessed a high speed, good protection, and a large aircraft capacity (though she was still smaller than the American carriers). Rounding out 1st Carrier Division was *Kaga*. Converted from a battleship, she possessed the lowest speed and was the least maneuverable of the Kido Butai's carriers, but could embark the most aircraft.

The two ships of the *Soryu* class epitomized Japanese carrier design philosophy with their combination of a relatively large aircraft capacity on a fast, light hull. Both carried an operational air group equivalent to the much larger *Akagi* and *Kaga*. Powerful machinery and a cruiser-type hull gave a very high speed, but protection over machinery and magazine spaces was entirely inadequate.

The 3rd Carrier Division of the Kido Butai was composed of the two ships of the *Shokaku* class. But *Shokaku* had been badly damaged during Coral Sea and was under repair. *Zuikaku* was untouched, but her air group had taken such a beating that she was also out of action. It is a sign of Japanese overconfidence that efforts were not made to supplement her aircraft and commit her to the forthcoming battle.

The salient strength of the Kido Butai was its ability to conduct coordinated, large-scale air operations. As a matter of course, during 1942 the Japanese were able to handle their carrier aircraft in a manner far superior to that of the Americans. This was combined with well-trained and experienced aircrews. Of the carrier bomber crews, 70 percent were veterans of Pearl Harbor. The figure for carrier attack plane crews was an even higher 85 percent.

However, despite relatively light losses Japanese aviation industry was unable to keep up. As a result, the four carriers at Midway carried 16 percent fewer aircraft than they had done at Pearl Harbor only a few months earlier. As proficient as the IJN was at massing and coordinating offensive air power, it also possessed an inability to defend its carriers properly. The defensive capabilities of the Japanese carriers were fatally compromised by a lack of radar and generally ineffective anti-aircraft defenses. This would be fully revealed at Midway.

When appointed to replace the unwell Halsey as commander of Task Force 16, Rear-Admiral Spruance had no experience as a carrier commander. However, he had a remarkably flexible and adaptable intellect and incisive but balanced judgment, which made his appointment most apposite for the particular conditions of Midway. He was in many senses the "right man for the right job." Although unknown to the Japanese before the battle, he was to establish himself from June 1942 onward as one of the foremost commanders of the US Naval forces in the Pacific War. (NARA)

THE US NAVY CARRIER FORCE

As Nimitz was planning his response to the expected Japanese advance into the Central Pacific, he had only the three carriers of the *Yorktown* class to oppose the Japanese following the loss of USS *Lexington* at Coral Sea just three weeks prior. The *Yorktown* class was designed with the benefit of fleet experience and proved to be very successful in service. The 4in side armor belt and 1.5in of vertical armor over the machinery spaces and their 5in/38 dual-purpose anti-aircraft guns would prove invaluable at Midway. So would the fact that American carriers routinely operated a deck park of aircraft meaning that they embarked more aircraft than their Japanese counterparts.

After the battle of the Coral Sea the salient weakness of the US Navy's carrier force in 1942 was its continued difficulty in conducting coordinated air operations. This was a problem which reached new heights at Midway. It meant that the vulnerable torpedo bombers attacked independently, with predictable results. The doctrine of independent strike by a single air group when combined with bad weather, poor communications, or bad navigation was a potential recipe for disaster. Only the courage and initiative of individual commanders compensated for this doctrinal weakness.

Nimitz planned that the two carriers of Task Force 16 (TF-16) under Spruance would constitute the main strike force: both carriers would launch an all-out strike once the

Such was the damage inflicted on the USS *Yorktown* in the battle of Coral Sea that the IJN presumed her sunk. Limping back to Pearl Harbor on May 27 she was placed in Dry Dock No. 1 and returned to service within a remarkable 48 hours. Although her many repairs were temporary at best, her presence at Midway was to prove decisive. (Via Roger Chesneau)

Japanese carriers were spotted. Task Force 17 (TF-17) under Fletcher, built around *Yorktown*, would serve as a search and reserve force to be employed at Fletcher's discretion. During the battle, Fletcher hedged his bets in order not to repeat the experience at Coral Sea: by keeping *Yorktown*'s air group in reserve, he would be ready to deal with any unexpected surprises.

At Coral Sea, American fighters had been allocated half to combat air patrol and half to strike escort. After the power of Japanese naval aviation was amply demonstrated, American fighter allocation was changed in favor of increased fleet air defense at Midway.

For the upcoming battle, and in accordance with existing doctrine, Nimitz decided to operate his carriers in two task forces. Accordingly, Fletcher decided to separate his two task forces by 10–15 miles, close enough for mutual fighter support. American naval intelligence was a key advantage for Nimitz at Midway, as it allowed him to position his forces to maximum benefit, but it did not mean that those forces were guaranteed success once the battle had been joined.

The flagship of the First Air Fleet for the *MI* Operation was the venerable *Akagi* ("Red Castle"). Originally designed as an *Amagi*-class battlecruiser she was converted following the Washington Naval Treaty to an aircraft carrier. She was launched in April 1925 with three flight decks forward. (Via Roger Chesneau)

OPPOSING PLANS

THE JAPANESE PLAN

The *MI* Operation was scheduled to open on the morning of June 3 with a devastating blow by Nagumo's carrier force against Midway, positioned in the North Pacific, between Hawaii and Tokyo. Nagumo's force of six carriers escorted by two battleships, two heavy cruisers, one light cruiser, and 11 destroyers (the same force employed to strike Pearl Harbor) would approach Midway from the northwest to knock out its air strength in a single blow. Of course, as at Pearl Harbor, strategic and tactical surprise was assumed. Further air strikes were envisioned on Midway on June 4 preparatory to a landing. On June 5, the Seaplane Tender Group would land on Kure Island 60 miles west of Midway to set up a seaplane base.

All of this was a prelude to the landing of 5,000 troops on Midway Atoll scheduled for June 6. Following the expected quick capture of the island, two construction battalions were tasked to quickly make the base operational. To accomplish this before the expected clash with the American fleet, they were given exactly one day. The base would become a veritable fortress with the fighters from Nagumo's carriers as well as six Type A midget submarines, five motor torpedo boats, 94 cannon, and 40 machine guns carried aboard the transports.

THE US PLAN

Despite popular myth, Nimitz's decision to engage the Japanese at Midway was not a desperate gamble against impossible odds but a carefully calculated plan with great potential to cause serious damage to the enemy. Good intelligence played a part. The Pacific Fleet's cryptologists had assembled a fairly close idea of the IJN's intentions. The main target of the operation was identified as Midway, where four to five large carriers, two to four fast battleships, seven to nine heavy cruisers, escorted by a commensurate number of destroyers, up to 24 submarines, and a landing force could be expected. Additional forces, including carriers, would be dedicated against the Aleutians. The operation would be conducted during the first week of June, but the precise timing remained unclear. All in all, this was a fairly close approximation to Japanese plans, but somewhat lacking in specifics.

To engage the Japanese, Nimitz carefully arrayed his available assets. Unfortunately for Yamamoto, his plans were nothing like what the Japanese assumed. Despite the constant suggestions from US Navy commander Admiral King that they be employed as aggressively as possible, Nimitz immediately decided that there was no place for the Pacific Fleet's seven remaining battleships. He did not want his carriers to be hamstrung in any way by the slow battleships and he had no assets available to provide them with adequate air cover or screening. The battleships remained out of harm's way in San Francisco.

The Pacific Fleet's striking power resided in its carriers. Two of these, *Enterprise* and *Hornet*, were assigned to Spruance as TF-16 and would be off Midway by June 1. The damaged *Yorktown*, still in TF-17, remained as Fletcher's flagship and would be in position off Midway by June 2. Fletcher would assume overall command of the two carrier groups when he arrived.

Nimitz held a major advantage in that the battle was being fought within range of friendly aircraft. Midway was jammed with as many aircraft as possible, including a large number of long-range reconnaissance aircraft, fighters to defend the base from air attack, and a mixed strike force of Marine, Navy, and Army Air Corps aircraft. Defending the base were a number of submarines and a garrison of some 2,000 Marines.

Employment of Midway's 115 aircraft was an important consideration, in particular the long-range PBY flying boats which were able to conduct wide-ranging searches, greatly reducing the possibility of a surprise air raid on the island. Nimitz agreed with his staff that the best position for the carriers was northeast of Midway. By being fairly close to Midway, they could respond quickly to attacking enemy carriers. Most important was the question of risk to the carriers. Nimitz never saw the battle as a death-struggle for control of Midway. His orders to Fletcher and Spruance provided the guidance that they were to "be governed by the principle of calculated risk which you shall interpret to mean the avoidance of exposure of your forces to attack by superior enemy forces without good prospect of inflicting, as a result of such exposure, greater damage to the enemy." On top of these written orders, Nimitz personally instructed Spruance not to lose his carriers. If required, he was to abandon Midway and let the Japanese attempt a landing. Even if captured, it could be recaptured later. It must be assumed that Nimitz provided the same instruction to Fletcher.

Finally, Nimitz believed that the IJN carriers would be operated in two separate groups, one likely attacking Midway and the other providing cover. Nimitz held high hopes that his carriers could ambush the Japanese carriers attacking Midway, followed by a second phase where three American carriers faced just two Japanese.

THE BATTLE OF MIDWAY

OPENING MOVES

On May 27, the 1st Kido Butai departed Hashirajima Anchorage one day later than scheduled. However, with the landing day on Midway determined by tidal conditions, the overall plan was not modified. This meant one day less was available to neutralize Midway before the scheduled landing. Another aspect of the tightly synchronized Japanese plan was also falling behind schedule. The submarines for the scouting cordon were also running late, with some arriving on station on June 3, not June 1 as planned. By this time the American carriers had already moved through the area. The commander of the 6th Fleet did not even think it was important enough to tell Yamamoto of this fact.

Meanwhile *Hornet* and *Enterprise* sortied on May 28. *Yorktown* was out of dry dock on May 29 following the completion of her repairs and departed the next day to join her sister ships. After leaving Pearl Harbor, TF-16 steered to the northwest to take its assigned position 350 miles northeast of Midway. TF-16 rendezvoused with *Yorktown* on June 2 at 1600hrs, 325 miles northeast of Midway. At this point, Fletcher assumed command. The assembled strength of the US Pacific Fleet, three carriers, eight cruisers, and 15 destroyers, now waited to combat the combined might of the IJN.

On the morning of June 3, *Yorktown* launched 20 Dauntlesses to conduct searches. Fletcher moved his carriers to a new position some 175 miles west of Point Luck in anticipation of a Japanese attack on Midway. Meanwhile, the 1st Kido Butai approached Midway from the north where the weather was very bad on June 2 and 3.

Though the Japanese plan had called for the battle to open with a surprise air attack on Midway, Nagumo's late departure meant that the first Japanese force to be spotted was the Invasion Force which continued to close on Midway on schedule and was already in range of Midway's air searches. At 0843hrs on the morning of June 3, PBYs from Midway spotted part of the Japanese force and an attack was launched at 1200hrs by B-17s. Though no hits were scored, the Japanese could not remain under the illusion that strategic surprise was still possible, a fact rammed home when a night-time torpedo-plane attack was also launched with partial success.

A squadron of Douglas "Devastator" torpedo bombers unfold their wings for a takeoff abroad the USS *Enterprise* during the battle of Midway, June 3–6, 1942. They are headed for an attack on the huge concentration of Japanese air and sea power off Midway. The carrier's scout and torpedo bombers scored direct hits on three Japanese carriers and a battleship. (Bettmann/Corbis)

ABOVE
Midway under attack pictured early on the first day of the Japanese offensive. (Tom Laemlein)

OPPOSITE
Raising the National Emblem during the height of the battle. This dramatic incident was not staged. Because word of the approach of Japanese forces came so early in the morning the flag was raised while the battle was in progress. (Tom Laemlein)

THE JAPANESE STRIKE MIDWAY

At 0430hrs on June 4, Nagumo started launching 108 aircraft to strike Midway. The strike was composed of 18 carrier bombers from *Akagi* and *Kaga* and 18 carrier attack planes from *Soryu* and *Hiryu*. Each carrier contributed nine fighters for escort. Six Wildcats and 18 F-2A Buffalos intercepted the Japanese 30 miles from Midway. The ensuing air battle, begun at 0620hrs, resulted in a disaster for the defenders. For a loss of 13 Buffalos and two Wildcats, Japanese losses were only one or two Zero fighters and three carrier attack planes. Most of the remaining Marine fighters were damaged; only two returned to Midway undamaged.

After brushing the Marines aside, the Japanese formation went on to strike their allocated targets. But no American aircraft was caught on the ground, and the defending anti-aircraft fire was extremely heavy. Following the bombardment of Midway, the leader of the Japanese strike, *Hiryu*'s Lieutenant Joichi Tomonaga, signaled to Nagumo "there is need for a second attack wave." Not only had the strike failed to meet its objectives, but the cost to the Japanese was very high, and these losses would be keenly felt later in the day.

Meanwhile the Marine force at Midway had launched their own counterattack against the invasion force and the IJN carriers with Devastators, B-26 Marauder Bombers, and a high-altitude attack from B-17s but no direct hits were scored.

THE CARRIER BATTLE OF JUNE 4

At 0430hrs, the American carriers were some 200 miles north-northeast of Midway. As a precaution, Fletcher launched ten scout dive-bombers from *Yorktown* to perform reconnaissance to his north out to 100 miles. Fletcher's major advantage during the day was that he could rely on Midway to conduct the bulk of his reconnaissance. After launching his scouts, Fletcher headed to the northeast just 215 miles east of Nagumo and well within the reach of Japanese scouts. All of the American advantages of superior intelligence would add up to nothing if the Japanese were successful in finding the Americans first.

To conduct his scouting, Nagumo devoted a total of seven aircraft. Six were ordered to fly to a range of 300 miles and the last out to 150 miles. Several of the aircraft took off behind schedule and were hampered by bad weather. At best, the Japanese reconnaissance efforts were half-hearted; at worst, they were negligent. Both the Americans and Japanese believed that victory in a carrier battle was decided by which side could attack first, thus making good reconnaissance essential. The greater American emphasis on this aspect of the operation paid early dividends on June 4.

At 0530hrs, the electrifying report "Enemy Carriers" was received by Fletcher from PBYs flying from Midway. This was followed at 0552hrs by a report from another PBY of "Many planes headed Midway, bearing 310 distance 150."

Once plotted out by Fletcher's staff, the Japanese force was 247 degrees at 180 miles from TF-16. This was just within the strike range of the American air groups; however, the report was in error. The Japanese carriers sighted were actually 200 miles from TF-16, thus placing them slightly out of range of a full strike. The Japanese carriers were 220 miles from TF-17. Moreover, the report of only two carriers corresponded with the intelligence provided by Nimitz and created the concern in Fletcher's mind that the other two Japanese carriers remained unlocated.

After quick deliberation, Fletcher ordered Spruance at 0607hrs to head south and strike the reported contact. Fletcher would follow after *Yorktown* recovered her scout aircraft launched earlier that morning. Spruance and his chief of staff decided on a 0700hrs launch.

Navy SBD Dauntless dive-bombers fly over a burning Japanese ship during the attack on the Japanese fleet off Midway. (Tom Laemlein)

It was calculated that by that time the Japanese would be some 155 miles from TF-16, within range of the short-legged American fighters and torpedo bombers. At 0638hrs, Spruance's flagship signaled to *Hornet* to launch at 0700hrs. At this point, Mitscher and Ring and the various squadron commanders of *Hornet*'s air group made a fateful decision. For reasons never fully explained, they decided to send *Hornet*'s strike group on a course of 265 degrees to the target, well to the north of the contact report. The report of only two carriers still weighed heavily with Fletcher. The other two Japanese carriers thought to be in Nagumo's force could be operating in another group, perhaps far from the reported contact. Until the situation was clarified, Fletcher decided to hold *Yorktown*'s aircraft in reserve. Around 0630hrs, *Yorktown* completed recovery of her ten scout aircraft and Fletcher headed to the southwest at high speed to follow Spruance.

Spruance had committed a total of 116 aircraft to the attack – 20 fighters, 67 dive-bombers, and 29 torpedo planes. However, the cohesion of the strike was already in question. Instead of two air groups heading to their targets in loose company ready to launch coordinated strikes, the American strike aircraft now proceeded in three groups due to a late launch from *Enterprise*. More importantly, each of the three groups was taking a separate course to the target.

NAGUMO'S DILEMMA

After his Midway strike departed, Nagumo still held a large reserve force in readiness. As per Yamamoto's orders, Nagumo was to maintain half his strike aircraft armed for attacks on naval units to counter any American ships making an appearance. Following the recommendation

from Tomonaga at 0715hrs advising that a second Midway strike was required, Nagumo decided to disobey Yamamoto's orders and ordered that his reserve aircraft be prepared for land attack in order to launch the second attack on Midway. This required that the carrier attack planes have their torpedoes exchanged for 800kg bombs and that the carrier bombers be loaded with high-explosive bombs, unsuited for attacking ships. In Nagumo's mind, this was justified since the search planes were scheduled to have reached their furthest points and had yet to report anything.

Just as this rearming process was beginning, Nagumo received very disturbing news. At 0740hrs, a search aircraft reported: "Sight what appears to be ten enemy surface ships, in position bearing 010 degrees distance 250 miles from Midway. Course 150 degrees, speed over 20 knots." Though this initial report made no mention of carriers, it obviously meant the US Navy was present in strength. At 0745hrs, Nagumo ordered the suspension of the rearming process of his reserve aircraft. Finally, at 0830hrs, Tone No. 4 filled out its incomplete earlier report delivering the alarming report "the enemy is accompanied by what appears to be a carrier."

Nagumo still retained a large strike force of 43 torpedo aircraft and 34 dive-bombers partially armed with high-explosive bombs. Nagumo's real problem was that he believed only six Zero fighters intended for strike escort were still available. The rest had been launched to fend off Midway's attacks. Compounding Nagumo's difficulties was the return of his Midway strike with many aircraft low on fuel or damaged. Predictably, the aggressive Yamaguchi advised Nagumo to launch an immediate strike against the American carrier, even if it was not properly escorted.

Since no immediate action was taken, the initiative again passed to the Americans when the Marine force at Midway attack arrived. After weighing all his options, Nagumo decided to take the cautious course. He would recover his Midway strike, and then proceed to the northeast to close with the Americans

No photograph survives from Japanese sources showing the air operations of the IJN Fleet at Midway. Although this picture dates from just prior to the Pearl Harbor strike in December 1941, it conveys very well a scene similar to that experienced aboard the flagship *Akagi* as it prepared to launch its Zero fighters early on the morning of June 4, 1942.

As part of the air search pattern instigated by Nagumo after the launch of the Midway strike force, the battleship *Haruna* catapulted its old and short-ranged Nakajima E8N "Dave" float-plane to survey to the north of the southward-moving carrier fleet. (Courtesy of Philip Jarrett)

while preparing a 1030hrs strike. This would include 34 carrier bombers, 43 carrier attack planes armed with torpedoes, and 12 fighter escorts. Until the strike could be launched, the combat air patrols (CAP) could provide defense against the brave but ineffective American attacks. At 0918hrs, the recovery complete, Nagumo changed course to the northeast and increased speed to 30 knots to close with the American force, believing that if he could have the time to prepare for his planned 1030hrs launch, his veteran aviators would make short work of the American carrier. In reality, whatever course Nagumo had decided upon, it was probably already too late. The American carrier aircraft launched at 0700hrs were already well on their way to the Japanese carriers.

THE DECISIVE PHASE

At 0815hrs, the radar aboard *Enterprise* detected an unidentified aircraft to the south approximately 30 miles away – the same reconnaissance aircraft that had reported to Nagumo. Fletcher now knew his carriers had been sighted. Not wanting to be caught with fueled and armed planes on deck, Fletcher decided to launch part of *Yorktown*'s strike. Between 0830 and 0905hrs, 17 dive-bombers, 12 torpedo bombers, and six fighter escorts were launched. The entire strike headed off on a course of 240 degrees from TF-17. Fletcher still retained a strike force of 17 dive-bombers together with six fighters.

Aircraft from three US carriers were now heading toward Nagumo's carriers. Aside from a single squadron remaining on *Yorktown*, this amounted to every strike aircraft that Fletcher could put in the air. Up until this point, the CAP over the 1st Kido Butai had done a superb job defending. However, the assailants they had faced so far were a makeshift force not well trained in attacking ships. If the American carrier aircraft could find their targets, Japanese air defense capabilities would be tested as never before.

The first to attack was *Hornet*'s torpedo plane squadron. Lieutenant-Commander John Waldron took his 15 Devastator aircraft on the course of 265 degrees, as briefed, flying at 1,500ft. At 0825hrs, he broke away from Ring's formation and took his squadron to the southwest where he was certain the enemy would be. He was exactly right. Waldron spotted smoke and then the Japanese carriers at 0915hrs. Commencing an immediate attack, Waldron's squadron went to wave-top level and began an attack run at the 1st Kido Butai which was heading directly toward them. Waldron picked out the nearest carrier to him, which happened to be *Soryu*. The Japanese had 18 fighters aloft on CAP, and, as the attack developed, *Akagi* and *Kaga* launched another 11. The only form of defense possessed by the Devastators was to fly as low as possible. This did not stop the slow aircraft from being hacked down mercilessly by the swarming Zeros. Between 0920 and 0937hrs, all 15 Devastators were destroyed but not until a single aircraft launched its torpedo at 800 yards against *Soryu*'s starboard side with no success. The sacrifice was important, not because it drew the Japanese CAP down to low altitudes but because it prevented the Japanese from spotting the American strike aircraft.

The next American aircraft to make an appearance were the 14 Devastators of VT-6 from *Enterprise*. Lieutenant-Commander Eugene Lindsey decided to head for the nearest carrier, *Kaga*, and conduct a split attack. The Japanese CAP was now up to 27 fighters and lookouts had spotted the approaching torpedo planes from the south at 0938hrs. Meanwhile, *Akagi* and *Soryu* launched another seven fighters at 0945hrs. The 14 Devastators began their attack runs under heavy fire, and this time at least five were able to launch against *Kaga*, but the extreme range and bad angles of the torpedo launch prevented any hits.

Circling overhead at 22,000ft during the slaughter of the American torpedo bombers were the ten Wildcats of Lieutenant Gray's VF-6. By 0950hrs, he had been overhead the 1st Kido Butai for 30 minutes, undiscovered by the Japanese the entire time. He had not heard the pleas of VT-6 for help as they commenced their attack, so, after making a contact report at 0956hrs, Gray returned to *Enterprise* minutes later.

The fate of *Hornet*'s strike is one of the most controversial aspects of the battle. Despite the fact that the Japanese lay on a course of 240 degrees from TF-16 when the PBY contact report was received, *Hornet*'s air group was ordered to fly a course of 265 degrees to the target. Commander Ring and his 34 Dauntlesses and ten fighters passed well north of 1st Kido Butai. Fortunately for the Americans, the fate of

A B-25 of 345th Bomb Group attacks the IJN during the battle for Midway. (Tom Laemlein)

> "Be governed by the principle of calculated risk which you shall interpret to mean the avoidance of exposure of your forces to attack by superior enemy forces without good prospect of inflicting, as a result of such exposure, greater damage to the enemy."
>
> **— NIMITZ'S ORDERS TO FLETCHER AND SPRUANCE**

Enterprise's dive-bombers was very different. The 33 aircraft under Lieutenant Commander McClusky departed on a course of 231 degrees and eventually tracked down the Japanese force albeit through a somewhat indirect route. As McClusky approached the target, the strike from *Yorktown* took a more direct route to the 1st Kido Butai. The performance of *Yorktown*'s Air Group was by far the best on June 4; generally missed in assessments of the chaotic American attacks that day on the 1st Kido Butai was that *Yorktown*'s dive-bomber and torpedo squadron launched a generally coordinated attack. By chance, this attack developed at the same time McClusky's aircraft arrived in the target area.

At the time of the approach of *Yorktown*'s air group and of McClusky's dive-bombers, 41 Japanese Zero fighters were already aloft on CAP or just scrambling but all were at low altitude, the result of just having dealt with the previous attacks.

At 1010hrs, the cruiser *Chikuma* gave the initial warning of another impending attack. She spotted the Devastators from VT-3 when they were still 14 miles from the nearest carrier and fired her main battery in the direction of the oncoming aircraft to alert the CAP. However, unlike the previous torpedo plane attacks, these had the advantage of an escort by six Wildcats; two of these provided close escort at 3,000ft with another four under Lieutenant-Commander John Thach maintaining watch from 5,500ft. A large number of Zero fighters were attracted to Thach's small formation. Up to 20 Japanese fighters launched continual attacks, shooting down one of Thach's Wildcats. The remaining three went into the defensive formation known as the Thach Weave and successfully warded off the Japanese fighters, shooting down three.

The two Wildcats on close escort successfully defended their charges, shooting down two Japanese fighters in the process. The result of the fighter duel between the six fighters and the 1st Kido Butai's CAP was that virtually all the defending fighters were drawn into the fight at low altitudes. Only a single Devastator was shot down before the torpedo planes leveled off at 150ft for their final attack run.

To present their stern to the approaching torpedo bombers, Nagumo decided to turn to the northwest. The squadron's commanding officer, Lieutenant-Commander Lance Massey, decided to pass up this poor attack angle and head to the north to attack the last carrier in sight, *Hiryu*. This forced the attackers (VT-3) to run parallel to the 1st Kido Butai, giving the Japanese CAP additional opportunities to attack.

As *Yorktown*'s torpedo bombers approached, no Japanese observer spotted the arrival of VB-3 at 15,000ft. Likewise, the arrival of McClusky's dive-bombers also went unnoticed. The 17 dive-bombers of VB-3 selected *Soryu* as their target. Of these, only 13 were still armed with bombs after a faulty electrical arming switch resulted in the loss of the 1,000lb bombs aboard the squadron commander's aircraft and three others. Beginning at 1025hrs, VB-3 scored three hits on *Soryu*. No aircraft were lost to anti-aircraft fire or CAP.

Of the 32 dive-bombers with McClusky, 30 dived on targets. According to doctrine, each of the two squadrons present would take a single target. McClusky ordered the leading squadron, VS-6, to hit the nearest carrier, *Kaga*, and for VB-6 to hit the more distant *Akagi*. However, in the confusion, both squadrons prepared to dive on *Kaga*. At 1022hrs, McClusky and his two wingmen, VS-6, and most of VB-6 commenced their dives on *Kaga*. With no CAP present and no anti-aircraft fire, the result was devastating. Four bombs hit the ship, turning her almost instantly into an inferno.

As the *Soryu* and *Kaga* were dealt mortal damage, it appeared that *Akagi* would survive unscathed. However, in one of the most important moments of the battle, Lieutenant Richard Best, commanding officer of VB-6, realized that *Akagi* might go untouched. Best and two other VB-6 aircraft aborted their dives on *Kaga* and proceeded north to attack *Akagi*. Attacking from *Akagi*'s port side, they gained total surprise. Best placed a 1,000lb bomb on the aft edge of the middle elevator. This then penetrated to the upper hangar where it exploded among the armed and fueled aircraft. The entire attack by *Enterprise*'s dive-bombers cost only two VB-6 aircraft, which were destroyed either by low-flying CAP on their withdrawal or by anti-aircraft fire.

Between 1035 and 1040hrs, the last attack of the morning against the 1st Kido Butai was completed. After taking his Devastators to a better attack position, Massey attempted to get *Hiryu* in a split attack. Five Devastators launched against *Hiryu*'s starboard side between 600 and 800 yards, but none hit. Ten of the 12 Devastators were shot down.

With this, the American attack was over. A total of eight bombs had been placed on three carriers. *Hiryu* was untouched by dive-bombing and torpedo attack and remained undamaged. Compared with the fatal damage suffered by the three carriers, aircraft losses mattered little. However, losses on both sides had been heavy. Of the up to 41 Japanese fighters on CAP, 11 were shot down, and three more ditched. In return, they inflicted crippling losses on the early piecemeal American strikes, but were unable to defend the carriers from dive-bomber attack.

Enterprise's and *Hornet*'s returning aircraft had a difficult time finding TF-16 because their carriers were not in the location where they had been briefed. Throughout the day,

A Japanese heavy cruiser of the *Mogame* class on fire after attack by planes of Task Force 16 during the battle of Midway. (Bettmann/Corbis)

A Japanese destroyer explodes as a result of the American carrier aircraft attacks. The splashes surrounding the destroyer give some indication of the level of attack. (Tom Laemlein)

Spruance's staff failed to perform basic functions adequately and 13 aircraft were lost at sea. *Hornet*'s air group had inflicted no damage on the enemy. In the process they had lost 15 torpedo planes and ten fighters, and only 20 of the 34 dive-bombers were recovered aboard the carrier. *Enterprise*'s strike fared better, but losses were still heavy. Her dive-bombers had inflicted mortal damage on two carriers. Only four torpedo bombers out of 14 returned, and of the 33 dive-bombers dispatched, only 15 returned.

THE JAPANESE RESPONSE

In the aftermath of the American dive-bombing attack, the condition of all three damaged Japanese carriers was perilous. Unless prompt and effective damage-control measures could be taken to avoid the spread of fire, all three would be lost. The fate of the smaller *Soryu* was the first to be decided. The three hits at approximately 1025hrs set off huge fires which quickly spread to the second hangar deck. At 1040hrs, the ship went dead in the water. *Soryu* sank that evening at 1913hrs with the loss of 711 officers and men, including her captain who refused to leave his ship.

The bombs that struck *Kaga* penetrated to the upper hangar deck, igniting fires from the aircraft and ordnance there. One of the four bombs hit the bridge, killing, among others, Captain Okada and the ship's damage-control officer. This left the fight against the raging flames under the control of the ship's inexperienced senior aviators. The flames could not be controlled and soon all power was lost. At 1925hrs, the ship was scuttled with destroyer torpedoes. Losses from her crew totaled 811 officers and men.

The death of *Akagi* was the most prolonged. Ordinarily, the single bomb hit at 1026hrs would not have been fatal, but the well-placed bomb had penetrated to the hangar deck where it ignited the fueled and armed carrier attack planes located there. The crew was unable to localize the flames to a single portion of the hangar deck, and they soon spread to the flight deck. At 1042hrs, the ship's steering failed. Nagumo could not command the 1st Kido Butai from a burning carrier with a jammed rudder and he was evacuated. After much anguish, Yamamoto personally ordered the ship scuttled the next morning. Over 200 of her crew were lost.

The morning's disaster left only a single carrier operational – *Hiryu*. On board Yamaguchi received orders to launch an immediate strike on the American carriers. Yamaguchi decided to commit *Hiryu*'s carrier bomber unit and to follow this up with a strike by *Hiryu*'s remaining carrier attack aircraft one hour later. Both would be given an escort of six fighters. *Hiryu*'s remaining air strength was not great: only 36 fully operational aircraft were on board – ten fighters, 18 dive-bombers, and eight torpedo planes. These would be reinforced by the 27 CAP fighters still aloft, but Yamaguchi would have to be careful about employing his sparse strike assets.

The 18 carrier bombers were all piloted by veterans and were considered an elite unit. They would have ample chance to prove it. Twenty-four aircraft, including escorts, were launched at 1050hrs, and by 1058hrs the group headed to the west. At this point, the American carriers were less than 100 miles away.

While the Japanese had decided on an immediate strike from *Hiryu*, they remained unclear on the composition of the American force they were facing. Nevertheless, determined to avenge the events of the morning, Nagumo ordered what remained of the 1st Kido Butai to head toward the Americans, now believed to be only 90 miles away. *Hiryu* would launch air strikes followed by what Nagumo optimistically believed would be an immediate surface engagement in which the Japanese heavy units would smash the Americans. The fanciful notion that the Americans would oblige Nagumo's desire for a surface engagement was shattered when at 1240hrs a reconnaissance plane reported that the US force was headed north. With the realization that his surface ships stood little chance of catching the American carriers, Nagumo changed course to due north.

When Yamamoto received the shocking news that *Akagi*, *Kaga*, and *Soryu* were on fire he issued a flood of orders in an attempt to retrieve the situation. At 1220hrs, he directed the Main Body south to assist Nagumo. While the transports of the Invasion Force moved to

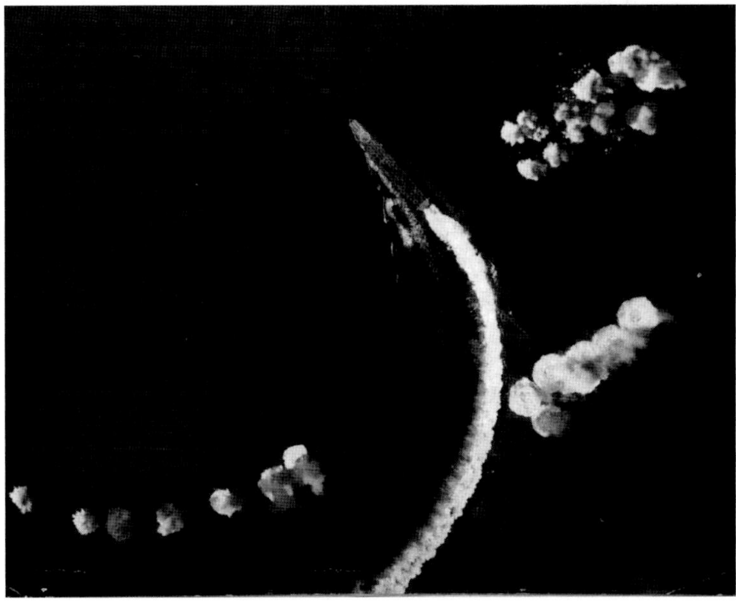

Akagi under attack by the Americans at Midway. It is possible to see that she was trying to evade the US aircraft by the line she was taking. (Tom Laemlein)

An illustration of the battle of Midway showing the intense air battle between the Japanese and American naval forces. (Photo by Hulton Archive/ Getty Images)

the northwest to await developments, the 2nd Kido Butai supporting the Aleutians operation was ordered to move south. At 1310hrs, he gave instructions for the airfield on Midway to be destroyed. With Midway eliminated, only the American carriers remained as a threat. These could be dealt with by strikes from *Hiryu* and an overwhelming surface attack.

HIRYU RETALIATES

En route to the American carriers, at about 1130hrs, the Japanese strike spotted six US aircraft. Impulsively, the aggressive fighter escort peeled off to engage. In the ensuing melee, two of the escorting Japanese fighters were damaged and were forced to return to *Hiryu*. Now the already inadequate strike escort was reduced to a mere four fighters.

The first indication for the Americans that the Japanese response was in progress was received at 1151hrs when *Yorktown*'s radar gained contact on an inbound group of unidentified aircraft to the southwest 32 miles from the ship. This development came at a bad time for the Americans. Twelve Wildcats had just been hurriedly launched at 1150hrs to clear the deck as a relief for the CAP and the six fighters concluding their CAP rotation were landing. Subsequently, the just-launched CAP was not well deployed and was not at its proper altitude.

However, as the American fighters climbed to 10,000ft they launched an attack on the Japanese carrier bombers whose Zero escorts were still trying to catch up. Seven carrier bombers were dispatched as the attackers closed in now with their fighter escort. The ensuing attack by the remaining seven carrier bombers was one of the most accurate of the entire war and fully confirmed the elite status of the *Hiryu*'s carrier bomber unit. Of the seven aircraft, three scored direct hits and two scored damaging near-misses – an impressive achievement. However, at the end of the attack, *Hiryu*'s carrier bomber unit had been shattered: 13 of 18 carrier bombers had been shot down with three Zero fighters also lost. *Yorktown* had come to a stop and was issuing thick, black smoke from the bomb hole amidships. The airmen of the *Hiryu*, under the direction of Lieutenant Michio Kobayashi, had seemingly dealt the American carrier serious damage. At 1323hrs, Fletcher shifted his flag to the cruiser *Astoria*, and Spruance dispatched two cruisers and two destroyers from TF-16 to assist *Yorktown*.

TOMONAGA ATTACKS *YORKTOWN*

Yamaguchi knew the only chance to get the Midway operation back on track was to at least disable the three American carriers. Quick and effective action by *Hiryu* still presented a chance to save the situation. At 1245hrs, one of the returning carrier bombers radioed that the strike had left one American carrier burning. Yamaguchi prepared a makeshift force of 16 aircraft drawn predominately from *Hiryu* but also *Akagi* and *Kaga*. At 1331hrs they departed to the east. At this point, TF-17 was just 83 miles away and TF-16 only 112 miles distant.

By the time Lieutenant Joichi Tomonaga's strike began its flight, *Yorktown*'s crew had put out the fires and restored the boilers to enable the carrier to steam at 25 knots. At about 1430hrs, when Tomonaga sighted a US carrier task force, he had no idea this was the previously damaged *Yorktown*. He immediately ordered an attack.

The Americans were already aware of Tomonaga's approach thanks to radar contact and CAP was prepared, supported by fighters from TF-16. Compared with the interception of *Hiryu*'s dive-bombers, this air battle did not go as well for the Americans. Several factors conspired to allow most of the attacking force to launch their weapons at *Yorktown*. These included an inadequate number of fighters deployed at improper altitudes and a more effective close escort by the Japanese fighters.

Of the four torpedoes fired, some launched only 600 yards away, two found their target. Both hit the port side with devastating effect. *Yorktown* came to a halt and took an immediate 23-degree list. All five carrier attack planes from the second group and four of their escorting fighters survived to return to *Hiryu*. For a cost of just five carrier attack planes and two fighters, Yamaguchi had disabled what he thought was a second American carrier. *Yorktown* would eventually sink as a result of this attack on June 6.

THE DEATH OF *HIRYU*

Fletcher's prudence in launching an earlier search now paid off. At 1445hrs, a *Yorktown* aircraft reported the position of *Hiryu*, placing her 160 miles northwest of TF-16. By 1542hrs, the strike was airborne and headed toward the Japanese carrier. As the US strike was launching, *Hiryu*'s second strike against *Yorktown* returned to its ship. To hit what he

This dramatic photo shows the moment that the Japanese score a hit on the American carrier *Yorktown* during the battle of Midway. The carrier would sink as a result of this attack. (Bettmann/Corbis)

believed was the third and final American carrier still to be operational, Yamaguchi planned a third strike at 1800hrs. For this strike, *Hiryu* could muster only four carrier bombers, five carrier attack aircraft, and nine escorts.

But IJN reconnaissance aircraft soon confirmed that in fact two American carriers remained operational. This news came just as a group of American dive-bombers arrived overhead the 1st Kido Butai, achieving complete surprise. At 1705hrs, the American dive-bombers began their attack. Caught unawares and with her CAP outnumbered by the attacking dive-bombers, the fate of *Hiryu* was all but sealed. Four bomb hits on *Hiryu* were enough to set the ship aflame and she eventually sank the following morning.

OPPOSITE
US soldiers stand silently at attention before the flag-draped bodies of their comrades, who died during the battle of Midway. (Bettmann/Corbis)

YAMAMOTO'S DECISION

The carriers committed to the Aleutians operation did not receive Yamamoto's orders to head south until 1500hrs on June 4 while in the middle of a strike and so could not depart until the following morning. Yamamoto viewed Nagumo's efforts at forcing a surface engagement as not aggressive enough, so at 2255hrs on June 4, he relieved Nagumo of his command except for the crippled *Akagi* and *Hiryu* and their escorts. Nobutake Kondo assumed command of the combined force for the coming night battle.

By 2330hrs, no contact had been made by the advancing Japanese forces and it was obvious that no surface engagement was forthcoming. To continue an advance to the east would put the ships in a vulnerable situation in the morning against American air attack. At 0015hrs on June 5, Yamamoto issued orders to Kondo and Nagumo to break off their advance to the east and fall back to join the Main Body. At 0020hrs, Kurita's cruisers were ordered to break off their planned bombardment of Midway. Finally, at 0255hrs, Yamamoto bowed to the inevitable.

In the immediate aftermath of the Japanese dive-bombing attack on *Yorktown*, corpsmen treat casualties in the area aft of the island. In the background is the No. 4 1.1in gun mount. (US Naval Historical Center)

He transmitted orders to the Combined Fleet canceling the Midway operation. Unfortunately for Kurita's close support group this order was not received until the morning of June 5 when they were only 50 miles from Midway. As a result they came under direct attack first from Midway-based aircraft and subsequently by Spruance's carriers. Eventually Spruance retired to the northwest to refuel. The battle was over.

AFTERMATH

There was no disguising the fact that the Japanese had been dealt a major defeat. All four carriers of the 1st Kido Butai had been sunk and all aircraft on those ships (248 in total) had been lost. Total Japanese dead were 3,057 personnel, most from the crews of the four carriers. Most significant among the carrier crew casualties was the loss of 721 aircraft technicians aboard. In addition to the losses to the IJN's carrier force, heavy cruiser *Mikuma* was sunk and heavy cruiser *Mogami* so badly damaged that she would not be operational again until 1943. The landing on Midway was never attempted. The only undisputed success of the whole undertaking was the capture of Attu and Kiska islands in the Aleutians on June 7.

For the Americans, the cost of inflicting a strategic defeat on the Japanese was relatively

Shown here under attack by B-17E Flying Forts, the 23,000-ton *Hiryu* was one of the last Japanese "treaty-class" medium attack carriers. Launched in 1939, she was sunk shortly after this photo was taken off Midway. (United States Naval Institute Photo Archive)

small. The most important loss to the Pacific Fleet was carrier *Yorktown*. The only other ship lost was the destroyer *Hammann*. A total of 144 aircraft were lost and 362 sailors, Marines, and airmen were killed.

By the time TF-16 returned to Pearl Harbor on June 13, it was obvious that Nimitz's gamble had delivered one of the most important victories in American naval history. In one encounter, the Pacific Fleet had blunted the offensive strength of the IJN. The loss of Nagumo's four carriers altered the balance of power in the Pacific. Only two Japanese fleet carriers remained to act as the centerpiece of a rebuilt carrier force. The Pacific Fleet possessed three fleet carriers, soon to be joined by a fourth, *Wasp*, from the Atlantic Fleet. Before Midway, the Japanese had the advantage of a numerically superior carrier force. After Midway, this advantage had been lost.

The battle also marked the end of the Japanese expansion phase in the Pacific War, as it ruined the IJN as a force capable of strategic offensive operations. The effects of the battle did not mean the end of the IJN as a fighting force, but it did wrest the initiative away from the Japanese. The Americans were quicker to respond to the changed circumstances than the Japanese by launching their first strategic offensive of the war – an attack against the Japanese-held islands of Tulagi and Guadalcanal in August.

N • PEARL HARBOR • CORAL SEA •

WAY • GUADALCANAL

ORIGINS OF THE CAMPAIGN

Guadalcanal was the first American amphibious counteroffensive of World War II. It was on this virtually unheard of island that the Americans shattered the myth of Japanese invincibility in the Pacific. Although the battles of Coral Sea and Midway are described as turning-point battles, it was at Guadalcanal that the Japanese war machine truly ground to a halt. The battle for Guadalcanal was a unique battle for many reasons. Both the American and Japanese forces fought at the farthest end of their supply lines. The battle itself would be among the longest in duration of the Pacific campaign. It would take six months of fierce and savage fighting in difficult terrain, testing the endurance of both sides, before the Japanese were driven off the island.

Ship losses off Guadalcanal, comparable to those suffered later off the Philippines and Okinawa, were so great that the waters along the north coast of Guadalcanal would become known as "Iron Bottom Sound" – a name that continues to this day. The bulk of the fighting was endured by the US Navy and the Marine Corps. However, US Army forces contributed significantly to the latter stages.

The Japanese advance had taken them to New Guinea and the Solomon Islands before pushing south and seizing Tulagi and Guadalcanal, where they began the construction of an airfield. The US was aware that the Japanese advance in the Pacific threatened the communications lifeline to Australia. Furthermore, American bases that lay in the path of the Japanese advance would be endangered. The Joint Chiefs of Staff concluded that an American offensive in the Pacific was now a matter of necessity. Once it was determined that the Japanese were constructing an airfield on Guadalcanal, the newly formed 1st Marine Division was given the mission of seizing that island.

OPPOSING PLANS

THE JAPANESE PLAN

The Japanese began construction of an airfield on Guadalcanal in mid-July 1942, with completion estimated by mid-August. According to Japanese documents captured later, the objective of capturing Tulagi in the Solomon Islands and building an airfield on Guadalcanal was to protect their flank while

OPPOSITE
Solomon Islands, August 1942. This dramatic picture shows the Guadalcanal landing, which was followed by six months of grueling fighting. (Bettmann/Corbis)

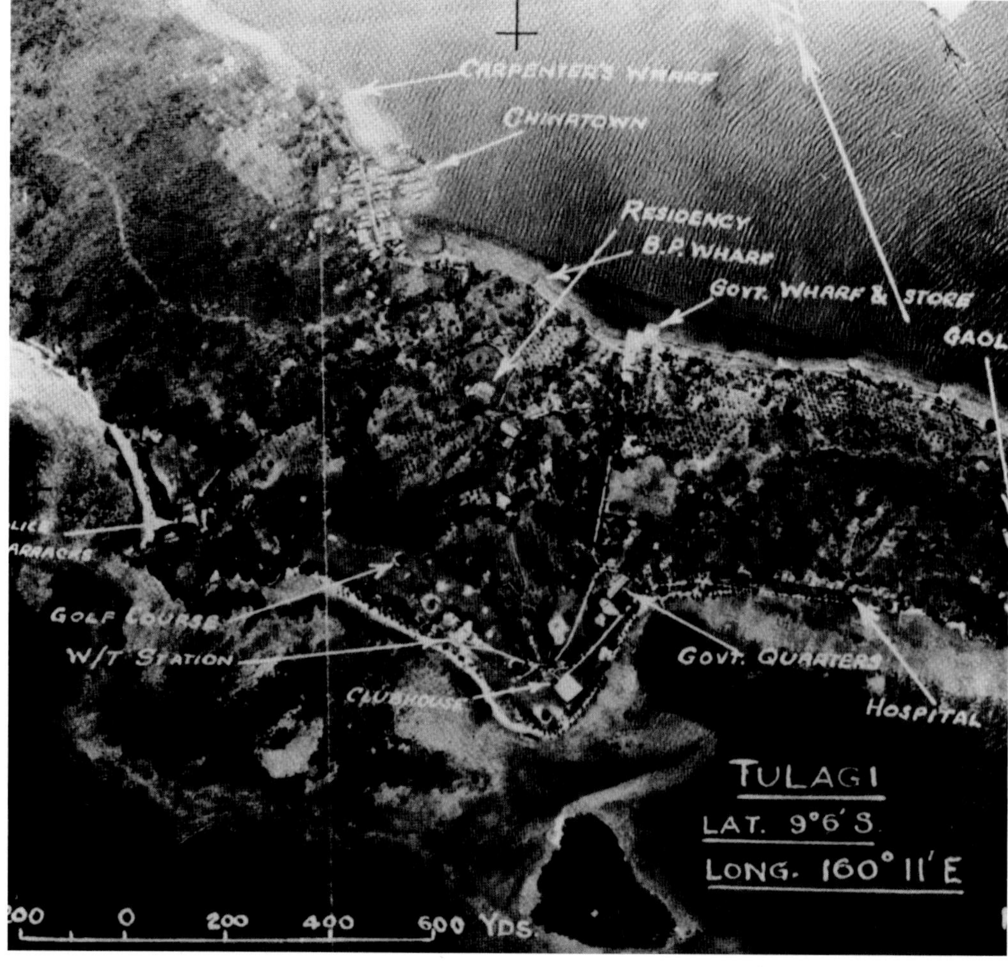

The landing on Tulagi was made on the beach just south of the golf course by the Marines of the 1st Raider Battalion, followed by the 2nd Battalion, 5th Marines. The Raiders then moved west and the 5th Marines moved east to capture the island. The date of the photo, May 17, 1942, indicates that it is an early intelligence photo and was probably used to plan the assault. (USMC)

they were carrying out their main attack on Port Moresby, New Guinea. The secondary objective was to secure a favorable base of operations to move south through New Caledonia to attack Australia. This attack was to take place after the capture of New Guinea.

THE US PLAN

The American plan for the invasion of Guadalcanal began with inter-service rivalries. After the battle of the Coral Sea, in early May 1942, General Douglas MacArthur, Commander of the Southwest Pacific Area (CINCSWPA), realized that the Japanese would eventually attempt to sever the lines of communication between Hawaii and Australia. He felt that a Japanese attack on New Guinea was inevitable. To prevent such an attack he wanted to take the offensive against the Japanese in the New Britain-New Ireland areas. An attack of this nature would force the Japanese out of the region and back to Truk, north of New Guinea. MacArthur's plan found favor with General George C. Marshall, US Army Chief of Staff. However, MacArthur did not have the resources available to launch such an offensive. Further, he had no troops under his command that had any experience of amphibious warfare. Simultaneously, Admiral Chester W. Nimitz, Commander-in-Chief Pacific Fleet (CINCPAC) and Pacific Ocean Area (CINCPOA), was contemplating a strike on Tulagi, a plan that found favor with Admiral Ernest J. King, Chief of Naval Operations. However, King felt that the immediate objectives should be in the Solomon and Santa Cruz Islands, with the ultimate objective in the New Guinea and New Britain areas. Nor could either side decide on an operation commander as and when an attack plan was formulated.

At the end of June the Joint Chiefs of Staff finally agreed on a compromise plan. It called for Admiral Robert Ghormley to command the Tulagi portion of the upcoming offensive; thereafter General MacArthur would command the advance to Rabaul. The American Navy with the Marine Corps would attack, seize, and defend Tulagi, Guadalcanal, and the surrounding area, while MacArthur made a parallel advance on New Guinea. Both drives would aim at Rabaul. The boundary between Southwest Pacific Area and the South Pacific Area was moved to reflect this, and South Pacific Forces were given the go-ahead to initiate planning. Ghormley in turn contacted Major-General Alexander A. Vandegrift, the Commanding General, 1st Marine Division (reinforced), to tell him that his division would spearhead the amphibious assault, scheduled to take place on August 1, 1942.

For General Vandegrift the problems were just beginning. He had not expected to go into combat until after January 1943. Only a third of his division was at their new base in Wellington, New Zealand; a third was still at sea; and the other third had been detached to garrison Samoa. In little less than a month Vandegrift would have to prepare operational and logistical plans, sail from Wellington to the Fiji Islands for an amphibious rehearsal, and then sail to the Solomon Islands to drive out the Japanese. In addition, there was limited available intelligence on the objective.

Realizing the enormity of the task ahead. Vandegrift asked for an extension of the invasion date. He was given one week: the amphibious assault would take place on August 7, 1942. There would be no further postponements, for the Japanese had most of the airfield completed.

The grouping of the Marines for the operation was based on intelligence estimates of Japanese forces in the area. It was estimated that of the 8,400 Japanese believed in the area, 1,400 were on Tulagi and its neighboring islands. The remaining 7,000 were thought to be on Guadalcanal, but this later turned out to be an erroneous estimate; only about half that number were there. It was anticipated that Tulagi would be the more difficult of the two amphibious objectives. The Marines going ashore there would have to make a direct assault against a small, defended island. To protect the flanks of the Marines landing on Tulagi, it was decided to first seize key points overlooking Tulagi on nearby Florida Island.

OPPOSING COMMANDERS

THE JAPANESE COMMANDERS

Japanese troops in the Solomon Islands in the summer of 1942 constituted a force to be reckoned with, but were not numerically superior, while the Japanese command structure was disjointed and plagued with a lack of cooperation between the Army and Navy. Army forces in the area centered on the Japanese 17th Army under the command of Lieutenant-General Harukichi Hyakutake, who was preoccupied with the conquest of New Guinea. The naval commander tasked with defense of the area was Vice-Admiral Gunichi Mikawa, a seasoned officer who had commanded the escort for Admiral Chuichi Nagumo's carrier force from Pearl Harbor to the Indian Ocean. Mikawa was in command of the 4th Fleet, which was not a large force and was composed of either middle-aged or older ships. Although Mikawa was tasked with defense of the area, he did not have control over the air units at Rabaul. They were controlled by Vice-Admiral Nishizo Tuskahara, Commander of the 11th Air Fleet. Mikawa was justifiably concerned with the command and control measures this caused and the general lack of preparedness.

THE US COMMANDERS

For the Guadalcanal campaign the American command was set up under Admiral Chester W. Nimitz although Ghormley would be in overall command of the operation, codenamed *Watchtower*. Ghormley, in turn, would appoint Vice-Admiral Frank Jack Fletcher as commander of the entire task force. This naval task force, designated an Expeditionary Force, was made up of two groups: the aircraft carriers constituted the Air Support Force, under Rear-Admiral Leigh Noyes; while other warships and the transports were organized as the Amphibious Force, under Rear-Admiral Richmond Kelly Turner. Major-General Vandegrift would command the Marines as part of the Landing Force.

Vice-Admiral Gunichi Mikawa was the architect of the battle of Savo Island. This battle was the worst defeat suffered by the American Navy since Pearl Harbor. Mikawa was appalled by the lack of a cohesive Japanese command in the Solomon Islands area. (Naval Historical Center)

OPPOSING FORCES

Guadalcanal would set the tone for the future campaigns of the war in the Pacific – not just one battle of quick duration, but a series of land, air, and sea battles "slugged out" along a narrow coastal belt, in restricted waterways and in the air space over Guadalcanal. The reason why the campaign was to be so prolonged was that neither side would be able to mass its forces at a critical juncture to obtain a decisive victory. The eventual outcome would be decided by the dogged determination of the American forces committed to the campaign and the release of critically needed supplies and equipment – coupled with luck.

THE JAPANESE FORCES

Initially, the Japanese were successful in the early naval battles. With the battle of Savo Island (August 8–9) they achieved a great naval victory that severely crippled the US Navy's ability to support the operations ashore and in the waters surrounding Guadalcanal. And, initially, with their land-based fighters they were also able to control the air space overhead. Their ground forces were seasoned fighters and had achieved notable military successes up to Guadalcanal.

Japanese soldiers were masters of jungle warfare but their tactics were poor and their tanks were inadequate. Communications in the jungle were also poor and tropical disease was a major problem – of the 21,500 casualties suffered by the Japanese in the campaign, 9,000 were to die of tropical diseases.

The Imperial Japanese Army (IJA) was fairly well organized at the regimental level and below, but rarely did it operate at a divisional level. It consistently underestimated the capabilities of its enemies, a course of action that would prove disastrous on Guadalcanal. The Imperial Japanese Navy (IJN) on the other hand was an efficient organization. Tactically it could operate by day as well as by night. It was a disciplined aggressive force that carried out its assigned tasks without hesitation, using its weapons systems with deadly efficiency. The most serious failing of the IJN was its inability to exploit its successes. Time and time again throughout the naval campaign the Japanese achieved a tactical victory and then departed. By exploiting their successes they could have achieved a strategic victory. In the air, the Japanese had clearly achieved a technological masterpiece with the Zero fighter. This aircraft, with its lightweight construction and high-rate of climb, could outmaneuver any American plane on Guadalcanal, but its missions were restricted due to limited fuel supplies.

THE US FORCES

The American troops who invaded Guadalcanal were for the most part untried volunteers. The majority of the equipment that the Marines had was World War I vintage and unsuited for conditions on Guadalcanal. Communications were a problem, but since the Marines had mostly internal lines, these were not as severe as the problems experienced by the Japanese. The tactics used by the Marines to encounter the Japanese were basic. Preparing to seize and then defend the airfield, they held the key terrain features that were encompassed by the Lunga Perimeter. On these they created strong points, forcing the Japanese to attack at a disadvantage. The Marines also discovered that in the jungle flanking attacks on dug-in positions worked much better than frontal assaults.

American artillery was accurate and the Stuart light tanks brought ashore by the Marines were utilized effectively. They were light enough to be employed in the jungle clearings and superior to their Japanese counterparts. Later, when the Army was brought in to reinforce and eventually to relieve the Marines, they could benefit from the Marines' experience and were better equipped.

The US Navy's entry to the campaign did not start off on a good note. The battle of Savo Island was the worst naval disaster since Pearl Harbor. Most of the equipment on board the ships was World War I vintage and radar was not effectively exploited. But it soon learned from these early errors.

TOP
At the start of the battle, the Japanese had air superiority, as shown by this downed Wildcat on Guadalcanal. (Tom Laemlein)

BOTTOM
During the battle for Guadalcanal, Marines used a variety of weapons, including two types of the Reising .45cal submachine gun, as well as the Browning Automatic Rifle (BAR). (USMC)

Damage control was a key aspect of the naval war; if a Japanese ship was damaged in a naval engagement it would have to be out of range of American aircraft from Guadalcanal by daylight – if not, it would be sunk by those planes. In contrast, damaged American ships could be repaired at a series of "local advanced naval bases" and be returned to fight again.

The Transport Division (TRANSDIV) was divided into two groups, X-RAY Guadalcanal and Y-OKE (Tulagi). The Marines of X-RAY, under Major-General Vandegrift, the Division Commander, were to land on Guadalcanal, while smaller, more specialized groups of Y-OKE were organized to assault Florida Island, Tulagi, Gavutu, and Tanambogo under the command of Brigadier-General William H. Rupertus, the assistant division commander. A total of 1,959 officers and 18,146 enlisted Marines and Navy Corpsmen comprised the amphibious landing force.

THE LANDINGS

It was still dark (0400hrs) on August 7, 1942, when the amphibious task force silently separated into two groups as it approached Savo Island. Prior to their arrival in the area, the task force had conducted an amphibious rehearsal in a remote portion of the Fiji Islands. The rehearsal, conducted in high surf conditions on beaches obstructed by coral reefs, was a disaster and was aborted to avoid injury to the personnel and damage to the precious landing craft, which did not bode well. The American amphibious forces were embarked on 19 transports and four destroyer/transports. There were five cargo ships, eight cruisers, 14 destroyers, and five minesweepers. The accompanying carrier support group consisted of three battle groups, *Saratoga*, *Enterprise*, and *Wasp*. One battleship, *North Carolina*, and a force of cruisers and destroyers screened the battle groups. This force stayed to the south of Guadalcanal while the amphibious force sailed north, dividing in two when they approached Savo Island.

The movement to the amphibious objective area was shielded from the Japanese on Guadalcanal by one of the many tropical rainstorms that frequent the region. Once the two groups separated they proceeded to their assigned beaches. After arriving on station, naval gunfire and carrier aircraft began to bombard their respective targets in accordance with the landing plan. The pattern of future campaigns in the Pacific was about to be demonstrated.

TULAGI

The Marine planners felt that before Tulagi could be taken, certain key terrain features on nearby Florida Island would have to be captured. At 0740hrs on August 7, 1942, 20 minutes before H-Hour, the first amphibious landing operation in the Solomon Islands was undertaken to secure a promontory that overlooked Beach Blue – the Tulagi invasion beach. A second unopposed landing was also made at Halavo to secure the eastern flank of the Gavutu landings.

Tulagi was attacked at 0800hrs, according to schedule. The first to see action were the Marines of the 1st Raider Battalion, commanded by Colonel Merrit A. Edson, and they were followed by the 2nd Battalion, 5th Marines. The assault waves made their way onto the beach through water ranging from waist to armpit level. Upon reaching the shore, the Raiders moved east and the 2nd Battalion moved northwest. Japanese resistance was encountered almost immediately but was systematically overcome. The advance continued slowly until dusk, when they consolidated and dug in for the night. This first night on Tulagi was to be indicative of many future nights in the Pacific: four separate attacks were launched by the Japanese to dislodge the Raiders from their positions; each attack was beaten back. Despite some further pockets of resistance, by nightfall on August 8, 1942, Tulagi was in Marine hands.

GAVUTU AND TANAMBOGO

These two small islets, connected by a causeway, were to be seized by two companies of the 1st Parachute Battalion. Gavutu, the higher in elevation of the two islands, was to be taken first. The amphibious assault was to take place at H-Hour + 4 (1200hrs) on August 7. The plan called for a landing on the northeast coast. The naval gunfire support for the Gavutu amphibious assault was so effective, however, that it actually began to work against the attackers: so complete was the destruction that the original landing site, a concrete seaplane ramp, was reduced to rubble. The landing craft were forced to divert farther north to land the Parachutists and in so doing were exposed to flanking fire from Tanambogo. Despite heavy casualties, the Parachutists took the northeastern portion of the island. However, a small detachment of Marine reinforcements, deployed during a night-time assault, was badly mauled.

On August 8, the 3rd Battalion, 2nd Marines, was ordered to reinforce the Parachutists on Gavutu and then attack Tanambogo. Supported by tanks from the 2nd Tank Battalion and with air and naval gunfire support, an amphibious landing was made at 1620hrs on August 8, 1942, on Tanambogo. Once a beachhead was established, reinforcements crossed the causeway, and by 2300hrs, two-thirds of the island was secured. After a lot of fighting during the night, the island was completely secured by late on the 9th. Once Tanambogo fell, organized resistance in the Tulagi, Gavutu, Tanambogo, and Florida Islands ceased. In all, the operation had taken three days. American losses overall were light, and the Japanese lost 1,500 troops. Only a handful of prisoners were taken.

A US Marine LVT shown landing at Guadalcanal. (Tom Laemlein)

GUADALCANAL

On Guadalcanal an unopposed landing was made at Beach Red, about 6,000 yards east of Lunga Point. It was spearheaded by the 5th Marines, followed by the 1st Marines, and by 0930hrs the assault forces were ashore and moving inland. Their plan was simple: the 5th Marines would proceed along the coast, securing that flank, while the 1st Marines would move inland through the jungle and secure Mount Austen, described as a grassy knoll and reportedly only a short distance away. Now came the realization that intelligence concerning the terrain on Guadalcanal was faulty. Mount Austen was both four miles away and the most prominent terrain feature in the area – it would not be captured until months later. The remainder of the first day was spent consolidating positions and attempting to disperse the supplies that were stockpiling on the beach. Meanwhile the strongest Japanese countermeasure came at 1400hrs in the form of an air raid by 18 twin-engined Type 97 bombers, two of which were shot down. A second wave of Type 99 Aichi bombers that came later was also repulsed with the loss of two aircraft.

At 2200hrs, General Vandegrift issued the attack order for the next day. With Mount Austen out of reach and only 10,000 Marines ashore, he ordered the airfield to be taken and a defensive perimeter set up. August 8, therefore, began with a westward advance by all Marine forces on Guadalcanal. The airfield remained the primary objective. Contact with small groups of Japanese began to occur as the Marines closed on the airfield. In the Lunga region, just south of the airfield, defensive positions consisting of trenches and anti-aircraft emplacements, well built and equipped, were discovered deserted. The airfield, nearly 3,600ft long and in its last stages of construction, was defended by a small group of Japanese who were overcome. By the end of the day, the airfield had been taken and a defensive perimeter established. It was later revealed that the Japanese had been aware of the impending American assault but had thought it was only to be a raid. Therefore Japanese troops in the area had been instructed to withdraw into the hills until the Americans departed. So far the Japanese resistance had been less than effective. In the air, attacks were repulsed with minimum damage to the Americans. However, the Japanese had no intention of giving up the Solomon Islands without a fight.

AUGUST

Early on August 8, part of the Japanese 8th Fleet under Admiral Mikawa made preparations to attack the American amphibious task force. Mikawa's battle group consisted of five heavy cruisers and two light cruisers plus a destroyer. With this formidable force he began to move south. En route, he was spotted by an Allied patrol plane and there began a tragic chain of events that would lead to one of the greatest naval disasters ever suffered by the American Navy.

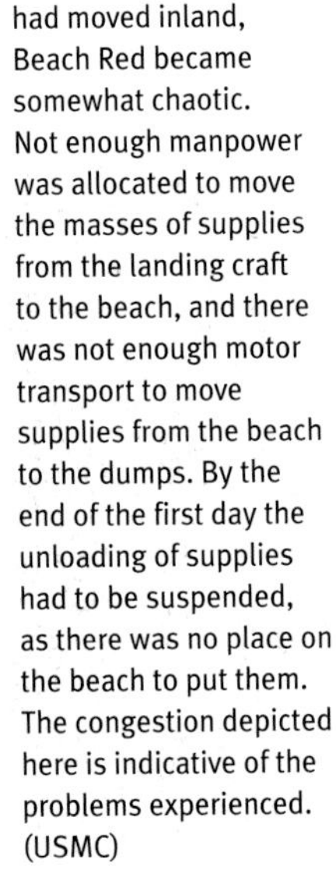

After the assault troops had moved inland, Beach Red became somewhat chaotic. Not enough manpower was allocated to move the masses of supplies from the landing craft to the beach, and there was not enough motor transport to move supplies from the beach to the dumps. By the end of the first day the unloading of supplies had to be suspended, as there was no place on the beach to put them. The congestion depicted here is indicative of the problems experienced. (USMC)

THE BATTLE OF SAVO ISLAND

Although there was considerable confusion about which direction the Japanese force was heading in, Rear-Admiral Turner positioned two destroyers, *Blue* and *Ralph Talbot*, northwest of Savo Island, to maintain a radar watch on the channel. He then positioned three cruisers, the *Australia*, *Canberra*, and *Chicago*, along with two destroyers, the *Bagley* and *Patterson*, to patrol between Savo Island and Cape Esperance. Three additional cruisers, *Vincennes*, *Astoria*, and *Quincy*, along with two destroyers, *Helm* and *Jarvis*, were to patrol between Savo Island and Florida Island. Two other cruisers and two destroyers guarded the transports. As these events were occurring, Admiral Fletcher, in command of the carrier support group, felt that operational losses to his aircraft and dwindling fuel oil for his ships limited his effectiveness. He requested and was granted permission to withdraw on August 9. Once Rear-Admiral Turner was aware of Fletcher's plans he also decided to withdraw his amphibious fleet which was vulnerable without air cover. This was despite the fact that the transports had not yet unloaded all supplies to the Marine force now on Guadalcanal.

But at 0145hrs on August 9, the Japanese naval force miraculously slipped past the radar picket destroyers. Launching a surprise night-time attack the Japanese scored a major victory. The Allies (both US and Australian ships were present) lost four cruisers, with one cruiser and one destroyer damaged. Fortunately, Admiral Mikawa did not attack the transport area. Had he done so he could have effectively curtailed American operations in the area. Instead he broke contact and headed back to Rabaul to be out of range of American carrier aircraft. Meanwhile, the damage inflicted by the Japanese on the amphibious task force delayed its departure on August 9. But by 1500hrs, the first group of ships had departed; the last group left at 1830hrs.

One of General Vandegrift's primary concerns was the threat of a Japanese seaborne invasion, so the bulk of the division's assets were set up to repel a counterlanding. Seen here are two Marines manning a M1917 (top) while a M3A1 light tank is dug in and camouflaged as part of a beach defensive position (bottom). (Tom Laemlein and USMC)

THE FIRST WEEK

With the withdrawal of the amphibious task force the Marines were left without air support. The withdrawal of the transports had left the Marines with only part of their supplies: ammunition was adequate, but food was a much more serious issue and by August 12 the division was on two meals a day. The captured airfield, renamed Henderson Field, would now have to be developed for the mission to be a

Before Guadalcanal the enemy advanced at his pleasure – after Guadalcanal he retreated at ours."

— ADMIRAL "BULL" HALSEY

success. Until it was completed, the Marines would be at the mercy of any Japanese air or naval attacks. By August 20, the Marines would have aircraft based on the island. Initially just 19 Wildcats and 12 dive-bombers were available but they were eventually supplemented by some Army Air Corps' P-400s.

In the first week the tone of the campaign was set. Daily – and this was to continue for months except when weather and American fighter aircraft were present – Japanese planes made incessant air raids. The targets were either Henderson Field or resupply shipping at Lunga Point. At night the perimeter was bombarded by Japanese warships. All in all, the situation looked pretty bleak for the Marines, virtually abandoned by the Navy. Having quickly established themselves ashore, they began to improve the perimeter. Considering a Japanese invasion more than likely, General Vandegrift concentrated the bulk of his combat units along the beach. Once the Lunga Perimeter was established, patrols were sent out to gain information on the Japanese forces on the island. So far as could be determined, the bulk of the Japanese forces were concentrated west of the perimeter, in the Matanikau River and Point Cruz area and a number of operations were launched to clear the defenders.

PREVIOUS SPREAD
Two American Marines firing a captured .50cal Japanese machine gun at Japanese planes during the battle for Guadalcanal in the Solomon Islands. (Hulton-Deutsch Collection/Corbis)

BELOW
Colonel Kiyono Ichiki was the leader of the 900-man Japanese force that attacked the Marines at "Alligator Creek." Contrary to popular belief, he did not commit suicide after burning his regimental colours after the aborted attack: last seen he was rallying his men as they attacked the Marines. More than likely he was killed attempting to cross the sand spit. (USMC)

THE FIRST BATTLE OF THE MATANIKAU

On August 19, a battalion-sized operation by the 5th Marines was launched against the Japanese in the Matanikau area, its mission being to drive the Japanese out of the region. Company B, 1st Battalion, was to approach using the coastal road and fight a spoiling action at the river mouth, while a second company (Company L, 3rd Battalion) was to move overland through the jungle and deliver the main attack from the south. The third company (Company I, 3rd Battalion) would make a seaborne landing to the west near Kokumbona village and cut off any retreating Japanese. The operation was a success and the Marines succeeded in destroying the small Japanese garrison in the area.

THE BATTLE OF THE TENARU

On August 13, the Japanese High Command ordered Lieutenant-General Haruyoshi Hyakutake's 17th Army at Rabaul to retake Guadalcanal. The naval commander for this operation was to be Rear-Admiral Raizo Tanaka. With no clear intelligence picture of the American forces on Guadalcanal, Hyakutake decided to retake it with 6,000 troops from the 7th Division's 28th Infantry Regiment and the Yokosuka Special Naval Landing Force. The spearpoint of the effort would be made by the reinforced 2nd Battalion of the 28th Infantry Regiment, led by Colonel Kiyono Ichiki. Ichiki and an advance element of 900 troops were taken to Guadalcanal and landed at Taivu Point on the night of August 18, 1942. At the same time 500 troops of the Yokosuka 5th Special Landing Force went ashore to the west at Kokumbona.

These landings were the first run of what would be nicknamed the "Tokyo Express" by the Marines. This was basically a shuttle run organized by Admiral Tanaka. Composed of cruisers, destroyers, and transports, it shuttled troops and supplies at night from Rabaul to Guadalcanal. The route they took down the Solomons chain was nicknamed the "Slot." After landing at Taivu, Colonel Ichiki established his headquarters, sent out scouting parties, and awaited the arrival of the remainder of his regiment. Once he had the rest of his troops and accurate intelligence on the Americans he would attack. The intelligence picture Ichiki had was that a raiding party of Americans was cowering in a defensive perimeter around the airfield. Ichiki's plan was to march to the former Japanese construction camp east of the Tenaru, establish it as his headquarters and then move against the Americans. But his scouting party was destroyed by a US Marine patrol. Fearing he had lost the element of surprise he decided to march westward with the troops he had to hand.

On the night of August 20/21, Marine listening posts detected the movement of a large body of Japanese troops. The listening posts had no sooner withdrawn than a severely wounded native, Jacob Vouza, a sergeant in the native police contingent, who had been tortured and left for dead by the Japanese, stumbled into the Marine lines and, before collapsing, imparted the news that the Japanese were going to attack. No sooner had Vouza arrived than the first Japanese, who were marching in formation, ran into a single strand of barbed wire placed across the sand bar at the mouth of the creek. This temporarily disorganized the leading elements of Ichiki's force, who were not expecting to run into any defensive positions so far east.

The ensuing battle that erupted, which would later be referred to as the battle of the Tenaru, was fierce and savage. Using human wave tactics, the Japanese attempted to crush Lieutenant-Colonel Edwin A. Pollock's 2nd Battalion, 1st Marines, which was defending the area.

The aftermath of the battle of the Tenaru clearly indicates the determination of the Japanese attackers. The dead Japanese in the foreground had actually penetrated to the west bank of the creek before they were stopped by the defending Marines. The Marines in the background are walking through the area to survey the aftermath of the battle. (NARA)

Unable to dislodge the Marines, Ichiki sent part of his force south along the east bank to cross the creek upstream in an attempt to outflank the Marines. This attempt failed. He then sent a company out through the surf in an attempt to break through from the north. This attempt also failed and Ichiki was killed. But the fight continued throughout the night. In the morning the Marines were still holding. It was then decided to conduct a double envelopment to eliminate Ichiki's force. Supported by light tanks, artillery, and newly arrived fighter planes, the 1st Battalion, 1st Marine Regiment, which had been held as division reserve, outflanked Ichiki's force and destroyed it. Of the original 900 Japanese troops, 800 were dead or dying on the sand bar and in the surrounding jungle. The cost to the Marines was light: 34 killed and 75 wounded.

THE BATTLE OF THE EASTERN SOLOMONS

While the issue on land was being decided the Japanese assembled a major naval task force under admirals Tanaka and Mikawa. At the same time an American naval task force under Admiral Fletcher which was operating southeast of the lower Solomons in what it believed to be a safe area, became engaged in the battle of the Eastern Solomons. Unaware of what had happened to Ichiki, the Japanese had planned on reinforcing him with a larger secondary force of about 1,500 troops. This force departed on August 19 in four transports screened by four destroyers. They were to land on Guadalcanal on August 24. To support the transports and operations ashore the Japanese dispatched two naval task forces composed of five aircraft carriers, four battleships, 16 cruisers, and 30 destroyers.

Three American carrier groups, comprising three aircraft carriers, one battleship, six cruisers, and 18 destroyers, were operating about 100 miles southeast of Guadalcanal. Somehow, an erroneous intelligence report on August 23 indicated that the large Japanese force, believed to be in the area, was returning to the Japanese base at Truk Island. Operating on this mistaken belief, one of the carrier groups based around *Wasp* departed from the group to refuel. This left two carrier groups formed around *Enterprise* and *Saratoga*.

Shortly afterward, patrol planes discovered the Japanese transport group 350 miles from Guadalcanal. The next day, August 24, American carrier planes discovered the Japanese forces, and at the same time Japanese carrier planes discovered the American forces. In the ensuing air-to-ship, air-to-air battle, the smaller American force turned back a larger Japanese force. The Japanese were able to land 1,500 troops and bombard Henderson Field; but they were not able to intervene in the ground fighting. Also, they were no longer able to control the air space over Guadalcanal. The Japanese lost the carrier *Ryujo*, one destroyer, one light cruiser, and 90 aircraft, with one seaplane carrier and a destroyer damaged. Shortly after the battle the American naval force departed. The Americans had sustained damage to one aircraft carrier, *Enterprise*, and had lost 20 planes. Far more serious losses followed. On August 31, the aircraft carrier *Saratoga*, patrolling west of the Santa Cruz Islands, was torpedoed. The aircraft carrier *Wasp*, on patrol southeast of the Solomons, was torpedoed and sunk on September 15. With one carrier sunk and two damaged, *Hornet* was the only remaining American aircraft carrier in the South Pacific. Meanwhile on Guadalcanal itself a second so-called "battle of Matanik" was fought with an attempt to place the 1st Battalion 5th Marines ashore west of Point Cruz but again no decisive results were achieved. The Japanese defenders eventually chose to retire and the Marines returned to the Lunga Perimeter.

SEPTEMBER

While the ground fighting was going on, important strategic developments were taking place. A Marine air wing was beginning to establish itself at Henderson Field. On September 3, 1942, the 1st Marine Aircraft Wing, under Brigadier-General Roy S. Geiger, arrived. With the arrival of the wing, the tide in the air would eventually be turned against the Japanese pilots.

THE TASIMBOKO RAID

In early September, the islanders reported that several thousand Japanese had occupied and fortified the village of Tasimboko, about eight miles east of Lunga Point. These reports were dismissed by Marine intelligence, but as

US Wildcats pictured on the captured Guadalcanal airfield, which was quickly renamed Henderson Field by the Marines. (Tom Laemlein)

a precautionary measure it was decided that an amphibious raid should be made against what was believed to be a small Japanese garrison force. Marines were drawn from the 1st Raider Battalion and the 1st Parachute Battalion under the command of Colonel Merritt A. Edson.

The Raiders landed at dawn September 8, followed shortly afterward by the Parachutists. As they moved west they met minimal resistance until they approached Tasimboko, when resistance dramatically increased. The Japanese troops, estimated at 1,000, were well armed and equipped. They were also supported by field artillery firing at point-blank range but the Marine force succeeded in occupying the village. There they discovered thousands of life jackets and multiple supplies. What they did not know was that the Japanese they had just fought were the rear party of the 35th Infantry Regiment (or Kawaguchi Brigade, as it was referred to). Totaling more than 3,000 troops commanded by Major-General Kiyotaki Kawaguchi, it had arrived between August 29 and September 1.

Two events saved the smaller Marine force from being destroyed by the numerically superior Japanese. First was the fact that Kawaguchi had begun to move southwest through the jungle. His intention was to move undetected to the south of Henderson Field and then launch an attack north from the jungle. Second, an American resupply convoy en route to Lunga Point was passing by the area. The Japanese incorrectly concluded that the convoy was reinforcing the Marine attacking force and a full-scale landing was being made. Kawaguchi and Edson would meet again, less than a week later, on a grassy ridge overlooking Henderson Field.

THE BATTLE OF "BLOODY RIDGE"

After Tasimboko it was decided to put the Raiders and Parachutists in a reserve position. They were to occupy a defensive position on a series of grassy ridges south of Henderson Field, near the division command post. But patrols and native scouts began to encounter increasing Japanese opposition. On September 10, native scouts reported that the Japanese were cutting a trail and were five miles from the perimeter. A major Japanese offensive was in the making. The ridge positions were also bombed in daily air raids. Unable to advance, the Marines consolidated their positions on the southernmost knoll of the ridge complex. This would be the start of a crucial battle that would be called the battle of "Bloody Ridge" – a turning point in the campaign.

To defend the area, Edson positioned his composite battalion of Raiders and Parachutists in a linear defense along the southernmost ridge and in the surrounding jungle. The western flank was anchored on the Lunga River. The attack began that evening with shelling from Japanese warships, followed by repeated probings of the Marine lines from the jungle to the south. Later that night the Kawaguchi Brigade repeatedly struck. Preceded by a 20-minute naval bombardment, powerful thrusts were directed from the west primarily against the companies that occupied the jungle terrain flanking the ridge. The Raiders were pushed back and the next day, September 13, Edson attempted to use his reserve companies to dislodge the Japanese who had established a western salient into his position. This daylight attack did not meet with success, so the Marines began to prepare for the inevitable night attack. Throughout the day Japanese planes attacked the Lunga Perimeter, sometimes bombing the ridge. The second night, Kawaguchi struck with two infantry battalions. He succeeded in driving the Marines back to the northernmost knoll of the ridge. But from this final position the Marines held back the Japanese onslaught. Kawaguchi knew that he would have to overwhelm the enemy if his attack on Henderson Field were to succeed; Edson knew that at this stage of the battle his troops were no longer just fighting to save Henderson Field – they were fighting to save their very lives.

At dawn on September 14, planes from Henderson Field and the 2nd Battalion, 5th Marines, supported the Raiders and Parachutists in driving the remainder of Kawaguchi's forces back into the jungle. Kawaguchi had been defeated; the majority of his troops were either dead or dying. The Marines lost 31 killed, 103 wounded, and nine missing; the Japanese lost more than 600 killed. For his heroic defense of "Bloody Ridge" Henderson Field, Edson would receive the Congressional Medal of Honor. While Kawaguchi was attacking the ridge, two other companies attacked the 3rd Battalion, 1st Marines, at "Alligator Creek" but this too was repulsed.

MATANIKAU ACTION

With all the Japanese attacks repulsed, Vandegrift decided to expand the Marine perimeter. Bolstered by the addition of the 7th Marines, recently transported from Samoa, Vandegrift tasked them with clearing the Japanese from the Matanikau area. The action was initially planned to be accomplished in two separate phases. A reconnaissance in force by the 1st Battalion, 7th Marines, was to be conducted from September 23–26 in the area between Mount Austen and Kokumbona. On September 27, the 1st Raiders Battalion was to conduct an attack at the mouth of the Matanikau River with the objective of pushing through to Kokumbona and establishing a patrol base there. The 1st Battalion, 7th Marines, under the command of Lieutenant Colonel "Chesty" Puller, set out as scheduled. Late in the evening of

This is the road that leads from "Bloody Ridge"' to the airport. In this picture it is very easy to see why the defense of Bloody Ridge was so critical. Once the Japanese advanced to the open plain in the foreground, they would have seized the airfield and driven a deadly wedge between the Marine forces. Had the Japanese succeeded, there is some doubt whether they could have been ejected. (USMC)

September 24 the battalion made contact with a strong Japanese force near Mount Austen.

General Vandegrift, fearing that Puller had made contact with a strong Japanese force, sent the 2nd Battalion, 5th Marines, to reinforce him. The combined force then continued its advance to clear the east bank of the Matanikau. As it approached the river mouth on September 26, the combined force came under fire. The 2nd Battalion, 5th Marines, succeeded in making its way to the mouth of the river, but could not force a crossing. It was decided to have Puller's Marines and the 2nd Battalion, 5th Marines, hold and engage the Japanese at the mouth of the river.

The 1st Raider Battalion, meanwhile, had set out from the perimeter. However, developments at Matanikau River resulted in the Raiders moving eastward and planning to strike the Japanese from the rear. The action began early on September 27 with the Raiders, now under Lieutenant-Colonel Sam Griffith (Edson having been promoted and given command of the 5th Marines), moving up to their intended crossing point. But concentrated enemy fire succeeded in stopping the assault and preventing the Raiders from deploying. From this point on, the American operation degenerated.

A message from the Raiders was interpreted incorrectly at division headquarters, and believing that the Raiders had successfully crossed the river, two companies from Puller's battalion were sent to assist in a shore-to-shore landing west of Point Cruz. The landing was unopposed but mortar bombs fell on the Marines just as they reached the ridges 500 yards south of the landing beach killing the commanding officer. A strong enemy column from Matanikau River then engaged the Marines. Now all three Marine forces were in combat with the Japanese but unable to support each other. The force west of Point Cruz realized they were in danger of being surrounded so since they had no radio equipment spelt out "HELP" using their T-shirts. This was spotted by a dive-bomber pilot who radioed a message to the 5th Marines. Puller subsequently left the Matanikau area to rescue his isolated companies. Using a small flotilla of landing craft the companies were finally evacuated at a cost of 24 killed and 23 wounded. The Japanese force was estimated to have been 1,800 strong with 60 killed and 100 wounded. Once the withdrawal was accomplished, the Marines along the Matanikau also pulled back to the perimeter, leaving the Japanese still in control of the region and ending the ground fighting for the month of September. Meanwhile the naval actions during the month had been limited to the nightly attempts to interdict the "Tokyo Express."

OCTOBER

MATANIKAU BATTLE

In October the Americans intended to drive the Japanese from their Matanikau stronghold, and intelligence reports indicated that the Japanese were massing in the region for another all-out attack. General Vandegrift planned for the 5th Marines (minus one battalion) to conduct a spoiling attack at the mouth of the Matanikau River, which would focus Japanese attention on that area; while the 7th Marines (minus one battalion), reinforced by the 3rd Battalion, 2nd Marines, would cross the river upstream, then turn north to clear the area on the west bank. The operation would be supported by artillery and from the air with the objective to prevent Japanese artillery from firing at Henderson Field.

Meanwhile the Japanese hoped to seize positions east of the Matanikau River to establish better positions for their artillery. Fortunately for the Marines, they put their plan into action first. The plan called for the 5th Marines to set up positions on the east bank of the Matanikau running south from the mouth by 1,800 yards. The main force, composed of the 3rd Battalion, 2nd Marines, and the 7th Marines would cross the Matanikau, moving northward, and then assault the Matanikau village. On October 7 the advance began. By noon, the 3rd Battalion, 5th Marines, had made contact with a Japanese company which they began to drive back. At 1830hrs on October 8 the Japanese attacked in force but were ultimately unsuccessful. On October 9 the main attack was launched. The 1st Battalion, 7th Marines, came across a large concentration of Japanese from the 4th Infantry Regiment camped in a deep ravine. Using artillery and mortars the Marines decimated the Japanese and more than 700 were killed.

THE JAPANESE COUNTEROFFENSIVE

The Japanese, who had been planning a full scale counteroffensive since August, had completed new preparations by October. The planned Army–Navy operation for the recapture of Guadalcanal was to be directed by General Hyakutake, commander of 17th Army.

The battle of Cape Esperance

This major counteroffensive was to be launched on three fronts. The first phase began at sea, with the battle of Cape Esperance. In this battle the opposing naval forces made contact near Savo Island. The Americans under Rear-Admiral Norman Scott took up a north–south position against the Japanese force that was moving at a right-angle toward it. Admiral Scott then executed a classic crossing the "T" maneuver, the main batteries of the American ships being brought to bear on the Japanese ships traveling in a lineahead formation. As a result the Japanese were forced to retire. On each side a destroyer was lost and a cruiser damaged. It was not a major victory, but the naval balance of power was starting to shift toward the Americans.

The battle for Henderson Field

On October 13, the Japanese struck Henderson Field with an intense aerial bombardment. Artillery fire followed and shortly before

The terrain the Marines moved through in the Matanikau region was hardly passable. Often the point elements had to blaze a trail through tangled terrain, and progress was extremely limited. In this picture, a machine gun crew struggles to get its ammunition cart up a slight slope. Working like this in the heat and humidity sapped the endurance of the Marines. (USMC)

midnight two Japanese battleships began a systematic bombardment. When they retired, bombers hit the airfield again. By the afternoon of October 14, Henderson Field was completely out of action. Only minimal operations could be carried out from a nearby grass runway. On October 15, five Japanese transports began to unload troops and supplies at Tassafaronga Point, and despite coming under US Navy fire managed to offload 3–4,000 troops and 80 percent of their cargo.

With the arrival of the last of his troops, General Hyakutake was confident of success. The plan of attack was to be four-pronged. Lieutenant-General Masao Maruyama was to lead the main force and attack from the south, near "Bloody Ridge." The second prong, under Major-General Tadashi Sumiyoshi, was to attack from the west with tank support and cross the Matanikau River. The third prong was to cross the Matanikau River a mile upstream and move north against the Marines while the fourth prong called for an amphibious assault at Koli Point. In the event this was canceled when the Japanese believed American resistance was about to collapse. The attack was to commence on October 22; however, movement through the jungle caused unexpected delays – delays that upset a very elaborately coordinated attack schedule. All supplies had to be man-packed, and the artillery pieces were the first to be left along the tortuous trail that made its way up and down the steep slopes south of Mount Austen. As a result, Maruyama was forced to delay his attack until the 24th.

Meanwhile Major-General Sumiyoshi, who was out of communication with Maruyama, began his attack on the afternoon of October 21 but was driven back. The following day was quiet until 1800hrs. But this time the Marines were ready. Artillery and a concentration of anti-tank weaponry waited for the Japanese. The massed Marine artillery fire virtually annihilated Sumiyoshi's troops and the Marines still held the western sector. The following night, October 24, during a rainstorm, Maruyama's forces launched their attack against the 1st Battalion, 7th Marines, commanded by Lieutenant-Colonel Puller.

The Japanese had finally hacked their way through the jungle and were just south of "Bloody Ridge" but were now only armed with machine guns – all the artillery and mortars had been abandoned in the jungle. Simultaneous with Maruyama's attack was the third prong attack on the southwestern side of the Marine perimeter. Puller's Marines were supplemented by the 7th Marines reserve force. The Japanese resolutely attacked during the night, but every charge was beaten back. The following day, October 25, became known as "Dugout Sunday" as the Japanese continuously shelled and bombed Henderson Field. That night Maruyama attacked with his 16th and 29th Infantry Regiments along the southern portion of "Bloody Ridge." Again the Marines and soldiers, supported by Marine 37mm anti-tank weapons firing canister rounds, repulsed the final assault. At dawn Maruyama withdrew, leaving more than 1,500 of his troops dead in front of the Marine lines. That same night the third prong forces also met with defeat when attacking the 2nd Battalion, 7th Marines, to the east of the Matanikau River. These unsuccessful Japanese attacks marked the end of their October counteroffensive. It would also be the high water mark for the Japanese in the campaign. Other battles, many just as fierce, were yet to be fought, but October would be the decisive month on land.

At sea, October ended with the battle of the Santa Cruz Islands. In that battle, a strong Japanese force that had been maneuvering in the area was attacked by a naval task force under Rear-Admiral Thomas C. Kinkaid. In the ensuing battle the Americans lost an aircraft carrier and a destroyer, while another aircraft carrier, a battleship, a cruiser, and a destroyer were damaged. The Japanese lost no ships while sustaining damage to three aircraft carriers and two destroyers; but their forces departed the area.

NOVEMBER

November was a month of change in the campaign. The South Pacific Area received a new commander: Admiral Ghormley was relieved and Admiral William F. "Bull" Halsey took command. With Halsey came the much-needed troops and supplies to maintain the American presence in the area.

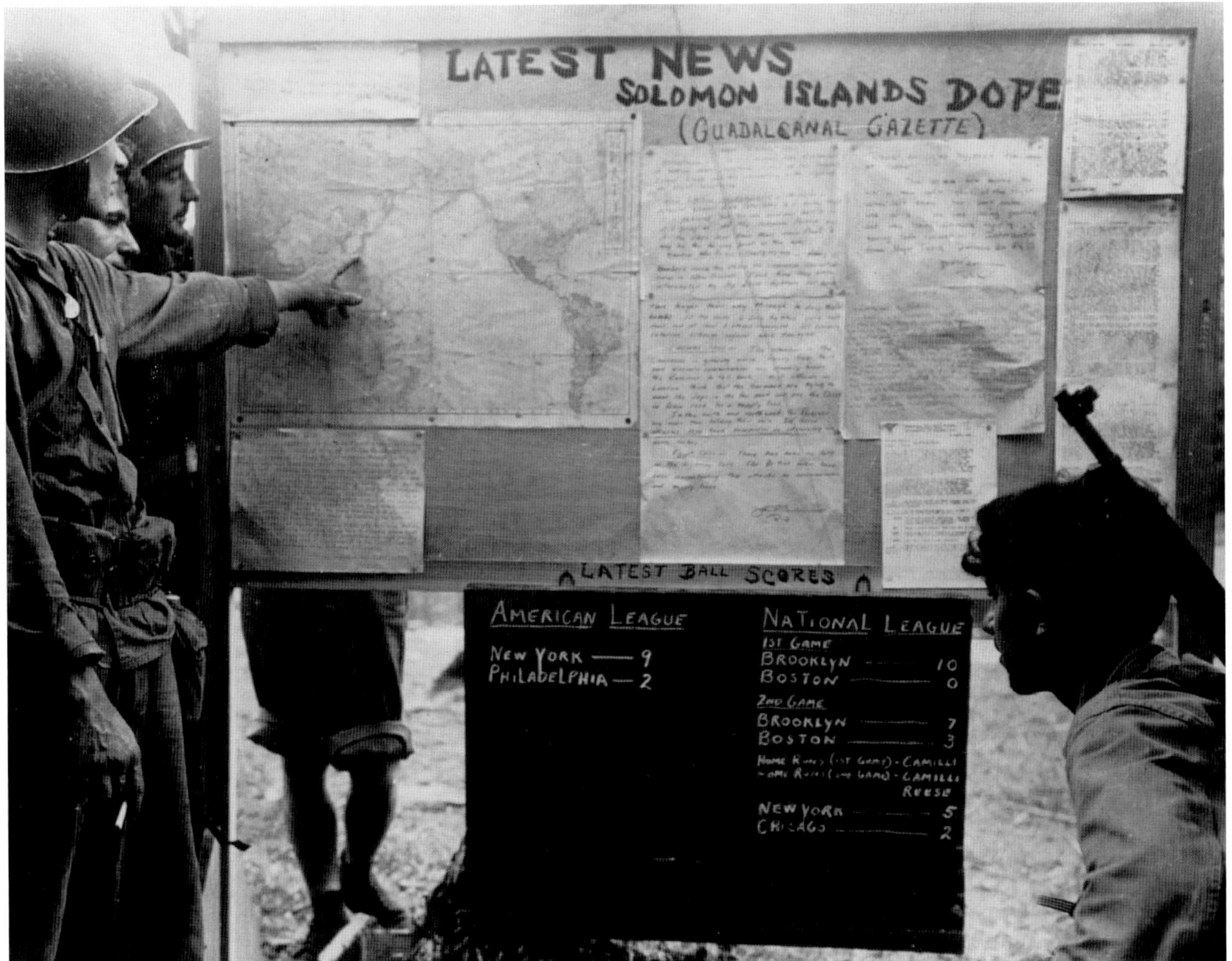

US Marines at the Guadalcanal battle front keep up with the news at home and check their position on the map at a news board, known as the *Guadalcanal Gazette*, set up for their benefit. Even in the midst of a long campaign, the sports results were of upmost importance. (Bettmann/Corbis)

again and began to surround them. Over the next few days all Japanese attempts to break out were foiled, and the Marines and soldiers, supported by artillery, began to reduce the pocket of resistance. By November 12, they had completed their mission. In this final eastern action, the Americans had lost 40 killed and 120 wounded; the Japanese had lost more than 450 killed.

THE FINAL NAVAL BATTLES

The Japanese attempted another reinforcing naval operation in the Second Naval Battle for Guadalcanal, but after a sharp engagement the Japanese were again turned back. The last naval action in November was the battle of Tassafaronga as a Japanese "Tokyo Express" destroyer force attempted to resupply the beleaguered Japanese troops. But this was intercepted by Rear-Admiral Carleton H. Wright. Each side lost a destroyer but again the Japanese were turned back. With the close of November, the Japanese no longer had control of the waters around Guadalcanal.

THE ARMY TAKES OVER

December saw some definitive changes in the campaign. The Lunga Perimeter was not much larger than it had been in the early days, but there were now enough troops to take decisive offensive action. The American Army was ashore in force, and was led by Major-General Alexander Patch, who had the Americal Division under his command. With Admiral Halsey in overall command, the bleak days were ending. Troops and equipment were pouring into Guadalcanal, and some of the worst-hit Marine units had been relieved and given a much needed rest. Meanwhile the new Army P-38 fighter aircraft was making its debut in the area, and B-17 bombers were now based at Henderson Field. With the tide of war turning it was decided to relieve General Vandegrift's 1st Marine Division. On December 9, after more than four months of protracted combat, the Marines were pulled out. Sick, tired, dirty, and exhausted, they were glad to leave their island purgatory. Command of the ground forces was now turned over to Major-General Patch of the Army, who was left with an experienced cadre of troops, for he still had a major portion of the 2nd Marine Division in his command. Intelligence reports indicated that 25,000 Japanese were still on the island – in comparison with 40,000 Americans. However, the exact disposition of the Japanese forces was not known, although it was generally assumed that they were in the Mount Austen and Kokumbona area, and were still being resupplied by the "Tokyo Express."

Mount Austen is not a single hill mass, but a spur of Guadalcanal's main mountain range with a 1,514ft summit covered in dense rain forest. For the American soldiers who would have to fight there, Mount Austen was a jungle nightmare. Supplies had to be man-packed up the steep slopes and casualties evacuated back the same way. The fighting was fierce, and the Japanese were well dug in. The attack, which began on December 17, 1942, was not over until January 1943. American soldiers of the 132nd Infantry bore the brunt of the fighting, until hard hit by fatigue and illness during 22 days of intense jungle warfare, they were relieved on January 4. They had lost 112 killed in contrast to Japanese losses in the region of 450.

With the start of the New Year, Major-General Patch, now commanding XIV Corps, (Americal Division, 25th Infantry Division, 43rd Infantry Division, and 2nd Marine Division), resolved to bring matters to a close and drive the Japanese from Guadalcanal: in a series of quick offensive actions, he decided to drive westward and crush Japanese resistance between Point Cruz and Kokumbona. In a one-week period the Marines advanced more than 1,500 yards to a position from which a Kokumbona offensive could be launched. In the process they killed an estimated 650 Japanese. While these gains were being made, the 35th Infantry was engaged in heavy fighting at the Gifu, on Mount Austen, and in the hilly jungle area to the southwest centering on a feature known as the "Seahorse," from its resemblance in an aerial photograph. In a difficult one-day battle the 3rd Battalion, 35th Infantry, seized the "Seahorse," effectively encircling the Gifu. But it would take an arduous two-week battle to seize the Gifu itself with advancements made in 100-yard increments. In a hellish battle in the jungle, a lone US tank supported by 16 infantrymen penetrated to the heart of the Gifu and then began a systematic destruction of pillboxes and Japanese soldiers. By the night of January 22/23, the Gifu was quiet. The reduction of the Gifu had cost the Americans 64 killed and 42 wounded; the Japanese had lost more than 500 killed. Meanwhile, in a final two-day offensive that ended on January 24, 1943, Kokumbona was captured. At the end of January, the final task facing XIV Corps was that of pursuing and destroying the Japanese before they could dig in or escape.

THE FINAL PHASE

By early February, Major-General Patch was convinced that the Japanese were planning a withdrawal, something he wanted to prevent. The American forces instituted a final pincer movement to trap the remaining Japanese troops. However, the US advance was too slow, and in the face of a determined Japanese delaying action 13,000 Japanese troops of the 17th Army were able to withdraw to Cape Esperance. The Japanese had been skillful and cunning. Nevertheless the essential significance of the campaign was unchanged. The first phase of the Solomons campaign was concluded as a victory for the Americans, and the first major step had been taken in the reduction of Rabaul.

AFTERMATH

Guadalcanal provided an archetype for jungle and naval warfare in the Pacific. It was a hard fought campaign that shattered the myth of Japanese invincibility. From the campaign a seasoned fighting force was created. Most important, the campaign validated the theories and practice of amphibious warfare that had been taught at the Marine Corps schools at Quantico, Virginia, in the late 1920s and 1930s. The important gain for the Americans was Guadalcanal itself. It would be developed into one of the largest advanced naval and air bases in the region and would be a springboard for future amphibious operations in the region. And by holding it the Americans had kept open the lines of communication with Australia.

The cost of the campaign had not been prohibitive for the Americans. Total Army and Marine losses were 1,600 killed and 4,700 wounded. The Japanese lost considerably more: 25,400 from all services. Naval losses were more even with each side losing about 25 major warships.

JADALCANAL • TARAWA

ORIGINS OF THE CAMPAIGN

Utilizing the islands and atolls ceded to them after World War I, Japan had constructed an outer ring of defenses, ranging from the Marianas to the Marshall Islands in the east. An attack on the island of Makin in the northern Gilbert Islands, by a Marine Raider Battalion in August 1942, alerted the Japanese to the vulnerability of the Gilberts, and the token force in the area was reinforced by a much larger contingent of troops. The island of Betio (pronounced "baysho") on the atoll of Tarawa was selected as a main base as it afforded the best site for an airfield, and construction battalions began building the island's defenses in September.

Lying some 2,500 miles southwest of Hawaii, Tarawa was the most southerly point in Japan's outer defense ring and it held a pivotal position on the lifeline from Hawaii and the United States to the South Pacific, Australia, and New Zealand. It was vital that this lifeline be maintained and most Allied operations in 1942 and early 1943 were conducted to that end. The invasion of Guadalcanal in 1942 and the operations in Papua New Guinea steadily rolled back the Japanese forward positions that threatened Australia.

Vice-Admiral Raymond A. Spruance and his planning team were reluctant to take too great a risk in what was to be the Marines' pioneering amphibious assault against the enemy. The decision was made to assault an island that could be readily taken with whatever resources were available at the time; a flawed decision as events were subsequently to prove.

The Gilberts had until recently been British territory and the Americans had access to a wide range of up-to-date information about the islands from British and Commonwealth expatriates. At a conference held in Hawaii in September 1943, Operation *Galvanic* was formulated and the first of the "island hopping" operations was approved.

OPPOSING COMMANDERS

THE US COMMANDERS

As a branch of the Navy, the operations of the United States Marine Corps in the Pacific came under the direct control of Admiral Chester W. Nimitz, Commander-in-Chief Pacific Fleet (CINCPAC) and Pacific Ocean Area (CINCPOA).

OPPOSITE
US Marines are seen firing from behind a sand bag entrenchment which they threw up as protection on the flat island of Tarawa where the highest point of land was only 12ft. (Bettmann/Corbis)

Betio Island from the west. Taken after the battle, this photograph shows the size of the island with its dominant airfield, and Green Beach in the foreground. It is difficult to comprehend that over 5,600 people died here in the space of 76 hours. (USAF)

Spruance continued to act for Vice-Admiral "Bull" Halsey who was then still in hospital; for the rest of the war he would act as the CINCPAC's chief strategist and right-hand man, planning almost every amphibious landing up to Okinawa.

The Marines earmarked for the operation, the V Marine Amphibious Corps (VMAC), were under the overall command of Major-General Holland M. Smith. His benign, grandfatherly appearance belied an explosive temper that prompted his Marines to adopt his initials "H. M." to "Howlin' Mad," a title that stuck for his entire career. Smith was a champion of amphibious warfare, and had helped pioneer the techniques years earlier in the Caribbean.

The outbreak of war found him in charge of Army and Marine amphibious training on America's West Coast, and he immediately became the prime choice for *Galvanic*.

The assault on Betio was allocated to the 2nd Marine Division under its commander, Major-General Julian C. Smith. He was an unassuming and experienced officer, with 34 years' service behind him including a spell fighting the "banana wars" – clandestine battles fought in the jungles of Haiti and Nicaragua in the 1920s and 1930s against revolutionaries.

Getting the Marines to the Gilberts, and putting them ashore was the job of the Commander of Task Force 54, Rear-Admiral Richmond Kelly Turner, a master of amphibious warfare who had previously organized the landings on Guadalcanal.

At a lower command level there were several officers whose contribution has been recognized as very significant to the success of *Galvanic*. Colonel David M. Shoup was 38 at the time of the battle, and had only limited combat experience. He was the divisional operations officer responsible for planning the attack down to the last detail. Although wounded coming ashore, after Shoup landed on D-Day he immediately set up a command post and directed operations throughout the most critical period of the battle, until relieved on November 21. His leadership and devotion to duty won him the Medal of Honor. Another key role was played by Major Michael Ryan, commanding officer of Company L of the 2nd Marines. When his battalion commander, Major Schoettel, failed to land on Red Beach 1, Ryan gathered together a mixture of scattered infantrymen, tank crews, amtrac drivers, engineers, and corpsmen to secure Green Beach, earning Ryan a much-deserved Navy Cross.

TOP

Colonel David M. Shoup. As divisional operations officer he planned the assault on Betio Island and was unexpectedly given the job of implementing his own plans. Shoup was awarded the Medal of Honor for his role in the battle, and in 1959 was appointed Commandant of the US Marine Corps. (USMC)

BOTTOM

Models of Betio Island, codenamed Helen, are displayed before the landings. (NARA)

ABOVE LEFT
US Marines seen sheltering behind an LVT on Tarawa beach. (Tom Laemlein)

ABOVE RIGHT
The Sherman tank played a pivotal role in the capture of Betio Island and provided invaluable assistance to the infantry in mopping up pockets of resistance. (NARA)

OPPOSITE
Japanese tanks were inferior to the American Shermans in all respects and as a result many were used as static artillery pieces. (Tom Laemlein)

THE JAPANESE COMMANDERS

The Gilbert Islands came jointly under the control of the Commander-in-Chief, South East Asia, Vice-Admiral Kusaka, and the Commander-in-Chief 2nd Fleet, Vice-Admiral Kondo. Their sole contribution was to make the decision to reinforce the Gilberts, and to bolster the air detachments in the Solomons. Once Operation *Galvanic* was under way Tarawa was virtually abandoned.

As commander of the 111th Construction Unit, the placement of the defenses of Betio and the construction of the airfield fell to Lieutenant Murakami. More an engineer than a fighting man, he performed a brilliant job and turned the island into what was, yard for yard, probably the best defended outpost in the Pacific.

Murakami's aim was to prevent the enemy from reaching the beaches. He knew that if the Americans could establish a landing force in substantial numbers at any point on the island it would only be a matter of time before the defenders would be overwhelmed. His obstacles included pyramid-shaped reinforced concrete tetrahedrons which were placed around half of the island on the coral reef, anti-boat barriers made of palm tree logs, and barbed wire.

Ashore were anti-tank ditches, dug a short distance back from the perimeter barricades, and extensive minefields. He turned Betio into what his compatriots called "a hornet's nest for the Yankees."

In September 1943, Rear-Admiral Keiji Shibasaki took over command of the island and its defenders. He boasted that, "The Americans could not take Tarawa with a million men in a hundred years." Himself a veteran of amphibious landings along the coast of China, he fully appreciated the difficulties facing the invader and planned accordingly.

OPPOSING FORCES

THE US FORCES

The Marines' only practical experience of amphibious landings to date had been at New Britain, New Guinea, and Guadalcanal where the landings had been opposed only lightly, if at all. At Tarawa the plan was for the Marines to assault an island that was known to be heavily defended. The outcome would decide the whole future of the Navy's proposed "island-hopping" strategy for the remainder of the Pacific War.

"The Americans could not take Tarawa with a million men in a hundred years."

— **REAR-ADMIRAL SHIBASAKI**, SEPTEMBER 1943

The 2nd Division, USMC

At the time of *Galvanic* the 2nd Division numbered around 20,000 men, composed of three infantry regiments, the 2nd, 6th, and 8th (the USMC traditionally refer to their regiments simply as "Marines"). An average regiment would comprise about 3,500 officers and men, and would have three rifle battalions consisting of three rifle companies, one weapons company, and one HQ company.

There were additional organic units within the division. A tank battalion of three companies of three tank platoons was using the Sherman M4-A2 medium tank. These were ideal for use against the Japanese in the Pacific where they completely outclassed the Japanese "Ha-Go" tanks. There was also a medical battalion and the amphibian tractor battalion who were the first to use the improved LVT-2 tractor universally known as the amtrac. The Marines at Tarawa, unlike those who fought at Guadalcanal, had modern infantry weapons including Garand M-1 semi-automatic rifles, Browning automatic rifles, and portable flame-throwers.

The US Navy

From the time of their embarkation in Wellington, New Zealand, on November 1, until they left the line of departure for the invasion beaches, the Marines of Holland Smith's V Amphibious Corps (VMAC) were the responsibility of the US Navy. The invasion force – Task Force 54 (TF-54) – was subdivided into two groups: the Northern Attack Force (TF-52) under Rear-Admiral Richmond Kelly Turner, which was to secure the island of Makin to the north; and the Southern Attack Force (TF-53) under Rear-Admiral Harry Hill, which would take Tarawa Atoll.

The fire support group, under Rear-Admiral H. F. Kingman, comprised the battleships *Tennessee*, *Maryland*, and *Colorado*; the heavy cruisers *Portland* and *Indianapolis*; the light cruisers *Mobile*, *Birmingham*, and *Santa Fe*; and the destroyers *Bailey*, *Frazer*, *Gansevoort*, *Meade*, *Anderson*, *Russell*, *Ringgold*, *Dashiell*, and *Schroeder*. The three battleships of the group were semi-obsolete ships that had been salvaged from the mud of Pearl Harbor after the 1941 attack. However, they still packed a hefty punch with their 14in and 16in guns, and were ideally suited to provide offshore bombardments.

For air cover, aerial bombing, and strafing during the operation, three aircraft carriers, the *Essex*, *Bunker Hill*, and *Independence*, of Rear-Admiral Montgomery's TF-50-3 would accompany the Southern Attack Force.

THE JAPANESE FORCES

The battle for Tarawa would see the first confrontation between the US Marines and Japan's Special Navy Landing Force (SNLF) – sometimes referred to as the "Imperial Marines." The SNLF could trace its origins to the earliest days of the Imperial Japanese Navy (IJN) when they were developed as small infantry units attached to naval ships. Over the years, however, they evolved into much larger combat units of highly trained and specialized amphibious infantry. In 1941 they had spearheaded the invasions of Guam, Wake Island, and the Solomons.

On Betio Island, Rear-Admiral Shibasaki commanded the 3rd Special Base Defense Force (formerly the 6th Yokosuka SNLF), the Sasebo 7th SNLF, the 111th Construction Unit, and a detachment of the 4th Fleet Construction Department; in all around 5,000 men. Because of the small area of the island, a considerable amount of which was taken up by the airfield and its facilities, Shibasaki concentrated his efforts on defeating the

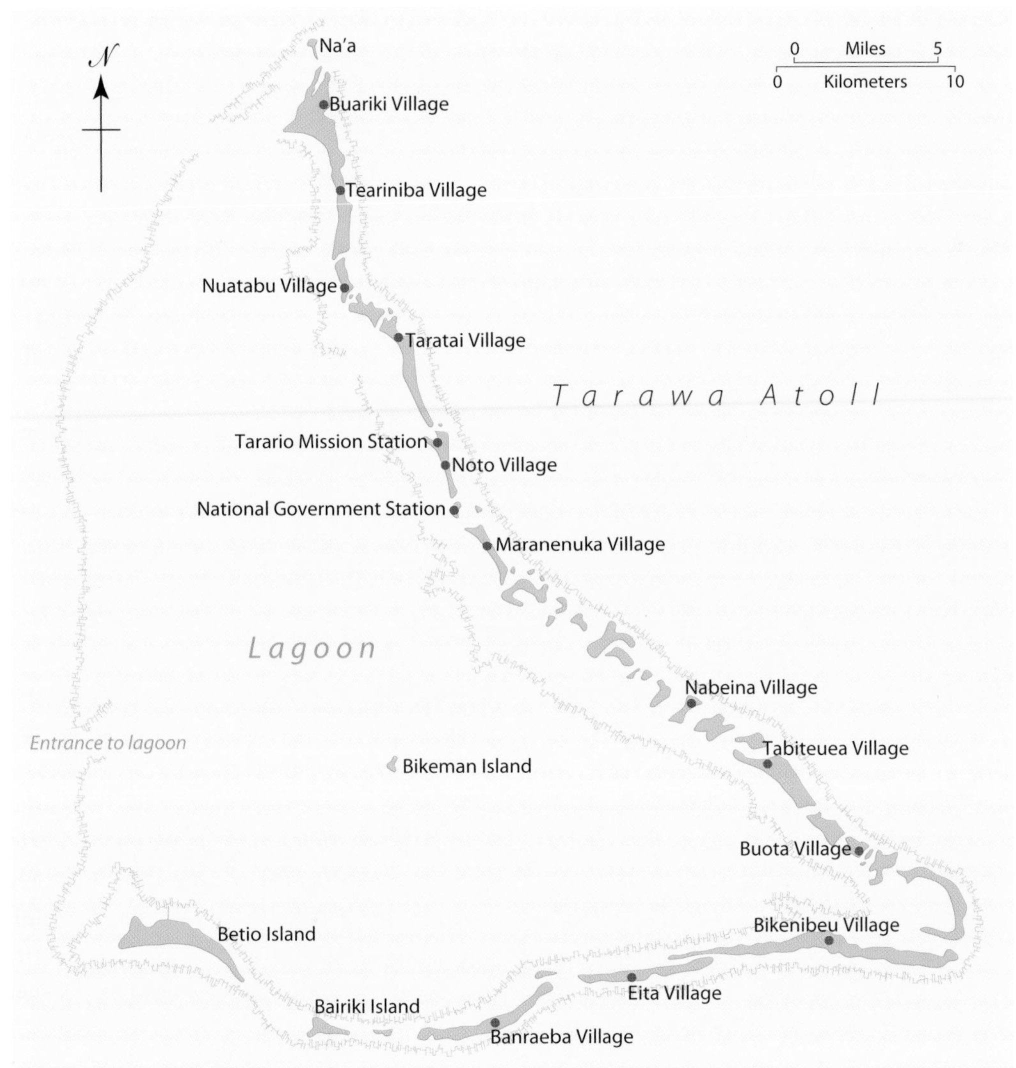

Map showing Tarawa Atoll, the scene of the Marines' "island hopping", which started at Betio on November 20.

invader at the water's edge. Consequently the beach defenses were formidable. Pride of place went to four 8in naval guns.

OPPOSING PLANS

THE US PLAN

A major factor of the Tarawa battle was speed: Nimitz ordered Spruance to "get the hell in there, and get the hell out." The fear of a major Japanese naval retaliation was paramount in the thinking behind this, the first of the Marines' "island-hopping" campaigns. However, a series of US offensives in the Solomon Islands in early 1943 had caused the Japanese to divert ships and aircraft from as far away as the Marshalls, the Marianas, and the Celebes, to counter a very real threat against their stronghold of Rabaul. The IJN took a serious view of the threat, and transferred a large number of ships from Truk to bolster the

Rabaul defenses. As a result the naval forces in the Marshalls were so weakened that they were incapable of repelling any major landings in the area.

The Gilbert Islands had been under British jurisdiction since 1915, and consequently the Marine planners were able to draw upon the experience of a number of British, Australian, and New Zealand expatriates nicknamed the "foreign legion." The all-important subject of tides worried Shoup and his staff. Betio Island was surrounded by a reef which extended for some 800–1,200 yards out to sea. The first three waves of 1,500 men were due to land in amtracs (LVTs), therefore the depth of water around the island was, theoretically, irrelevant. However, the remainder would come ashore in Higgins boats – Landing Craft Vehicle Personnel (LCVPs) – shallow-draught, 36ft long boats with wide ramps, which drew only 3–4ft of water when loaded.

Opinions among the "foreign legion" were varied; some thought that there would be enough water to allow the Higgins boats to clear the reef, but Major Frank Holland, who had lived in the Gilberts for 15 years, and had studied the tides, was appalled. He knew that there would be a "dodging" tide at that time, giving no more than 3ft of water over the reefs. If his predictions were correct the second wave of Higgins boats would be grounded before reaching the beaches.

Julian Smith had intended to land with two regiments abreast and with one in reserve, but Holland Smith announced that the 6th Marines would be held as corps reserves. This, coupled with a decision by Nimitz to limit the pre-invasion bombardment of Betio to around three hours on the morning of D-Day (to achieve "strategic surprise"), meant that the Marines would be mounting a frontal attack with only a 2–1 superiority; well below the desired minimum.

Colonel Shoup and the 2nd Division planners had decided to attack from the lagoon side, which was minimally less well defended, and offered calmer waters for the amphibious assault craft. The assault plan was relatively straightforward. The transports would assemble to the west of the atoll and disembark the Marines. The landing craft would make their way to the boat rendezvous area, just outside of the gap in the western reef, from where they would move in

BELOW LEFT
"Alligator assault," Tarawa, 1943. Tarawa marked the first tactical employment of tracked landing vehicles as assault craft. The Alligators negotiated the barrier reef and delivered 1,500 Marine riflemen to the beach, but were too few and too shot-up to shuttle the remainder of the assault force from the reef. (USMC)

BELOW RIGHT
Blackened by fire and pock-marked by machine-gun fire, the Sherman medium tank "Colorado" sizzles in the lagoon. "Colorado" recovered from being set ablaze from a Japanese shell and rendered invaluable support to the infantry. Tarawa marked the Sherman's combat debut in the Pacific, although few survived the battle. (USMC)

predetermined waves to the line of departure some 7,000 yards inside the lagoon. From there the Marines were released from Navy control and the assault waves, headed by the amtracs, would make the final dash of around 6,000 yards to the beaches.

The three landing beaches were designated from west to east as Red 1, 2, and 3. The 3rd Battalion, 2nd Marines, under Major John Schoettel, were to land on Red 1: a deep cove, its eastern half was protected by a log barricade and covered from both sides by heavy machine guns and artillery. Red 2 stretched for about 500 yards from the eastern end of the cove to a quarter-mile long pier, and was assigned to the 2nd Battalion, 2nd Marines, under Lieutenant-Colonel Herbert Amey. There was a 3–4ft-high log wall along the entire length of this beach, and from the pier to a point level with the end of the airfield runway. Red 3 stretched for 800 yards intersected by the short Burns-Philp pier; here the 2nd Battalion, 8th Marines, under Major Henry Crowe, would land.

The western end of Betio had been designated as Green Beach and the southern shore as Black 1 and 2 but no landings were planned here on D-Day.

THE JAPANESE PLANS

Shibasaki's prime objective was to prevent the invader reaching the beaches. He knew his first defense was a natural one: the shelf-like reef surrounding the whole island, which was to prove almost catastrophic to the Marines. At the water's edge a log barricade surrounded most of the island, and behind it, at strategic points, were coastal guns ranging in caliber from 3.1in to 8in, dual-purpose anti-aircraft guns and more than 30 other pieces ranging from 3in pack howitzers to 0.5in machine guns. In the center of the island the airfield, with its 4,000ft runway, was dominant. Anti-tank ditches were dug at both ends of the airfield and near to the 8in Vickers guns. Offshore concrete, log, and barbed wire barricades were so placed that, by avoiding them, the landing craft would enter "killing channels" covered by the main gun batteries. Shibasaki and his engineers had concentrated the defenses on the southern shore of the island from where they expected the Marines to land due to the natural geography of the island atoll.

THE BATTLE OF TARAWA

D-DAY

In the pre-dawn darkness of November 20 the invasion fleet lay off the coast of Betio. The planners had called for a raid on the island by B-24 Liberator bombers of the 7th Air Force. But the raid never materialized; this was the first of a number of "foul-ups" that were to rob the Marines of an opportunity to cut back on the enemy's firepower on the beaches.

By 0300hrs the transports were in position and the long and laborious task of disembarking the troops and filling the landing craft began. The amtracs and LCVPs went into the water, came alongside the troop transports, and the precarious business of loading the Marines got under way. Although they had practiced many times before leaving New Zealand, the maneuver was fraught with danger. Climbing down netting on the side of a tall troopship, laden with anything up to 100lb of equipment, in almost total darkness in a choppy sea was not the ideal way of leaving ship.

At around 0500hrs a Kingfisher spotter-plane was launched from Hill's flagship, the

NEXT SPREAD
The Japanese caused devastating damage to the amtracs approaching Red Beach 1. Here abandoned LVTs and floating bodies at the log barricade bear witness to the effectiveness of the defenses. (NARA)

Maryland. Its job was to observe the imminent naval bombardment and radio back corrections to range and direction. Seeing the flash from the ship's catapult, the Japanese manning the 8in gun at Temakin Point opened fire on the *Maryland*. The battleships and cruisers swung around, and fired in retaliation. Marines in their landing craft watched in awe as the massive shells howled over their heads and the sky was lit up with monstrous flashes.

The seawall, almost the only cover on the beachhead from the accurate Japanese gunfire, gave the Marines time for a brief respite before they went "over the top" to attack the airfield. (NARA)

Aboard the old battleship *Maryland*, the terrific concussion from the broadsides from the 16in guns caused lights to go out and radios to malfunction. From that moment, until the end of the battle, communications between Hill and the rest of his command would be a serious problem. At 0530hrs it became evident that the troopships were out of position – a strong southerly current had carried them within range of the enemy shore batteries. The shelling was abruptly terminated as the ships scurried to their new positions, followed by flotillas of landing craft.

Shibasaki was now fully aware that the Americans intended to attack from the north. He was also aware of the problems still facing the enemy: the natural protection of the coral reef and the low tide that morning. When to his relief the massive bombardment suddenly stopped, he immediately began moving men and equipment from the southern shore to the north.

Shortly after 0600hrs, the minesweepers *Pursuit* and *Requisite* began sweeping the entrance to the lagoon, and immediately came under fire from shore batteries. Once the passage was clear the destroyers *Ringgold* and *Dashiell* entered the lagoon and engaged the enemy with their 6in guns. The *Pursuit* meanwhile took up position at the line of departure and shone her searchlight to guide the landing craft.

It was at 0735hrs that the main bombardment by the support group got under way. In a spectacular display of pyrotechnics the battleships and cruisers raked the island. Many Marines could have been forgiven for thinking that the Betio defenses had been obliterated but the post-action review was to show that the Navy had achieved few of its aims. The ground had been well and truly churned over, but the bulk of the Japanese defenders and their weapons were still in place, awaiting the first wave of Marines.

For the landing craft the haul to the beaches seemed unending. First they had to assemble between the transports and the entrance to the lagoon; from there it was a three and a half-mile trip to the line of departure and a further three miles to the beaches. By the time they landed some of the troops would have been pitching about on the sea for nearly six hours.

At 0900hrs Hill ordered the end of the bombardment. He was worried that the smoke and dust rising from the island would affect the accuracy of his gunfire, and that the LVTs now approaching the beaches would be hit. The result was that the Japanese had a vital ten minutes in which to reorganize and bring their guns to bear on the rows of lumbering craft now approaching the end of the pier.

Braving anti-aircraft fire, Lieutenant-Commander MacPherson dived in low ahead of the flotilla and took a look at the reef. What he saw filled him with horror: instead of the 4–5 feet of water expected, the sea was so low that in places large areas of coral were drying in the sun. Major Holland's predictions, largely ignored by the planners, would haunt many people before the end of D-Day.

RED BEACH 1 – MORNING

As the amtracs of the 3rd Battalion, 2nd Marines entered the cove that formed Red Beach 1 they came under murderous fire from in front and from both sides. The fire from the east shore was particularly fierce. Here the enemy had in place 3in and 1.4in guns, together with numerous single and twin machine-gun emplacements. This area was destined to be the last part of Betio to be subdued by the Marines. In the face of such heavy fire many amtracs veered away to the west, coming ashore at the junction of Red Beach 1 and Green Beach, where they encountered a 5ft high seawall, and few Marines could get onto the land.

Private First Class Bob Libby from the 3.16in mortar platoon of the 3rd Battalion should have been in the third wave of Higgins boats heading for Red 1. The account of his arrival on the beach is an explicit illustration of the horror of Tarawa:

About 500 yards out our Higgins boat rammed into the reef, and everyone was ordered over the side. I landed in water well over my head, having missed the reef due to the boat being held up against it. Kicking myself from the bottom, I rose to the surface and found a footing on the reef itself. A quick look round revealed nightmarish activity; I noticed our boat drifting ashore and struck to my right, my intention being to keep the boat between me and the heavy fire coming from shore as long as I could. It was possible to keep a watch for machine gun fire skipping off the surface, a move to one side or the other allowed passage for this while still moving slowly toward the beach. Everywhere and anywhere I looked there were knocked-out amphibious tractors burning fiercely, landing craft being blown apart. The walking wounded were moving in the opposite direction making their way to drifting boats. The water around me was red or pink with a churning mass of spouting geysers; bodies were floating on the surface everywhere I looked; here a man moving along was no longer seen. The sound of screaming shells passed overhead, the unmistakable crack of rifle fire zipped around my ears, the screams of the wounded were almost lost in this cacophony of sound. If anyone can think up a picture of Hell, I don' t think that it would match up to that wade-in from the reef to the shore at Tarawa, with floating bodies and bits of bodies, the exploding shells, and burned-out craft; there was no hiding place, no protection: my only armor was the shirt on my back. It took about half an hour from leaving my boat to put foot on dry land.

RED BEACH 2 – MORNING

In the waters off Red Beach 2 a disaster was brewing. The last of the Marine regiments to land, Lieutenant-Colonel Amey's 2nd Battalion, 2nd Marines, were faced with rows of dug-in enemy emplacements. The objective was to land

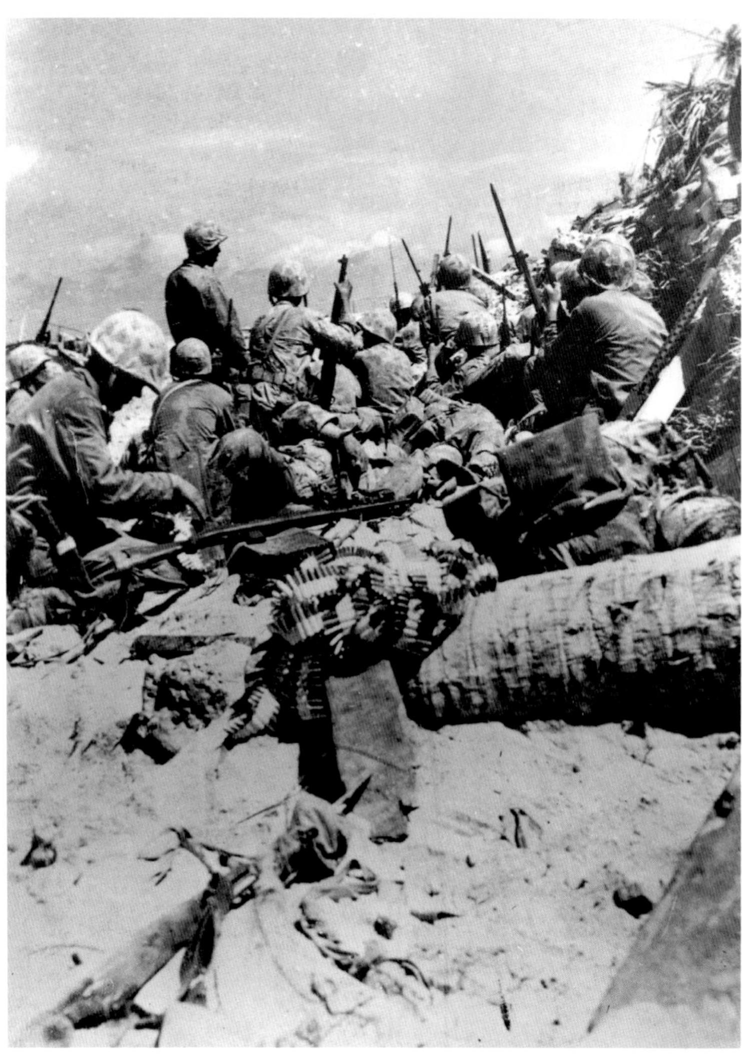

Marines huddle under cover of a sand bank, probably on Red Beach 2. The man on the left checks his .30in machine gun ammunition belts which were vulnerable to sand and grit. Losses during the landings left the assault battalions short of support weapons. (NARA)

Company F on the left and Company E on the right, and for Company G to be in support; but as the first waves of amtracs came within range of the Japanese positions a hail of anti-boat artillery and small-arms fire shredded the water. The coxswains, desperate to escape the blistering barrage, put their vehicles ashore wherever they could find space. As the survivors ground ashore the troops leaped over the sides and headed for the only cover that was available: a log barricade that ran the full length of the beach.

Amey was only 200 yards from the beach when his amtrac became entangled in the barbed-wire barricade and would not budge. The colonel and his HQ went over the side and crouched alongside the craft to escape the hail of bullets lashing the water all around them. After a while there was a lull in the fire, and the group headed to the shore on hands and knees to present a smaller target. When the water became too shallow the colonel stood up and shouted: "Come on – these bastards can't stop us!" and splashed toward the shore: he was hit in the chest and throat by a burst of machine-gun fire and died instantly. With Amey was Lieutenant-Colonel Walter Jordan from the 4th Division, who had come along as an observer. As he was the senior officer present he found himself acting commander of 2nd Battalion, 2nd Marines.

On the left-hand side of the beach Company F lost almost half of its strength as the troops attempted to get to the beach and over the log barrier at the water's edge. Those who made it formed themselves into small units a few yards inland, armed only with light machine guns and other small arms. Most radios were saturated with seawater and were unusable, and runners soon fell prey to enemy snipers.

Company E had landed at the junction of Red Beaches 1 and 2 after their amtrac had veered away in the face of heavy mortar and rifle fire. Despite a storm directed at them they succeeded in silencing one Japanese strongpoint, but as the platoon leader fell dead they took cover in a large shell hole. Company G landed somewhere between the other two, taking heavy losses before they reached the barrier. The beach was already crowded with casualties as men attempted to locate the source of the enemy fire.

RED BEACH 3 – MORNING

The destroyers *Ringgold* and *Dashiell*, already stationed in the lagoon off Red Beach 3, were an enormous asset to the men of the 2nd Battalion, 8th Marines. Maintaining a constant barrage along the shore they kept the defenders buttoned up long enough for "Jim" Crowe's team to come ashore with minimal losses, and only 25 casualties in the first wave of LVTs. Crowe, the only one of the three battalion commanders to get ashore on D-Day, had to wade in when his Higgins boat ground to a halt on the reef. Even so he arrived only four minutes behind the last wave of amtracs.

The only part of the beachhead where significant gains could be made appeared to be to the east. Here Crowe's executive officer was able to push beyond the short pier, but was soon forced back. Crowe responded by sending Company G across their flank, reinforcing it against the counterattack that he was sure would come at any moment. Like most other regimental commanders that day, he found his radio to be inoperable and sent runners toward the pier in an attempt to make contact with the Marines on Red Beach 2 at his right.

OTHER OPERATIONS

While the three assault regiments were attempting to consolidate their beachheads, Colonel Shoup was desperate to get ashore. From the mixed reports that he had received it was obvious that things were not going to plan.

His initial attempts to land had come under heavy fire, but he and his HQ finally got ashore around 1030hrs. Sprinting across the beach he received shrapnel wounds in his leg when a mortar shell exploded nearby, but he waived medical help and set up his headquarters at a bunker just inland on Red 2. Shoup's attempts to assess the situation were frustrated by the failure of the man-pack radios, and few dispatched runners returned. Gradually however, information did begin to filter through. Shoup became aware that some troops had managed to get ashore on Red 1, and that the battalion commander, Major Shoettel, was still out in the lagoon. But he did not know that Major Ryan had landed and was rallying the stragglers at the western end of the beach. Lieutenant-Colonel Jordan had succeeded in making contact, and was told to retain command of 2nd Battalion, 2nd Marines, most of whom were huddled behind the seawall. On Red 3 he learned that some forward positions were near to the airfield taxiway, and that further east a few Marines were nearly 200 yards inland.

Shoup then gave the 1st Battalion, 2nd Marines, under Major Wood Kyle, instructions to land on Red 2 and to attempt to work westward to Red 1. However, there was another delay as Kyle searched desperately for enough amtracs to house his Marines. When the battalion finally started for Red 2 they met such a heavy and accurate barrage that many

Admiral Harry Hill and staff view the attack on Tarawa Island from the bridge of USS *Maryland*. (Bettmann/Corbis)

landing craft veered away to the west, ending up at the extremity of Red 1 where they were recruited by Major Ryan.

At around 1130hrs Shoup ordered Major Ruud's 3rd Battalion, 8th Marines, to land on Red 3 in support of "Jim" Crowe. There were no amtracs available at the line of departure, and Ruud and his men were left to come ashore the hard way, by Higgins boat. The Japanese gunners had now worked out the range to perfection, and the first salvos arrived just as the boats reached the reef. As the ramps came down the Marines – most of them laden with heavy equipment – leaped into the water amid a furious barrage from the artillery at the eastern end of Betio. From the shore, Crowe's men could only watch in horror as the figures struggled forward amid exploding landing craft and spouts of artillery fire. Seeing his men facing annihilation, Major Ruud took the courageous decision to order the fourth wave back.

Julian Smith was now left with only one reserve unit, Major Lawrence Hays' 1st Battalion, 8th Marines, and they were ordered to the line of departure in readiness. At 1330hrs Julian Smith radioed Holland Smith asking V Corps of the 6th Marines to be returned to his command. Permission was granted at 1430hrs, and he now felt confident enough to ask Shoup where he wanted the 1st Battalion to land. His message never got through, so he instructed Hays to land at the extreme eastern end of Betio and work his way northwest to link up with Shoup on Red 2. Yet again the communications foul-up persisted, and this message went missing, with the result that the batallion spent the remainder of D-Day and the following night embarked in their landing craft awaiting instructions.

Admiral Spruance aboard the *Indianapolis* was short of information, and could see that the operation was faltering. His staff were of the opinion that he should step in and take control, but he declined; he had selected his team and they must be allowed to conduct the battle as they saw fit.

RED BEACH 1 – AFTERNOON

Major Ryan found himself in charge of a bewildering mixture of men on Red 1. He had the remains of three rifle companies, one machine gun platoon, plus the remnants of Major Kyle's 1st Battalion, 2nd Marines. Over the course of the morning he had also acquired various amtrac drivers, heavy weapons men, engineers, signalers, and corpsmen. On the eastern side of the cove the formidable cluster of Japanese defenses that had caused such havoc that morning were still intact, and Ryan realized that his best chances lay in attacking south along Green Beach. He got a message to Shoup at 1415hrs informing him of his situation, and proceeded to carve out a beachhead by overrunning several enemy pill-boxes. However, he had nothing but infantry weapons available to him, and he decided that his best option was to consolidate his position for the night.

RED BEACHES 2 AND 3 – AFTERNOON

By late afternoon of D-Day the Marines had a toehold on parts of Red Beaches 2 and 3. The battleships and cruisers continued to pound the eastern end of the island to prevent reinforcements from moving westward, and the fighters and dive-bombers from the carrier support group strafed and bombed anything that moved outside the Marines' perimeter. Sherman M4-A2 medium tanks had been specially prepared for the landings: 6–8ft long extensions were attached to the exhausts and air intakes, to be discarded when they got

Admiral Shibasaki's concrete bunker. It was here, on D-Day, that the Admiral and his entire HQ staff were killed by naval gunfire. This photo, taken after the battle, shows an abandoned Type 95 tank and indicates the terrific pounding that the structure suffered during the course of the battle. (USMC)

ashore, and all openings below the anticipated water line were sealed with a tarlike compound. Special reconnaissance platoons had been formed to guide the tank drivers through the reef. Many would be killed attempting to plot a safe route. Remarkably, despite the fact that the floats did not work properly and the ropes became soggy with salt water, of the eight tanks only one flooded out with the remainder making it ashore on Red Beach 2. On Red Beach 1, six Shermans were landed but due to flooding and getting bogged down in shell-holes, only one, "China Gal" eventually succeeded in joining Major Ryan's force, albeit with her main 3in gun inoperable.

THE DEFENDERS

The Japanese force put up a fiercely determined defense. Their well-coordinated and accurate fire, particularly from Red Beaches 1 and 2, had caused grievous casualties to the initial row of amtracs, and the Marines, who had been compelled to wade ashore from their LCVP Higgins boats when they ground to a halt on the reef, had been decimated. Shibasaki's four months of intensive training was paying off, although he would no doubt have regretted that he had concentrated on the southern and western defenses, anticipating that these were the most likely site for the American landings. His ambition to encircle the islands with mines, tetrahedrons, and barricades had also been thwarted by lack of time. The 3,000 mines that remained in storage were a reminder that the reefs could have been an even more formidable barrier to the invaders.

It was sometime on the afternoon of D-Day that an incident was to occur that would

US Marines charge across open ground from the beach at Tarawa to the airport, which was the principal prize for which the bloody fight was waged. One man carries a spade to dig himself in. The Americans suffered the greatest losses of their history in this battle, but they virtually wiped out the entire Japanese garrison. (NARA)

irrevocably alter the course of the battle in favor of the Americans. A sharp-eyed Marine somewhere on the island spotted a group of Japanese officers standing in the open and called in naval gunfire from the *Ringgold* and *Dashiell* who obliged with a salvo of 5in rounds fuzed as air bursts. The group turned out to be Admiral Shibasaki and his staff. In a gesture of benevolence, they had decided to give up their concrete blockhouse HQ for use as a hospital, and to move to a secondary command post a few hundred yards away. The resultant explosion killed Shibasaki and his entire staff.

The importance of Shibasaki's death cannot be overestimated; had he lived he would doubtless have launched a massive counterattack on the night of D-Day against the precariously positioned Marines. There were scarcely 3,000 ashore, clinging to isolated pockets no more than a few yards inland, with little artillery support and few tanks. The Japanese were known to excel in night-time fighting, while the Marines favored defensive positions at night. What would have happened had this attack occurred is open to speculation: at best the Marines would have been subjected to a massive assault along the length of their front, with the inevitable huge casualties; at worst it could have been a monumental disaster.

D-DAY+1

The American foothold on Betio was tenuous. On the right of Red Beach 1, Major Ryan and his assorted band held a strip of the island about 250 yards wide and 300 yards long, with the sea on both sides. They were short of supplies and had no means of evacuation. On the combined Red 2 and 3 beachheads the troops were in sporadic contact with each other but there was a 600-yard gap between them and Ryan. Their line ended 300 yards from the main pier, and to the east, near the Burns-Philp wharf, a few Marines had forced their way inland to within yards of the main runway of the airfield.

The Americans were unaware of the death of Shibasaki: for decades it was assumed that he died sometime near the end of the battle. The absence of the anticipated attack was a puzzle to the staff of V Corps but deprived of their leader and senior staff the Japanese defenders lacked direction. There was some sporadic fire from the Japanese lines during the early hours, and aircraft from the Marshall Islands made an unsuccessful attempt to bomb shipping to the west of the island, but on the whole the night was fairly uneventful. With daylight came the heat and an awful smell. The scores of bodies littering the beaches and shoreline were starting to decompose where they lay; the area was still far too dangerous for the burial parties to move in, and the stench would become one of the battle's enduring memories for the Marines as the death toll reached the thousands over the next two days.

Colonel Rixey had brought some of his artillery ashore the previous night and now it was brought into action. Siting two of his howitzers at the eastern end of Red 2 he began pounding the strongpoints at the end of the cove, enabling Major Hays' 1st Battalion, who had already endured 24 hours in their Higgins boats without food, drink, or toilet facilities, to get ashore with slightly fewer casualties although the enemy firepower had already exacted a heavy toll prior to disembarking. At 0800hrs Hays reported to Shoup with what remained of his battalion; casualties were around 50 percent, and a great deal of equipment had been lost in the water.

As the day wore on and the tide rose, a flow of heavier equipment such as anti-tank guns, jeeps, bulldozers, and half-tracks would get ashore, but for the moment Shoup would have to make do with what he had. The principal objective for D+1 was to reach the far side of Betio, cutting the Japanese garrison in two, and to link up with Major Ryan. His surviving Marines were sent to bolster the troops on the right flank of Red 2, but even with the help of a tank to beef-up the attack, little headway was made and a grim stalemate set in.

The Japanese had used the first night to consolidate their inland defenses. The Marines who had succeeded in crossing the western taxiway of the airfield on D-Day were now trapped in a "triangle" formed by the taxiways and the main runway. The Japanese had set machine guns to cover this area; anyone attempting to cross them faced almost certain death. The Marines in the "triangle" – mainly companies A and B of Wood Kyle's 1st Battalion, 2nd Marines – were virtually cut off from Red Beach 2. Shoup was determined to get his men across Betio, and after a concerted bombardment by carrier planes, these Marines raced across the 125-yard strip between the "triangle" and the sea, occupied a 200-yard long trench, and dug in. Later in the afternoon, Shoup sent Colonel Jordan and his 2nd Battalion, 2nd Marines, command over to the south side where Jordan assumed command. It had been hoped that this combined group would have been able to strike past and link up with Crowe, who was pressing inland from Red 3, but Jordan radioed back that he had fewer than 200 men, including 30 wounded, and that ammunition, grenades, food, and water were in very short supply. Given the circumstances, Shoup told him to consolidate his position and he would endeavor to send supplies across by amtrac.

Meanwhile, over on Green Beach, the most significant gains of D+1 were being made by Major Ryan and his assortment of Marines. Bolstered by the arrival of "China Gal" and "Cecilia," another Sherman that had bogged down on D-Day but had now been recovered, Ryan was preparing to advance along the length of Green Beach to Temakin Point, the southwest extremity of Betio, under the cover of a naval bombardment.

Green Beach after the landing of Major Jones' 1st Battalion, 6th Marines, on D+1. The collection of rubber boats lie abandoned on the shore, and a few amtracs are at the water's edge. Nearby troops assemble on the beaches. (US Navy)

Even after D-Day, bodies remained unburied on the beaches and around pillboxes and log emplacements all over the island. It was scenes such as this, authorized for publication by President Roosevelt, that brought the horror of total war home to the American public. (NARA)

When the barrage lifted, the Marines swept forward with "Cecilia" clearing the way for the infantry, and by 1100hrs the advance party were standing alongside the 8in Vickers guns at Temakin Point. In one short and brilliantly coordinated attack Ryan had cleared Green Beach, leaving it open for the 6th Marines to make their much delayed landing. It is little wonder that Julian Smith would declare it "the most cheering news of D+1."

At 1600hrs on D+1 Ryan and his group held Green Beach to a depth of 100–150 yards; on Red 2 the elements of 1st Battalion, 8th Marines, held the beach as far as the Japanese strongpoint at the edge of the cove; and 3rd Battalion, 8th Marines, were deployed near the Burns-Philp wharf on Red 3. Inland, 2nd Battalion, 8th Marines, had pushed forward to the edge of the airfield's main runway, and on the south coast parts of 1st and 2nd Battalions, 2nd Marines, had a 200-yard enclave, with the enemy to their east and west. The way was now open for unopposed landings on Green Beach by 1st Battalion, 6th Marines, including some tanks. The end of D+1 saw the Marines in a much more favorable position. The failure of the enemy to counterattack on day one had given the Americans the advantage, and from there onward the issue was not in doubt. Supplies were streaming in and at 2030hrs Colonel Merritt Edson, the divisional chief-of-staff, arrived to take over command from the almost exhausted Shoup. Although Edson was officially to take over on Betio, Colonel Shoup remained ashore until the end of the battle.

From somewhere on the island a last message was flashed to Tokyo: "Our weapons have been destroyed. From now on everyone is attempting a final charge; may Japan exist for ten thousand years."

D-DAY+2

For the third day of the battle Edson and Shoup decided on a three-front attack. Jones' 1st Battalion, 6th Marines, were to pass through Ryan's men and attack eastward, between the southern limit of the airfield and the sea, to link up with elements of 1st and 2nd Battalions, 2nd Marines, on the southern shore. At the same time Major Hays' 1st Battalion, 8th Marines, were to strike west from their positions on Red 2 in an effort to reduce the stubborn pocket of gun emplacements at the junction of Red 1 and 2. The third phase was to be an eastward thrust against the enemy inland from the Burn-Philp wharf by Colonel Elmer Hall's 2nd and 3rd Battalions, 8th Marines. It was a bold plan, especially considering that only Jones' men were fresh; the others had been fighting ceaselessly for two days and nights with limited supplies of water, and little food. Meanwhile, Lieutenant-Colonel Kenneth McLeod and the Marines of the 3rd Battalion, 6th Marines, who had been kept in readiness at the point of departure since 1600hrs the previous day by a series of contradictory instructions, finally came ashore on Green Beach at 0800hrs, much to their relief.

Just after 0800hrs, Jones and his troops came up against surprisingly light resistance and covered 1,000 yards in less than three hours. Jones pressed on eastward, and cleared a cluster of pillboxes and bunkers. Despite the assistance of Stuart light tanks and half-tracks, by the end of the day the "Pocket," as it became known, had not been cleared as Edson and Shoup had hoped. In fact this would remain the last position on Betio to fall to the Americans. Major Crowe's composite unit from the 2nd and 3rd Battalions, 8th Marines, was to advance eastward, pushing beyond the Burn-Philp wharf and toward the eastern end of the main runway. They had to deal with a steel pillbox and a machine gun emplacement.

Crowe's men then surged forward to the end of the runway, where they joined the left flank of Jones' column. Apart from the Pocket, and a few isolated groups of enemy troops, the Marines (to all intents and purposes) held the western two-thirds of Betio. General Julian Smith had come ashore during the morning on Green Beach, and after a brief inspection transferred to the command post of Red 2 to join Edson and Shoup.

At around 1930hrs that night a small raiding party probed the defenses of the 1st Battalion, 6th Marines. At 0300hrs a second, and much larger, assault was mounted. Screaming "Marines you die!" and "Japanese drink Marine blood!" several hundred charged across the battalion front. This was the famous "banzai" charge that was soon to become familiar to Marines throughout the Pacific theater. Although it was successfully repelled, dawn revealed the extent of the carnage. Japanese dead numbered 325 for 173 Marine casualties including 45 dead. The enemy's great banzai had failed – for the Japanese left on Betio there was little hope.

D-DAY+3

As November 23 dawned the final major actions of the battle took place. Destroyers and carrier planes had battered the area from 0700hrs to 0730hrs, prior to the Marines moving out.

"The Marines fought almost solely on esprit decorps, I was certain. It was inconceivable to most Marines that they should let another Marine down, or that they could be responsible for dimming the bright reputation of their Corps. The Marines simply assumed that they were the world's best fighting men."

— **ROBERT SHERROD**, 1943, REGARDING THE BATTLE OF TARAWA

Supported by Sherman and Stuart tanks, McLeod's men made good progress despite facing some suicidal resistance, accounting for some 475 of the enemy for the loss of only nine killed and 25 wounded. At 1300hrs a sweaty Marine stepped onto the sand spit at the far tip of Betio and swilled the dust from his face; the whole eastern half of the island was in American hands.

The only sizeable body of the enemy still remaining were the defenders of the Pocket; the determined gun crews holed up in their formidable emplacements at the boundary of Red Beaches 1 and 2. Fire from 75mm artillery pieces, pounding the complex from close range, and the determined assaults by the infantry with flamethrowers and demolition charges, finally wore the defenders down. A small number surrendered, more committed suicide among the smoking debris and at 1300hrs Shoup was able to notify Julian Smith that the Pocket had finally fallen.

Mopping-up operations continued for days as the Marines checked all of the burned and shattered pillboxes and bunkers and at noon on November 24, Julian Smith and Holland Smith, who had arrived from Makin, witnessed a simple flag-raising ceremony as the Stars and Stripes and the Union Jack, to signify that Tarawa was a British possession, were raised on two battered palm trees.

All that remained was to mop up the remainder of Tarawa Atoll in a series of smaller, although still taxing operations. As recalled by Private First Class Herbert Deighton, "We chased the Japs all the way up the Atoll until we were on the last but one island: Buariki." But by November 27 the battle for Tarawa was finally over.

AFTERMATH

With the battle over the 2nd and 8th Marines shipped out for Hawaii almost immediately; the relatively less-mauled 6th Marines stayed on to garrison the islands until they were turned over to the US Navy on December 4. At CINCPAC headquarters on Hawaii the "inquest" got under way at once – the next amphibious assault was planned for the Marshall Islands in early February 1944 and the lessons learned at Tarawa had to be discussed and implemented straight away. These included the condemnation of the use of warships as communications centers, the ineffectiveness of the naval barrage at the start of the operation, and the lack of effective waterproof covering for the man-pack radio.

Four Medals of Honor were awarded for the action on Betio, three of them posthumously. Other outstanding achievements were recognized, notably the capture of Green Beach on D+1 by Major Ryan and his gathering of the survivors of the landings on Red Beach 1. In retrospect, the capture of Green Beach was the factor that turned the tide of the battle irrevocably in the Marines' favor, and gained Ryan a much deserved Navy Cross.

Despite the many errors and omissions, the battle was won in 76 hours of some of the most savage fighting of the Pacific War and it uplifted the spirit of the America people after years of depression. One newspaper heading read: "Last week some 2,000–3,000 United States Marines, many of them now dead or wounded, gave the nation a name to stand beside those of Concord Bridge, the *Bon Homme Richard*, the Alamo and Belleau Wood – that name is Tarawa."

MARSHALL ISLANDS

ORIGINS OF THE CAMPAIGN

The seizure of the Marshall Islands in the Central Pacific, controlled by Japan since 1914, had long been recognized as a necessity in a war with Japan. As far back as 1921, Marine Major E. H. "Pete" Ellis had formatted a hypothetical plan to seize four of the Marshalls' atolls to serve as staging bases for further naval operations against Japan. The US 5th Fleet had already seized the Gilberts after the bloody November 1943 battles for Tarawa. Meanwhile, US and Australian forces were advancing in New Guinea. A major issue was to decide which atolls in the Marshalls would be seized as the Japanese had bases on six atolls plus Kusaie and Wake Islands. Admiral Nimitz proposed Kwajalein (the main base near the Marshalls' geographic center), Maloelap, and Wotje (the latter two being closer to Pearl Harbor). These three atolls held 65 percent of the air bases in the Marshalls and the other bases could be neutralized without necessarily being physically occupied. On December 7, Kwajalein became the primary objective and D-Day was set for January 17 although this was later pushed back to January 31 with Majuro Atoll to the east as a secondary objective. The other bases were to be neutralized by air and naval bombardment throughout the campaign and the bypassed islands would continue to be neutralized from the new American bases established on the captured atolls.

OPPOSING PLANS

THE US PLAN – OPERATIONS *FLINTLOCK* AND *CATCHPOLE*

While the Marshalls campaign consisted of a series of relatively small-scale and short duration battles far easier than the hard-fought later campaigns such as Iwo Jima or Okinawa, it was nonetheless complex with battles fought on seven main islands scattered over a large area and made more complex by the scores of other islands that had to be reconnoitered and cleared. Staffs at all levels were hampered by changes in plans, a shortage of time, and lack of precise information on the objectives.

Operation *Flintlock* was divided into phases. The main phase was the seizure of Kwajalein and Majuro atolls between January 29 and February 8. Phase II was the seizure of

OPPOSITE
Marines from the 4th Division take cover after being fired upon when their landing craft landed on Kwajalein Atoll. (The Mariners' Museum/Corbis)

US bombs blast Japanese airbase in Marshall Islands. Blazing Japanese installations send up huge puffs of white smoke as Roi island, Japanese airbase on Kwajalein Atoll in the Marshall Islands, rocks under the shattering impact of American bombs. Carrier-based US planes raided the island stronghold in preparation for landings by US Marine assault troops. American forces captured Kwajalein during the continuing offensive in the Central Pacific. (Topfoto)

Eniwetok Atoll scheduled for February 17–23. This was essentially a separate operation – *Catchpole*. The remaining phase would become known as *Flintlock, Jr* and involved the clearing of the largely unoccupied remaining Marshalls between March and April.

Preliminary bombardment to soften the many island garrisons and neutralize airfields began on December 4, 1943, with carrier- and land-based aircraft attacking Roi, Kwajalein, Mille, Ebeye, and Wotje. There were no new attacks until January 1944, when land-based aircraft from the new Gilberts airfields began frequent raids on all Japanese installations, with the result that by D-Day there were no operational Japanese aircraft in the Marshalls. The plan was for Amphibious Reconnaissance Company, V Amphibious Corps (VAC), to reconnoiter Majuro Atoll before midnight on D-1 to determine Japanese troop locations. If there were Japanese troops present, 2nd Battalion, 106th Infantry, would assault the islands. The Marine 1st Defense Battalion would then occupy the atoll, airfield construction would begin, and the atoll would be prepared as a fleet anchorage. Once Majuro was secured, US forces would reconnoiter nearby Arno Atoll.

Two forces would assault Kwajalein Atoll in a three-phase plan (not to be confused with *Flintlock*). The Northern Troops and Landing Force – 4th Marine Division – would assault Roi-Namur while the Southern Troops and Landing Force – 7th Infantry Division – landed on Kwajalein Island. Phase I would first clear Japanese lookouts from outlying islets near the objective islands to allow artillery to support the main assaults. Other islets flanking the lagoon entrances would also be secured.

Phase II, the main assault, would commence on D+1 and it was projected that the islands would be secured within two days. Phase III entailed clearing the atoll's remaining islets.

The original date for the 2nd Marine Division assault on Eniwetok was March 19, 1944, with 27th Infantry Division taking Kusaie Island to the southeast at the end of the month. When it became apparent that Kwajalein would be easily secured, it allowed the Joint Expeditionary Force Reserve to be released to take Eniwetok and D-Day was set for February 17. The somewhat impromptu planning lasted from February 3–15. However, the battle for Eniwetok would prove to be tougher than the US troops originally envisaged as a result of the recent arrival of Japanese reinforcements.

The destruction on Kwajalein Island from naval bombardment prior to its capture. (Bettmann/Corbis)

THE JAPANESE PLAN – *Z* OPERATION

After the loss of the Solomons and Aleutians, the Imperial General Headquarters established a new National Defense Zone on September 30, 1943. This line ran along the south edge of the Netherlands East Indies facing Australia, turned north through eastern New Guinea, then ran through the Carolines, anchoring on the great bastion of Truk, and through the Marianas, Volcano, and Bonin Islands. The Marshalls were not encompassed within the "Tojo Line," as the National Defense Zone was known, and the bases there were to fight a delaying action while preparations continued on the main line of defense.

To defend the "Tojo Line," Admiral Mineichi Koga, commander of the Combined Fleet, planned the *Z* Operation. Key positions along the defensive line were strengthened and reinforced. The plan was based on a mutually supporting system of naval and air bases scattered in-depth throughout the region. Island garrisons possessed their own air units to protect themselves but additional air units would flow into the area's surrounding bases to strengthen the defense and attack the approaching invasion fleet from what Japan viewed as "unsinkable aircraft carriers." In due course the Combined Fleet would arrive from Truk and engage the American fleet in the long-sought decisive battle.

Island garrisons under direct attack were to use their own initiative. They were to establish defenses designed to destroy the enemy at the water's edge. If the enemy were to force a landing, the garrison was to conduct persistent counterattacks to delay the invaders as long as possible.

The overall concept of the *Z* Operation was based on airpower, both land and carrier-based, but the Japanese failed to appreciate that, before attacking the targeted islands, the Americans would eliminate all Japanese aircraft in the entire region.

Roi (top) and Namur Islands displaying the damage caused by bomber strikes between November 7, 1943, and January 17, 1944. The islands' lagoon side is to the left. Roi-Namur was a rare instance where island codenames actually related to physical characteristics. "Burlesque" (Roi) was bare of vegetation while "Camouflage" (Namur) was covered with undergrowth.

OPPOSING COMMANDERS

THE US COMMANDERS

Rear-Admiral Richmond Kelly Turner had taken command of 5th Fleet Amphibious Force, in August 1943, to perfect landing force operations in preparation for attacks on the Gilberts and Marshalls. He commanded both the Joint Expeditionary Force and the Northern Attack Force for the Saipan and Tinian operations, and would later oversee the Guam and Okinawa landings, and he directed the amphibious forces of both 3rd and 5th Fleets. Major-General Harry Schmidt (USMC) took command of V Amphibious Corps (VAC) on July 12, 1944, a position he would hold for the rest of the war, including the assault on Iwo Jima.

Major-General Charles H. Corlett (US Army) took command of the 7th Infantry Division in April 1943, and he also doubled as commander of Amphibious Training Unit 9, the Kiska Task Force, and was the ground force commander for the invasion of Kiska Island in the Aleutians. After Operation *Flintlock* he went on to serve in Europe. Brigadier-General Thomas E. Watson of the USMC led the brigade-sized Tactical Group 1 (TacGrp 1) during the capture of Eniwetok, subsequently taking command of the 2nd Marine Division in April 1944.

THE JAPANESE COMMANDERS

Rear-Admiral Michiyuki Yamada (Imperial Japanese Navy, IJN) graduated from the Naval Academy in 1914 and became a flyer in 1918. He commanded land-based flying units early in the war and was given command of the 24th Air Flotilla on January 20, 1943, before being promoted to Rear-Admiral later that year.

Rear-Admiral Monzo Akiyama (IJN) assumed command of the 6th Base Force responsible for defense of the Marshalls in November 1943. On February 2, 1944, he was killed on Kwajalein.

Major-General Yoshimi Nishida (Imperial Japanese Army, IJA) was the commander of the 1st Amphibious Brigade at Eniwetok. He died in his headquarters on Parry Island, Eniwetok, on February 23, 1944.

OPPOSING FORCES

THE US FORCES

The Joint Expeditionary Force (Task Force 51) was responsible for the whole of the Marshalls' operation under Rear-Admiral Turner's 5th Amphibious Force. TF-51's 297 ships were organized into three attack forces to seize northern and southern Kwajalein Atoll and Majuro Atoll. These were backed by the Reserve Force, the Fast Carrier Force (TF-58), and Defense Forces and Land-Based Air (TF-57) with 7th Air Force and Navy land-based and patrol aircraft. TF-51 included 11 aircraft carriers, seven old battleships, 12 cruisers, 75 destroyers, 46 transports, 27 cargo ships, five landing ships, dock (LSD), and 45 landing ships, tank (LST). The Fast Carrier Force amassed 12 more carriers, eight battleships, six cruisers, and 34 destroyers. 5th Fleet (TF-50), under Admiral Spruance, oversaw the entire operation.

The Southern Attack Force, directly under Rear-Admiral Turner's command, would seize Kwajalein with the 27th Infantry Division. The Northern Attack Force commanded by Rear-Admiral Richard L. Conolly would deliver the 4th Marine Division to Roi-Namur. The Reserve Force, under Captain D. W. Loomis, carried TacGrp 1, which would later be tasked to seize Eniwetok. The Majuro Attack Group was commanded by Rear-Admiral Harry W.

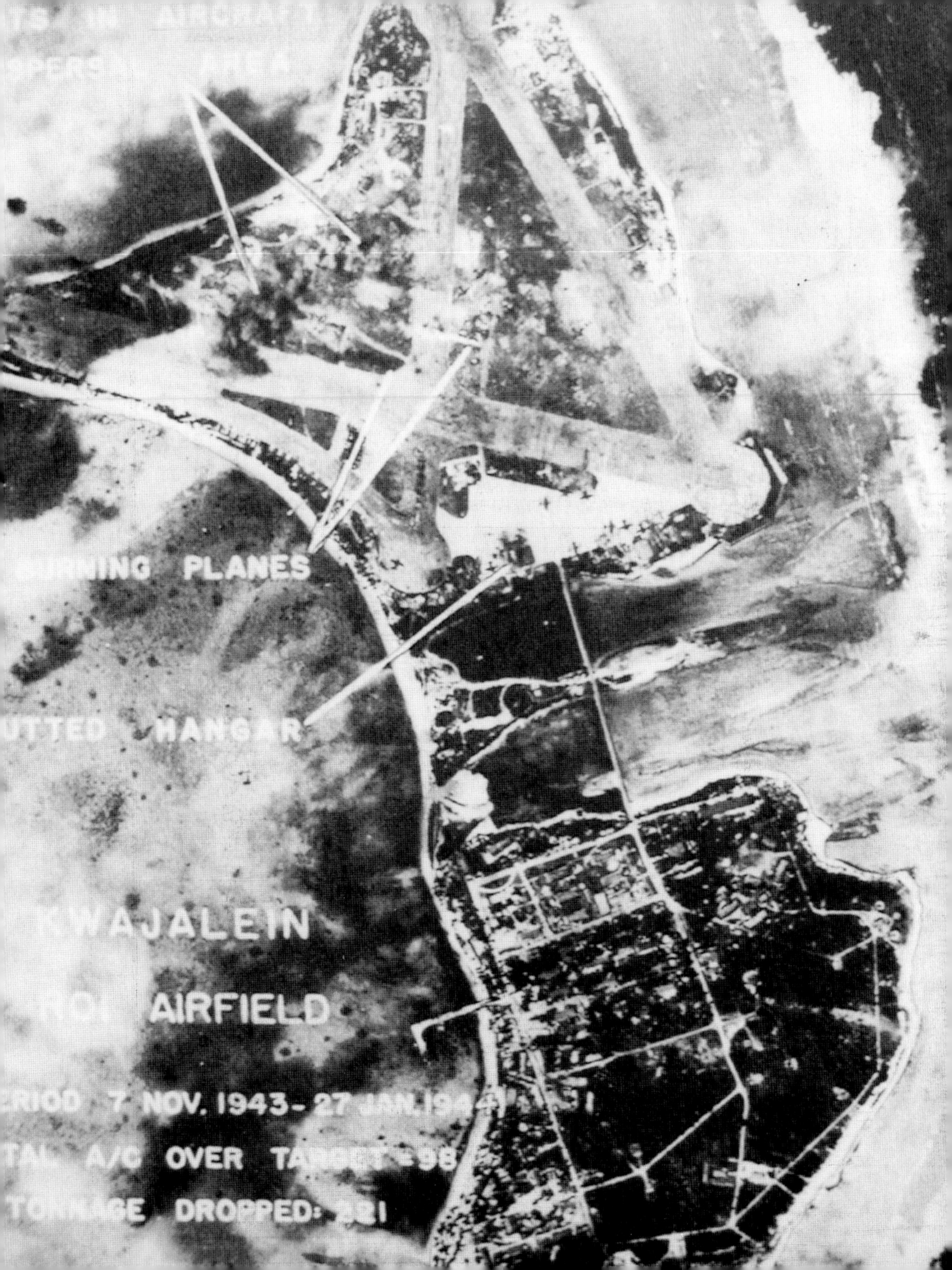

URNING PLANES

UTTED HANGAR

KWAJALEIN

AIRFIELD

ERIOD 7 NOV. 1943 - 27 JAN. 1944

TAL A/C OVER TARGET = 98

TONNAGE DROPPED: 221

Hill and carried a small Army and Marine force to occupy Majuro Atoll.

VAC doubled as the Expeditionary Troops, deploying with only minimal corps troops, since it would not fight as a unified corps, but rather land its two divisions at opposite ends of Kwajalein Atoll, their primary objectives being 43 miles apart. The 4th Marine Division, "The Fighting Fourth," had departed for the Central Pacific in January 1944 with 24,902 troops. The 7th Infantry Division's 21,768 troops were attached to VAC on December 11 in preparation for the Kwajalein assault.

VAC formed TacGrp 1 on November 1, 1943, on Oahu around the 22nd Marines (Separate) to serve as the reserve landing force. The 22nd Marines possessed organic units, more normally attached from divisional units in the event the regiment was assigned to a division: engineer, medical, motor transport, pioneer, and M4A2 tank companies; reconnaissance, ordnance, and supply and service platoons; plus a 75mm pack howitzer battalion. This gave the reserve landing force 3,701 Marines and 5,624 soldiers. Army and Marine units detached from VAC would augment the Group to 10,269 for the late February assault on Eniwetok Atoll. Garrison forces would include 6,217 Army, 9,454 Marine, and 15,278 Navy personnel, some of whom were drawn from the assault troops.

The Majuro Landing Force (aka "Sundance" Landing Force) consisted of the 2nd Battalion, 106th Infantry and Amphibious Reconnaissance Company, VAC, with 1,459 soldiers and 136 Marines.

Colonel Franklin A. Hart, commander, 24th Marines, discusses the landing plan for Namur Island with his regimental staff. The white tags on the terrain board identify defenses, installations, and key terrain features.

THE JAPANESE FORCES

The Japanese 4th Fleet was not a conventional fleet, but rather an operational command, with few assigned ships, responsible for the defense of the Japanese Mandate. Once the American fleet arrived in the Marshalls, the 4th Fleet would have little effect on the battle and the forces there. The immediate headquarters responsible for the Marshalls was the 6th Base Force on Kwajalein. Also located on Kwajalein were the 6th Submarine Base Force, 6th Communications Unit, 61st Guard Force, a detachment of the 4th Fleet Construction Unit (Korean laborers), a company of the Yokosuka 4th Special Naval Landing Force (SNLF), 952nd Air Unit, and numerous unassigned casuals and stragglers. The 1st Company, 3rd Mobile Battalion, 1st Amphibious Brigade, was assigned to defend Kwajalein while the 2nd Mobile Battalion (less 1st and 2nd companies, but with attachments totaling 729 men) was caught on Kwajalein while en route to Wotje. There were about 5,000 personnel on Kwajalein, 933 of them IJA. Some 500 personnel were located on nearby Ebeye Island.

Roi-Namur was defended by a detachment of the 61st Guard Force, a detachment of the 4th Fleet Construction Unit, Headquarters 24th Air Flotilla and its 275th, 281st, and

LEFT
Rear-Admiral Michiyuki Yamada commanded the 24th Air Flotilla based on Roi-Namur and died during the pre-invasion bombardment of Namur.

RIGHT
Rear-Admiral Monzo Akiyama was the commander of the 6th Base Force responsible for the guard forces and other defense forces in the Marshall Islands.

735th Air Units. The 22nd Air Flotilla had been assigned to the Marshalls, but in late November the 24th Air Flotilla deployed from Japan with 30 fighters and 40 bombers. Another 18 fighters and some torpedo-bombers were also sent from Rabaul. There were some 3,000 IJN personnel on Roi-Namur.

Jaluit, Maloelap, Wotje, and Mille were defended by the 62nd, 63rd, 64th, and 66th Guard Forces, respectively, plus detachments of 4th Fleet, 6th Base Force, and 24th Air Flotilla. 3rd Battalion, 170th Infantry Regiment of the 52nd Division was located on Mille with IJA South Sea garrison detachments located on the others. The following strengths are the IJN and IJA totals with the IJA in parentheses: Jaluit – 2,200 (620), Maloelap – 3,100 (404), Wotje – 3,300 (667), Mille – 5,100 (2,530). The 6th Base Force was also responsible for the defense of Kusaie and Wake Islands.

The Japanese defenders of Eniwetok, including remaining air and ground crews, numbered some 3,500. The main defense force was the 1st Amphibious Brigade. It had a headquarters, three 1,036-man mobile battalions, a 76-man machine-cannon unit and a 66-man tank unit with nine Type 95 light tanks. The brigade headquarters was on Parry Island with 1,115 troops plus 250 IJN personnel. The 1st Mobile Battalion held Eniwetok with 779 troops. The 3rd Mobile Battalion defended Engebi with 692 troops, some 500 IJN personnel plus the 61st Guard Force detachment.

Altogether there were 28,000 IJN personnel, IJA troops, and laborers in the Marshall Islands.

Japanese defenses

While Truk in the Carolines was heavily fortified as the 4th Fleet's home base, few other islands in the Mandate possessed fortifications other than air, seaplane, and naval bases. Coast defense and anti-aircraft guns were few

Marines of the 22nd Regiment aim machine gun fire at a Japanese target 400 yards up the beach at Eniwetok during the attack that took place between February 17–23. (Bettmann/Corbis)

while the natural vegetation and few natural obstacles or dominating terrain features gave little opportunity to establish an effective defense. The fringing reefs would present an obstacle to conventional landing craft, but not amtracs. The Japanese expected any assault to come from the ocean side, where the reef was narrower than on the lagoon side, exposing debarking troops for less time, and ships could approach closer to the shore. For this reason the Japanese concentrated their defenses on the ocean side. But anti-boat obstacles and underwater mines could not be emplaced on this side because of heavy surf.

Reinforced platoon strong points were positioned along the ocean side consisting of clusters of trenches, foxholes, and machine-gun positions. Concrete machine gun pillboxes and gun emplacements were built on some islands, but were few and far between. Many of the permanent buildings such as headquarters or signal centers were constructed of reinforced concrete and, while they provided cover, were not sited as defensive positions. Most defenses consisted of fighting trenches without revetments, two-three-man foxholes, and simple machine gun bunkers with light overhead cover.

OPERATION *FLINTLOCK*

On December 4, 1943, two American carrier groups attacked Kwajalein and Wotje Atolls, destroying several aircraft and sinking seven freighters. Importantly, reconnaissance aircraft managed to get complete aerial photography of all the islands – vital for the forthcoming operation.

TF-51 departed the Hawaiian Islands on January 22–23, 1944, heading southeast for 2,200 miles. On January 29, four carrier groups began attacking the islands with 700 aircraft, supplemented by the bombardment of warships offshore. On the 30th the Northern and Southern Attack Groups separated and headed for the north and south ends of the huge Kwajalein Atoll. The 4th Marine Division had departed California on January 13 for the then longest shore-to-shore amphibious assault in history – 4,300 miles.

IJN units were conspicuous by their absence in the Marshalls. The two commanders of elements of the Japanese 2nd Fleet had conferred and concluded that without carrier air support their forces were too weak to challenge the US 5th Fleet. They withdrew to Truk on December 7.

OCCUPATION OF MAJURO

The Majuro Attack Group departed Hawaii, accompanying the Reserve Force, on January 23. The group split off from the main task force on the 30th and headed for Majuro Atoll, 280 miles southeast of Kwajalein. Aboard was the "Sundance" Landing Force, detached from the 27th Infantry Division, and the Amphibious Reconnaissance Company, VAC, totaling 1,600 troops. At about 2300hrs on January 30 a platoon of the reconnaissance company landed in rubber boats on Calalin Island, making them

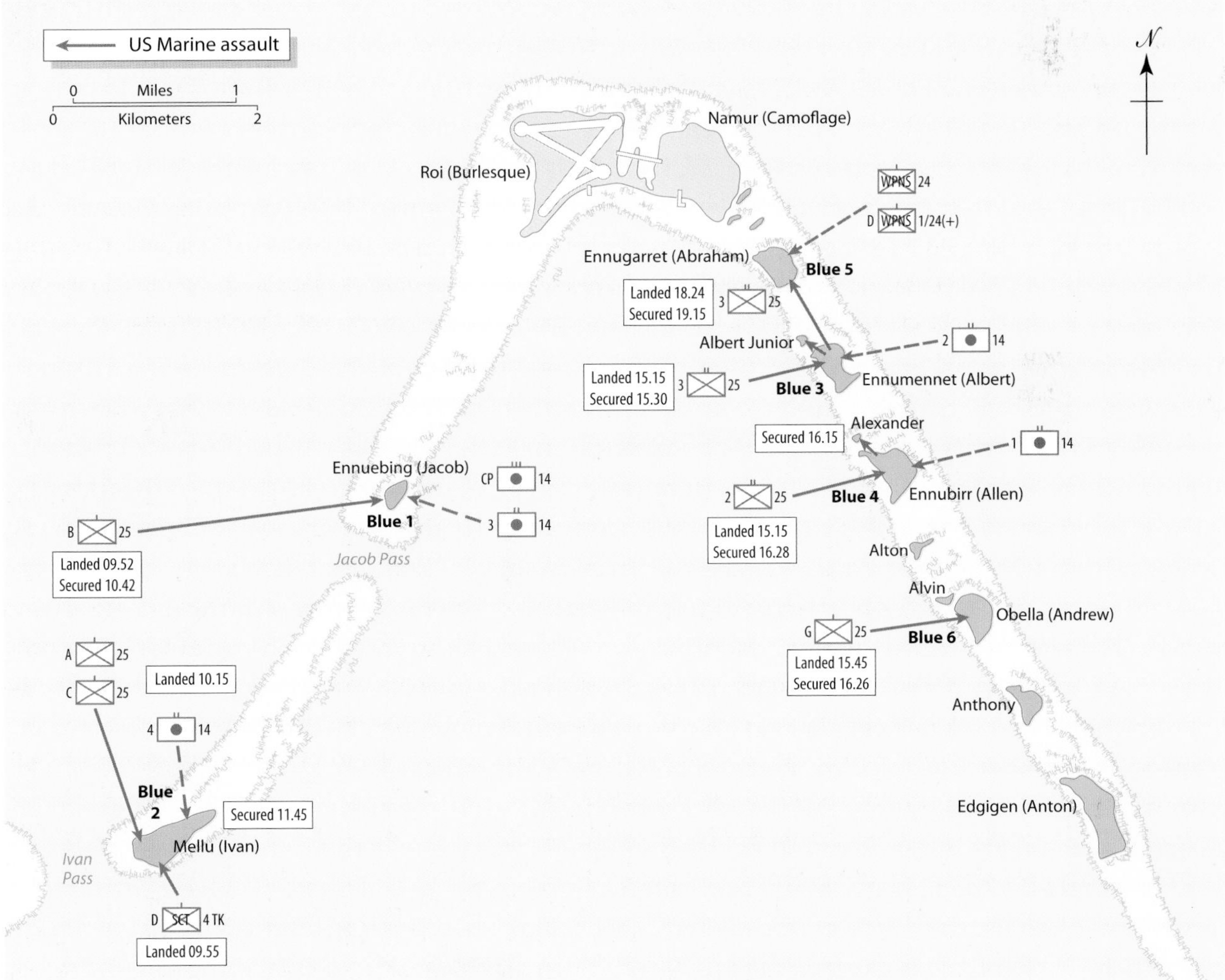

Map showing the Roi-Namur islands and the Marine advance. (Osprey Publishing Ltd.)

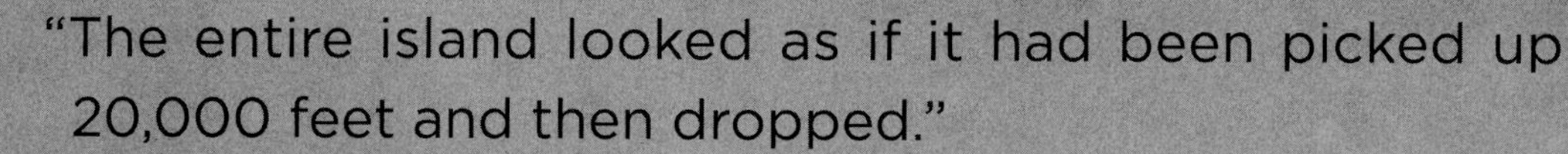

"The entire island looked as if it had been picked up 20,000 feet and then dropped."

— **PARTICIPANT OF THE ACTION AROUND THE MARSHALL ISLANDS,** DESCRIBING THE DESTRUCTION OF KWAJALEIN

the first American troops to land on any territory that Japan had possessed since before the war. The rest of the company landed on other islands and found the Japanese had already abandoned the atoll. The force also occupied Darrit and Dalop Islands with air and fleet facilities subsequently built.

ROI-NAMUR ASSAULT

The Northern Attack Force (TF-53), with the 4th Marine Division, arrived off Roi-Namur in the pre-dawn hours of January 31 (D-Day) with three battleships, five cruisers, three escort carriers, 21 destroyers, five sub-chasers, 11 minesweepers, 13 attack transports, seven troop transports, three attack cargo transports, one destroyer-transport, two LSDs, 20 LSTs, and two tugs. "Ivan" and "Jacob" would be seized from the seaward side to allow the Northern Attack Force to enter the lagoon for the main attack the next day. The troops boarded landing craft at 0530hrs to be boated to a transfer point, where they would in turn board amtracs unloading from LSTs.

H-Hour for "Ivan" and "Jacob" was 0900hrs, A-Hour for "Albert" and "Allen" was 1130hrs, and B-Hour for "Abraham" was 1600hrs following preparatory bombardment and air-strikes from carrier-based planes on all five. The rough sea and inadequate rehearsals back in California soon began to show their effects. The swells slowed the amtracs to half speed and wind-driven spray drowned radios. The area in which the transfer from LCVPs to amtracs was taking place became congested and confused. H-Hour was reset for 0930hrs.

At 0952hrs, Company B, 2nd Battalion, 25th Marines, finally came ashore on "Jacob" and overran the island in 15 minutes. It was declared secure at 1042hrs, the 19 defenders killed or captured. Difficulties were encountered at "Ivan" to the southwest. Surf, winds, and reef conditions slowed the amtracs. Strafing attacks prevented the enemy from taking advantage of the delay, and although the 12.7cm battery opened fire it was easily silenced. Following the landings the island was secured at 1145hrs.

Now the action shifted east to a string of islets running to the southeast. Here the landings would occur from inside the lagoon. A-Hour was set for 1100hrs. The LCI(G), gunfire, and air strike plan was similar to the earlier assault. The 2nd Battalion troops had been in their LCVPs since before dawn while they served as the "Jacob/Ivan" reserve. The amtracs from that assault met the 2nd and 3rd battalions, 25th Marines, the latter still aboard its transport, but again rough seas delayed the transfers. LVTs became scattered and some followed the wrong control craft. A-Hour was changed to 1430hrs as stray amtracs were rounded up and communications problems persisted.

The amtracs finally entered the lagoon through "Jacob Pass" and headed for "Andrew," "Allen," and "Albert," A-Hour was now set at 1500hrs as the amtracs struggled across the

ABOVE
A Marine light machine gun crew fights on the front line of action on Namur during the battle for the Marshall Islands. (Bettmann/Corbis)

OPPOSITE
US Marines rest on Namur Beach soon after landing in February 1944. (Bettmann/Corbis)

Suicide was preferable to capture for most Japanese soldiers, and these scenes were seen throughout the American campaign in the Pacific. Note that these soldiers used their toes to pull the triggers. (Tom Laemlein)

lagoon. "Albert" and "Allen" were secured at 1530hrs and 1628hrs, respectively.

The 3rd Battalion, 25th Marines was then ordered to secure "Abraham," the closest islet to Namur. Amtracs were still in short supply and the original 1600 B-Hour had passed. "Albert Junior," a tiny islet 200 yards off "Albert," was secured and machine-guns emplaced to support the "Abraham" assault. Only four amtracs were available, but the assault went in at 1824hrs. Six Japanese were killed, the rest fled to Namur, and the islet was secured at 1915hrs with only one marine wounded. The amtracs shuttled in troops armed with halftracks, anti-tank guns, mortars, and machine guns, which were emplaced to support the Namur landing.

Regardless of repeated delays the "Ivan" Landing Force had accomplished all its D-Day missions. Roi-Namur was now cut off, supporting artillery was in place, and the assault troops were more than ready to get off their ships after 19 days at sea.

Roi Island, February 1 (D+1)

The Roi and Namur assaults were conducted simultaneously, but for clarity are described separately. Unit locations are described from left to right as if viewed from behind the US front line.

The original plan called for the assault troops to be boated by LCVPs from their transports to the tractor LSTs where they would have the luxury of boarding the amtracs in the holds of the "large slow targets." This was planned to take place outside the lagoon, but because of the problems encountered the day before with the rough conditions, the LSTs entered the lagoon after first light to provide the amtracs a shorter and smoother ride, conserve fuel, and reduce turnaround delays. At 0650hrs the USS *Tennessee* opened direct fire with its 14in guns against the blockhouse on the sandspit linking Roi-Namur. The Roi bombardment commenced at 0710hrs with the 14th Marines artillery on the adjacent islets joining in followed by air attacks. W-Hour was 1000hrs.

The 23rd RCT, under Colonel Louis R. Jones, was aboard its 4th Amphibian Tractor Battalion amtracs and ready to go, though a bit behind schedule because of problems disembarking the amtracs. The 24th RCT, destined for Namur, was having more serious difficulties, so W-Hour was set back to 1100hrs. Although the 23rd RCT reached the line of departure on time, the assault was again delayed, but naval gunfire continued. The bombardments were lifted at 1150hrs and the 23rd RCT made its run to Roi, hitting the beaches at 1157hrs.

Red 2 was 550 yards wide on the western half of the south coast and Red 3 was on the eastern half. 1st and 2nd battalions, 23rd

Marines, respectively, would land on these beaches with two companies abreast. The O-1 Line ran across the island west to east roughly 200–300 yards inland with its east end on the causeway. Amphibian tanks of companies A and C, 1st Armored Amphibian Tractor Battalion, came ashore at 1133hrs. Companies A and B of 1st Battalion, 23rd Marines, followed the amphibian tanks ashore and quickly reached the O-1 Line.

On Red 3, E and F of the 2nd Battalion, 23rd Marines, came ashore at 1150hrs. They had been preceded by 18 amphibian tanks. Enemy resistance on Red 3 was just as weak as on Red 2. Large numbers of positions had been destroyed by the bombardment and survivors were dazed. The command post of 2nd Battalion, 23rd Marines was in operation by 1215hrs, by which time E and F had reached the O-1 Line.

The light resistance actually led to difficulties controlling the troops, a phenomenon seldom seen in other Pacific island assaults. Encouraged and relieved by the inconsequential resistance, squads and platoons began a disordered headlong dash across the island but were eventually recalled to the O-1 line for coordinated attacks. The subsequent "re-assault" of Roi's northern two-thirds kicked off at 1530hrs preceded by a naval gunfire barrage commencing 20 minutes earlier. The earlier disorganized charge had served to confuse the enemy, and he had not yet recovered to face this new even more devastating coordinated attack. At 1802hrs Roi was declared secure.

The torpedo warhead warehouse on Namur detonates at 1305hrs. This photograph was shot from the Roi beachhead. This explosion caused half of all the 24th Marines' casualties.

Namur Island, February 1–2 (D+1–D+2)

The 24th RCT under Colonel Franklin A. Hart began experiencing difficulties even before reaching the line of departure. The unit was to be landed by the 10th Amphibian Tractor Battalion, which had supported the assault on the neighboring islands the day before. Parent LSTs were not equipped with recognition lights and fuel-hungry amtracs could not find their mother ships. Fearing insufficient fuel for their own amtracs, LST skippers turned away stranger amtracs. Many failed to report back to the LSTs in the dark and spent the night sitting on islets. Others were damaged or suffering mechanical problems. At 0630hrs Colonel Hart reported to General Schmidt, "We are short 48 LVTs" (of 110 allotted). A frantic search was made for stray amtracs, but to no avail in the short time remaining.

Both the assault battalions' reserve companies had received their full complement of amtracs. 3rd Battalion, 24th Marines, redistributed its reserve amtracs to the assault companies, while 2nd Battalion replaced Company G with its reserve Company E. At the last minute Company G arrived aboard scrounged amtracs and LCVPs and Company A, 1st Battalion, 24th Marines was returned to its parent battalion. Not surprisingly the organization of the assault waves was confused and control officers were still trying to sort them out when the signal was given to attack. Colonel Hart attempted to halt the 3rd Battalion, 24th Marines, which had began to advance but, seeing the Roi assault was under way, desisted realizing that it could endanger the entire operation.

Green 1 encompassed the sandspit and the western third of Namur's south coast. The Yokohama Pier marked the boundary between Green 1 and Green 2 to the east, which extended to "Sally Point." The pier also marked the battalion boundary between 2nd and 3rd battalions, 24th Marines, which ran to "Natalie Point" on the north shore. The O-1 Line ran from the causeway east along a main road although the wreckage of the many blasted buildings and dense brush caused a great deal of control and orientation problems.

Army infantrymen pause below Eniwetok Island's 9ft embankment, which had halted amphibian tanks attempting to move inland. An M1917A1 heavy machine gun is being emplaced to cover their advance. (Tom Laemlein)

The 3rd Battalion came ashore on Green 1 at 1200hrs with companies K and I attacking north. At 1300hrs the battalion reached the O-1 Line. The 2nd Battalion hit Green 2 at 1155hrs. Amtracs were supposed to carry the troops 100 yards inland, but an anti-tank ditch blocked both amtracs and tanks. This led to congestion on the narrow beach. By 1300hrs most of companies F and E had reached the O-1 Line, but resistance was stiffening.

As Company F approached the O-1 Line near the east coast an assault team breached a large concrete structure with a shaped charge. Japanese in the vicinity began withdrawing as Marines threw satchel charges into the hole, unaware that it was a torpedo warhead bunker. A massive explosion obliterated the structure and blocks of concrete, palm trees, wood, torpedo warheads, and other debris rained down over the island. Two nearby structures also exploded, although these blasts were not as large as the original; they were probably ammunition bunkers detonated when the first bunker exploded. A cloud of black smoke rose 1,000ft skyward and most of the island was immediately covered by a blast of smoke and dust. The explosion, which left a 100ft water-filled crater, left 20 Marines dead and 100 wounded across the island. Company F lost 14 dead and 43 wounded.

More tanks were landed and the assault passed the O-1 Line, achieving greater depth on the left. Japanese resistance was increasing with the defenders taking advantage of the rubble and dense brush, and 37mm canister rounds were used to blast away foliage. The division advance control point was established on Green 1 between the sandspit and the pier at 1630hrs. At 1930hrs Colonel Hart ordered his unit to dig in for the night. Nightfall was 1945hrs.

Using palm fronds as concealment, two Marines of the 4th Marine Division take a careful look around before advancing on Namur during the battle for the Marshall Islands. (Bettmann/Corbis)

At first light the tanks were in position to help beat off a counterattack, which struck the gap that had developed between companies I and B. The tanks moved forward to engage the attackers as Company L moved in to close the gap and contain any breakthrough. The attack was defeated and the Marines had advanced some 50 yards. Colonel Hart launched his own attack at 0900hrs. By 1215hrs, the 3rd Battalion, 24th Marines had secured “Nora Point” on the northwest corner. However, the 2nd Battalion’s tank support was late so its attack was delayed an hour. The two battalions met at “Natalie Point” on the north end at 1215hrs. Mopping-up continued in the rear and the island was declared secure at 1418hrs.

The 4th Marine Division had performed well for its first operation, suffering just over 1,000 casualties in the process. Fire discipline had been lax, as expected of green troops, and control measures loose, but this was all part of learning their trade. It was felt that if sufficient amtracs had been available on time Namur could have been secured on D+1. The 25th RCT went on to clear 47, mostly unoccupied, Kwajalein Atoll islets from February 2–5.

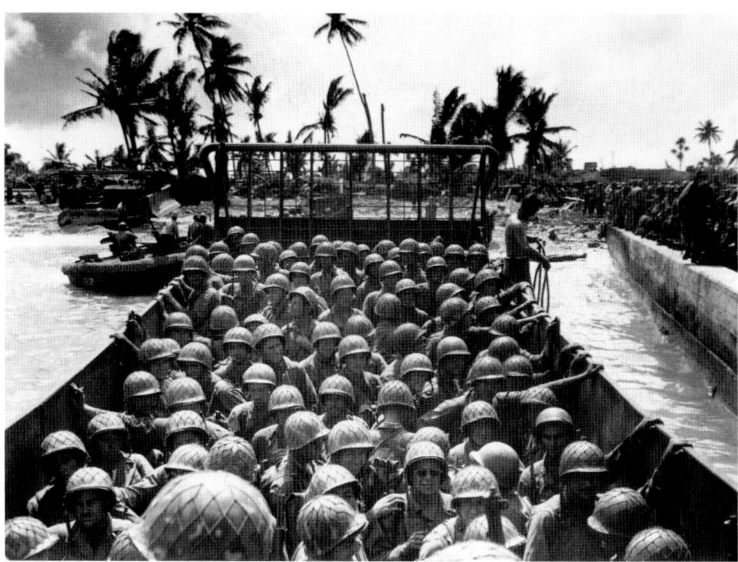

KWAJALEIN ASSAULT

In the moonless pre-dawn hours of D-Day, January 31, the Southern Attack Force (TF-52) with the 7th Infantry Division, slipped into its transport and fire support areas six–ten miles southwest of Kwajalein Island. The force consisted of four battleships, three cruisers, three escort carriers, 18 destroyers, three sub-chasers, five minesweepers, 18 attack-transports, five troop-transports, two attack cargo-transports, two destroyer-transports, two LSDs, 20 LSTs, and three tugs.

Kwajalein – neighboring islands, February 1 (D+1)

Two destroyer-transports raced ahead of the task force closing on "Cecil" and "Carter" guarding the lagoon's entrance, a half-mile apart and the latter nine miles northwest of Kwajalein. Two composite company-size units had been formed from the 7th Cavalry Reconnaissance Troop and Company B, 111th Infantry and attached to Colonel Wayne C. Zimmerman's 17th RCT. Troops A and B were made up of roughly half of each unit. The reconnaissance elements' rubber boats would be towed by launches to within 800 yards of the islets and would then paddle ashore to mark landing sites. The rifle platoons would then come ashore in LCVPs. Once "Cecil" and "Carter" had been secured the cavalry troop elements on the two islets were to be reconstituted and then reconnoiter "Chauncey" while the infantry held "Cecil" and "Carter."

Even with delays and minor problems Troop A landed on what they thought was "Cecil" at 0545hrs. Four Japanese defenders had been killed and two captured before the US troops realized they were on the wrong islet – "Chauncey" one mile northwest of "Cecil." They discovered a beached Japanese tug and left a small element to watch it as the rest of Troop A re-embarked at 0929hrs. They then landed on "Cecil" at 1124hrs, found it clear of enemy, and declared it secure at 1235hrs.

Troop B landed on "Carter" at 0620hrs; although the dense brush slowed the reconnaissance, they discovered a Japanese force, and all 20 defenders were killed with one American wounded. "Carter" was declared secure at 0948hrs. On "Chauncey" the infantrymen discovered a force of over 100 Japanese hidden in the islet's center; almost half the Japanese troops were killed and the US infantry withdrew losing two men.

"Carlson" was two miles northwest of Kwajalein Island and 900 yards southeast of "Carter," and separated by a shallow reef from "Carlos" 4,300 yards to the northwest. 17th RCT was tasked to secure both "Carlson" and "Carlos." The two assault battalions transferred from their transports to LCTs where they boarded the amtracs for the actual assault. At 0810hrs the cruisers began a sustained bombardment of the two objective islands as well as of Kwajalein, "Burton," and "Beverly." They were joined by the two battleships, which had already been pounding Kwajalein since 0618hrs. "Carlos" was secured at 1615hrs. The 2nd Battalion, 17 RCT, landed on the northeast end of "Carlson" at 0912hrs. Resistance had been expected, but other than scattered rifle fire, which wounded one man, there was no serious enemy action and "Carlson" was declared secure at 1210hrs. The field artillery and warships continued to bombard Kwajalein and "Burton" through the night.

Kwajalein Island, February 1 (D+1)

H-Hour for Kwajalein was set for 0930hrs, February 1. The power of the pre-assault barrage was unprecedented in the Pacific; 36,000 rounds of naval gunfire and artillery plus sizeable air attacks pummeled the island. Alternating barrages of naval gunfire and 96 carrier aircraft sorties hit the island as the assault waves disembarked from their LSTs on the ocean side. LCI(G)s spewed forth rockets and poured in automatic cannon fire as the amtracs, with 20 in the first wave mounting portable flamethrowers, churned toward the shore. The landing force was released at 0900hrs.

The landing beaches, Red 1 and Red 2, were on the island's westernmost end, with Red 1 to the north and Red 2 to the south. 184th RCT under Colonel Curtis D. O'Sullivan, landing on 250 yard-wide Red 1, would be led in by the 3rd Battalion, with Company L on the left and I on the right. Company B, 767th Tank Battalion followed, it ashore and then came 2nd and 1st Battalions.

32nd RCT commanded by Colonel Marc J. Logie assaulted 300-yard wide Red 2. Each

OPPOSITE TOP
US Army .30cal machine guns on Kwajalein beach. (Tom Laemlein)

OPPOSITE BOTTOM
Palm-studded "Carlos" Island, a South Pacific paradise in the Marshalls, falls to American invasion forces driving ashore in Coast Guard-manned landing craft as part of the assault on the Marshall Islands. (Bettmann/Corbis)

24th Marines assault troops pinned down on a Namur beach. The crate in the foreground contains medical supplies indicated by the red cross on a white swatch. The yellow half-circle symbol identifies the 4th Marine Division and the numbers within the symbol the specific unit.

beach was covered by a strong point, but these had been largely obliterated. Small numbers of defenders managed to reoccupy craters and wreckages, and a few pillboxes had survived. The current forced amtracs to veer to the right, but most landed on the assigned beaches at 0930hrs. Fire was weak and the assault troops suffered few casualties.

Undestroyed seawall sections, craters, stumps, and debris halted many amtracs and tanks, some still in the water. They maintained a torrent of machine gun fire as artillery from "Carlson" shifted inland. Marshes were found in the dense brush behind the beaches. Many amtracs, instead of turning to the flanks to circulate back to the LSTs, instead turned around on the beach causing congestion as more amtracs rolled in. The reef halted later waves in LCVPs and the troops waded ashore.

The assault troops had pushed 250–300 yards inland to the edge of the radio direction finding station in a large clearing. The two lead companies of each assault battalion skirted the clearing through the coastal vegetation and then fanned out. Between 1430 and 1450hrs, they reached a road crossing the island 800–900 yards from the island's west end. The follow-on battalions mopped up and the reserve battalions secured the beachheads. The advance turned into a slow crawl as every surviving pillbox, trench, and shelter was laboriously cleared. So many scattered field works were encountered that the advance slowed to a crawl and there was now a 300-yard gap along the runway between the two battalions. Company E, 2nd Battalion, 32rd Marines, covered the gap and before dawn Company C moved forward to guard the area. The Japanese attempted several concentrated attacks and endlessly attempted to infiltrate the US positions. Nonetheless, American casualties were startlingly light until this point; 21 dead and 87 wounded in the two assault regiments.

Kwajalein Island, February 2–4 (D+2–D+4)

A coordinated attack was to be launched at 0715hrs. Tanks were moved forward and 2nd Battalion, 184th RCT, would attack through 3rd Battalion. Artillery began a preparation followed by air strikes and naval bombardment. Initially good progress was made but then the advance was slowed because of resistance, obstacles, and rubble. The 2nd Battalion did not quite make it to the objective line, halting 150–220 yards short, but the 3rd Battalion, 32nd Marines, made it to the line ... barely. Company G relieved F at 1630hrs. The day's casualties for both regiments were 11 dead and 241 wounded. Enemy prisoners reported only a few hundred defenders remaining, their communications disrupted, and the defenses severely battered. The forward companies were alerted to expect a banzai attack that night. There were probes and a great deal of small arms, grenade, and mortar fire, especially after midnight, but the promised attack never materialized. The next day's (D+3) assault would commence at 0715hrs.

Preceded by preparatory fires as was the previous day's attack, 1st Battalion, 184th RCT led off on the left with companies A and B passing through 2nd Battalion. They were soon held up by strong resistance in a group of shattered buildings along the lagoon shore. From this point the island's northern end was covered with buildings and four strong points remained on the ocean side and north end. Company A pushed farther north and attempted to attack from the flank through the Admiralty Area, but became bogged down. The 3rd Battalion, 32nd Marines, on the ocean side advanced with companies L and I taking

Troops advance on Kwajalein covered by an M4A2 tank of the 767th Tank Battalion. The blasted vegetation proved to be an obstacle to foot and vehicle movement.

the lead. Company K soon relieved L, although it had to swing into the 1st Battalion, 184th RCT zone through part of the Admiralty Area to do so: good progress was made.

At 1330hrs the new attack was launched with C and A from 1st Battalion, 184th RCT attacking west into the built-up area as Company B secured the area's south flank. They reached the lagoon by 1800hrs, halting for the night. The day's casualties had been high, 54 dead and 255 wounded. More Japanese had been killed than were expected still to be on the island. The battalions were still 200–350 yards short of their objective line.

After sunset the Japanese counterattacked but were defeated. Additional counterattacks were broken up before they began by massed mortar and artillery fire. A sizeable number of enemy remained in the 400 by 1,000 yard north end and constant blasting by artillery, mortars, naval gunfire, and air strikes could not reduce them. It was taking longer than expected to secure the island, mainly due to the stiff resistance of the IJA's 2nd Mobile Battalion and SNLF troops.

The US regimental and divisional command posts launched the final D+4 attack to clear the island in the belief that the forward troops were somewhat farther north. Far too many small pockets remained in the rear and the reserve battalions were experiencing difficulties rooting them out. The attack was launched at 0715hrs, supported by tanks, and immediately ran into stiff resistance. The advance was slow and confused, with many attacking platoons tied down clearing pockets of defenders. Comparatively large numbers of prisoners began to surrender, mostly Koreans. At 1610hrs, Major-General Corlett finally declared the island secure, even though the north end was not cleared until 1920hrs with mopping-up operations continuing.

EBEYE ISLAND ASSAULT

Once it was determined the reserve regiment would not be needed on Kwajalein, preparations began for the Ebeye, or "Burton," Island assault just over 20 miles north of Kwajalein. Scheduled for 0930hrs on February 3 (D+3), the island had been shelled and bombed since D-1; in addition 155mm batteries on "Carlson" had added their firepower. Two cruisers and artillery blasted the island as the amtracs went in. 1st Battalion, 17th RCT, landed with Company C on the left and A on the right against light fire at 0935hrs. Company B followed with Company C, 767th Tank Battalion. The battalion pushed quickly across the island and then worked north. The 3rd Battalion landed to mop up the south end. The advance continued north until 1900hrs when they halted for the night midway up the island's length. Throughout the night Japanese attempts to organize counterattacks were harassed by US artillery and naval gunfire.

The attack resumed at 0730hrs on February 4, but it was soon held up by Japanese who had reoccupied pillboxes on the ocean coast, although these were soon overcome. At 1130hrs, the 3rd Battalion passed through the 1st as the attack reached the seaplane apron. On the left, Company L advanced behind tanks across the open apron as K on the right pushed through the hangar area and reached the island's north end; "Burton" was declared secure at 1337hrs. Some 450 Japanese were killed and seven captured. US losses were seven dead and 82 wounded.

Most of "Burton" was heavily wooded, but was virtually blasted clean of vegetation. In the upper left is a concrete air-raid shelter with its typical two entrances.

ENIWETOK ASSAULT

Brigadier-General Thomas Watson's TacGrp 1, VAC, was given the task of securing Eniwetok, having served as the Fleet Reserve at Kwajalein. Additional units augmented the Group for Operation *Catchpole*. D-Day was set for February 17 and the force departed Kwajalein on 15th aboard the Eniwetok Expeditionary Group (TG-51.11). Carrier strikes had been conducted against the atoll since the end of January.

At the same time *Catchpole* was launched, TF-57, the Fast Carrier Force, attacked Truk (February 17–18). Much of the Japanese Combined Fleet had withdrawn to the Palaus, but the strikes sank 39 warships, auxiliaries, and merchantmen, as well as destroying over 200 aircraft. Operation *Hailstone* neutralized the Japanese Navy's "Gibraltar of the Pacific," eliminating the need for a costly amphibious assault on the atoll.

Naval shelling of Engebi, Eniwetok, Parry, and Japtan Islands began in the early morning hours, to be joined by air strikes after dawn. The ships of the Expeditionary Group steamed

An American plane sweeps overhead to strafe the enemy hidden in their coral trenches. A group of Marines lie prone in the sand peppering the Japanese across smoking No-Man's Land with rifle fire. (Bettmann/Corbis)

single file through two passages in broad daylight, three battleships, three cruisers, 15 destroyers, one sub-chaser, four minesweepers, seven attack-transports, two attack cargo-transports, six cargo ships, two destroyer-transports, two tugs, an LSD, and nine LSTs. Four escort carriers, their screening destroyers, and auxiliaries remained outside the lagoon. A fleet carrier and two light carriers provided additional support. One US Navy officer remarked that it was "one of the most thrilling episodes that I witnessed during the entire war."

All three main landings were led by Company A, 708th Amphibian Tank Battalion. The 708th Amphibian Tractor Battalion provided the troop amtracs. The separate 22nd Marines under Colonel John T. Walker would take on most of the workload. Colonel Russell G. Ayers' 106th Infantry, detached from the 27th Infantry Division, and with its 2nd Battalion still on Majuro, would back up the Marines.

Eniwetok's neighboring Islands, February 17–18 (D-Day–D+1)

As the larger warships blasted the main islands, destroyers shot up "Camellia" and "Canna" to the southeast of Engebi. Elements of Amphibious Reconnaissance Company, VAC, were landed by amtrac on "Camellia" at 1320hrs and on "Canna" at 1330hrs. Finding them unoccupied, they secured them by 1400hrs on D-Day. "Zinnia" was secured by the 17 Company D (Scout), 4th Tank Battalion, as were four other islets west of Engebi in the early morning of D+1 to prevent the enemy escaping from Engebi. There had been a great deal of confusion during the positioning of ships for this phase, but it was nonetheless accomplished on schedule.

ENGEBI ISLAND, FEBRUARY 18–19 (D+1–D+2)

W-Hour was 0845hrs on D+1 (February 18), and after heavy preparatory shelling and bombing, which detonated the main ammunition dump, the assault amtracs followed the LCI(G)s toward Engebi. Each battalion landed with all three companies in line. The landings were on the island's central southwest shore, with 2nd Battalion, 22nd Marines, coming ashore on Blue 3 as 1st Battalion landed on White 1, while the 3rd was the Regimental Reserve. Tank Company, 22nd Marines, and a platoon of Cannon Company, 106th Infantry, followed. Marine tanks easily knocked out their dug-in Japanese counterparts. By 1030hrs, 2nd Battalion, 22nd Marines had cleared most of the island's west half, much of which was occupied by the airstrip. Resistance continued at "Weasel" and "Newt" points, but they were cleared by 1310hrs. The northeast shore, riddled with Japanese defenses, proved a tougher job, however.

On the right, 1st Battalion quickly split with Company A driving north to "Newt Point" and C toward "Skunk Point" on the southeast corner. The Japanese there attempted to escape north and found themselves in the wide gap between the two assault companies. This allowed them to fire into Company A's flank. Covered by dense brush and palms, the area also had numerous Japanese spider-hole defenses. But by 1450hrs, Brigadier-General Watson could declare the island secure. The assault had been executed so quickly that even the experienced IJA defenders were unable to offer any meaningful organized resistance. By-passed Japanese troops and infiltrators caused difficulties through the night, but mopping-up continued and Engebi was formally secured at 0800hrs on February 19. US losses were 85 dead and missing and 166 wounded.

ENIWETOK ISLAND, FEBRUARY 19–21 (D+2–D+4)

106th RCT was in position off Eniwetok early on the morning of February 19, with an assigned Y-Hour of 0900hrs. New intelligence indicated Eniwetok was more heavily defended than expected so Y-Hour was postponed as the Marine tanks were being transported by LCMs from Engebi 25 miles to the north and were delayed by choppy seas. Arriving just in time the assault commenced with the lead troops coming ashore at 0916hrs.

The beaches were just to the west of the center-point of the island's northwest coast. 3rd Battalion, 106th RCT, hit Yellow 1 with Company L swinging east followed by I, with K pushing across the island to reach the opposite coast at 1030hrs. Part of K also swung wider inland and pushed east. The battalion's job was mainly to screen the east flank while the southwest third of the island was secured. 1st Battalion landed on Yellow 2 to the west of the 3rd. The Japanese battalion commander withdrew half his troops to the southwest end and sent the others to counterattack the 3rd's right flank. The attacks were beaten back by 1245hrs, but American casualties were high.

The 3rd Battalion was ordered ashore to land on Yellow 2 at 1425hrs, and passed through the 1st an hour later. Both battalions would launch an attack toward the southwest end at 1515hrs. The 106th commander ordered that the attack be continued after dark but the attack did not go well for the Marines, who felt night attacks were futile in rugged terrain and would allow many enemy positions to remain undetected. While the Army battalion received adequate illumination from ships in the lagoon, the Marines did not and had no tanks available either. A gap developed between the two battalions and the Marines lagged behind. At 0333hrs, 1st Battalion, 106th RCT, reached the end of the island, but 3rd Battalion, 22nd Marines, was 100 yards to their left rear. The Japanese attempted to probe and infiltrate through the night. The attacks were fought off and the advance to the coast continued.

The 3rd Battalion, 106th RCT, also attempted to continue its attack during the night, but this proved futile as the troops lacked the confidence and experience for such a difficult task. The battalion halted at 0430hrs, about a third of the way from the island's north end. The attack was renewed at 0700hrs on February 21. Resistance dwindled as the advance continued and the north end was reached at 1630hrs. The island was declared secure at 1721hrs. Army and Marine losses were 37 killed in action and missing, and 94 wounded in action.

While the fight for Eniwetok was under way Amphibious Reconnaissance Company, VAC, occupied Japtan at 1800hrs on February 19 after first securing ten unoccupied islets on the atoll's eastern rim.

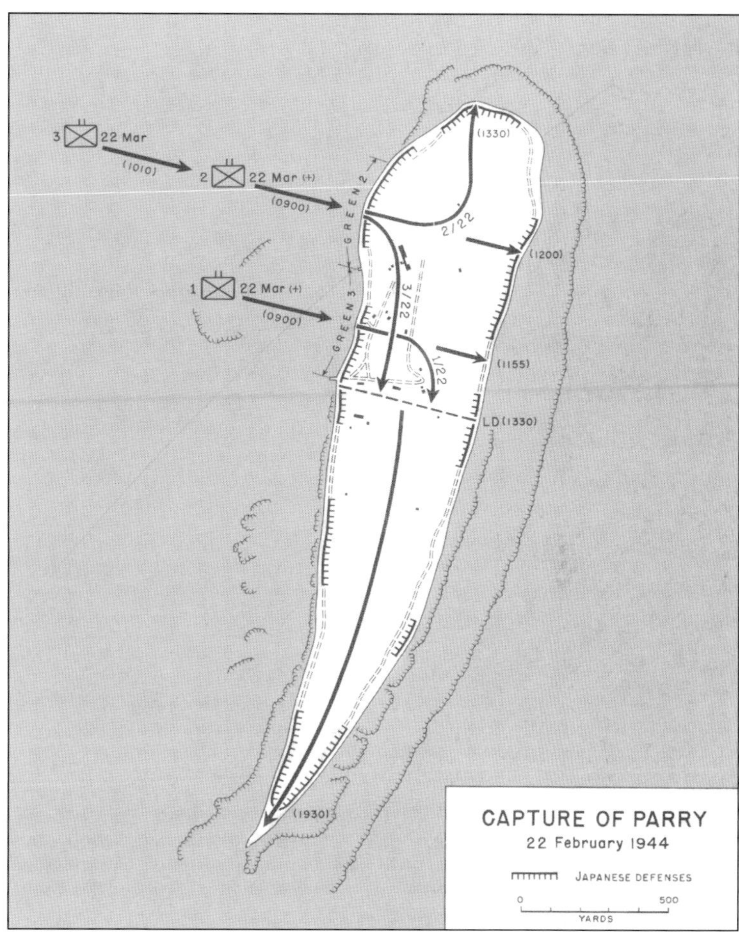

An original US military map showing the capture of Parry Island.

PARRY ISLAND, FEBRUARY 22–23 (D+5–D+6)

Brigadier-General Watson tentatively planned the Parry assault for February 21, to be carried out by the battalions that had seized Engebi. They reported their readiness in the afternoon of the 20th. Because action was bogged down on Eniwetok, the assault was postponed until the 22nd. Up to this point the 22nd Marines had lost 380 troops, but was still capable of attacking heavily defended Parry. In light of the resistance encountered on the other islands the naval and artillery bombardment plan was increased in weight. Z-Hour was set for 0900hrs, February 22.

The field artillery battalions began shelling at 0600hrs. 2nd Battalion, 22nd Marines landed at 0900hrs on Green 2 near Parry's northwest corner, but 200 yards farther south than intended, with part of the battalion landing on about two-thirds of Green 3 to the south. Mines were encountered on the beach, causing some casualties. In the line were, from left to right, companies G, F, and E. Companies G and F swung left to reach the north end by 1330hrs while Company E drove straight across to reach the ocean shore by 1200hrs. While the troops were consolidating after the landing, a group of 150–200 Japanese were discovered marching north and were wiped out in minutes.

These Marines are photographed resting after a weary battle to conquer Eniwetok Atoll in the Marshall Islands. (Bettmann/Corbis)

The 1st Battalion, 22nd Marines, also landed at 0900hrs on Green 1 just north of the island's central portion. It was 200 yards too far south, only landing on the extreme south edge of its assigned beach. Marine medium tanks soon came ashore and it was at this point that three dug-in Japanese light tanks behind Green 1 decided to attack, rather than earlier when the infantry were vulnerable. The Shermans immediately destroyed them before they inflicted any damage.

The attack south was launched at 1330hrs, after a short artillery barrage. Progress was rapid even though numerous spider-holes were encountered. The battalions were 450 yards from the island's southern tip when they halted for the night. Regardless, the regimental commander radioed Brigadier-General Walker, "I present you with the island of Parry at 19.30."

AFTERMATH

In the early morning hours of February 12 six four-engined H8K "Emily" flying boats raided Roi, bombing the huge Marine and Navy ammunition, fuel, and supply dump that had been established in the island's center. Some 85 percent of the supplies and 35 percent of the equipment were destroyed, 30 men killed, and 300 wounded, mostly Seabees. Despite the occupation of Kwajalein, Majuro, and Eniwetok Atolls, Operation *Flintlock* was not yet over. The 22nd Marines, operating from Kwajalein, conducted Operation *Flintlock, Jr* between March 7 and April 5, 1944. Its goal was to destroy any remaining Japanese elements, installations, and materiel in the Lesser Marshalls and inform native inhabitants that the US was in control while establishing good relations with them. The 22nd Marines secured 14 mostly unoccupied atolls and islands with a total of 29 landings, resulting in almost 100 Japanese killed and a few captured. Only two Marines were killed.

The Japanese still held out on Mille, Maloelap, Jaluit, and Wotje Atolls and Kusaie, Wake, and Nauru Islands. Rear-Admiral Masuda Nisuka commanded the 13,000 personnel from Jaluit. Beginning on March 4, the 4th Marine Base Defense Aircraft Wing, headquartered on Majuro, and 7th Air Force commenced a concerted campaign to neutralize the Japanese garrisons, which continued until the war's end. Navy Aviation and Army Air Forces had previously destroyed most Japanese aircraft on these islands. The 13,000 tons of aerial-delivered ordnance, coupled with frequent naval shelling, killed 2,564 Japanese and 4,876 died of disease and starvation. The remaining

Japanese survivors would finally surrender on September 2, 1945.

The capture of the Marshall Islands would mean that numerous airfields, as well as seaplane bases, submarine bases, and fleet anchorages could be established to support later operations in the Pacific Theater. Without these resources, the US would have struggled to secure victory in the later, more difficult campaigns. Operation *Flintlock* was also particularly important because it illustrated that the many hard lessons learned at Tarawa had been successfully implemented. While there were instances of confusion and misunderstood orders, overall the multiple landing operations went very well and in many ways set the standard for future operations.

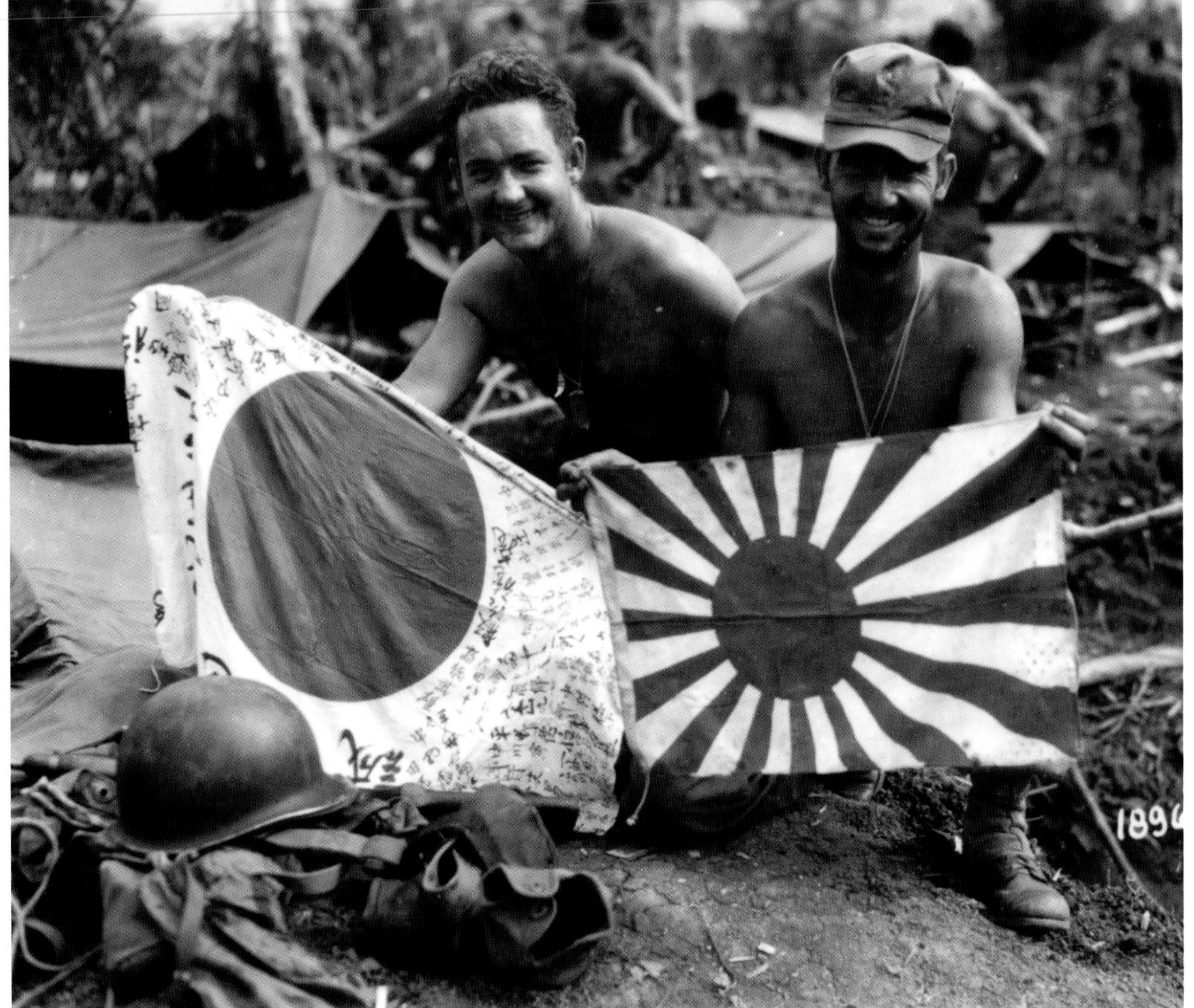

US Marines showing off trophies taken during the island hopping campaign. (Tom Laemlein)

3. That the invasion of Leyte be undertaken at the earliest possible date.

Nimitz reacted quickly to Halsey's suggestions and in turn sent his own communiqué to the Joint Chiefs of Staff. The resulting decision, made on September 14, the day before D-Day on Peleliu, was to speed up the landings on Leyte by two months. Points 1 and 2 of Halsey's recommendations were, however, ignored: a decision that would cost the 1st Marine Division and the 81st Infantry Division over 9,500 casualties.

Nimitz never fully explained his decision to overrule Halsey, saying only that the invasion forces were already at sea, that the commitment had already been made and that it was too late to call off the invasion. The Palau Islands had excellent airfields from which the Japanese could coordinate air attacks against the Philippine invasion force. Also, there were several thousand first-rate troops who could be sent to reinforce the Philippine garrison. Both factors, Halsey insisted, could be dealt with by the use of air strikes and naval bombardments, without having to commit ground troops, but Nimitz overruled him.

For the Japanese the Palau Islands were already part of the "National Defense Zone" to be defended at all costs. Premier Togo had instructed Lieutenant-General Sadao Inoue's 14th Division to be transferred from Manchuria to the Palau Islands in anticipation of the Allied invasion. The Palau Islands formed part of the Japanese Mandated Territory (which included Marshall, Mariana, and Caroline Islands) seized during World War I. Before the arrival of Lieutenant-General Inoue and his forces, the Palau Islands were defended by troops under the command of Major-General Yamaguchi. Yamaguchi's troops would bolster Inoue's forces for the defense of the Palaus.

The Japanese, after detailed surveys, correctly assumed that the Allies would probably assault from the south, with landings on Peleliu (for the airstrip) and Angaur, and then make their way up the Palaus chain, heading for Koror and Babelthuap.

So, the stage was set for one of the most controversial campaigns of the Pacific War and one of the bloodiest battles in US Marine Corps history.

OPPOSING PLANS

THE US PLAN – *STALEMATE II*

The assault plans were greatly revised following key intelligence reports from reconnaissance from US submarines and an underwater demolition team (UDT) of frogmen. It was realized that the island of Babelthuap was both heavily garrisoned and unsuitable for the construction of large air facilities so there was no justification for an invasion. This was in contrast to Peleliu which already had an excellent operational airfield and there was space on Anguar for further facilities. Following the fall of the island of Saipan in July 1944 several key intelligence reports on troop strength of the Peleliu and Anguar garrisons were also seized. As a result of all these reports a revised plan under the codename of Operation *Stalemate II* was agreed upon with D-Day set for September 15.

Operation *Stalemate II* called for the island of Peleliu to be assaulted by 1st Marine Division and the Angaur landings to be undertaken by the 81st Infantry Division. The floating reserve would be the 77th Infantry

Division, with the 5th Marine Division in support. The second phase of *Stalemate II* required XXIV Corps to assault the islands of Yap and Ulithi to the northeast of the Palaus on October 8.

To support Phases I and II, the 3rd Fleet (Western Pacific Task Force) split its forces. The Covering Forces and Special Groups (TF-30) were retained directly under Halsey's control. The Third Amphibious Force (TF-31) was divided into the Western Attack Force (TF-32) for Peleliu and Angaur under Rear-Admiral George H. Fort and the Eastern Attack Force (TF-33) for Yap and Ulithi under Vice-Admiral Theodore S. Wilkinson, the commander of the Third Amphibious Force. TF-32 itself was split into the Peleliu Attack Group (TG-32.1) with the 1st Marine Division directly under Admiral Fort and the Angaur Attack Group (TG-32.2) with the 81st Infantry Division under Rear-Admiral William H. P. Blandly. The Western Fire Support Group under Rear-Admiral Jesse B. Oldendorf consisted of five battleships, five heavy, and three light cruisers, and 14 destroyers. Eleven escort carriers of Escort Carrier Group under Rear-Admiral Ralph A. Ofstie provided close air support, combat air patrols, and anti-submarine patrols, although some were detached during the operation reducing the force to seven.

The initial assault on the designated beaches (codenamed "White" and "Orange") called for the three regimental combat teams, the 1st, 5th, and 7th Marines, to land abreast on 2,200-yard wide beachhead, each with one of their three battalions as regimental and divisional reserve. The 1st Marines would land on the left flank on White Beach 1 and 2 and push inland to a pre-determined point, then wheel left to attack the southwest end of the Umurbrogol Mountains, which extended up the

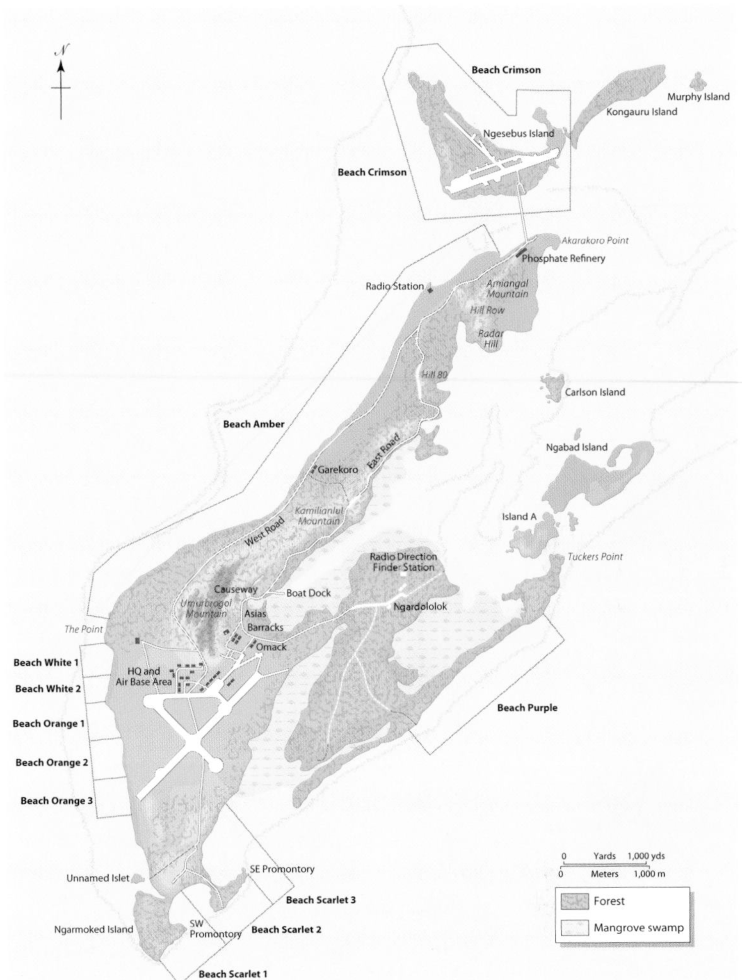

A map showing Peleliu Island which the US Marines attacked in September 1944 as part of Operation *Stalemate II*. (Osprey Publishing Ltd.)

northeast peninsula. The 1st Marines would then push northeast to the northern tip of Peleliu and on to Ngesebus Island, supported by the 5th Marines on their right flank.

In the center, the 5th Marines would land two battalions; one each on Orange Beach 1 and 2. The battalion on the left would link up with the 1st Marines, the other would drive straight across the airfield to the eastern shore. The 3rd Battalion, the regimental reserve, would land at H+1 (1 hour after the initial landing), pass between the other two battalions, and then participate in the movement northward.

Men of the 1st Marine Division practice boarding and debarking from DUKWs, amphibious 2.5 ton trucks, used by the Marines for the first time on Peleliu. However, DUKWs carrying artillery and ammunition following the assault waves were destroyed because of their lack of armor.

The 7th Marines, on the right flank, would land two battalions in column on Beach Orange 3. The two battalions were to drive across to the eastern shore on the flank of the 5th Marines, then wheel right and mop up the isolated enemy forces in a drive to the southeastern tip of the island. The 11th Marines together with artillery support from III Amphibious Corps (IIIAC) would provide direct fire support in the subsequent days.

The 81st Infantry Division was allocated to assault the island of Angaur, but only when the assault on Peleliu was considered "well in hand." Angaur would be assaulted by two of the 81st Infantry Division's three regimental combat teams (RCTs), the third being detached to seize Ulithi. The date for the invasion of Angaur would be set by the 1st Marine Division commander, Major-General William Rupertus.

Landings would be made on two of Angaur's beaches simultaneously. The 322nd RCT would land on the northern Beach Red, then it would push inland, moving south and west across the island with its left flank tying in with the other assault combat team, the 321st RCT. Landing on the eastern Beach Blue, the 321st RCT would move inland west and south across the island, with its right flank tying in with the 322nd RCT's left until the island was secure.

THE JAPANESE PLAN – DEFENSE OF THE PALAUS

The 14th Division, under Lieutenant-General Inoue, established his headquarters on Koror Island and deployed units to garrison Babelthuap, Peleliu, and Angaur, which he considered likely targets for invasion by the Americans. For the defense of Peleliu, Colonel Kunio Nakagawa had split the island into four defense districts. The North District was defended by the 346th Independent Infantry Battalion, 53rd Independent Mixed Brigade (IMB); South District by the 3rd Battalion, 15th Infantry; East District by the 3rd Battalion, 2nd Infantry; and finally the West District by the 2nd Battalion, 2nd Infantry. The 1st Battalion, 2nd Infantry, the 14th Division Tank Unit, and Engineer Company served as the Peleliu Sector Unit Reserve.

In addition there were to be support units of artillery, tanks, and engineers. The Japanese planned for both defense of the beaches as well as a defense in depth, following along the lines set out by Koror headquarters in its "Palau District Group Training for Victory" order of July 11, 1944, which stated: "... we must recognize the limits of naval and aerial bombardment. Every soldier and civilian employee will remain unmoved by this, must strengthen his spirits even while advancing by utilizing lulls in enemy bombardment and taking advantage of the terrain according to necessity." This Nakagawa would do to great effect, taking full advantage of the numerous coral caves and sinkholes, particularly in the area of the Umurbrogol Mountains. There were to be no mass suicidal banzai charges, but instead a long drawn-out battle of attrition, intended to bleed the Americans white. Peleliu would be the first occasion on which American troops encountered these tactics, but they would meet them again in the future on Iwo Jima and Okinawa.

The Americans anticipated that the operations on Peleliu and Angaur would be over within one week, Major-General Rupertus declaring: "It will be a short operation, a hard-fought 'quickie' that will last four days, five at the most, and may result in a considerable number of casualties. You can be sure, however that the 1st [Marine] Division will conquer Peleliu." Rupertus was right about the "considerable casualties," but the 1st Marine Division would not take Peleliu alone, and it would be months, not days, before Peleliu was conquered.

OPPOSING COMMANDERS

THE US COMMANDERS

Although in overall command of *Stalemate II*, the naval commanders of Third Amphibious Force had little input in the planning of the invasion of the Palaus and released control of the tactical situation once the ground troops had landed.

Major-General Roy S. Geiger, commanding officer of IIIAC, was still battling away on Guam while much of the initial planning was conducted but would return in time for the actual landings. But it was Major-General William H. Rupertus, USMC – Commanding General, 1st Marine Division – who was in command of the assault troops on Peleliu. Rupertus had lost his wife, daughter, and son in an epidemic while based in China before the war. This had a profound effect on him personally and left him with bouts of depression, which had a serious effect on his relationships with subordinates, as would become apparent during the battle for Peleliu. He also had an obvious mistrust of the Army, common among Marine officers, and had also broken his ankle during the practice Guadalcanal landings. If Geiger had been aware of his injuries he might well have replaced him.

At regimental level, it is probably difficult to find a more distinguished group of commanders in the US Marine Corps. Colonel Lewis B. "Chesty" Puller was commander of the 1st Marines. Puller's idea of a commander was

BELOW, LEFT TO RIGHT
Colonel Puller (left), commander of the 1st Marines. He had served in the Caribbean, Haiti, Nicaragua, and China before the war. His versatility and leadership in New Britain earned him the promotion to command the 1st Marines by February 1944.

Colonel Harris (center), commander of the 5th Marines, seen here on Peleliu conferring with Major-General Geiger and William H. Rupertus prior to 5th Marines operations in northern Peleliu.

Colonel Hanneken, commander of the 7th Marines. Hanneken had served as chief of staff and assistant Division commander, 1st Marine Division, prior to being given command of the 7th Marines in February 1944.

one who leads from the front and by 1944 his leadership had become legendary and his command of the 1st Battalion, 7th Marines, on Guadalcanal, won him his third Navy Cross. Colonel Herman H. "Hard Headed" Hanneken, commander of the 7th Marines, was like Puller a veteran of the pre-World War II Haitian and Nicaraguan campaigns, where he had won the Medal of Honor. He had a well-earned reputation as a tough and fearless commander. Colonel Harold "Bucky" D. Harris, commander of the 5th Marines, was the youngest of the three regimental commanders and the only one not to have served as an enlisted Marine having been transferred from an intelligence officer position. Although Harris was new to the 5th Marines and to commanding troops in combat, the regiment would perform extremely well under his command.

Major-General Paul J. Mueller, US Army, was the commanding general of 81st Infantry Division. Mueller had fought as a battalion commander in World War I and had held numerous staff assignments between the wars.

Lieutenant-Colonel Kunio Nakagawa, Commander of the 2nd Infantry Regiment (Reinforced), appointed to the defense of Peleliu and Angaur. A most able tactician, as he was to prove on Peleliu, he probably ranked with General Kuribayashi, the defender of Iwo Jima, as one of Japan's most talented tacticians.

THE JAPANESE COMMANDERS

Lieutenant-General Sadao Inoue, Imperial Japanese Army (IJA), commander of the 14th Division was Prime Minister Tojo's choice to command the 12,000 reinforcements headed for the Palaus. Inoue took command of all the Japanese forces on the islands and doubled as Commander, Palau District Group. He was fiercely dedicated to his heritage of five generations of military ancestors.

Upon his arrival on Koror, where he established his headquarters, Inoue appointed Colonel Kunio Nakagawa as Peleliu's new commander, with his 2nd Infantry (Reinforced). Colonel Nakagawa (IJA), commander of the 2nd Infantry and Peleliu Sector Unit, was a highly able commander who would make full use of all his defenses and troops on Peleliu, making the Americans pay dearly for every inch, as he had been ordered to do. However, in his new position he outranked the original Peleliu commander, Vice-Admiral Yoshioka Ito. The appointment of an Army colonel over a Navy vice-admiral caused a great rift between the rival forces, which deteriorated into farce. To resolve matters Lieutenant-General Inoue sent Major-General Kenjiro Murai from his headquarters on Koror Island to Peleliu to provide the Army with sufficient rank to satisfy the vice-admiral's honor, although the defense of Peleliu seems, to practical purposes, to have remained in the hands of Colonel Nakagawa.

There is evidence suggesting a rift between Major-General Murai and Colonel Nakagawa toward the end of the battle for Peleliu with Murai supporting a final glorious charge and Nakagawa preferring the original defensive attrition policy. Inoue supported Nakagawa stating to Murai: "it is easy to die but difficult to live on. We must select the difficult course and continue to fight because of the influence on the morale of the Japanese people. Saipan was lost in a very short time because of vain banzai attacks with the result that the people at home suffered a drop in morale." Major-General Murai accepted Inoue's counsel and no banzai charge occurred; instead he continued the defensive fight to the end, alongside Nakagawa.

OPPOSING FORCES

THE US FORCES

Pre-invasion bombardment would be provided by the 14in guns of five battleships with support from eight heavy and light cruisers. In addition, aircraft from three fleet carriers, five light carriers, and 11 escort carriers would assist in the "softening up" of Peleliu to commence on D–3 (September 12) and continue up until D-Day itself.

The 1st Marine Division had been raised in February 1941 and the "Old Breed" had seen extensive service in Guadalcanal and New Britain. The division had received 4,860 much needed replacements by June. The 1st Tank Battalion had recently received 75mm M4A2 Shermans. There were also three amphibian tractor battalions to support the assault which had some of the new model 75mm howitzer-armed LVT(A)4s. Rifle company machine gun platoons were equipped with flamethrowers and demolition kits as well as bazookas to attack pillboxes and caves.

The 81st Infantry Division had been reactivated (it had originally served in World War I) in June 1942. The new division was raised from a small regular army cadre and supplemented with newly commissioned reserve officers and conscripted troops. The division had undergone jungle training so although the troops were acclimatized and had undertaken training in rugged terrain with limited visibility, little had been done to prepare them specifically for *Stalemate II*. Angaur was to be its first combat action. The attached 710th Tank Battalion had M4A1 Sherman tanks as well as some M10 tank destroyers, which were invaluable for blasting out caves. The Army's amphibian tractor battalions, like the Marines, were equipped with LVT(2) and LVT(4) amtracs.

Calisthenics before breakfast. Men of the 1st Marine Division exercising on Pavuvu prior to debarkation for Peleliu, in an effort to bring their physical fitness up to scratch.

Assault troops for Operation *Stalemate II* numbered approximately 2,647 officers and 44,914 enlisted men, of whom 1,438 officers and 24,979 enlisted were Marines.

THE JAPANESE FORCES

The 14th Division under Lieutenant-General Inoue arrived in the Palaus from Manchuria via Saipan in April 1944. The division had been raised in 1905 and served in the Russo-Japanese War, the Siberian Expedition, and the Manchurian Incident. Between 1932 and 1944 it served three tours in China and Manchuria. The regiments of the 14th were equipped with a variety of defensive weapons including anti-tank guns and artillery including 18 75mm guns allocated to defend areas as necessary. There were also six flamethrowers and nine light tanks attached to the "heavy" 2nd Infantry regiment.

Lieutenant-General Inoue also assumed command of the 53rd IMB and other Imperial Japanese Army elements in the Palaus (6,500 men under the command of Colonel Nakagawa). He had already determined that Peleliu, Ngesebus, and Angaur in the south of the Palaus chain would be the first of the islands to be assaulted by the Allies and as such would form the mainstay of his defense.

The 3,800-man 53rd IMB was commanded by Major-General Takso Yamaguchi and was mostly concentrated on Koror. Yap Island was defended by 4,000 troops of the 49th IMB, 3,000 Imperial Japanese Navy (IJN) personnel of the 46th Base Force, and 1,000 laborers. Ulithi Atoll had already been abandoned by the Japanese several months before the US landing. Other IJA combat units on Peleliu included a light anti-aircraft unit and several mortar companies.

IJN forces in the Palaus were under the command of Vice-Admiral Yoshioka Ito. The IJN had by 1944 constructed numerous reinforced concrete blockhouses and bunkers and dug an extensive tunnel system near the end of the northeast peninsula as well as taking full advantage of Peleliu's natural caves. This elaborate, multi-level tunnel system could shelter 1,000 troops. Guard forces manned eight 120mm dual-purpose, and about three 200mm coast defense guns. Some aircraft units manned around 30 twin-barreled 25mm automatic guns and at least a dozen 20mm cannons were recovered from destroyed aircraft and set up on make-shift mounts to protect the airfields. In all there were approximately 4,000 IJN personnel on Peleliu.

Angaur was defended by the 1st Battalion, 59th Infantry (Reinforced), detached from the 14th Division and dubbed the Angaur Sector Unit, under the command of Major Ushio Goto. It mustered approximately 1,400 officers and enlisted men. The battalion was reinforced with a few IJN-manned 80mm coast defense guns, a 75mm mountain gun battery, a 20mm machine cannon company, 37mm and 47mm anti-tank gun platoons as well as some mortar platoons.

Estimates vary, but there were approximately 21,000 IJA, 7,000 IJN, and 10,000 laborers in the Palau Islands.

THE PELELIU ASSAULT

D-DAY

After an uneventful 2,100-mile voyage from their practice landings on Guadalcanal, men of the 1st Marine Division and the 81st Infantry Division prepared for battle. They climbed into LCVPs and LVTs, better known as amphibian tractors or "amtracs."

At 0530hrs naval support ships had begun the pre-landing bombardment of the beaches from a range of 1,000 yards. This lifted at 0750hrs to make way for carrier-borne aircraft to strafe the beaches in front of the first landing waves, while the naval bombardment moved to targets inland. The plan called for the first assault waves to be in LVTs. Subsequent support waves would transfer at the reef's edge from LCVPs to amtracs, returning from the beaches. Essentially it was the same plan as used at Tarawa in 1943 but this time with the support of armored LVTs with 75mm howitzers to provide suppressing fire. Preceding the first assault waves were 18 landing craft, infantry (gun) (LCI(G)) equipped with 4.5in rocket launchers.

However, as the LVTs crossed the line of departure and raced for the beaches, it soon became apparent that there were still plenty of live Japanese on Peleliu. Artillery and mortar fire began to fall among the amtracs – 26 were destroyed on D-Day. The first Marines to hit the beaches were men of the 3rd Battalion, 1st Marines. They landed on Beach White 1 at 0832hrs, just two minutes behind schedule, and within the next four minutes there were Marines on all five landing beaches. On Beach White the 1st Marines landed as planned, with the 2nd Battalion on the right and the 3rd on the left, with the 1st Battalion scheduled to land at approximately 0945hrs as regimental reserve.

LVT(A)4s plow toward the Peleliu landing beaches on D-Day, as the massive naval and aerial bombardment continued. Admiral Oldendorf claimed to have run out of targets for his pre-invasion bombardment and sent numerous vessels on to support the invasion of the Philippines. His opinion of the effects of his bombardment proved sadly exaggerated.

On White 2, the 2nd Battalion landed successfully and proceeded to push inland against moderate Japanese defenses. They advanced, supported by some of the armored LVTs until their M4A2 Sherman tanks could get ashore, to reach a line approximately 350 yards inland through heavy woods by 0930hrs. Here the battalion halted, at the far side of the woods and facing the airfield and buildings area. Tying in with the 5th Marines on their right flank, they held pending a solution to the problems the 3rd Battalion were facing.

As soon as the 3rd Battalion hit Beach White 1, they faced stubborn and violent opposition from strongly emplaced Japanese small arms fire to their immediate front, as well as from artillery and mortar fire that was blanketing the whole beach area. To make matters worse, no sooner had the lead elements landed and advanced less than 100 yards inland, than they found themselves confronted by a most formidable natural obstacle, a rugged coral ridge, some 30ft high. This had not shown up on any maps. Worse, the face of this ridge (christened “the Point” by the Marines) was honeycombed with caves and firing positions which the Japanese had blasted into the coral, and resisted all initial assaults. Even the tanks once they arrived stumbled into a wide, deep anti-tank ditch, dominated by the ridge itself.

All efforts failed to close the gap which had developed on the left. Late in the afternoon, a foothold was gained on the southern area of the Point, which improved the situation somewhat. But there was still great cause for concern, compounded by the fact that five LVTs carrying the 1st Marines command group had been badly hit whilst crossing the reef, with resultant loss of communications equipment and operators. Only much later in the day did divisional command become fully aware of the precariousness of the 1st Marines’ position.

After more than eight hours of possibly the most fierce fighting of the Pacific War so far, two gaps in the 1st Marines’ lines were so

Marines hit the beach at Peleliu only to face stronger enemy forces than anticipated. (Bettmann/Corbis)

serious as to endanger the entire division's position on D-Day. All possible reserves were committed, including headquarters personnel and at least 100 men from the 1st Engineer Battalion. Together they formed a defense in depth against the threat of a Japanese counterattack. Fortunately for the Marines, no such counterattack occurred.

It became apparent to the Marines that the Point was unassailable from the front and so eventually units fought inland and assaulted it from the rear. These units, commanded by Captain George P. Hunt, fought their way along the Point for nearly two hours, during which time they succeeded in neutralizing all of the enemy infantry protecting the major defensive blockhouses and pill boxes. Captain Hunt and his surviving 30 or so men would remain isolated for the next 30 hours, all the time under attack from Japanese infiltrators trying to take advantage of the gap in Company K's lines. When relieved, Hunt only had 18 men standing to defend the Point.

The 5th Marines fared a little better. The 1st Battalion landed on Orange 1 and the 3rd on Orange 2. On both beaches they met only scattered resistance, and little more as they moved inland. Instead of the unmapped coral ridges faced by the 1st Marines, the 1st Battalion, 5th Marines, advanced through coconut groves which afforded ample cover, reaching their first objective line and tying in with the 2nd Battalion, 1st Marines, on the left by 0930hrs in front of the airfield. Here, the battalion halted. This was partly because of the lack of progress by the 1st Marines on the extreme left against the Point, and also due to the murderous Japanese artillery and mortar fire which was sweeping the airfield and open ground to their immediate front.

On Orange 2, the 3rd Battalion, 5th Marines, did not fare as well as their counterparts in the

1st Battalion had on Orange 1. The LVT carrying most of the battalion's communications equipment and personnel was also destroyed on the reef. According to plan, Company I landed on the left and Company K on the right, with Company L landing shortly afterward as battalion reserve. On the left, all went comparatively well with Company I making contact with the 1st Battalion, 5th Marines, and advancing inland along with them.

On the right however, Company K ran into difficulties when elements of the 7th Marines landed on Beach Orange 2 instead of landing on their intended beach of Orange 3, the confusion delaying Company K's advance. They did not draw abreast of Company I until 1000hrs. The 3rd Battalion's situation deteriorated somewhat after the advance inland was resumed as companies K and I lost contact in the dense scrubland. By the afternoon, the regimental reserve, 2nd Battalion, 5th Marines, had landed to relieve Company I although the poor mapping of the area continued to add to the confusion. More bad luck befell the 3rd Battalion when, at about 1700hrs, a Japanese mortar barrage struck the command post. Colonel Shofner and several other members of the command staff were wounded and had to be evacuated, which severely disrupted the effectiveness of the 3rd Battalion as a unit for the rest of the day.

On the extreme right the 7th Marines were to land on Beach Orange 3. The 3rd Battalion landed first, followed by the 1st, the latter encountering difficulties as the reef was cluttered with natural and man-made obstacles. The slow progress of the amtracs meant they came under considerable fire. This caused many amtrac drivers to veer off to the left, resulting in their landing on Orange 2 instead of Orange 3. Much valuable time was lost in getting the 7th Marines back on course. But by mid-morning there was an unexpected coincidence: the flank battalions of the two assaulting regiments in the center and right were both the 3rd Battalions from the 5th and 7th Marines, with both containing companies I, K, and L. The confusion resulted in a gap between the two regiments as the 3rd Battalion, 7th Marines, paused to take stock of the situation, whereas 3rd Battalion, 5th Marines, was actually pushing ahead.

In the meantime, 1st Battalion, 7th Marines, had landed as planned on Orange 3 at 1030hrs with slightly more success than the 3rd, although some elements still ended up on Orange 2. As the Battalion reeled right as planned, they faced a dense swamp, not shown on any map, which was heavily defended. It took considerable time to work around the swamp and it was not until 1520hrs that Colonel Gormley was able to confirm that he had reached his objective line.

The lack of progress on the right worried General Rupertus and his concern over the loss of momentum resulted in his first committing the divisional reconnaissance company ashore and later still attempting to commit the divisional

NEXT SPREAD
This shattered Japanese plane, its tail assembly and wings torn off and even its "Red Ball" insignia punctured by shells, was found by US Marines when they captured Peleliu airfield. (Topfoto)

BELOW
On the heels of a terrific air-sea bombardment, assault troops of the 1st Marine Division storm ashore on Peleliu Island. Their amphibious tractors rest in the shallow water behind them while the vast invasion armada stretches far out on the horizon. (Bettmann/Corbis)

"It will be a short operation, a hard-fought 'quickie' that will last four days, five at the most, and may result in a considerable number of casualties. You can be sure, however that the 1st [Marine] Division will conquer Peleliu."

— **MAJOR-GENERAL WILLIAM RUPERTUS**

reserve. Gains for the Marines on D-Day were disappointing compared to the optimistic predictions. The 1st and 5th Marines had fallen short of their targets and the 7th Marines were the only ones to make any reasonable progress inland. The gap that remained in the middle of the 3rd Battalion, 5th Marines, on the left posed a threat to the entire south-facing line.

A Japanese tank stopped by mortar and bazooka fire on Peleliu. During the Japanese counterattack it became apparant that their tanks were no match for the Marine artillery, anti-tank guns, and Shermans. (Tom Laemlein)

One major Japanese counterattack occurred at around 1650hrs on D-Day, consisting of a tank and infantry sortie in force across the northern portion of the airfield. This attack had been expected by the Marines and accordingly the regimental commanders had brought up artillery and heavy machine guns as well as tanks to support that area. Thanks to poor tactics by the Japanese tank drivers the attackers were subjected to murderous flanking fire and the attack faltered.

Several smaller counterattacks occurred up and down the line during the afternoon and night of D-Day, none of which amounted to much. One thing was noted by the Marines with regard to the Japanese counterattacks and that was the fact that these were coordinated and disciplined attacks, rather than the frenzied banzai suicide charges experienced before. This was the first indication that something different was in store for the attacking Marines on Peleliu.

D+1 TO D+7

Major-General Rupertus and his staff landed on D+1 at 0950hrs and assumed direction of operations, taking over the command post that had set up in the large anti-tank ditch just inland of Beach Orange 2 on D-Day. As the area was still under Japanese fire from time to time, this was a somewhat uncomfortable position for Rupertus, particularly as his leg and broken ankle were still in a plaster cast. Plans were drawn up, based on the original battle plan for the advance across the island, in spite of the fact that the D-Day objectives had not been achieved.

The 1st Battalion, 7th Marines, attacked southward. Most of the Japanese defenses in this area faced seaward in the anticipation of this area being part of possible landings and, as such, 1st Battalion were assaulting these defenses from their less protected flanks and rear. Nevertheless, the area was still honeycombed with casemates, blockhouses, bunkers, and pillboxes, all mutually supporting. The going was grim and deadly. The southern shore was finally reached around 1025hrs.

One other factor hampering the Marines' progress was the temperature on Peleliu. During the day, it was over 100°F and the strains of protracted fighting and dehydration were beginning to tell. The advance was halted around 1200hrs until water and fresh supplies could be brought up. The rest of D+1 was spent bringing up supplies, together with tanks which assisted in reducing the remaining Japanese defenses.

D+2 saw the 7th Marines pushing further south, assaulting the southeast and southwest promontories of the southern shore. The entire southeast promontory was taken by 1320hrs. The southwestern promontory, much larger than the southeastern promontory, was the target of 1st Battalion. With the assistance of some tanks this too was finally in Marine hands by nightfall.

During the night of D+2/D+3, additional armor was brought up and at 1000hrs of D+3 the advance was resumed. Again progress was painfully slow with many reserve elements being attacked by Japanese from bypassed caves and underground emplacements. With the taking of the two promontories, the southern part of Peleliu was secured. Headquarters reported "1520 hours D+3, 7th Marines mission on Peleliu completed." Unfortunately, this was not quite the case.

While the 7th Marines were successfully securing the south, the 5th Marines in the center prepared to expand on their gains of D-Day, battling against heavy resistance and mangrove swamp conditions. By D+2 the 5th Marines were continuing to advance to the northeast, but they began to come under flanking fire from Japanese positions on the high ground to the front of the 1st Marines. The 1st Battalion, 5th Marines, reached its objectives by mid-morning of D+2 where it held until relieved by the 3rd. But when the 3rd Battalion tried to resume the advance in the afternoon it became pinned down from heavy flanking fire on its left. On the right, the 2nd Battalion had more success being concealed in the woods from Japanese artillery and mortar fire and was able to advance to beyond its objective line, though the heat and terrain began to take their toll on the Marines. By nightfall of D+2 the 2nd Battalion was tied in with the 3rd on the left and the shoreline on the right. D+3 (September 18) saw the 5th Marines making slow but continuous progress and by D+4 the eastern and southern shorelines had been reached and just two days later (D+6) the whole peninsular had been secured.

On D+1 Major-General Rupertus, upon arriving at the beachhead command post, had ordered the 2nd Battalion, 7th Marines (the division reserve) transferred to Puller's hard-pressed 1st Marines in an effort to "maintain momentum." After bitter fighting, Marine infantry supported by tanks captured a 500-yard segment of the ridge and a concerted counterattack by the Japanese on the night of D+1 was beaten off, but the hard fighting had taken a toll. On D+2 elements of the 1st Marines came into contact for the first time with the Umurbrogol Mountains. Aerial photographs did little justice to the real nature of the mountains described later in the 1st Marines regimental narrative thus: "a contorted mass of coral, strewn with rubble crags, ridges and gulches."

Marines on call in fire-support from their position 20 yards from the beach. (Tom Laemlein)

By D+2 the 1st Marines had already suffered over 1,000 casualties and as a result all three battalions were assembled in line on the regimental front, the 3rd on the left flank, the 1st in the center, and the 2nd on the right flank, with the newly arrived 2nd Battalion, 7th Marines, in reserve.

The remnants of Colonel Puller's 1st Marines on their way out of the line having been relieved by elements of the 7th Marines. They were initially told this was only a brief respite for a few days, but it was clear the 1st Marines were a spent force and Major-General Geiger ordered them to return to their base on Pavuvu.

The men of the 2nd Battalion, 1st Marines, scaled the slopes of the first ridge (christened Hill 200) and, after bitter hand-to-hand fighting and many casualties, by nightfall had secured the crest of the hill but immediately came under fire from the next ridge (Hill 210), and thus the pattern was set. In the center, the 1st Battalion progressed well, until confronting a substantial reinforced concrete blockhouse which should have been destroyed by pre-invasion bombardments. On the left the picture was a little brighter as the 3rd Battalion was able to advance along the comparatively flat coastal plain but had to call a halt when it was in danger of losing contact with 1st Battalion, 1st Marines, on its right flank.

By D+3 Puller's 1st Marines had suffered 1,236 casualties yet Puller was still being urged on by Major-General Rupertus to "maintain the momentum" and, as a result, all available reserves including pioneers, engineers, and headquarters personnel were committed as infantrymen. D+3 was a repeat of D+2 and would be repeated day after day. The 2nd Battalion took Hill 210, whilst the Japanese counterattacked Hill 200, forcing the Marines to withdraw. After a harrowing night of counterattacks what was left of the 1st Marines plus the 2nd Battalion, 7th Marines, resumed the attack on D+4 after a naval and artillery barrage. Once again progress was best on the left, the 3rd Battalion, 1st Marines pushing forward but again having to halt. In the center, the reserve battalion slogged from ridge to ridge suffering heavy casualties and the 2nd Battalion, 1st Marines, on the right pushed on over similar terrain against stiff resistance, which got worse with each successive ridge.

Although 2nd Battalion, 1st Marines, did not know it, they were attacking what was to become the final Japanese pocket in the Umurbrogol Mountains. By the end of D+4 the 1st Marines existed in name only, having suffered almost 1,749 casualties – six fewer casualties than the entire 1st Marine Division lost on Guadalcanal. On D+6, after another day of bitter hand-to-hand fighting, Puller was visited by IIIAC commanding general Roy Geiger. Upon his return to division headquarters, after seeing first hand the conditions, Geiger ordered Rupertus to replace the 1st Marines with the 321st RCT of the 81st Infantry Division, now on Angaur, and send Puller and his crippled unit back to Pavuvu. The 1st Marines by this time reported 1,749 casualties. One Marine later described the fighting in the Umurbrogol, which attests to the level to which the 1st Marines had deteriorated:

I picked up the rifle of a dead Marine and I went up the hill; I remember no more than a few yards of scarred hillside, I didn't worry about death anymore, I had resigned from the human race. I crawled and scrambled forward and lay still without any feeling toward any human thing. In the next foxhole was a rifleman. He peered at me through red and painful eyes. I didn't care about him and he didn't care about me. As a fighting unit, the 1st Marines was finished. We were no longer human beings, I fired at anything that moved in front of me, friend or foe. I had no friends, I just wanted to kill.

SIDESHOWS ON ANGAUR AND ULITHI

The IIIAC Reserve for Operation *Stalemate II* was the 81st Infantry Division, to be used as necessary and then to assault Angaur with two of its three RCTs but only when the situation was "well in hand" on Peleliu.

On September 16 (D+1) 1st Marine Division commander Major-General Rupertus gave the assurance that "Peleliu would be secured in a few more days" and so, on Rupertus' report, Lieutenant-General Geiger issued orders for the assault on Angaur to proceed. F-Day, the Angaur assault, was set for September 17 (D+2 on Peleliu).

Angaur Island lies seven miles southwest of Peleliu. Here Major Ushio Goto of the 1st Battalion, 59th Infantry (Reinforced) detached from the 14th Division, would make his last stand with some 1,400 troops. He had divided the island into four defense sectors and a small central reserve. Major Goto had

Protestant Chaplain Rufus W. Oakley holding services within a few hundred yards of Japanese positions on Peleliu, well within range of their mortars if they had chosen to throw them. (Topfoto)

expected the Americans to land on the superb beaches on the southeast of the island, codenamed Beaches Green 1 and 2 by the Americans; and therefore constructed his most formidable coastal defenses of steel-reinforced concrete bunkers and blockhouses, numerous anti-boat gun emplacements, machine gun nests, and rifle pits. But American reconnaissance had spotted this and instead the amphibious assault would take place on Beaches Red and Blue.

As planned the 322nd RCT landed on Beach Red on the northeast coast and 321st RCT landed on Beach Blue on the upper southeast. Both RCTs encountered only small-scale resistance during the landings but soon after the push inland they found the dense scrub forests infested with Japanese machine guns and snipers. The advance was slow and costly but by nightfall both RCTs had reached their objective lines.

On the third day (September 19), after a night of many Japanese small-scale counterattacks, 321st RCT pushed on and succeeded in cutting the island in two. The 321st RCT assaulted the Beach Green defenses from inland and with the

Map showing the capture of Angaur. (Osprey Publishing Ltd.)

aid of tanks and support weapons they were able to reduce the fortifications one by one. By the end of the third day, there remained only two areas still in Japanese hands; the biggest and most formidable being in the northeast centered on Romauldo Hill, a series of coral ridges and outcrops even more rugged than, but not as large as, on Peleliu. With the situation reportedly well in hand on Peleliu and Angaur, the IIIAC Reserve, the 81st Infantry Division's third RCT, the 323rd, was sent on to its secondary target of Ulithi Island as planned which was easily seized as it had already been abandoned.

In fact it would take another four weeks of bitter hand-to-hand fighting before Major Goto and his men, well armed with rifles, machine guns, and mortars, and dug well into the mass of caves and tunnels in the Romauldo Hills, were crushed, and then only with the extensive use of flamethrowers, grenades, and demolitions alongside the sheer determination of the Wildcats. October 22 marked the end of formal Japanese resistance. Casualties for the 81st were comparatively light compared to those on Peleliu; 260 killed, 1,354 wounded, and 940 incapacitated for non-combat reasons. The Japanese lost an estimated 1,338 killed and 59 taken prisoner.

"A HORRIBLE PLACE"

The 81st Infantry Division's 321st RCT began arriving from Angaur on September 23 and began to relieve Puller's battered 1st Marines who were initially withdrawn to the south of the island to rest. They attacked the northeastern peninsula on D+11. These had been dubbed Hills 1, 2, and 3, and Radar Hill, known as "Hill Row," and were actually the southern arm of the Amiangal Ridge. They were defended by some 1,500 infantrymen, artillerymen, and naval construction troops plus reinforcements from Koror. As the right progressed the 2nd Battalion, 5th Marines side-stepped to the west and pushed on to the north, leaving the 1st Battalion to continue the assault, and by nightfall had taken the southern end of the final ridge. What the 2nd did not know was that they were facing the most comprehensive cave system on Peleliu which was the underground home of the Japanese naval construction units who were, luckily for the Marines, better miners than infantrymen.

Fighting continued all day D+11 and D+12 with several small-scale counterattacks during the night but by the end of D+12 the 2nd Battalion had secured the northern shore (Akarakoro Point) though if the Marines held the area above ground, the Japanese still held it underground! It would take weeks for the Marines to finally quash all resistance on Akarakoro Point, and then only by blasting closed all the tunnel entrances, sealing the Japanese defenders inside to their fate. After two days of bitter fighting the Marines blasted and burned their way to the tops of Hill Row and by D+14 all but the Umurbrogol Pocket had been taken.

THE POCKET

The assault on the Japanese defenses in the Umurbrogol Pocket now took on the air of a medieval siege. With the attacks from the north by the 321st RCT the encirclement of the Pocket was complete whilst the 7th Marines continued to press from the south and west. The Pocket was now down to 1,000 yards by 500 yards in size, not much bigger than ten football fields.

Major-General Rupertus then made a less than sound decision by ordering the 1st Tank Battalion to return to Pavuvu. Their heavy firepower would be sorely missed in the final days of the campaign. To compound matters, a three-day typhoon also struck, making it impossible to land rations, fuel, or ammunition to the American troops. The bitter fighting continued and by now the 7th Marines had been in the Umurbrogol for two weeks. The 7th Marines landed on D-Day with 3,217 men, of whom 1,486 were now dead, wounded, or missing. They had sustained 46 percent casualties in a little under three weeks of fighting and their four battalions, including the attached 3rd Battalion from the 5th Marines, were now close to company-strength. General Geiger suggested to Major-General Rupertus that he should relieve the 7th Marines. Rupertus turned to his only remaining regiment, the 5th Marines.

With the introduction of the 5th Marines to the assault on the Pocket, Colonel Harris implemented two new "policies," which would remain in place until the end of the fighting. First, the attack on the Pocket would be made exclusively from the north, which offered the best opportunity to chip away at the many ridges one at a time. Second, aerial reconnaissance conducted by Colonel Harris during the first week on Peleliu showed him how formidable the Umurbrogol was. Now stripped of overlaying vegetation the numerous steep ridges, hills, sinkholes, gorges, and caves, to say nothing of the formidable Japanese defenses, became apparent, and it would clearly only be taken using siege tactics.

Tanks and infantry of 81st Infantry Division move into the Horseshoe in the Umurbrogol Pocket. On the left is "Five brothers;" the small pond barely seen above the large sinkhole in the foreground was the only source of fresh water for the Japanese and many were killed attempting to fill canteens under cover of darkness.

He intended to "be lavish with ammunition and stingy with men's lives."

This soon reaped rewards. By D+28 the Pocket had been reduced to an area 800 yards long by 500 yards wide. Nakagawa reported to Koror by radio that he was down to fewer than 700 effective troops. Despite the savagery of the fighting Rupertus still turned down the assistance of the 81st Infantry Division. However, events overtook Rupertus; first the 81st's detached RCT – the 323rd – arrived from Ulithi, then Admiral Wilkinson, the overall commander at Peleliu, was ordered to return to Hawaii and Admiral Fort replaced him. Upon taking command, Admiral Fort sent a communiqué stating that Peleliu had been secured, meaning the airfield was usable, much to the amazement of the men still fighting there, and that the "Assault Phase" of Operation *Stalemate II* was complete. Lieutenant-General Geiger was therefore directed to relieve the 1st Marine Division and turn the islands over to the 81st Infantry Division to mop-up and garrison as originally intended.

In fact it would take the 81st Infantry Division nearly six weeks, using essentially the same siege tactics as the Marines, to reduce the Pocket in painstakingly slow fighting ridge by ridge. On D+70 Colonel Nakagawa sent his final message to his superiors on Koror. He advised them he had burned the 2nd Infantry's colors and had ordered his men to "attack the enemy everywhere." During the night of D+70/71, 25 Japanese were killed attempting infiltrations and, the following morning, a captured soldier confirmed that both Colonel Nakagawa and Major-General Murai had committed ritual suicide in their command post.

Japanese hand-drawn artillery caught in the open on the east–west road have suffered the full wrath of Navy and Marine fighter-bombers. With total air superiority, the American air support made short work of any Japanese caught in the open.

AFTERMATH

With the operation over there was time to reflect on the battle and evaluate the human cost. The Marines lost 1,050 killed in action, 250 died of wounds, 5,450 wounded, and 36 missing. Total casualties by regiment were: 1st Marines – 1,749, 5th Marines – 1,378, and 7th Marines – 1,497. The 81st Infantry Division casualties on Peleliu were 1,393, of whom 208 were killed in action. A further 260 were killed and 1,354 wounded on Angaur. Japanese dead on Peleliu were estimated at 10,900 including those lost at sea in reinforcement attempts and raids. Only 202 prisoners were taken; mostly Korean and Okinawan laborers. Virtually the entire 1,400-man garrison of Angaur was wiped out with only 59 prisoners being taken.

Although the fighting was officially over and Peleliu declared secure, groups and individual Japanese troops still remained in isolated pockets and caves, mainly in the Umurbrogol

"... we must recognize the limits of naval and aerial bombardment. Every soldier and civilian employee will remain unmoved by this, must strengthen his spirits even while advancing by utilizing lulls in enemy bombardment and taking advantage of the terrain according to necessity."

— **JAPANESE ORDER**, JULY 11, 1944

---

mountains. Three months after the fighting in the Umurbrogol Pocket was over, the huge tunnel complex was still occupied by a handful of IJN and IJA troops. After several attempts by the Americans to persuade them to surrender – to no avail – the entrances were blasted closed. To everyone's amazement, in February 1945, five surviving Japanese managed to dig their way out to the surface, only to be captured.

Marine aircraft began arriving soon after D-Day on Peleliu and would eventually be joined by Navy sea search units who would assist in rescue operations for sailors and downed airmen. The Kossol Passage north of Babelthuap remained in use as a fleet anchorage and, in conjunction with Ulithi, supported operations in the Philippines. Angaur was occupied by Navy Seabees, who started work constructing a 7,000ft airfield for the Army Air Forces, even before the island was secured. It was later used by the 494th Heavy Bombardment Group which flew B-24 Liberators in support of US troops fighting in the Philippines. Raids were also flown against Koror and Babelthuap, still occupied by General Inoue.

The 81st Infantry Division remained on Peleliu and Angaur mopping up, clearing the battlefield of months of damaged equipment and materiel and guarding against possible seaborne raids from the north. The 81st departed between December 1944 and February 1945. Both the 81st and the 1st Marine Division would later fight on Okinawa.

Years after the end of the war, rumors persisted on Peleliu about surviving Japanese soldiers still hiding out in the mountains and swamps; eventually 120 Marines were sent to the island to search for survivors who were said to be preparing to attack Navy dependent housing. After several attempts to coax them out failed, a Japanese admiral was brought to Peleliu to convince the survivors that the war was over and it was acceptable to give themselves up with honor. Eventually on April 22, 1947, a lieutenant emerged along with 34 bedraggled soldiers – their battle for Peleliu was finally over. This was the last official surrender of World War II.

Whether Peleliu needed taking or not remains a subject of some deliberation by generals and historians alike, but some facts are clear:

1. MacArthur's flank was secured for his return to the Philippines and the danger of

This Japanese monument remembers the soldiers who fought the Americans in the battle for Peleliu. (Dave G. Houser/Corbis)

Japanese air strikes or troop reinforcements from the Palaus was removed. However, this danger was minimal as all Japanese aircraft in the Palaus had been destroyed and few of the Japanese barges were capable of the 700-mile open-sea trip to the Philippines.

2. Several thousand first-rate Japanese troops had been eliminated and the remaining troops in the Western Carolines could be contained by air and sea operations originating from the new American airbases on Peleliu and Angaur.
3. The change in Japanese tactics served as an early warning to the Allies of what to expect in the forthcoming operations. This made the 1st Marine Division and 81st Infantry Division two of the divisions best prepared for the coming battle on Okinawa.

TARAWA • MARSHALL ISLAND

ORIGINS OF THE CAMPAIGN

By the summer of 1944 Admiral Chester W. Nimitz had secured the Marianas, while General Douglas MacArthur controlled the whole length of New Guinea. Although there was a strong case for then attacking islands within striking range of Japan itself, as proposed by Nimitz, MacArthur argued emotionally for the Philippines. This was strategically a long left hook but also, MacArthur reasoned, a moral obligation to liberate a nation loyal to the US and potential post-war source of trade. MacArthur won: the Philippines would indeed be next.

OPPOSING COMMANDERS

THE US COMMANDERS

Strategic control of the 3rd Fleet was exercised by Nimitz who, based at Pearl Harbor, vested tactical control in Admiral "Bull" Halsey. In both character and manner the two men contrasted considerably. Nimitz had a sure strategic sense, never rushing to a decision. Halsey was the archetypal salt horse, his major characteristic was a pronounced tendency to aggression, offset by a popular touch that endeared him to subordinates and public alike.

Vice-Admiral Marc A. Mitscher, in tactical command of the fast carrier force (Task Force 38 – TF-38), was a career naval aviator. In 1944 he was 57 years of age but his post made heavy demands on him. In July 1945, as the final battle for Japan was shaping up, he was posted ashore but died just 19 months later.

MacArthur was officially Supreme Commander of the Southwest Pacific Area, but referred to himself as Commander-in-Chief. His family had strong ties with the Philippines and their people, and the Japanese occupation had initiated in him something of a personal crusade for their deliverance. Despite having a senior subordinate commander for each of the three major services, MacArthur ran his staff along Army lines, the other service representatives acting as technical consultants.

Vice-Admiral Thomas C. Kinkaid had commanded the 7th Fleet since November

OPPOSITE
General Douglas MacArthur wades ashore at Leyte. This for MacArthur was the vindication of a personal crusade and commitment to the people of the Philippines. (NARA)

Vice-Admiral Kurita commanded the Centre Group, which incorporated two of the most powerful battleships ever built, *Yamato* and *Musashi*. (NARA)

1942. Well trusted by MacArthur, he had twice been transferred by him to relieve existing commanders. His attention to detail was to prove important in coming events.

Rear-Admiral Jesse B. Oldendorf was a career naval officer who had previously seen action at Peleliu and would command Task Force 77 (TF-77) during the battle of Surigao Strait.

THE JAPANESE COMMANDERS

Admiral Soemu Toyoda, Chief of the Naval General Staff, was an excellent strategist but had a poor relationship with the Imperial Japanese Army (IJA). Vice-Admiral Jisaburo Ozawa, in contrast, worked well with the Army but showed little interest in his personal advancement, later refusing promotion to full admiral. Known as a first-class fighting admiral, he was an able tactician and had specialized in torpedoes and night-fighting.

Vice-Admiral Takeo Kurita had never attended War College but was a specialist in torpedo warfare. Vice-Admiral Shojo Nishimura was rated more highly than Kurita by the experienced Ozawa. Like Kurita, he was an able sea officer and a torpedo specialist.

OPPOSING FORCES

THE US FORCES

As far as operations in the Pacific were concerned, all Allied ships involved belonged to, or were controlled by, either the US 3rd or 7th Fleet. The 3rd Fleet was part of Nimitz's command, its flag officer being Halsey. Its overall remit was to "cover and support" the Leyte expansion. The 7th Fleet came under MacArthur, and was commanded by Kinkaid. Its task was to "transport, establish and support forces ashore in the Leyte area."

The 3rd Fleet

The 3rd Fleet consisted almost entirely of Task Force 38 (TF-38), which was organized in four fast carrier task groups. In all, TF-38 comprised about 90 ships, fairly evenly disposed between the four task groups, each a self-contained combat unit, capable of undertaking independent missions consisting of, typically, two attack carriers, two light carriers, one or more battleships, up to four cruisers and a destroyer squadron, usually of 16 destroyers organized in four divisions.

To meet the high attrition rates of TF-38's carriers there were also 11 escort carriers carrying replacement aircraft, ammunition ships, and salvage tugs. This large and valuable fleet train had its own escort screen, comprising 18 destroyers and 26 destroyer escorts.

At the "sharp end" of the 3rd Fleet were its carriers. Excepting the 1938-built *Enterprise*, all attack carriers were of the new 33,400-ton

Essex class. Light carriers were all of the new 14,200-ton *Independence* class, converted from heavy cruiser hulls and capable of over 31 knots.

An *Essex*-class ship carried an air group typically comprising 40–45 fighters (F6F Hellcats), 25–35 dive-bombers (SB2C Helldivers), and 18 torpedo bombers (TBF/TBM Avengers).

The 7th Fleet

Very much subordinated to the Army and geared to assist in its amphibious operations, the 7th Fleet was considered a "brown water" navy. Headed by a handful of cruisers and destroyers, it comprised mainly amphibious craft and, incongruously, submarines. Kinkaid's command was manifestly unsuitable and inadequate for mounting the planned assault on the Philippines. Nimitz therefore temporarily transferred from the Pacific Fleet what was virtually a fleet in itself. These temporary additions were organized as three further task forces, namely TF-77, 78, and 79.

TF-77 was used by Kinkaid to identify any special attack force and, during the Leyte operation, it had no overall commander but comprised several task groups and task units. Most important of these was TG-77.4, the escort carrier force which, commanded by Rear-Admiral Thomas L. Sprague, was charged with providing air support over the assault area while TF-78 and TF-79 had to transport and land the military. It was their landing that triggered the naval actions that resulted in the battle of Leyte Gulf.

An armada of American ships steaming along the coast of Leyte Island. The American investment in the campaign almost guaranteed success. (NARA)

THE JAPANESE FORCES

By mid-1944, the Imperial Japanese Navy (IJN) was in dire trouble, dangerously short of aircraft and fuel. In contrast, by fall 1944 the US Navy had mushroomed. Aircraft carriers had emerged as queens of the board and air superiority had become essential, not only for victory but also for sheer survival. The best area that the Japanese fleet could hope to defend was one bounded by a line from Japan to the Ryukyus, thence to Formosa and the Philippines, as there would be limited air cover provided from land-based aircrews. To counter an assault on various points of this periphery, the Japanese developed four so-called SHO plans, all relying on effective integration between naval forces and land-based air power.

Although reduced by nearly three years of war, the Japanese fleet remained formidable. It could still muster seven battleships, 11 carriers, 13 heavy, and seven light cruisers. Destroyers, so essential to any operation, had been reduced from 151 to just 63, while only 49 submarines remained.

Superficial comparison with Halsey's 3rd Fleet might lead to an assumption that a "decisive battle" was not out of the question, for the American admiral's strength stood at seven battleships, eight attack, and eight light carriers, eight heavy, and nine light cruisers. Halsey, however, was concentrated where his opponents were not. Halsey's ships were all modern, all well-trained, and could, to an extent, be replaced. He also had Kinkaid's 7th Fleet as back-up.

Japanese ships were of varying vintage and their radar and communications much inferior to those of the Americans (although, as events were to show, equipment is only as good as those using it). The crucial factor, however, was that between them, the 3rd Fleet's carriers could muster 800 or more aircraft.

OPPOSING PLANS

THE US PLAN

The proposed landings in Leyte Gulf involved two beaches. Designated Northern and Southern, each was about three miles in length, and about 11 miles wide, with two attack forces assigned to each.

The major purpose of the landings, as envisaged by the Joint Chiefs of Staff was effectively to separate Japanese forces based in the major islands of Luzon in the north and Mindanao in the south. This would permit the establishment of a springboard from which the strategically essential island of Luzon could be taken, while containing and by-passing the non-essential territory of Mindanao.

MacArthur controlled not only the strike capacity of the 7th Fleet's considerable force of escort carriers but Army Air Forces Southwest Pacific. To complicate matters, there were two further army air commands in the theater – XIV and XX Army Air Forces – while there was also the British Pacific Fleet. The latter staged a major diversion in the Indian Ocean but the Japanese were not fooled.

JAPANESE PLAN

The IJN knew that it would have to await trained replacements before being able to engage the US Navy in the "decisive battle" that doctrine demanded. The pace of the Allied advance, however, meant that the desperately required breathing space would not be granted to them. All pointers indicated that the Philippines would be the next objective and that, of the four variations on the SHO-GO contingency plan, SHO-1 would be the one most likely to be implemented. It would have to be pursued with what forces were to hand.

OPPOSITE
A Grumman Avenger stands ready for launch on a US carrier while a destroyer follows in its wake. (NARA)

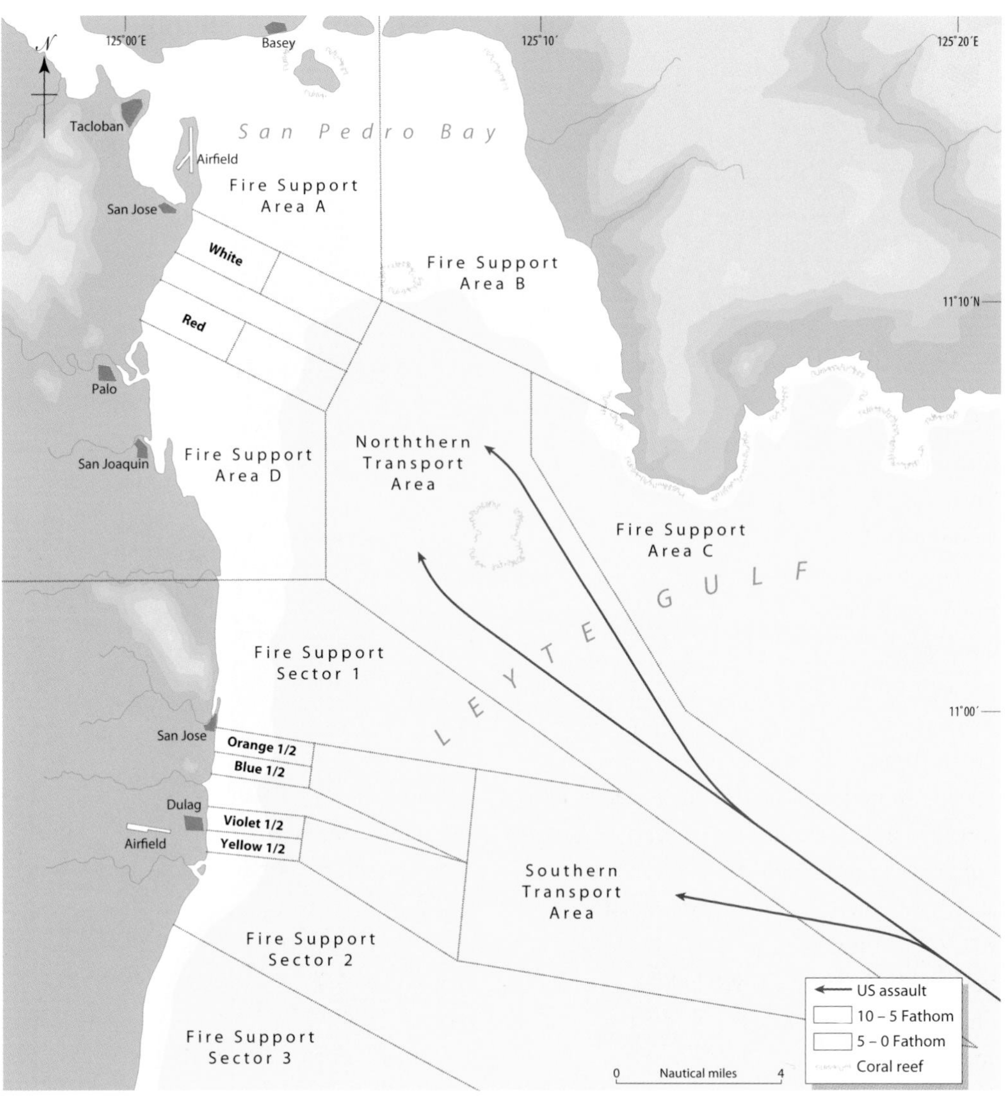

Map showing the organization and approach routes of the Leyte assault. (Osprey Publishing Ltd.)

The IJN's Chief of Staff, Admiral Shigeru Fukudome, had not admitted to either Toyoda or Ozawa the true state to which land-based air had been reduced, but it was already accepted that any Allied invasion fleet would need to be destroyed by surface action rather than by air attack.

The Japanese plan thus centered on getting a sufficiently powerful force to the invasion zone. As the 3rd Fleet would prevent this, the obvious ploy was to lure it elsewhere. An irresistible bait existed in Ozawa's toothless carrier force. It was no time to be considering long-term implications: the threat was imminent and, should the Philippines be lost, there would be little reason to have conserved the fleet.

Hastily modified to suit prevailing circumstances, SHO-1 now took the following form. Ozawa himself would lead the decoy carrier force, which would trail its coat to the northeast of Luzon, safely distant from the likely locations of Allied landings. With the 3rd Fleet's carrier groups thus removed, Japanese surface action groups would hit the invasion area at first light, arriving from north and south simultaneously.

Kurita, with the more powerful contingent, would proceed to form the northern jaw of the pincer charged with closing on the invasion zone. The weaker part, under Nishimura, would aim to arrive at the same time to attack from the south. As it lacked the necessary firepower, it was to be joined by a further force. This, under Vice Admiral Kiyohide Shima, would have to come all the way from Japan.

Last-minute adaptations to SHO-1 caused major shortcomings, with the various commanders having little or no knowledge of each other's movements. Fukudome, for instance, was not ordered to cover Kurita's Center Group, having been instructed only to use his air power to destroy the Allied landing force. Nishimura and Shima, who needed to combine to maximize their strength as the Southern Force, had received no instructions to do so. Shima was the senior commander, yet would fail to use his initiative to take charge of the situation. For the moment, the Japanese simply watched and waited for the next Allied move.

ACTION AND REACTION

OPENING MOVES (OCTOBER 17–22)

American intelligence appreciations prior to the Leyte landings were sketchy and inaccurate. The IJN was thought to have "no apparent intent to interfere." In an appreciation of possible Japanese reaction to the landings issued by General MacArthur's headquarters, it was stated specifically that approach by their fleet via either the San Bernardino or the Surigao Strait would be "impractical because of navigational hazards and the lack of maneuvering space."

In contrast, the Japanese assessment appears remarkably precise, predicting that the blow would fall in the Philippines during the final ten days of October. The likely location would be Leyte. Without certainty, however, the executive order for SHO-1 could not be given.

The approach to Leyte Gulf from the open sea to the east is constricted somewhat by several small islands. These afforded the Japanese useful locations for gun batteries and observation posts while confining any shipping to specific channels which could be, and indeed were, mined. At first light on October 17, therefore, companies of the 6th Ranger Battalion were landed on the islands to deal with any such enemy positions as minesweepers moved in.

These activities were sufficient to convince the Japanese of American intentions. At 0809hrs on October 17, therefore, Toyoda issued an alert for SHO-1 to ships and units of the Japanese fleet. Still cautious about

LCTs stand off the beaches of Leyte while troops wade ashore. Bombardments from battleships and cruisers darken the sky. (Associated Press © EMPICS)

Zeros readying for take-off from a Japanese carrier. (NARA)

committing his forces irrevocably, however, he delayed transmission of the executive order until 1110 on October 18. This meant that the earliest time for the actual Japanese attack on the Allied amphibious fleet had to be set for first light on October 22. Even this date then had to be set back a further three days, due to difficulties loading the airwings onto carriers and the supply of fuel.

Some 48 hours before the first of the Allied assault forces positioned themselves in the pre-dawn darkness of the Leyte Gulf, Kurita sailed from Lingga Roads. At 0100hrs on October 18 his flagship led to sea a truly formidable surface fighting force. It included the 68,000-ton super-battleships *Yamato* and *Musashi*, whose size and main battery of nine 18.1in guns would never be surpassed. In support were five older, but fully modernized, capital ships *Nagato*, *Fuso*, *Yamashiro*, *Kongo*, and *Haruna*, 11 heavy and two light cruisers, and 19 destroyers.

Kurita was bound for Brunei Bay, where his force arrived without incident. Here, it refueled and awaited final orders, which arrived on the afternoon of October 20, by which time the initial Allied assault on Leyte Gulf had been successfully concluded.

A few hours later, and far to the north, Ozawa's decoy Northern Force slipped unnoticed out of the Inland Sea. It was led by the fleet carrier *Zuikaku* which, as the only survivor of the six carriers that had ravaged Pearl Harbor, bore what the Americans term the "Indian sign" – she was a marked ship. In company were three light carriers, two hybrid battleship/carriers (with no aircraft), three light cruisers, and nine destroyers. In view of his force's role, it was ironic that Ozawa passed through the American submarine standing patrol line without being observed or reported.

Also starting from Japanese home waters on October 21 was Shima's force. Already the weakest of the formations, it had been

OPPOSITE
A map showing the Japanese plan of attack. (Osprey Publishing Ltd.)

reduced by having several of its units earmarked for a diversionary troop landing. His effective remaining force comprised two heavy and one light cruiser, and seven destroyers.

Shima's orders were ill-defined, charging him to "support and cooperate" with Nishimura's group, which was hived off Kurita's main force at Brunei Bay. Kurita, with what we will term the Center Group, sailed at 0800hrs on October 22. This force had to synchronize its attack, at dawn on the 25th, with that of the Southern Force, yet it had further to travel.

As the Japanese moved purposefully on their assigned missions, the Allied fleets, predominantly American, went about their pre-landing business. Hoping for a challenge from the whole IJN, Halsey kept the 3rd Fleet to the east of Luzon, at no great distance from the location toward which Ozawa was, in fact, making.

KURITA'S CENTER GROUP

Ambush in the Palawan Passage (October 21–23)

Although well aware that the IJN was on the move, the American high command had little idea of where. Movements so far were beyond the range of search aircraft. Over a dozen American submarines were, however, in Philippine waters and it was this service that made contact and drew first blood.

Due to time constraints Kurita took the Palawan Passage from Brunei Bay to the central Philippines. This is a relatively straightforward route for navigation but narrow due to shallow reefs. This ensured

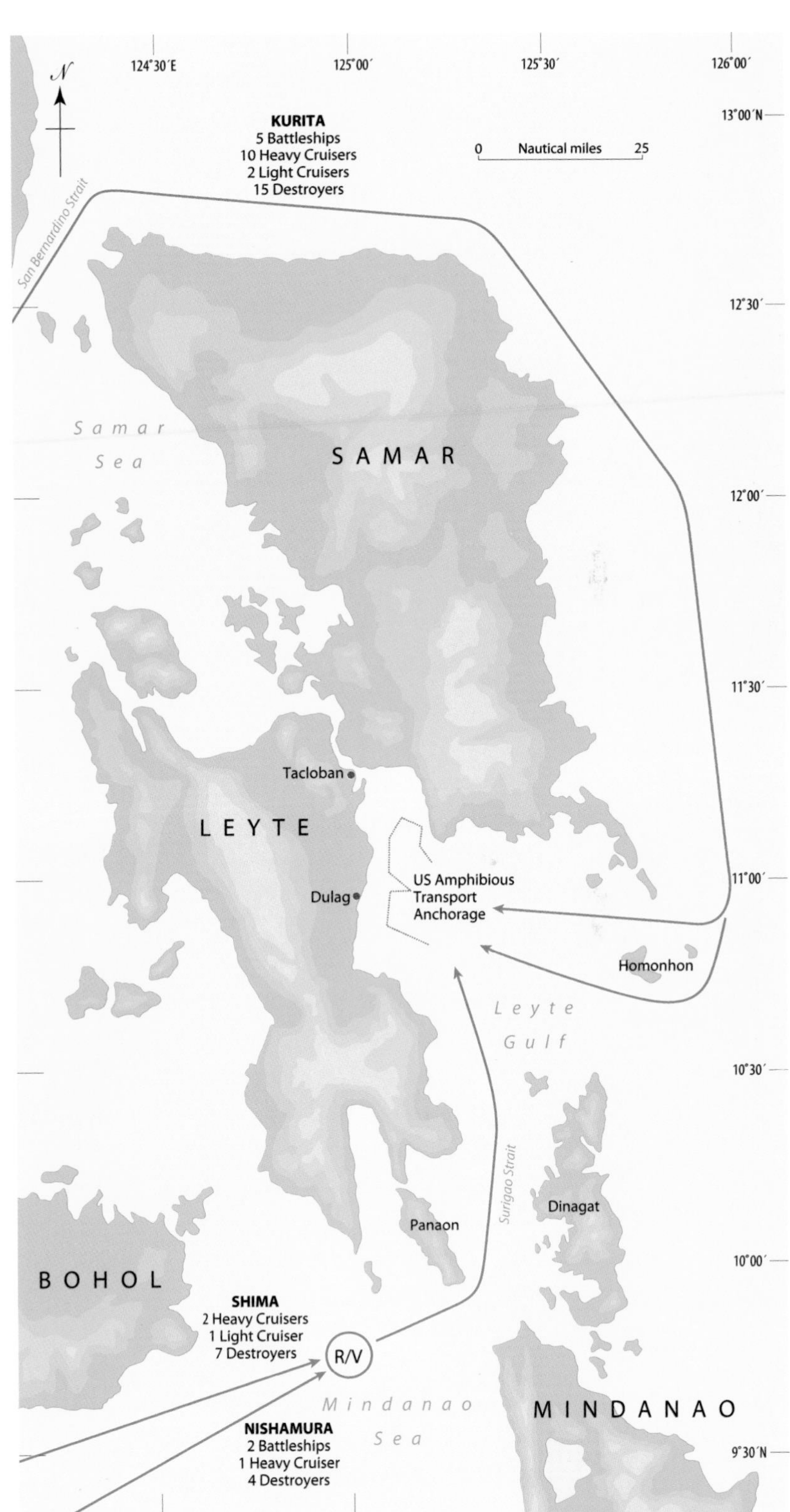

USS *Dace*, one of the submarines that ambushed Admiral Kurita's Center Force in the Palawan Passage. (NARA)

that any enemy vessel in transit was certain to be noticed by a submarine patrol.

At 0245hrs on October 23, although it was still dark, the US Navy submarine *Darter* could make out the Japanese formation as it paralleled it at 15 knots. Just 20,000 yards distant was a submariner's dream, a huge assembly of warships, the targets overlapping. Kurita was steaming in two main columns, each in two parts and comprising battleships led by two or three heavy cruisers.

Darter and her partner submarine *Dace* moved into an attacking position. Kurita's flagship *Atago* was sunk obliging Kurita and his staff to swim for it. Sorely injured, the *Takao* fell out of line and reversed course.

Not only had the two submarines severely mauled the Japanese Center Group, they had also gravely dented its flag officer's confidence as he was pulled from the sea by a destroyer and transferred to the battleship *Yamato*. His vital communications personnel had either been killed, scattered around the fleet, or were returning in the shattered *Takao*. Kurita pressed on, but his force and composition were now known. By midnight October 23–24 the formation was heading eastward toward Mindoro and, as daylight strengthened on the 24th, it rounded the island's southern tip to enter the Sibuyan Sea. Kurita had been bloodied but was still dangerous, on time, and headed for the critical San Bernardino Strait. It was now Halsey's job to stop him.

Battle of the Sibuyan Sea (October 24)

By dawn on October 24 Rear Admiral Frederick Sherman's TG-38.3 was off Luzon, Rear Admiral Gerald Bogan's TG-38.2 (incorporating Halsey's flagship, *New Jersey*) was east of the San Bernardino Strait, and Rear Admiral Ralph Davison's TG-38.4 was abreast of Leyte Gulf. All launched reconnaissance at the earliest possible moment to establish the new position, course, and speed of the reported fleet.

Heading toward the area east of the Philippines, where Halsey calculated that the Japanese would be, an aircraft from the TG-38.2 carrier *Intrepid* located Kurita at 0625hrs by chance rounding the southern tip of Mindoro. A surprised Halsey had to accept that Kurita was, in fact, headed for the San Bernardino and was going to offer battle. He immediately ordered both Sherman and Davison to close Bogan's group at their best speed.

While this order was being complied with, a scout aircraft reported a new Japanese fleet, heading east across the Sulu Sea. This was Nishimura's van group of the Southern Force and Halsey again made a correct assessment, that it, too, was bound for Leyte Gulf, but this time via the Surigao Strait to its south. Although Halsey's latest orders to the carrier groups were taking Davison's, the southernmost carrier group, beyond the range at which he could engage Nishimura, Halsey remained confident that Kinkaid had means sufficient to deal with the problem posed by Nishimura.

Significantly, the autocratic MacArthur, insistent upon maintaining the independence of his command, forbade any direct means of communication between the 3rd and 7th Fleets so Halsey and Kinkaid could not confer directly but only via the main fleet radio station. Messages between the admirals could thus take hours, arrive out of sequence or even fail to arrive at all. Dawning clear and bright, the morning of October 24 saw Mitscher's three task groups ranged down the eastern side of the Philippines – Sherman to the north, Bogan (with Halsey) in the center, and Davison to the south. With a battle looming, the admiral took the precaution of recalling Vice Admiral John McCain's group (TG-38.1), now 300 miles away en route to Ulithi, the US Navy's South Pacific anchorage. McCain's was the most powerful of the four groups, but its return would be slowed by a refueling rendezvous.

With Sherman drawing most of Fukudome's venom, Bogan and Davison concentrated on dealing with the largest of the enemy formations, that of Kurita. From 0810hrs, when the Japanese were sighted in the Tablas Strait, they were hit by a series of air strikes – a total of 259 sorties.

Within the Center Group, the huge *Yamato* and *Musashi* stood out and the latter was eventually sunk. After the third air strike, Kurita briefly lost confidence, reversing course and losing a vital four hours or so before again, at 1715hrs, assuming his easterly track for the strait. His force had been reduced by a battleship, four heavy cruisers, and several destroyers. He remained, however, a potent threat.

Halsey's returning aviators were in exuberant spirits with over-optimistic assessment of their results. Halsey chose to believe that Kurita's Center Group no longer represented a threat. His mind was elsewhere for, somewhere out there, yet unaccounted for, were the Japanese carriers. These were what he wanted to destroy.

A Dauntless takes off from an American carrier during the battle for Leyte. (Tom Laemlein)

OZAWA'S NORTHERN FORCE

For Ozawa, his mission was painful. Instead of the usual 250 aircrew, he could barely muster 100 part-trained aircrew and his role was simply to be discovered by 3rd Fleet search aircraft then, using his precious carriers as live bait, to lure Halsey as far north as possible, clearing the way for Kurita to sweep Leyte Gulf clean of amphibious shipping. Having left the Inland Sea on October 20 the Northern Force had kept well to the west to avoid being spotted by American reconnaissance aircraft already operating out of Saipan in the Marianas. Ozawa did not wish to be located until Kurita was well advanced, for his early destruction would achieve nothing.

At 1430hrs on October 24 Ozawa detached his two hybrid battleship/carriers *Ise* and *Hyuga* (each lacking aircraft but still mounting eight 14in guns), together with a light escort, to make a direct challenge.

The ships were sighted at 1540hrs by a pair of aircraft from Davison's group which, together with Bogan's, was still occupied in flying strikes against Kurita as he advanced across the Sibuyan Sea. Land-based Japanese air activity was tailing off and Sherman was able to follow up the sighting by putting up further search aircraft. This, at 1640hrs, finally located Ozawa, reporting the Northern Force's composition as four carriers, two light cruisers, and about five destroyers. As all his force had now been sighted, Ozawa re-concentrated the formation.

The Japanese battleship *Yamato* is hit by a bomb near her forward turret while under attack in the Sibuyan Sea. She survived the attack. (NARA)

Halsey was now in something of a quandary. Ozawa's position was almost 200 miles north of his northernmost carrier group, Sherman's TG-38.3. It was too late to launch a strike and have the aircraft return in daylight (night flying was still a specialty). Left to himself, Ozawa might pull further to the north and use his already longer-range aircraft in a shuttle-bombing attack, flying from their carriers to airfields in Luzon, refueling and re-arming before flying back to their ships, attacking Sherman on both legs of the flight. Gambling that Kurita was, as reported, a spent force, Halsey summoned Rear-Admiral "Mick" Carney, his Chief of Staff, and gave the fateful order: "Mick, start 'em north."

HALSEY'S 3RD FLEET

Halsey's decision (October 24–25)

His mind made up, Halsey ordered Bogan and Davison, at 2022hrs on October 24, to concentrate on Sherman's group and to move north to attack Ozawa at dawn on the 25th. For good measure, he also instructed the returning McCain's TG-38.1 to refuel as quickly as possible and to rejoin the task force. Halsey was determined to direct a major action from the bridge of his flagship. It was just what the Japanese had intended.

Between them, his group had discovered and reported the full strength of the Northern Force, at that stage still split. Why should Halsey have doubted that this was the total enemy strength when, hours before, he had

A Japanese warship sinks off Leyte Island after an attack by US Army and Navy planes supporting landings at Ormoc Bay. Halsey believed most of the central Japanese fleet to be in a similar state, so set off after Ozawa, who was being used as bait. (Bettmann/Corbis)

accepted the aviators' inflated reports of damage to Kurita? By midnight on October 24–25, the whole of the 3rd Fleet was heading northward at high speed. The three carrier groups duly rendezvoused at 2345hrs, at the very time that a surprised and relieved Kurita was threading his Center Group through the now unwatched San Bernardino Strait. Halsey was focused on nailing Ozawa and he ordered away night-flying search aircraft. These confirmed, a little after 0200hrs, not only Ozawa's presence but also that the Japanese were barely one hundred miles ahead.

Captain Arleigh Burke, Mitscher's Chief of Staff, suggested that, to avoid the risk of the vulnerable carriers blundering into heavy enemy units before dawn, it would be wise to form TF-34 promptly and to have it stationed ahead as a battle line. Halsey accepted the advice and, at 0240hrs, Vice Admiral Willis Lee's ships pulled away at high speed.

Halsey informed Nimitz, King, MacArthur, and Kinkaid of the move, the last two recipients indirectly. His signal terminated in a rather enigmatic "Own force in three groups concentrated." Kinkaid must have received the message quickly for at 0312hrs, obviously uncertain of what Halsey really meant, he posed the direct question: "Is TF-34 guarding the San Bernardino Strait?"

Again, indirect signal routing proved to be a major problem for Halsey did not receive this pointed query until 0648hrs. At 0704hrs he answered unequivocally: "Negative. Task Force 34 is with carrier groups now engaging enemy carrier force." Kinkaid was totally dismayed but, within minutes, it would get worse.

KURITA'S CENTER GROUP

The battle off Samar (October 25)

Kurita was now well behind schedule and there was no longer any hope of synchronizing his attack on Leyte Gulf with that of Nishimura and Shima from the south. At 2320hrs the last of the *Independence*'s night-fliers parted company with the Japanese force as they were re-directed by Halsey to locate Ozawa's Northern Force. Their reports of the Center

Group's progress had been transmitted, mainly for Kinkaid's benefit but, thanks to the cumbersome communications system between the 3rd and 7th Fleets, there is no record that Kinkaid ever received them.

By 0035hrs on the 25th the whole of the Center Group had exited the strait and, surprised at the lack of even an American picket there, Kurita cracked on down the coast of Samar, on the shortest route to his objective.

Kinkaid possessed within his 7th Fleet very considerable firepower, a contributory factor in Halsey's decision making. Its strength, however, was vested in ships intended to support amphibious warfare, not to fight major actions; its battleships over-age veterans and its carriers all escorts. The escort carriers were organized as TG-77.4 under the command of Rear Admiral Thomas Sprague and subdivided into three task units – Taffy 1 (Sprague's own), 2 (Rear Admiral Felix Stump), and 3 (Rear Admiral Clifton Sprague – no relation). At full strength, each task unit could deploy about 150 aircraft. The units worked independently with, perhaps, 50 miles between them. On the morning of October 25, Taffy 1 was the southernmost, operating off northern Mindanao. Taffy 2 was directly east of Leyte Gulf, while Taffy 3 was to its north, off the coast of Samar and directly in the path of Kurita's Center Group.

Kinkaid had been up all night, as reports came in regularly regarding the progress of the Japanese Southern Force. At 0155hrs and as yet only with reservations about whether Halsey was holding the ring to the north, he ordered Sprague to conduct air searches from dawn.

As daylight strengthened on the morning of October 25, Kurita became increasingly apprehensive. During the previous 48 hours he had survived having his flagship sunk under him, but had lost track of many of his trusted staff. He had been strafed, bombed, and torpedoed for hours by almost unopposed airstrikes, and had been obliged to leave the stricken *Musashi* to her fate. Now, suspiciously, as if encouraging him on, he had been allowed to pass an unguarded choke point and gazed at an empty horizon.

Kurita was certain that the 3rd Fleet was lurking close at hand and, shortly, the whole of its mighty air strength would be hurled at him. His doubts seemed to be realized when his radars detected aerial activity ahead. At 0627hrs as the sun rose on a clear morning, Kurita changed his force's disposition from night cruising order to an anti-aircraft formation. Even as the smaller units were positioning themselves around the larger, lookouts reported the horizon ahead to be peppered with masts. Within minutes came the unwelcome news that the masts were those of aircraft carriers.

His fears realized, Kurita resolved to sell his force's existence for as high a price as possible. With no time to waste, he countermanded his earlier order for his force's redisposition and, instead, signaled "General Attack," an instruction for each commanding officer to work independently. In place of a formidable battle line of four battleships and six heavy cruisers, Kurita's ships were rushing pell-mell at what was assumed to be an overwhelming enemy force.

In fact, Kurita had seen only what he had expected to see. What lay in his path was not the 3rd Fleet, which Halsey had taken far to the north, but the escort carriers of Clifton Sprague's Taffy 3. At 0645hrs an American aircraft reported that it was being fired upon by a strange force of warships. These were already appearing and observers expressed disbelief as the massive Japanese superstructures eased above the horizon.

US GM FM-2 Wildcat fighters of the type used in the battle off Samar. Flying from the decks of the CVEs of Taffies 2 and 3, the Wildcats contributed to the US success against overwhelming odds. (NARA)

As the first lines of shell splashes marched across his force, Sprague ordered a course change to the east, which opened the range while allowing him to launch aircraft and urgent pleas for assistance were broadcast.

Friendly forces reacted quickly, but Taffy 1 was about 130 miles distant, Taffy 2, 50 miles. All carriers dispatched aircraft in a "come-as-you-are" mode. From his headquarters ship, Kinkaid had his fighter detection unit send all airborne aircraft to Sprague's assistance. Taffy 3's carriers meanwhile, adopted a circular formation of about 2,500 yards' diameter. Their escorts, belching smoke, threw themselves at their enormous adversaries in real and simulated torpedo attack. The Japanese had opened fire at about 30,000 yards and, what with the mass of smoke and the varying courses adopted by Sprague's ships, took some time to get on target. Ominously, the range was closing rapidly and the tattered formation of the enemy ships was allowing them to work round on either flank.

For 15 minutes at 0705hrs a heavy rain squall enveloped the beleaguered CVEs, giving Sprague the opportunity to make some ground toward the sanctuary of Leyte Gulf itself. Kurita meanwhile, was greatly troubled by the uncoordinated attentions of seemingly dozens of aircraft, most of which did not bomb but pressed home strafing attacks. In truth, of course, there simply had not been the time to arm them. Amazingly, the Japanese observers were unfamiliar with the distinctive silhouette of a CVE and, still imagining themselves to be faced with the 3rd Fleet, the ships hesitated to close to lethal range. Sprague's men were surviving thus far through the sheer ferocity of their response.

Inevitably, however, the Americans began to take damage. The destroyer *Johnston* was buried in enemy fire. Her fellow destroyers, *Hoel* and *Heermann*, fared similarly, but their "fierce face" tactics, threatening the enemy with torpedoes that they no longer possessed, caused the Japanese to fragment even further by virtue of individual ships' evasive tactics. Before she sank, the *Hoel* had been struck by about 40 shells of all calibers.

Visibility, thanks to rain and smoke, now varied between 100 and 25,000 yards. At any glimpse of the carriers, the enemy fired opportunistically. Pressed hard, Sprague ordered away the four little destroyer escorts, which had torpedo tubes but had never used them. Now the ships were ordered to plug the gaps in the smoke and to attack with torpedoes on opportunity. This was learning the hard way. Nimble, they escaped damage for a while by "chasing salvoes," but there were just too many salvoes. By 0845hrs Kurita had lost all tactical control, but the prospects for Sprague looked bleak indeed.

The remaining Japanese cruisers had ordered themselves into a column which overhauled the Americans on their port side, while the destroyers tried again to starboard. Astern were the heavy units with the remainder of the Center Group.

All Sprague's CVEs were now making their best speed on a southwesterly course. So close were the enemy cruisers that the CVEs were using their single 5in guns to return fire through gaps in the smoke but the *Gambier Bay* was sunk. The enemy was not having it all his own way, however, for, even as the *Gambier Bay* rolled over at 0905hrs, a group of dive-bombers from the *Kitkun Bay* put a devastatingly accurate attack into the heavy cruiser *Chokai*, which sank in about 20 minutes.

Japanese cruiser *Chikuma* evades attack during the battle off Samar. A bomb has already blown off part of her stern. *Chikuma* played a leading role in the battle, focusing much of her attack on the US CVE *Gambier Bay*. (NARA)

By 0924hrs the tophamper of the Japanese battleships was visible from Taffy 2, close enough also to attract a few ranging salvoes. Stump had already dispatched four strikes and, at 0935hrs, sent off a fifth. Kurita was aware that he, too, was accumulating cripples. These would hamper any rapid retirement and, worryingly, his totally disordered force was now running into a second carrier group. Now hardly 50 miles distant from his Leyte objective, Kurita was still convinced that he was battling the 3rd Fleet. He also reasoned that the delay caused by this opposition would have allowed the Americans to have cleared the gulf of all amphibious shipping and transports. Even if he succeeded in fighting his way through, therefore, he would face certain annihilation for no return. Fatigued by his recent experiences, his resolve wavered.

In truth, there was little more to prevent Kurita from pressing on, clear to the invasion zone, but never was the expression "the Fog of War" more appropriate.

At 0911hrs Kurita ordered his scattered units to retire northward and to re-form. The Japanese commander had also been receiving disquieting signals regarding the fate of the Southern Force (see below) and, so a now-unmolested Kurita spent over three hours steering an apparently aimless course off Samar, determining what best to do. At 1310hrs, Kurita ordered retirement and the surface action off Samar was over.

OZAWA'S NORTHERN FORCE

The battle off Cape Engaño (October 25)

Heading north at easy speed to avoid over-running the enemy by night, Halsey transferred tactical command to Mitscher. By 0430hrs on October 25, night reconnaissance reports, now some two hours old, had placed Ozawa's force at conflicting distances ahead, and search radar displays were being carefully monitored. Mitscher was not one either to waste time or to be surprised by events. Preceded by numerous search aircraft, the first strike began to get airborne at 0540hrs. Having gained a specified distance ahead of the fleet, this force had been ordered to orbit until contact with Ozawa was established. This came at 0710hrs. The Japanese were some 200 miles east of Cape Engaño in northern Luzon, just 150 miles from Halsey and, thanks to Mitscher's prescience, only 80 miles from the waiting air strike.

By 0800hrs the first Helldivers plummeted from the high blue. The enemy combat air patrol (CAP) was barely a dozen strong and easily dealt with by the upper escort. Evading the dive-bombers put the Japanese formation into disarray, allowing the torpedo-carrying Avengers their chance to select individual targets. Their weapons were released from about 1,500 yards.

The attack was pressed home through heavy anti-aircraft fire. The carrier *Chitose* went down at 0937hrs. The carrier *Zuiho* took a single bomb but survived. Wearing Ozawa's flag, the primary target, *Zuikaku*, was struck by a torpedo near the end of the strike and Ozawa transferred to the light cruiser *Oyodo*.

As the Japanese no longer had air cover, the Americans were able to vector-in follow-up strikes. The second attack, much smaller, concentrated on the carrier *Chiyoda*, several bombs setting her well ablaze. The third strike, of a massive 200 aircraft, arrived at about 1310hrs. Ozawa's undamaged ships were found to be in two main groups, moving at high speed. The third strike then concentrated on the already-damaged *Zuikaku*, eventually sinking it at 1415hrs. At 1410hrs, to avoid further losses, Ozawa left the *Chiyoda* to her fate.

US CVEs off Samar make smoke while fleeing from the Japanese Center Group. Fortunately for Taffy 3, Admiral Kurita thought he had encountered a full-scale carrier group and was more cautious than he would otherwise have been.

At 1145hrs, a fourth strike came in. This finally put paid to the *Zuiho* before concentrating on the *Ise*. But, maneuvering violently, the *Ise* came through. At 1610hrs Mitscher ordered away his fifth and largest attack but again the *Ise* and *Hyuga* survived. As a final gesture, a small sixth strike arrived before 1800hrs. Most of its fliers were now on their third sortie of the day and fatigue meant that the Japanese attracted no further damage. Ozawa, however, had lost three carriers as a result of air attacks, while the fourth, the abandoned *Chiyoda*, was sunk by gunfire from American cruisers at about 1700hrs. Still, he had not only succeeded totally in his intention to draw off Halsey's 3rd Fleet but he also brought home the bulk of his remaining force.

For Halsey, October 25 was probably the worst day of his long career. By now receiving favorable reports of Mitscher's first air strike, Halsey assumed that the lack of aerial opposition was due simply to the Japanese being caught by surprise. Knowing that a

These Helldivers, seen here over the Marshall Islands, were used to great effect in the battles of the Leyte Gulf, inflicting considerable damage on the Japanese naval assets. (Tom Laemlein)

second strike was airborne and that Ozawa was already badly hit, Halsey re-directed McCain's TG-38.1, the most powerful of his four carrier groups, to proceed from its refueling "at best possible speed" to Kinkaid's assistance. For the moment, Lee's TF-34 remained heading north. Around 1000hrs Kinkaid appealed again: "My situation is critical. Fast BBs [battleships] and support by air strikes may be able to keep enemy from destroying CVEs and entering Leyte." If Halsey was dismayed by this, he was almost immediately galvanized by a signal from Nimitz himself from Pearl Harbor: "Turkey trots to water GG Where is repeat where is Task Force Thirty Four RR The World wonders." With the beaten and scattered remnants of the enemy's Northern Force just 40 miles from his 16in guns and the action that he so desired, Halsey divided his forces. Ordering Sherman and Davison to finish off Ozawa, he put about both TF-34's battleships and Bogan's TG-38.2 for Leyte Gulf. The time was 1055hrs.

HALSEY'S 3RD FLEET

The run to the south (October 25)

Halsey was now in limbo. There were enemies to the north and south but both beyond reach. Kurita's Center Group hovered menacingly while its admiral prevaricated. Taffy 3 had slipped away but this did not mean the end of the escort carriers' ordeal, for Sprague's Taffy 1 was facing its own challenge. Taffy 1 had sent off a 28-plane strike at daybreak, directed at the Japanese Southern Force. Within the hour it was dispatching every other available aircraft to the assistance of Taffy 3. In the midst of all this furious activity, nobody had time to consider the near non-existent threat from enemy land-based aircraft.

At 0740hrs, six Japanese aircraft appeared from the direction of Mindanao and dived on the ships below. This was the first deployment of the new corps of *Kamikaze* ("Divine Wind"), units piloted by men prepared to sacrifice themselves in disciplined, premeditated attack. As Taffy 1 cleared its debris and tended the injured, it was Clifton Sprague's Taffy 3 that was singled out for further punishment and *St. Lo* was sunk.

KURITA'S CENTER GROUP

Kurita's deliverance (October 25–26)

While Kurita agonized as to whether he should retire, he was hit at 1220hrs by a final ragged strike mounted by Taffies 2 and 3. Savaged by surface gunfire and by Kamikaze attack, the CVE groups were still full of fight. At 1040hrs, in one of the most distant carrier strikes of the war, McCain's ships had launched 100 aircraft from a range of 335 miles. Due to the need for maximum fuel, only bombs, no torpedoes, could be carried. The attack developed at 1315hrs but McCain's aircraft caused little damage to Kurita.

Meanwhile, Kurita and Halsey were closing rapidly. The night-fliers of the *Independence* again established first contact, actually sighting the enemy Center Group, at 2140hrs, as it entered the San Bernardino Strait in single column. Halsey ordered both carrier groups to be ready at daybreak, in order to "kick the hell" out of them.

Having rendezvoused at 0500hrs on the 26th, the two carrier groups began launching a first strike an hour later. The Japanese were not located, however, until 0810hrs, when a second strike was dispatched. A third left at 1245hrs. Weariness had now blunted the attack, however, and Kurita was fortunate in losing only a light cruiser and a destroyer.

THE SOUTHERN FORCE

The approach phase (October 24)

In following the fortunes of the Japanese Center and Northern forces it has been necessary, to avoid confusion, to ignore the progress and the fate of the Southern Fleet of Nishimura and the rear group of Shima. Although ordered to support and cooperate neither attempted to communicate with the other.

Nishimura's van group made steady progress until 0905hrs on October 24, when search aircraft from Davison's TG-38.4 reported it to be about 50 miles west of the most southerly point of Negros and dive-bombed but to little effect. Shima's rear group was sighted some three hours later also steering round to Negros. Reported again at about 1240hrs, Nishimura then went unobserved for nearly 12 hours because Davison's task group, along with the others, had been ordered north by Halsey. On advising the latter that his aircraft were tracking a substantial Japanese force, Davison was told that the 7th Fleet had adequate resources to deal with it. This was despite the sighting reports so far being contradictory with respect to ship numbers and types. The result, however, was that Kinkaid's main firepower was drawn south to deal with the Southern Force at a time when it would be urgently needed off Samar to deal with Kurita's Center Group. At a time when Kinkaid needed regular reports of the enemy's progress, the support of Davison was removed. The 7th Fleet Commander was thus reliant upon radar-equipped PBYs, which failed to find the Japanese at all.

KINKAID'S 7TH FLEET

Kinkaid's dispositions (October 24)

Early in the afternoon of the 24th Kinkaid alerted all units to the strong likelihood of an enemy attack during the coming night, and charged Rear-Admiral Jesse B. Oldendorf, overall commander of the bombardment groups, to plan the necessary 7th Fleet dispositions to meet it. Oldendorf then turned geography to his advantage. What the Japanese had hoped would be an unobtrusive route to Leyte Gulf, Oldendorf then turned into a blind alley.

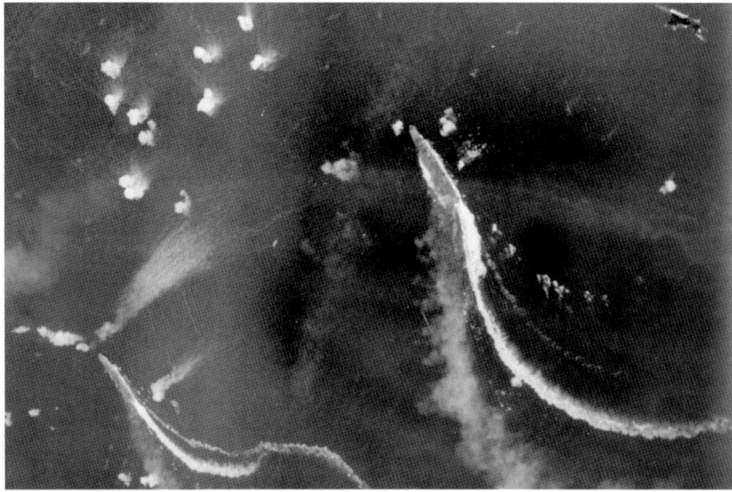

Japanese carriers *Zuikaku* (left) and *Zuiho* (right) maneuver while under attack in the battle off Cape Engano. (NARA)

Among his various naval assets, Kinkaid could count 39 PT boats. Now lacking effective night-flying reconnaissance aircraft, Oldendorf organized the craft in 13 three-boat sections and stationed them over the 100 miles or so between Bohol Island and Surigao Strait. Their task was to lie silently, report the passage of the enemy, and then to attack, section by section.

As Halsey was assumed to be controlling the northern approaches to Leyte Gulf, a maximum number of surface combatants were used in Oldendorf's planned deployments. Twenty-eight destroyers would ambush the Japanese in the strait itself. Those Japanese ships that had survived the attacks so far would then be approaching the upper end of the strait, only to find Oldendorf's heavy units disposed across their path, blocking the exit. The six battleships (placed under the tactical command of Rear-Admiral George L. Weyler) would steam in open water and in battle line, allowing their full broadside to be brought to bear in unobstructed fire. Nor was this the sum total of the forces arrayed against the enemy. On the flanks of Weyler's battle line, plugging the gaps between its extremities and the neighboring shorelines, cruiser forces were deployed. On the left, under Oldendorf himself, were three heavy and two light cruisers. On the right were one heavy cruiser and two light. The action, seemingly inevitable, would be fought in darkness, with neither side able to employ aircraft. It would be the last example of such.

THE SOUTHERN FORCE: BATTLE OF SURIGAO STRAIT

Phase I (October 24–25)

At 2236hrs, PT-131 detected Nishimura's van group on radar. At this point, the *Mogami* and three destroyers had been sent ahead, the two battleships, and a single destroyer, *Shigure*, trailing. The latter ships, threatened from their starboard side, turned toward their assailants. Immediately, the PT boats were in desperate action as the *Shigure* fixed them by searchlight and engaged them with all available weapons. As was too often the case with light forces, the PTs had received very little exercise in torpedo attack.

Other PT boat section attacks did not fare much better as the Japanese demonstrated their aptitude for night-fighting. Reassured by this successful defense and progress to date, Nishimura signaled at 0100hrs to Kurita (whose

Kamikaze strikes against the American forces were a common feature of the Pacific War by late 1944. These attacks showed the determination of the Japanese and inflicted a large amount of damage on the US fleet. They also struck fear into the hearts of the American troops. (Tom Laemlein)

Center Group had already exited the San Bernardino) and to Shima, that he would pass Panaon Island, and thus enter the Surigao Strait, at 0130hrs. For this final approach, he closed up his formation. Two destroyers probed ahead, followed at about 4,000 yards by the flagship *Yamashiro*, herself flanked by the remaining two destroyers.

Five more PT sections were waiting in the eight-mile gap between Panaon and Mindanao. At this point the Japanese were vulnerable as they made a six-point alteration in course to take them into the strait proper. Their defense was as alert and effective as ever, and the small American craft were again brushed aside. At 0213hrs the van group successfully fought off the last of the light craft. Three further sections of PTs lay ahead, but these were ordered to stay clear to enable the destroyers to commence their attacks. The failure of the PT boats would have been complete had they not also attacked Shima's rear group. This force was rounding Panaon at about 0325hrs when PT-137 succeeded in putting a single torpedo into the light cruiser *Abukuma*. She fell out of line and remained afloat, to be sunk the following day by US Army bombers. Thirty PTs had seen action, firing a total of 34 torpedoes for one hit. Ten boats had been damaged by return fire, one of them sinking. Could the destroyers fare any better?

Phase II (October 25)

Some 10,000 yards south of Weyler's battleships, Destroyer Squadron 54 (Desron 54) was likewise patrolling across the northern end of the Surigao Strait. As reports on Nishimura's progress were then received from the PTs, Oldendorf forwarded them to the destroyermen who were ordered to attack with torpedoes only, with no use of guns to betray their positions. Having delivered its attack, each division was to turn toward the shoreline in order to remain concealed and also to keep the range clear for Weyler's battleships when they opened fire. Having enjoyed a quiet half-hour since the last PT-boat attack, the Japanese had, none the less, remained vigilant. At 0300hrs, as the destroyers swung hard left in sequence to release their torpedoes, the night was, once again, lanced by Japanese searchlights but at 9,000 yards these failed to illuminate the destroyers. First the battleship *Fuso* was struck then the *Yamashiro*

and three destroyers, one of which was sunk and the other two badly damaged.

Now it was the turn of the Desron 24, the six destroyers covering Oldendorf's right flank cruisers. These proceeded down the western side of the strait, organized in two divisions with one direct hit scored on the *Yamashiro* and finishing off the *Fuso* and the *Michishio*. At this stage, the badly damaged *Yamashiro* was slowed, but still on course. On her starboard quarter was the as yet undamaged *Mogami* and just one surviving destroyer, *Shigure*, when Weyler's battle line opened fire.

Phase III (October 25)

Nishimura has to be credited with raw courage as he led his already tattered squadron into this inferno. By 0400hrs the *Yamashiro* could be seen on fire at so many locations that her every detail was clear-cut. Flooding uncontrollably, she slowly rolled over and, at 0419hrs, went down, taking with her Vice-Admiral Nishimura and the majority of his crew. The *Mogami* was also on fire and her commanding officer dead although she did avoid complete destruction by the US battleships and destroyers. Recognizing the hopelessness of the situation the commanding officer of the lone Japanese destroyer *Shigure* decided to retire into the relative safety of darkness and eventually stumbled upon the head of Shima's rear group which had retired after being unable to contact Nishimura.

Phase IV (October 25)

Shima, having signaled his intentions to Tokyo, recalled his destroyers and, at 0425hrs, commenced his retirement. It was several minutes before it became apparent on Oldendorf's plotting tables that the remnants of the enemy's Southern Force were, in fact, retiring. Perhaps due to reaction and fatigue, Oldendorf's pursuit seemed half-hearted, begun at only 15 knots.

At 0520hrs, in gathering daylight, Oldendorf gained sight of his quarry. Still "burning like a city block," the unfortunate *Mogami* attracted fire but again survived, however, by 0730hrs the cruiser *Asagumo* had been sunk. But then came the news that Sprague's CVEs were in action with Kurita's heavy forces. For the moment, Shima's luck held as his pursuers, already short on fuel and ammunition, worked up to maximum speed in the opposite direction to assist in the crisis developing around Leyte Gulf.

MOPPING UP

The closing phases (October 25–27)

Subsequent to the major actions described above it will be apparent that, at some point during October 25, no fewer than three Japanese admirals, Shima, Kurita, and Ozawa, were in retreat and seeking to save as great a proportion

OPPOSITE
The battle of Ormac Bay was just one element of the fighting in and around the Leyte Gulf. It stemmed from the Japanese operations to reinforce and resupply their forces still situated on Leyte. At first the US thought they were trying to evacuate their troops, but by November the picture was clearer and it became apparent that they were attempting to land 34,000 troops. The US then began to intercept the convoys, as seen here with this B-25 strafing a Japanese ship. (Tom Laemlein)

The Australian cruisers HMAS *Shropshire* (left, foreground) and HMAS *Australia* (right, foreground) took part at Leyte Gulf, with *Shropshire* present in the cruiser line at Surigao Strait. (NARA)

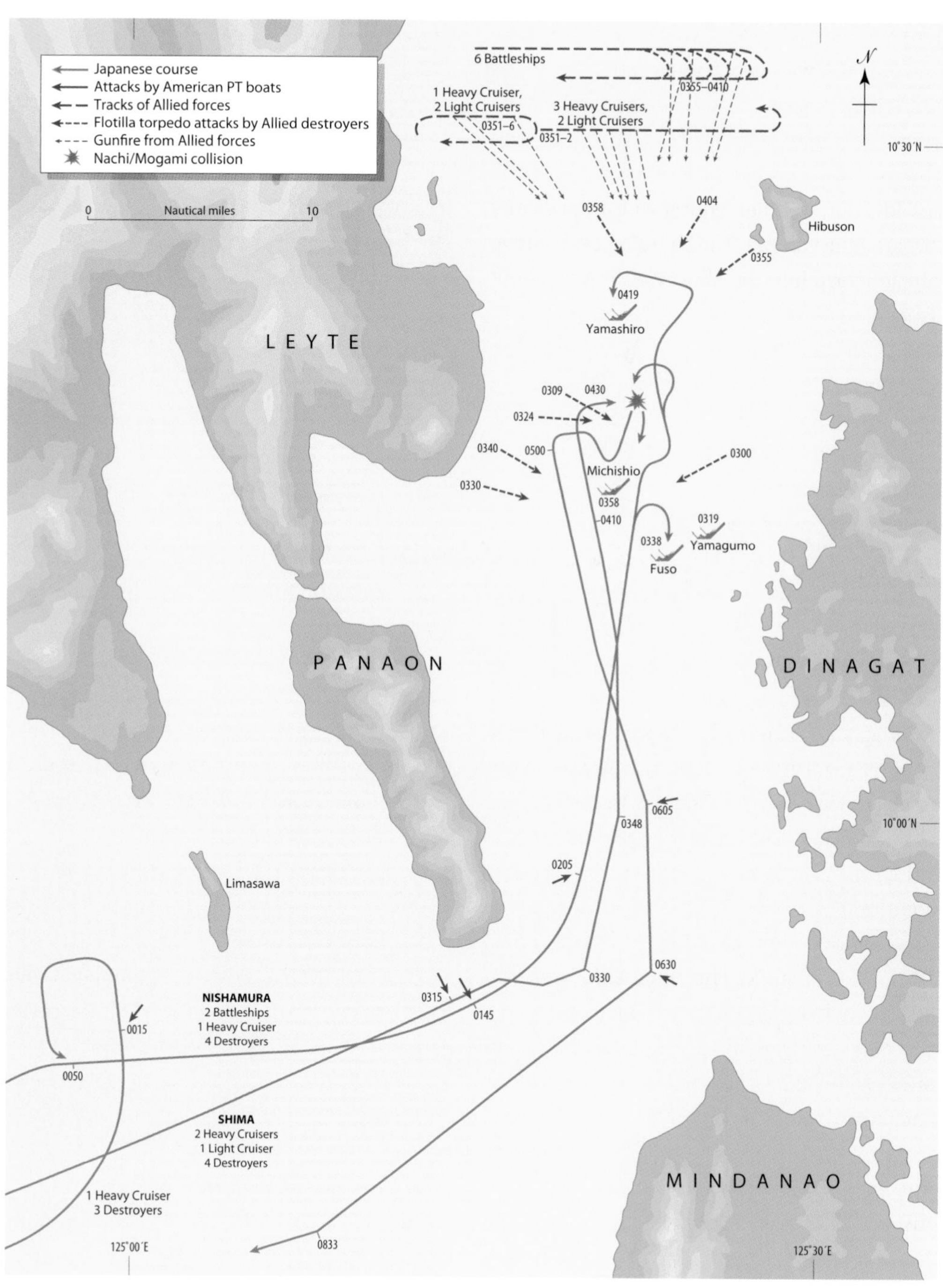

A map showing the main movements and key events of the battle of the Surigao Strait. (Osprey Publishing Ltd)

of their defeated forces as possible. It remained the task of the Americans to capitalize on their disorder and to pick off the damaged and the vulnerable. Chronologically, the first group to seek safety in retirement was the Southern Force, which turned about at 0425hrs. As Oldendorf vacillated about further surface action to annihilate Shima, Sprague's CVEs took the initiative and dispatched an air strike at 0545hrs. It was 0910hrs before this found the gravely damaged *Mogami* and she was finally sunk. Once freed from the attentions of Kurita's Center Group, Sprague's CVEs again attended to Oldendorf's earlier request with a valedictory strike against Shima. The aircraft found Shima, already deep into the Mindanao Sea, at about 1500hrs on the 25th, but were able only to damage a destroyer.

Meanwhile Kurita began his withdrawal by signal at 1236hrs on October 25. It disappeared back into the San Bernardino Strait between 2100 and 2200hrs although the destroyer *Nowake* was sunk.

On October 26 Kurita was attacked by three air strikes from US carriers and land-based B-24s although thanks to his timely retirement Kurita, too, had preserved a good proportion of his force. From about 0630hrs on October 25 Ozawa's Northern Force was headed in a generally northern direction, still attempting to entice Halsey's 3rd Fleet north.

Although he had dispatched TF-34 southward at 1115hrs, Halsey held back a squadron of four cruisers with which to finish off Ozawa's stragglers and the stricken *Chiyoda* was sunk. The *Hatsuzuki* was also subsequently sunk by US destroyers and the light cruiser *Tama* was sunk by a US submarine at 2310hrs on October 25. In its sacrificial role, the Northern Force lost all its four carriers, together with a light cruiser and three destroyers. Nevertheless, Ozawa, his mission successful, brought back his two battleships, another light cruiser, and five destroyers.

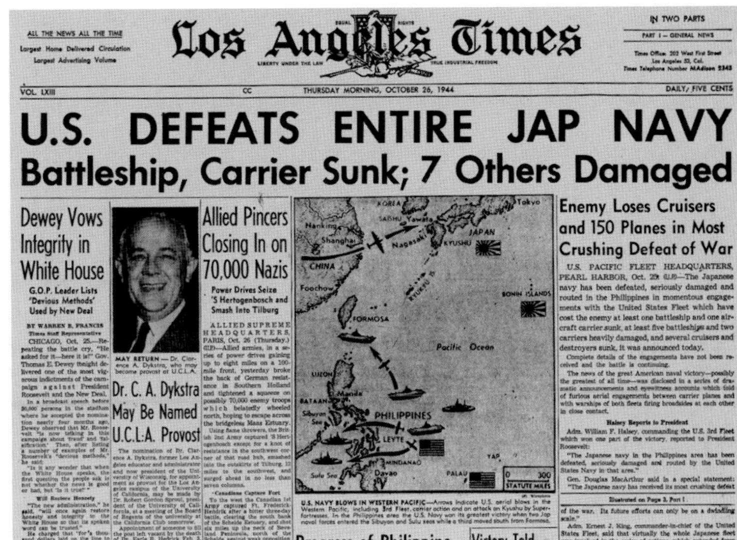

ALL THE NEWS ALL THE TIME
Largest Home Delivered Circulation
Largest Advertising Volume

Los Angeles Times

EQUAL RIGHTS — LIBERTY UNDER THE LAW — TRUE INDUSTRIAL FREEDOM

IN TWO PARTS
PART I — GENERAL NEWS
Times Office: 202 West First Street
Los Angeles 53, Cal.
Times Telephone Number MAdison 2345

VOL. LXIII — CC — THURSDAY MORNING, OCTOBER 26, 1944 — DAILY, FIVE CENTS

U.S. DEFEATS ENTIRE JAP NAVY

Battleship, Carrier Sunk; 7 Others Damaged

Dewey Vows Integrity in White House

G.O.P. Leader Lists 'Devious Methods' Used by New Deal

BY WARREN B. FRANCIS
Times Staff Representative

CHICAGO, Oct. 25.—Repeating the battle cry, "He asked for it—here it is!" Gov. Thomas E. Dewey tonight delivered one of the most vigorous indictments of the campaign against President Roosevelt and the New Deal.

In a broadcast speech before 30,000 persons in the stadium where he accepted the nomination nearly four months ago, Dewey observed that Mr. Roosevelt "is now talking in this campaign about 'fraud' and 'falsification.'" Then, after listing a number of examples of Mr. Roosevelt's "devious methods," he said:

"Is it any wonder that when the White House speaks, the first question the people ask is not whether the news is good or bad, but 'Is it true?'"

Will Restore Honesty

"The new administration," he said, "will once again restore honesty and integrity to the White House so that its spoken word can be trusted."

He charged that "for a thousand dollars laid on the line to

MAY RETURN—Dr. Clarence A. Dykstra, who may become provost at U.C.L.A.

Dr. C. A. Dykstra May Be Named U.C.L.A. Provost

The nomination of Dr. Clarence A. Dykstra, former Los Angeles educator and administrator and now president of the University of Wisconsin, for appointment as provost for the Los Angeles campus of the University of California, may be made by Dr. Robert Gordon Sproul, president of the University of California, at a meeting of the Board of Regents of the university at the California Club tomorrow.

Appointment of someone to fill the post left vacant by the death of Dr. Earle R. Hedrick Feb. 3, 1943, is known to be considered a matter of increasing urgency

Allied Pincers Closing In on 70,000 Nazis

Power Drives Seize 'S Hertogenbosch and Smash Into Tilburg

ALLIED SUPREME HEADQUARTERS, PARIS, Oct. 26 (Thursday.) (U.P.)—Allied armies, in a series of power drives gaining up to eight miles on a 100-mile front, yesterday broke the back of German resistance in Southern Holland and tightened a squeeze on possibly 70,000 enemy troops which belatedly wheeled north, hoping to escape across the bridgeless Maas Estuary.

Using flame throwers, the British 2nd Army captured 'S Hertogenbosch except for a knot of resistance in the southwest corner of that road hub, smashed into the outskirts of Tilburg, 12 miles to the southwest, and surged ahead in no less than seven columns.

Canadians Capture Fort

To the west the Canadian 1st Army captured Ft. Frederick Hendrik after a bitter three-day battle, clearing the south bank of the Schelde Estuary, and shot six miles up the neck of Beveland Peninsula, north of the Schelde, against weak opposition. The latter drive resulted in the capture of Rilland, six miles

U.S. NAVY BLOWS IN WESTERN PACIFIC—Arrows indicate U.S. aerial blows in the Western Pacific, including 3rd Fleet carrier action and an attack on Kyushu by Superfortresses. In the Philippines area the U.S. Navy won its greatest victory when two Jap naval forces entered the Sibuyan and Sulu seas while a third moved south from Formosa.

Progress of Philippine Victory Told

Enemy Loses Cruisers and 150 Planes in Most Crushing Defeat of War

U.S. PACIFIC FLEET HEADQUARTERS, PEARL HARBOR, Oct. 25. (U.P.)—The Japanese navy has been defeated, seriously damaged and routed in the Philippines in momentous engagements with the United States Fleet which have cost the enemy at least one battleship and one aircraft carrier sunk, at least five battleships and two carriers heavily damaged, and several cruisers and destroyers sunk, it was announced today.

Complete details of the engagements have not been received and the battle is continuing.

The news of the great American naval victory—possibly the greatest of all time—was disclosed in a series of dramatic announcements and eyewitness accounts which told of furious aerial engagements between carrier planes and with warships of both fleets firing broadsides at each other in close contact.

Halsey Reports to President

Adm. William F. Halsey, commanding the U.S. 3rd Fleet which won one part of the victory, reported to President Roosevelt:

"The Japanese navy in the Philippines area has been defeated, seriously damaged and routed by the United States Navy in that area."

Gen. Douglas MacArthur said in a special statement: "The Japanese navy has received its most crushing defeat

Illustrated on Page 3, Part I

of the war. Its future efforts can only be on a dwindling scale."

Adm. Ernest J. King, commander-in-chief of the United States Fleet, said that virtually the whole Japanese fleet was involved in the series of actions, which extended from the mid-Philippines invasion zone to the waters between

Front page of the *Los Angeles Times*, October 26, 1944, reporting on the United States victory over Japanese naval forces at the battle of Leyte Gulf. (Topfoto)

AFTERMATH

An American Naval War College publication of 1936 noted that, in naval warfare, "mistakes are normal, errors are usual; information is seldom complete, often inaccurate and frequently misleading." This passage could have been written after the battles for Leyte Gulf. Between October 23 and 26, the landings in the Philippines triggered a series of clashes that, together, constitute the greatest naval engagement of all time. But poor communication procedures prevented a great victory from becoming total victory. Following the battle of the Philippine Sea in the preceding June, the IJN needed time to re-train. The Americans correctly denied it that time by obliging it to make a total commitment over Leyte. Although a considerable proportion of the Japanese surface fleet yet survived, it was never again able to seriously challenge American naval supremacy.

ORIGINS OF THE CAMPAIGN

As the final days of 1944 ebbed away the Japanese were facing defeat on all fronts as they prepared to defend the homeland at the inner limits of their defensive perimeter. The unique strategic location of the island of Iwo Jima, midway along the B-29 Superfortress route from the Marianas to Tokyo, made it imperative that the island should come under American control. Prior to the occupation of Saipan, Tinian, and Guam in the summer of 1944, the B-29s had been limited to carrying out raids on southern Japan from bases in central China. With the problem of transporting all of their fuel by air over thousands of miles of inhospitable country and the limitations of small bomb loads, the attacks had little impact. But now, with the construction of five huge airfields on the US-held islands, only 1,500 miles from the Japanese mainland, the way was open for the 20th Air Force to mount a massive campaign against the industrial heartland of Japan.

A new strategy of "area bombing" by the 20th Air Force was planned. The only obstacle on the flight path was Iwo Jima. It housed two airfields with a third under construction, and a radar station that could give two hours warning of an impending raid. The US Air Force desperately needed to eliminate the threat of fighter attacks from the Iwo airfields and to neutralize the radar station there. With the island under American control there would be the added bonuses of a refuge for crippled bombers, facilities for air-sea rescue flying boats, and, more importantly, a base from which P-51 Mustang long-range escort fighters could operate.

At Iwo Jima the amphibious techniques which had been developed over the previous three years were to receive the supreme test as three Marine divisions pitted themselves against more than 21,000 deeply entrenched Japanese troops led by a brilliant and determined commander, Lieutenant-General Tadamichi Kuribayashi. "Do not plan for my return," he was to inform his wife from Iwo Jima. Sadly his words would also be the epitaph for nearly 6,000 US Marines.

Lieutenant-General Smith, Commander Fleet Marine Forces Pacific and a veteran of Tarawa and Marianas, called the battle: "The most savage and most costly battle in the history of the Marine Corps."

OPPOSITE
This dramatic shot from the rear of a landing craft shows the chaos into which the Marines were deposited – volcanic ash up to their ankles, enemy pillboxes, and bunkers straight ahead, and more troops arriving every five minutes. (NARA)

OPPOSING COMMANDERS

THE US COMMANDERS

On October 3, 1944, the Joint Chiefs of Staff issued a directive to Admiral Chester W. Nimitz, Commander-in-Chief Pacific Fleet (CINCPAC) and Pacific Ocean Area (CINCPOA), to occupy the island of Iwo Jima. As with previous amphibious landings in the Marine Corps "island hopping" campaign, he entrusted the planning and implementation of the assault, codenamed Operation *Detachment*, to his experienced trio of tacticians, Spruance, Turner, and Smith who had masterminded almost every operation since the initial landing at Tarawa in 1943.

Rear-Admiral Raymond A. Spruance had been Nimitz's right-hand man since his outstanding performance at the battle of Midway. His quiet unassuming manner concealed a razor sharp intellect and an ability to utilize the experience and knowledge of his staff to a remarkable degree. Rear-Admiral Richmond Kelly Turner, the Joint Expeditionary Force Commander, was by contrast notorious for his short temper and foul mouth, but his amazing organization skills placed him in a unique position to mount the operation. Dovetailing the dozens of air strikes and shore bombardments, disembarking thousands of troops and landing them on the right beach in the right sequence was an awesome responsibility fraught with the seeds of potential disaster, but Turner had proved his ability time and time again. Lieutenant-General Holland M. Smith, Commanding General Fleet Marine Force Pacific, was nearing the end of his active career. His aggressive tactics and uncompromising attitude had made him many enemies including MacArthur and at Iwo Jima he was content to keep a low profile in favor of Major-General Harry Schmidt, V Amphibious Corps Commander.

The Iwo Jima landing would involve an unprecedented assembly of three Marine divisions: the 3rd, 4th, and 5th under the command of Major-General Graves B. Erskine, Major-General Clifton B. Cates, who had won the Navy Cross, and Major-General Keller E. Rockey, respectively. Responsibility for preparing and executing Marine operations for *Detachment* fell to V Amphibious Corps

FROM LEFT TO RIGHT
Fleet Admiral Chester Nimitz. (US Navy)

Admiral Raymond Spruance. (NARA)

Rear-Admiral Richmond Kelly Turner's organizing skills were legendary. With the exception of Peleliu, he masterminded every landing in the Pacific from Guadalcanal to the final battle at Okinawa. (US Navy)

Lieutenant-General Smith was a volatile leader. He is seen here in his two-toned helmet alongside the Secretary of the Navy (with binoculars) and a group of Iwo Jima Marines. (NARA)

Landing Force Commander Major-General Harry Schmidt. A veteran of the Saipan invasions, he would have the honor of fronting the largest Marine Corps force ever committed to a single battle.

THE JAPANESE COMMANDERS

In May, Lieutenant-General Tadamichi Kuribayashi had been summoned to the office of the Japanese Prime Minister, General Hideki Tojo, and told that he would be the commander of the garrison on Iwo Jima. Kuribayashi, a samurai and long-serving officer with 30 years distinguished service, had spent time in the United States as a deputy attaché and had proclaimed to his family: "the United States is the last country in the world that Japan should fight." Kuribayashi succeeded in doing what no other Japanese commander in the Pacific could do – inflicting more casualties on the US Marines than his own troops suffered.

General Kuribayashi wasted no time in re-organizing the inadequate defense system that he discovered upon his arrival on the island. Here he is seen with members of his staff directing operations. (Taro Kuribayashi)

OPPOSING FORCES

THE US FORCES

The American Marine force totaled over 70,000 men including many seasoned veterans. On February 15, the invasion fleet left Saipan, first the LSTs carrying the first waves of troops from the 4th and 5th Divisions and the following day the troop transports with the remainder of the Marines and the tanks, supplies, artillery, and supporting units.

THE JAPANESE FORCES

The Japanese High Command realized the importance of Iwo Jima and as early as March 1944 began to reinforce the island. The 145th Infantry Regiment and the 109th Division (including the 26th Tank Regiment) were drafted to the island. Naval units including anti-aircraft and engineering groups were also present. At the time of the Marine landing, February 19, 1945, the total Japanese garrison numbered 21,060, considerably more than the American calculation of 13,000.

OPPOSING PLANS

THE US PLAN

The plan of attack devised by Schmidt's V

With Mount Suribachi in the foreground, the invasion beaches can be seen on the right of the picture, stretching northward to the East Boat Basin. Isolating the volcano was the number one priority for the Marines and involved crossing the half-mile neck of the island as rapidly as possible. (US Navy)

OPPOSITE, BOTTOM
Three of the old battleships of the US Navy get into position prior to "softening up" the island in preparation for the landings. Their 16in shells were ideal for reducing the concrete bunkers that dotted the Iwo Jima coastline. (National Archives)

Amphibious Corps looked deceptively simple. The Marines would land on the two-mile long stretch of beach between Mount Suribachi and the East Boat Basin on the southeast coast of the island. These beaches were divided into seven sections of 550 yards each. Under the shadow of Suribachi lay Green Beach (1st and 2nd Battalions, 28th Regiment), flanked on the right by Red Beach 1 (2nd Battalion, 27th Regiment), Red Beach 2 (1st Battalion, 27th Regiment), Yellow Beach 1 (1st Battalion, 23rd Regiment), Yellow Beach 2 (2nd Battalion, 23rd Regiment), Blue Beach 1 (1st and 3rd Battalions, 25th Regiment). Blue Beach 2 lay directly under known enemy gun emplacements in the quarry overlooking the East Boat Basin, and it was decided that both the 1st and 3rd Battalions of the 25th Regiment should land abreast on Blue Beach 1. General Cates, the 4th Division commander, said: "If I knew the name of the man on the extreme right of the right hand squad (on Blue Beach), I'd recommend him for a medal before we go in."

The 28th Regiment would attack straight across the narrowest part of the island to the opposite coast, swing left, isolate and then secure Mount Suribachi. On their right, the 27th Regiment would also cross the island and move to the north, while the 23rd Regiment would seize Airfield No. 1 and then thrust northward toward Airfield No. 2. The 25th Regiment, on the extreme right, would neutralize the high ground around the quarry overlooking the East Boat Basin.

THE JAPANESE PLAN

The American armada was soon spotted by Japanese naval patrol aircraft and the Iwo Jima garrison was put on immediate alert. General Kuribayashi had earlier issued his troops with a document called "The Courageous Battle Vows" which stated that each man should make it his duty to kill ten of the enemy before dying. With his defenses prepared and his men ready to fight to the death, Kuribayashi waited patiently for the approaching invader. General Kuribayashi had sent all civilians back to the mainland and had instigated a massive program of underground defenses creating an extensive system of tunnels (some even featuring operating theaters), caves, gun emplacements, pillboxes, and command posts. Kuribayashi had studied earlier Japanese defense methods of attempting to halt the enemy at the beachhead and had realized that they invariably failed. He knew that the Americans would eventually take the island but he was determined to exact a fearful toll in Marine casualties before they did so.

The geography of the island virtually dictated the location of the landing sites for the invasion force. From aerial photographs and periscope shots taken by the submarine USS *Spearfish*, it was obvious that there were only two stretches of beach upon which the Marines could land. Kuribayashi had come to the same conclusion months earlier and made his plans accordingly.

THE INVASION

D-DAY: "A NIGHTMARE IN HELL"

As a prelude to the landings Schmidt had requested ten continuous days of shelling by Rear-Admiral William Blandy's Amphibious Support Force (TF-52). Admiral Hill rejected the request on the grounds that there would be insufficient time to re-arm his ships before D-Day. Eventually he was offered a mere three days of "softening up" before his Marines went ashore. Spruance's comment – "I know that your people will get away with it" – was to sound hollow as the battle progressed.

The three days of bombardment were a bitter disappointment. Hampered by poor weather Schmidt complained: "We only got about 13 hours worth of fire support during the 34 hours of available daylight." By contrast, D-Day, Monday February 19, 1945, dawned sunny with unlimited visibility. During the night Admiral Marc Mitscher's TF-58, a vast armada of 16 carriers, eight battleships, and 15 cruisers, fresh from highly successful attacks against the Japanese mainland, arrived off Iwo Jima accompanied by Admiral Raymond Spruance in his flagship USS *Indianapolis*.

As the battleships and cruisers pounded the island and swarms of carrier-based aircraft mounted air strikes, the disembarkation of thousands of Marines from troopships and LVTs was gathering momentum. To spearhead the attack 68 LVT(A)s – armored amphibious

The west side of Mount Suribachi is wreathed in smoke as the pre-invasion bombardment gets under way. Spectacular as it was, Smith was disappointed with the results and criticized the Navy for their failure to destroy most of the enemy installations before the Marines landed. (US Navy)

Instead of the straightforward exit from the beaches that the Marines had been led to expect, they came upon terraces of black volcanic ash, some of them up to 15ft high, and there were long delays in getting troops, tanks, and artillery inland. (NARA)

tractors mounting a 75mm howitzer and three machine guns – were to venture 50 yards onto the beachhead to cover the first wave of Marines, but the first of a number of planning "foul-ups" was to frustrate their deployment. Along the whole of the landing beach there were 15ft-high terraces of soft black volcanic ash. The troops sank up to their ankles, the vehicles to their hubcaps, and the LVTs and Sherman tanks ground to a halt within yards of the shore.

In keeping with General Kuribayashi's strategy, Japanese resistance had been relatively subdued; he wanted the Americans to land substantial numbers onto the beaches before unleashing his coordinated bombardment. A steady stream of small arms and machine gun fire whined across the beaches and the occasional crump of a mortar shell sent sand flying, but the most formidable enemy was the sand itself. Marines were trained to move rapidly forward; here they could only plod and various items were rapidly discarded.

As the first waves of Marines struggled to move forward, successive waves arrived at intervals of around five minutes and the situation rapidly deteriorated. A little after 1000hrs the full fury of the Japanese defenses was unleashed. From well-concealed positions a torrent of artillery, mortar, and machine gun fire rained down on the crowded beaches.

By 1040hrs Harry Hill had 6,000 men ashore and the bulldozers that had arrived in the early waves were hacking away at the terraces. Some tanks were breaking through to solid ground and troops were finally escaping the horror of the beaches where Kuribayashi's artillery and mortars were wreaking havoc. Robert Sherrod, a noted war correspondent for *Time-Life*, aptly described the scene as "a nightmare in hell."

At the extreme left of the beachhead, Green Beach, the terrain was less difficult where the volcanic ash gave way to rocks and stone at the base of Mount Suribachi, defended by Colonel Kanehiko Asuchi and 2,000 men. Here Colonel Harry Liversedge's 28th Regiment began their dash across the half-mile isthmus below the volcano in an attempt to isolate this strategically vital position.

The 1st Battalion, ignoring this threat to their left flank, pressed on toward the far shore but soon encountered Captain Osada's 312th Independent Infantry Battalion and fierce fighting erupted around a series of bunkers and pillboxes. Some were destroyed and others bypassed in the mad dash to cross the island.

At 1035hrs six men of Company B, 1st Battalion, reached the west coast, soon to be joined by the remnants of Company C and Suribachi was isolated, albeit precariously. On

Red Beaches 1 and 2, the 27th Regiment under Colonel Thomas Wornham were having great difficulty in moving forward. The Japanese artillery bracketed the crowded beach and casualties mounted by the minute. To their right on Yellow 1 and 2, the 23rd Regiment under Colonel Walter Wensinger had come face to face with a mass of blockhouses and pillboxes. Battling against shredding machine gun fire, Sergeant Darren Cole, armed only with grenades and a pistol, single-handedly silenced five pillboxes before being killed by a hand grenade and became the first of the Marine Corps 27 Medal of Honor recipients during the battle.

At the extreme right, Blue Beach 1, Colonel John Lanigan's 25th Regiment moved straight ahead to avoid the obvious danger presented by the high ground at the quarry on their right flank, making a two-pronged attack with the 1st Battalion pressing inland as the 3rd Battalion swung right to assault cliffs at the base of the quarry.

A few tanks of the 4th Tank Battalion had finally succeeded in getting ashore on Blue 1 at around 1020hrs while at 1400hrs the 3rd

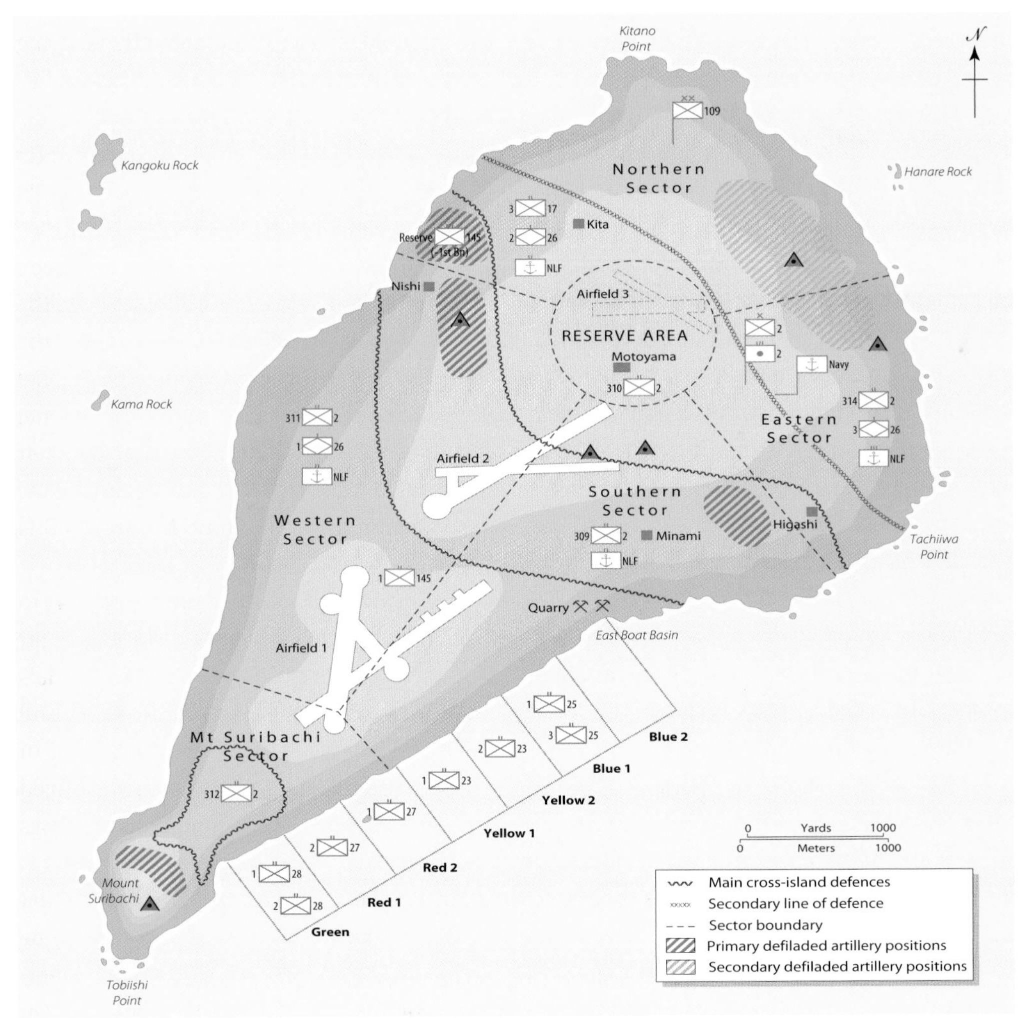

Map illustrating the Japanese defenses and US landings on Iwo Jima. (Osprey Publishing Ltd.)

Battalion under their commander "Jumpin' Joe" Chambers began scaling the cliffs around the quarry. The enemy resistance was fanatical and the Marines were soon down to 150 men from the original 900 who had landed at 0900hrs.

At the base of Mount Suribachi the 28th Regiment were consolidating their positions. By afternoon a few Sherman tanks that had penetrated the beachhead were moving up to provide valuable assistance by destroying many Japanese pillboxes with their 75mm guns, and by evening Suribachi was securely isolated from the rest of the island. The grim task of occupying this formidable bastion would have to wait until later.

In the center, the 27th and 25th Regiments were gradually extricating themselves from the Red and Yellow beaches and moving toward Airfield No. 1. The Seabees (Naval Construction Battalions) did sterling work to clear the beaches despite experiencing high casualties, which allowed a normal rate of landings to resume. Even so, in virtually every shell hole there lay at least one dead Marine.

By 1130hrs some Marines had reached the southern end of Airfield No. 1 which was sited on a plateau whose perimeter rose steeply on the eastern side. The Japanese mounted a fierce defense, hundreds being killed and the remainder pouring across the runway or disappearing into the pipes of the drainage system.

As evening approached, the Marines held a line running from the base of Mount Suribachi across the southern perimeter of Airfield No. 1 and ending at the foot of the quarry, but had not reached the 0-1 line, the unrealistic D-Day objective. Aboard the command ship *Eldorado*, "Howlin' Mad" Smith studied the day's reports. Progress had not been as good as he had hoped and the casualty figures made grim reading: "I don't know who he is, but the Japanese General running this show is one smart bastard," he announced to a group of war correspondents.

D+1 – D+5: "INFLICT MUCH DAMAGE TO THE ENEMY"

D+1

A 4ft high surf on the beaches and a bitterly cold wind did little to raise the spirits of either the Marines or their commanders on Tuesday, D+1. Having isolated Mount Suribachi, the 28th Regiment were faced with the unenviable task of capturing it, while to the north the remainder of the invasion force were poised to mount a concerted attack to secure Airfields 1 and 2.

Attacking on a broad front with artillery and aerial support, the Marines could only gain 75 yards of ground by 1200hrs in the face of fierce resistance from defenders commanded by a Colonel Atsuchi. Tanks had joined the battle at around 1100hrs following long delays in refueling and added valuable support, but the Japanese had a huge advantage in their prepared positions on the higher ground.

Little progress was made in the afternoon and the Marines dug in and awaited reinforcements and additional tanks for an all-out assault the following day. The Japanese were determined that there should be no respite for the enemy and commenced a barrage all along the front line. During the night, Japanese troops began to gather near the eastern slopes of the volcano but the destroyer USS *Henry A. Wiley* blasted them under the glare of searchlights, and the night-time counterattack was halted.

Section Chief Marine Private First Class R. F. Callahan calls in 155mm artillery fire against a Japanese position. (USMC)

To the north, the other three regiments began their offensive at around 0830hrs, with the right flank anchored at the quarry and the left swinging north in an attempt to straighten the line. The Marines encountered strong opposition. Mid-afternoon saw the arrival of the brand new battleship USS *Washington* which blasted the cliffs around the quarry with her massive 16in guns causing a landslide that blocked dozens of enemy caves.

By 1200hrs the majority of Airfield No. 1 was in American hands, a bitter blow to Kuribayashi, and the Marines now had an almost straight front line across the island although the D-Day 0-1 objective still eluded them. General Schmidt decided to commit the 21st Regiment of the 3rd Division (the Joint Chiefs of Staff had hoped to keep the whole of the 3rd Division intact for the upcoming invasion of Okinawa). However, the high seas and congested beaches frustrated the landings and the regiment was eventually ordered back.

D + 2

Wednesday's plan looked deceptively straightforward – the 28th Regiment would begin its final assault on Mount Suribachi and the remainder would move north on a broad front. But the deteriorating weather and 6ft waves meant the beaches were once again closed to landings.

Supported by a blistering artillery and naval barrage, as well as napalm and machine-gun fire from over 40 carrier planes, the 28th Regiment launched its assault on Mount Suribachi at 0845hrs. The gunfire denuded the ground before it, revealing chains of blockhouses and connecting trenches with little or no cover between the two front lines and hazardous rows of barbed wire. Once again the vitally needed tanks were delayed due to fueling problems.

The 3rd Platoon in the center met heavy opposition but the late arriving tanks helped their progress. By evening the regiment had formed a semi-circle around the north side of

A machine gun crew sit among a pile of spent ammunition somewhere just south of Mount Suribachi. (NARA)

the volcano and moved forward 650 yards on the left, 500 yards in the center, and 1,000 yards on the right – good progress under the circumstances.

To the north, the 4th and 5th Marine Divisions moved against a complex of well-hidden enemy positions and casualties soon began to mount. Near the west coast, Sherman tanks led an advance of over 1,000 yards by the 26th and 27th Regiments and the D-Day 0-1 line was finally reached. On the east side of the island, the 4th Division could only take 50 yards of ground in the rugged and hazardous terrain around the quarry despite being reinforced by an extra company. Captain "Jumpin' Joe" McCarthy, commanding officer of Company G, 2nd Battalion, 24th Regiment, stated: "We landed with 257 men and received 90 replacements. Of that total of 347 only 35 men were able to walk off the island when the fighting was over."

General Schmidt again disembarked the 21st Regiment of the 3rd Division and they came ashore on Yellow Beach. The Japanese continued their disruptive fire throughout the night and between 150 and 200 troops gathered at the end of the runway of Airfield No. 2 and rushed the lines of the 23rd Regiment at 2330hrs. A combination of artillery and naval gunfire annihilated them before they could reach the Marines.

D + 3

There was no let-up in the weather on Thursday as Marines of the 28th Regiment prepared to renew the attack on Suribachi. The Shermans were mired in mud and the Navy declined to supply air support in the appalling weather. It was to be up to the foot soldier with rifle, flamethrower, grenade, and demolition charge to win the day. Colonel Atsuchi still had 800–900 men left and they had no intention of allowing the Americans an easy victory. Major Youamata announced: "The Americans are beginning to climb the first terraces toward our defenses. Now they shall taste our steel and lead."

Throughout the day the Marines attacked the Japanese positions on the lower slopes of Suribachi. There was little room for maneuver and it was impossible to use support fire from artillery and tanks to maximum advantage because of the close proximity of the lines. By afternoon, Marine patrols had worked their way around the base of the volcano and it was surrounded. The bitter fighting on the northern slopes had reduced the Japanese garrison to a few hundred men and many were infiltrating the Marine lines through the maze of tunnels and joining Kuribayashi's forces in the north. Others moved upward toward the summit. The final assault would have to wait until the following day.

The sweep to the north continued with Harry Schmidt placing the newly landed 21st Regiment in the center of the line between the 4th and 5th Divisions around Airfield No. 2. Here Colonel Ikeda with his 145th Regiment had the strongest section of the Japanese defenses. The new 3rd Division men had a

Marine artillery was vital in the support of the front line troops. Most of the Marine advances were accompanied by massive bombardments from both offshore naval units and forward artillery. (NARA)

Near the base of Mount Suribachi, Marines destroy an enemy position with demolition charges. The dash across the base of Suribachi was accomplished in good time, the capture of the volcano taking days longer. (USMC)

baptism of fire as they stormed the heavily defended ground south of the airfield and the day's gains amounted to a mere 250 yards.

On the eastern flank near the quarry, "Jumpin' Joe" Chambers had rocket firing trucks brought forward to pound the enemy hideouts, resulting in dozens of Japanese fleeing to the lower ground where they were decimated by machine gun fire. Chambers was himself badly wounded in the afternoon and evacuated to a hospital ship.

The Japanese mounted a series of strong counterattacks throughout the day which were repulsed by heavy artillery fire, and as the weather deteriorated further the fighting died down. Casualties still crowded the beaches as the rough seas prevented LSTs from evacuating the wounded, and behind the lines near Airfield No. 1, the 4th Division cemetery was inaugurated. Up till now the dead had been left in rows under their ponchos, "stacked like cordwood" as one Marine described it.

"Howlin' Mad" Smith aboard the USS *Auburn* was counting the cost. Three days of battle and the Regimental Returns listed 2,517 casualties for the 4th Division and 2,057 for the 5th: 4,574 dead and wounded and the 0-1 line had just been reached. Little did he know that as his Marines approached the hills, ravines, canyons, gullies, and cliffs of the north the worst was yet to come.

D + 4

February 23 was the day that the 28th Regiment finally captured Mount Suribachi. With much improved weather, Lieutenant-Colonel Chandler Johnson gave the order to occupy and secure the summit and Marines from the 3rd Platoon started out at 0800hrs. A 40-man patrol led by Lieutenant Hal Schrier labored up the northern slopes, laden with weapons and ammunition. The going became increasingly difficult but the opposition was surprisingly light. At 1000hrs they reached the rim of the crater and engaged a number of the enemy who attacked them with hand grenades. At 1020hrs the Stars and Stripes were raised on a length of pipe. Throughout the southern half of the island the shout was "the flag is up" and troops cheered and vessels sounded their sirens.

With about one third of Iwo Jima in American hands and a great improvement in the weather, General Harry Schmidt landed to set up his HQ. It was decided that the 3rd Division would maintain the center with the 5th Division in the west and the 4th in the east. The Navy would continue to add support with gunfire and carrier aircraft, and the tanks of all three divisions would come under a single command, under Lieutenant-Colonel William Collins of the 5th Division.

The rest of D+4 was largely a day of consolidation and replenishment; however, Schmidt was planning a major offensive for the following day to break the stalemate.

D + 5

True to his word, Schmidt provided a tremendous naval barrage all along the front line. Masses of aircraft added bombs and rockets, and the Marine artillery and mortars expended huge amounts of ammunition.

Accompanied by a tremendous naval barrage and aerial support, the attack was spearheaded by the 21st Regiment deployed in the area between the two airfields. Massed tanks were scheduled to precede the infantry but Colonel Ikeda had anticipated this move, and the taxiways of both airfields were heavily mined and covered by anti-tank guns. Deprived of their armor, the Marines had no alternative but to clear the bunkers and pillboxes the hard way, with small arms, grenades, and flamethrowers. In what looked more like an episode from World War I, the Marines charged the high ground and the Japanese retaliated by leaving their positions and engaging the Americans in hand-to-hand fighting. In a frenzied melee of clubbing, stabbing, kicking, and punching, the Marines finally occupied the higher ground.

On the right flank, the 24th Regiment of the 4th Division were battling for "Charlie Dog Ridge," an escarpment south of the main runway of Airfield No. 2. Supported by howitzers and mortars they blasted and burned their way to the top sustaining heavy casualties. At 1700hrs Colonel Walter Jordan ordered the men to dig in for the night. By Iwo Jima standards the overall gains for the day had been impressive, but so too had the casualty figures. Between D+1 and D+5, 1,034 men had died, 3,741 were wounded, five were missing and 558 were suffering

From this picture it is clear to see that the Marines had technology and equipment on their side. (Tom Laemlein)

OPPOSITE TOP
The flamethrower was the most practical weapon for clearing the enemy from caves, pillboxes, and bunkers. Horrific in its effect, it saved the lives of countless Marines who would otherwise have had to prise the enemy out in hand-to-hand fighting. (Tom Laemlein)

BELOW
At 1020hrs the Stars and Stripes were raised on a length of pipe as Leatherneck photographer Lou Lowery recorded the moment. Around 1200hrs, a larger flag was raised to replace the smaller one. The event was photographed by Associated Press cameraman Joe Rosenthal, and this became the most famous picture of World War II. (US Navy)

from battle fatigue. Less than half of the island had been secured and the battle had a further 30 days to run.

D+6 – D+11: INTO THE MEATGRINDER

D + 6

Schmidt was intent on pressing northward across the plateau and Airfield No. 3 to split the enemy in two. Other factors also influenced the commander's choice. The west coast of the island had accessible beaches which were desperately needed to unload the vast amount of equipment and supplies still stacked in the armada of transports. With Okinawa only two months away these ships were urgently needed elsewhere, but at the moment the Japanese still commanded the heights northwest of Airfield No. 2 from which they could shell the western coast with impunity.

Even though the southern end of the island was still within range of many of the Japanese guns, the area around Airfield No. 1 was being turned into a construction site as over 2,000 Seabees worked on the runways so that B-29s and P-51s could land there in the future.

The thrust to the north began on D+6, Sunday, February 25. As the 3rd Battalion moved against high ground at the end of the main runway of Airfield No. 2, 26 Shermans rumbled out to spearhead the attack and ran into a fusillade of enemy fire. The strongest point in the Japanese defenses was "Hill Peter," a 360ft high prominence just off the runway. This was stormed repeatedly but by 1430hrs the Marines had only gained 200 yards. The 2nd and 1st Battalions had slightly better luck and were north of the airfield, although "Hill Peter" remained in enemy hands.

The 5th Division on the left was already 400 yards ahead of the 3rd Division lines and was ordered to stay where it was, but on the right the 4th Division faced a complex of four formidable defense positions that became known collectively as the "Meatgrinder." The first was Hill 382 (named from its elevation above sea level), with its slopes peppered with countless pillboxes and caves. Four hundred yards to the south lay a shallow depression called the "Amphitheater," and immediately to the east was "Turkey Knob," a hill surmounted by a massive blockhouse. The fourth obstacle was the ruins of the village of Minami, now studded with machine gun emplacements. This collective killing ground was defended by Major-General Senda and his 2nd Mixed Brigade.

The 23rd and 24th Regiments, some 3,800 men of the 4th Division, prepared to take on the "Meatgrinder" and at 0800hrs the now customary naval barrage and aerial attack preceded the assault on Hill 382. Vicious hand-to-hand fighting ensued as the survivors withdrew under cover of smoke. Day one in the "Meatgrinder" was a complete stalemate. About 100 yards had been gained at the cost of nearly 500 casualties.

US Marines also cleared Iwo Jima with the aid of the bazooka. (Tom Laemlein)

D + 7

On Monday, February 26, once again the day's gains on Hill 382 were insignificant. To the west the 5th Division set its sights on Hill 362A, 600 yards south of the village of Nishi and surrounded by pillboxes and caves. Tanks ground through the rocks to give support but the complex proved impregnable. A little to the right, the tanks smashed through the enemy defenses to a depth of 100 yards and the 27th Regiment advanced up the west coast assisted by off-shore gunfire. Day two of the battle for Hill 382 saw the 24th Regiment replaced by the 25th Regiment. The initial attack looked promising with a gain of over 100 yards until heavy machine gun fire from "Turkey Knob" brought the advance to a halt.

The 23rd Regiment to the left worked its way through a minefield beside the perimeter track of the airfield and advanced but was halted by heavy enemy fire with 17 Marines lost. It was during this engagement that

PREVIOUS SPREAD
As tanks assemble near Airfield No. 2, Marines of Company G, 24th Regiment, relax before renewing the attack on enemy pillboxes in the area. (USMC)

19-year-old Private Douglas Jacobson killed 75 of the enemy in less than 30 minutes and earned himself the Medal of Honor.

D + 8

"Hill Peter" still stood out like a sore thumb at the front of the 3rd Division line and at 0800hrs two battalions of the 9th regiment, Lieutenant-Colonel Randall's 1st and Lieutenant-Colonel Cushman's 2nd, moved forward to secure the complex. Inching forward against murderous machine gun and mortar fire the 1st reached the top of the hill but was pinned down by fire from bypassed positions at its rear. In the early afternoon another concerted effort was launched and elements of both battalions relieved the beleaguered Marines.

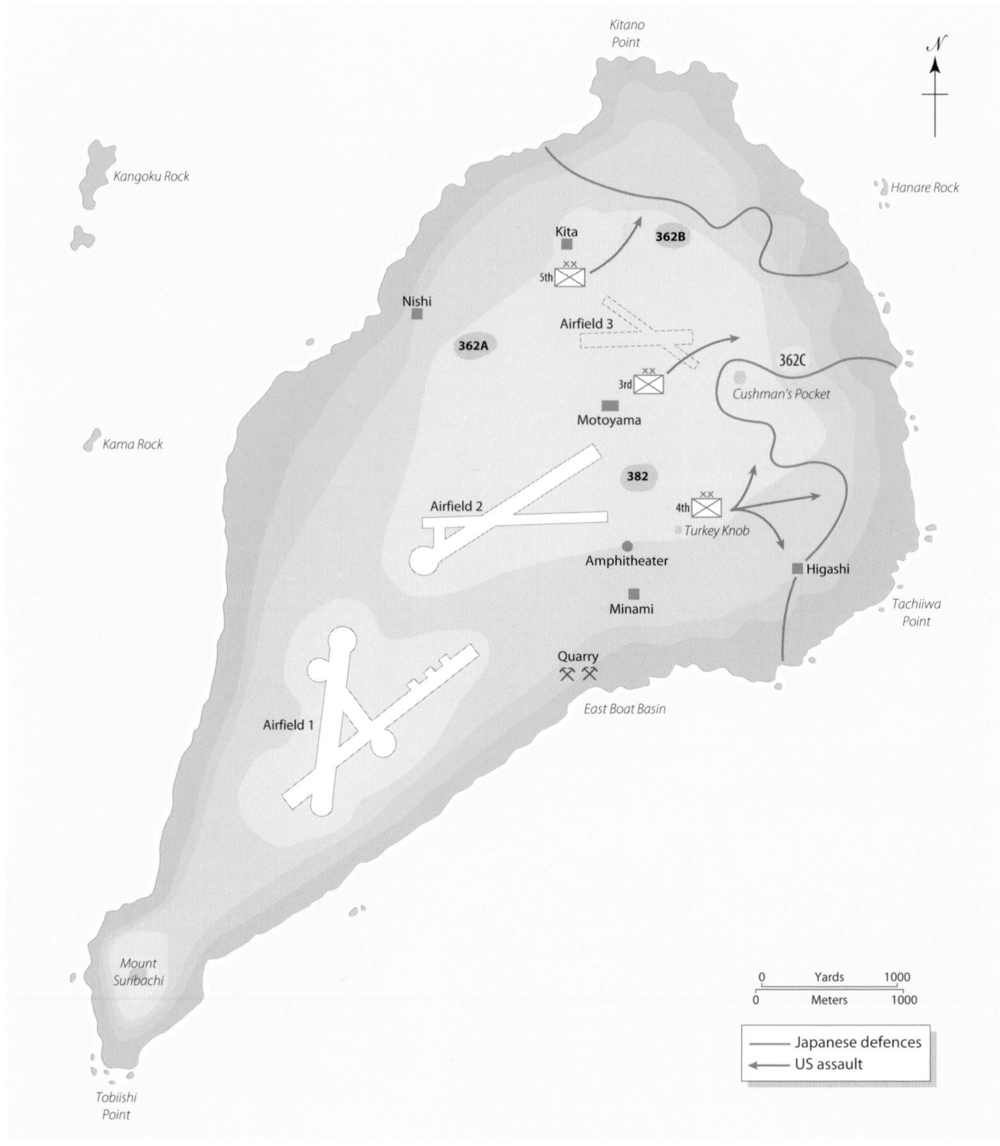

A map showing US gains by D+19. (Osprey Publishing Ltd)

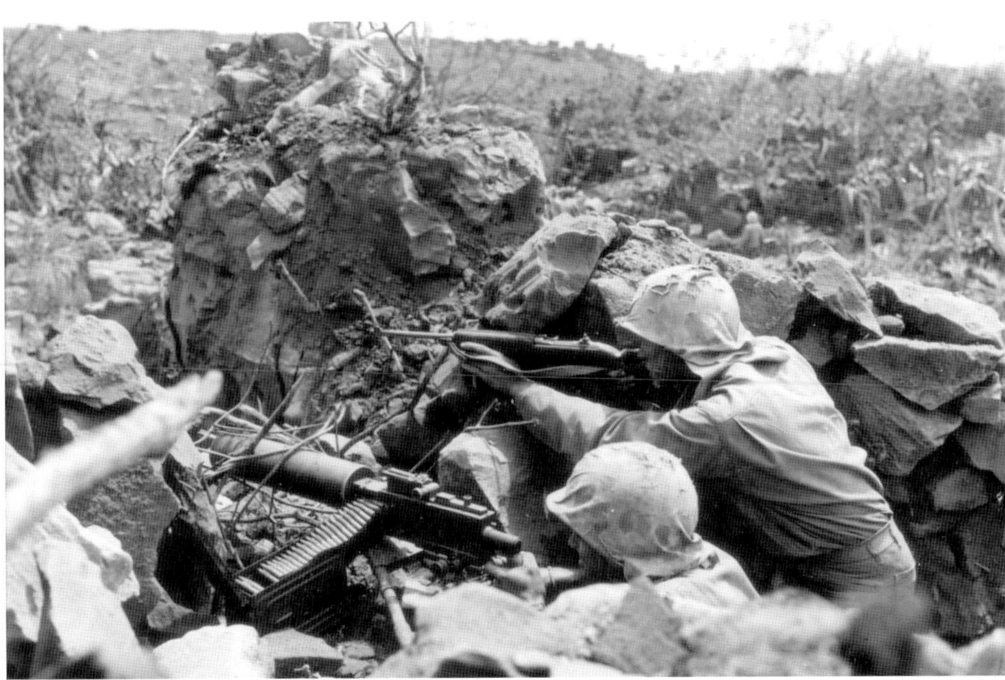

Marines from the 4th Marine Division slowly clearing Iwo Jima. (Tom Laemlein)

To the east the 4th Division appeared to be bogged down before the seemingly impregnable "Meatgrinder" and all day the battle seesawed up and down the hill. At the foot of the hill the Marines finally completed an encircling maneuver after bitter hand-to-hand fighting, and the last hours of daylight were spent in consolidating their precarious gains.

As the battle moved further north the tanks found it more and more difficult to operate among the gullies and boulder-strewn terrain. The battle was developing into a horrific man-to-man slog in which casualties escalated by the day and prisoners were a novelty.

D + 9

Although this was the day that Schmidt had predicted as the end of the battle, his orders for the day were for the 3rd to press forward toward the north coast. Relieving the battered 9th, the 21st Regiment moved out at 0900hrs and, under a huge naval and artillery barrage that appeared to have stunned the enemy, made good progress. At one point they were confronted by some of the few remaining "Ha-Go" tanks of Baron Nishi's 26th Regiment, but these flimsy vehicles were mostly wiped out. The Japanese soon recovered and by afternoon resistance had stiffened to such an extent that a second massive artillery barrage was called in and by 1300hrs the troops were again on the move. This time the momentum was maintained as the Marines stormed their way into the ruins of the village of Motoyama, once the largest settlement on Iwo Jima.

Over on the 5th Division front, the Marines were still confronted with Hill 362A – the top dotted with anti-tank guns and mortars and the slopes bristling with machine guns. The only gains of the day were made by the 1st Battalion who gained 300 yards near the base. The impasse at the "Meatgrinder" continued as the 4th Division continued to batter Hill 382 and "Turkey Knob." Attempts to encircle these

TOP
As the 5th Division advanced up the west coast, many enemy gun positions were captured. Here a Marine stands guard over a Japanese coastal artillery piece. (NARA)

BOTTOM
A couple of Marines utilize a captured Japanese Nambo machine gun as the fighting in the north intensifies. (NARA)

positions were frustrated, and as smoke shells covered the withdrawal of forward troops, the operation was closed for the day at 1645hrs.

D+10

After a night overlooking Airfield No. 3, the 21st Regiment of the 3rd Division moved forward against surprisingly light resistance and by 1200hrs was across the main runway. Tanks rolled forward to stiffen the attack and all went well until the forward troops reached Hills 362B and 362C, two more heavily defended bastions barring the way to the coast, and the advance ran out of steam.

On the west coast, the 28th Regiment, the conquerors of Mount Suribachi, were now bolstering the 5th Division front as all three battalions were pitted against the complex of strong points north of Hill 362A. The day started with naval shelling and the 1st and 2nd Battalions stormed the slopes and reached the summit as the Japanese had abandoned the site through a labyrinth of caves and had taken up new positions on Nishi Ridge, a ragged cliff line 200 yards further north.

For the 4th Division, Hill 382 was the key to the impasse. Until it was taken the whole of the eastern side of Iwo Jima would be firmly in enemy hands, and in the pre-dawn darkness the 24th Regiment moved up to replace the 23rd. In a day of unremitting savagery the battle flowed back and forth. The generals were becoming increasingly concerned about the combat efficiency of their units. It was not unusual to see command pass from captain to lieutenant to sergeant, and in some cases to Private First Class (Pfc).

D+11

The pressure continued on Hill 382 as "Zippos" (flamethrower tanks) expended over 1,000 gallons of fuel on the caves, but the Japanese simply retired to the depths of their tunnels. Meanwhile the 26th Regiment, in some of the fiercest fighting of the day, secured a foothold on the summit of Hill 382. Casualties were horrendous, one unit losing five officers in rapid succession.

In the center, hopes of a dash to the north coast were fading. Although the sea was only 1,500 yards away the 3rd Division had yet to deal with Hills 362B and C. Four thousand men headed out in a two-pronged assault, one group headed for Hill 362B while the other deployed around Airfield No. 3. The approach to the hill was a flat area overlooked by artillery and offering virtually no cover. Tanks were brought forward and under their cover an advance of 500 yards was made to the base of the hill.

Colonel Chandler Johnson's 28th Regiment on the west coast was determined to secure Nishi Ridge. Advancing along the left side of Hill 363A they came under heavy fire but pushed on to the ravine between the hill and the ridge where they had a clear area from which the Shermans could blast the cliff face although Johnson himself was killed.

D+12 – D+19: DEADLOCK

D+12

Casualty figures were reaching epidemic proportions. By D+12 the Marine figure stood at 16,000 of whom more than 3,000 were dead. The Japanese numbers were staggering. Of the 21,000 troops under Lieutenant-General Kuribayashi's command on D-Day, a mere 7,000 remained and still the battle raged.

In a grim day's fighting during which they suffered severe casualties, the 26th Regiment, 5th Division, finally stormed to the top of Hill 362B although the enemy still occupied much of the surrounding area. But the best news of the day came with the capture of Nishi Ridge by the 28th Regiment.

The 3rd Division again pitted themselves against the "Meatgrinder" and the 24th Regiment successfully surrounded Hill 382. But it was the only significant material gain of the day despite the award of an astonishing five Medals of Honor for acts of bravery.

D+13

In deteriorating weather, carrier plane sorties and naval bombardments were called off because of poor visibility. In the knowledge that the battle was swinging irrevocably in favor of the Americans, Lieutenant-General Kuribayashi radioed Tokyo: "Our strong points might be able to fight delaying actions for several more days. I comfort myself a little seeing my officers and men die without regret after struggling in this inch-by-inch battle against an overwhelming enemy..." The general's predictions were, if anything, on the pessimistic side as his garrison would prolong the battle for another three weeks.

As tanks and rocket launchers pounded the amphitheater in the east, the 3rd Division in the center were unable to make any significant progress. In the west the 5th Division continued to engage the more exposed positions with flamethrowers and grenades, but little progress could be reported over the entire front. It was clear that the Marines desperately needed a break after two weeks of the bloodiest fighting the Corps had ever experienced.

Near the beach, rows of dead lie under their ponchos: burial parties check identification and personal possessions. (NARA)

The Superfortress "Dinah Might" was the first B-29 to land on the island. The arrival attracted a great deal of attention, as crowds of Marines and Seabees gathered to see the huge bomber. (NARA)

The highlight of the day was the arrival of the first B-29 Superfortress bomber to land on Iwo Jima. The damaged aircraft had struggled back from a mission southwest of Tokyo. The bloody sacrifices of the Marine Corps in securing the island were beginning to pay dividends in the lives of what were to be thousands of Air Force crewmen.

D+15

D+14 had been a day of rest for the weary Marines and a chance to replenish supplies, albeit still under enemy fire. D+15 saw a return to a full-scale onslaught. The Navy and Marine artillery mounted one of the heaviest bombardments of the battle and within 67 minutes the artillery fired 22,500 rounds supported also by naval bombardments and carrier fighter planes.

Between 0800hrs and 0900hrs the 4th and 5th Divisions moved forward but resistance was as fierce as ever. The 21st and 27th Regiments on the west coast were halted by shredding machine gun and mortar fire before they had gone more than a few yards, and support from "Zippo" flamethrower tanks had little effect. Marine Dale Worley wrote: "They have almost blown Hill 362 off the map. There are bodies everywhere and the ground is spotted with blood. The smell is sickening."

In the center the 3rd Division also made little progress while in the east the best advance of the day was a mere 350 yards by the 3rd Battalion of the 24th.

D+16

General Erskine planned for a night-time attack to infiltrate enemy lines for about 250 yards and capture Hill 362C, the last major obstacle between the 3rd Division and the sea. At 0500hrs the 3rd Battalion of the 9th Regiment under the command of Lieutenant-Colonel Harold Boehm moved silently forward and for 30 minutes their luck held until an alert enemy machine gunner opened up. Pressing forward, Boehm and his men stormed to the top of the hill. But any euphoria was short lived, as Boehm checked his maps and realized that he was atop Hill 331 and not 362C. In the darkness and driving rain, one Iwo Jima hill looked much like another. Calling in artillery support, Boehm and his battalion pushed forward despite heavy opposition from the front and both flanks, and by 1400hrs finally reached the real objective.

As he was moving toward Hill 362C, the 1st and 2nd Battalions were advancing on Boehm's right flank, but soon encountered heavy resistance from their front and from bypassed positions. Lieutenant-Colonel Cushman and his 2nd Battalion had stumbled across the remains of Baron Nishi's Tank Regiment and soon found themselves surrounded. It was not until the next day that the remains of Cushman's battalion could be extricated with the aid of tanks. Bitter fighting was to continue in this area for another six days in what was to become known as "Cushman's Pocket." On the 5th Division front, the 26th Regiment, approaching a ridge just north of the ruins of Nishi Village, found the enemy opposition to be almost nonexistent when suddenly the ridge disappeared in a massive explosion. The Japanese had mined their command post and it was left to the Marines to recover the bodies of 43 of their comrades.

In a clever maneuver in the 4th Division sector, the 23rd and 24th Regiments moved to the east and then swung sharply south, edging the Japanese toward the 25th Regiment which had assumed a defensive line. Realizing that they were trapped, the Japanese elected for a banzai attack, against the direct orders of Kuribayashi. At around 2400hrs a large column of men was highlighted in the cross-flares from the naval destroyers and was decimated for no gain. The morning revealed the extent of the carnage. A body count showed almost 800 Japanese dead, probably the largest number of casualties that they suffered in a single day and a justification of Kuribayashi's reluctance to sanction the attack. Marine casualties were 90 dead and 257 wounded.

D+17–D+18

D+17, March 9, witnessed steady but unspectacular progress, despite another two young Marines both being awarded posthumous Medals of Honor. The final breakthrough to the sea was achieved by a 28-man patrol led by Lieutenant Paul Connally. As the men swilled their faces in the icy water, mortar rounds began falling among them and there was a mad scramble back to the safety of the cliffs. Connally had filled his water bottle with sea water and sent it to General Erskine with the message "for inspection, not consumption." That same night, as the Marines bedded down after another

The battle for Iwo Jima was a long, drawn out process, with Marines using various weapons against their enemy. A Carbine and Garand can be seen in this picture. The general destruction of the island following the naval bombardment is plain to see. (Tom Laemlein)

As the Marines made their way across the island, scenes such as this dead Japanese gunner at his post were everyday occurances. (Tom Laemlein)

frustrating day which saw only minor gains on the 4th and 5th Division fronts, the drone of hundreds of aircraft was heard as they skirted the east of Iwo Jima for the first of the "area bombing" raids on Tokyo.

D +19

It was obvious to both sides that, by March 10, the battle was reaching its climax. Cushman's Pocket was proving a tough nut to crack and the "Meatgrinder" and "Turkey Knob" were still to be taken. However, the Japanese were nearing the end of their endurance as diminishing numbers and chronic shortages were taking their toll. In the northwest corner of the island Lieutenant-General Kuribayashi prepared his final enclave, one which was significantly called "Death Valley" by the Marines. Located about 500 yards south of Kitano Point, it was a nightmare of rocks, caves, and gullies where the 1,500 remaining troops prepared for the end.

D+20 – D+36: "GOODBYE FROM IWO"

The Japanese were now confined to three distinct areas: one was Cushman's Pocket, the second an area on the east coast between the village of Higashi and the sea, and the other was Death Valley. Conventional battle was abandoned as the infantry slugged it out with a desperate enemy. Tanks could only operate in the few areas where bulldozers could clear a path for them. Artillery fire was reduced dramatically as the front lines merged, and many gunners found themselves donning combat gear.

"Among the Americans who fought on Iwo Jima, uncommon valor was a common virtue."

— ADMIRAL CHESTER NIMITZ

In the northwest, the 5th Division regrouped and re-armed in preparation for the final assault on Death Valley (or "The Gorge" as the Marine maps labeled it). Meanwhile the 3rd Division fought a bloody battle in Cushman's Pocket, slowly grinding down the fanatical remnants of Baron Nishi's command. The Baron, himself, partially blinded in the fighting, held out until the end and his body was never discovered.

General Senda was still holding out in an area east of Higashi. Prisoners estimated his strength at around 300 men, and in an attempt to reduce the carnage, General Erskine arranged for loudspeakers to broadcast to the Japanese to explain the futility of further resistance. However, the equipment failed to work and his efforts were in vain. The slaughter continued for four more days until the whole garrison was eliminated.

With only Death Valley to secure, Harry Schmidt could be forgiven for thinking that the battle was all but over. He sadly misjudged Kuribayashi, and another ten days of savage fighting and 1,724 casualties lay ahead. Death Valley was around 700 yards long and between 300 and 500 yards wide with dozens of canyons and gullies leading off on both sides. In a cave somewhere in this labyrinth the general planned his final stand.

Corpsmen and stretcher-bearers evacuate some of the wounded to landing craft on the beach. In a cynical move to placate public alarm at the mounting casualty figures, Iwo Jima was declared "secure" on March 14. In a ceremony held in the shadow of Mount Suribachi, Harry Schmidt's personnel officer read the statement as an artillery barrage thundered in the north of the island, almost drowning out his words. The irony of the situation was obvious to all. (NARA)

Prisoners were rare on Iwo Jima. A group of curious Marines stop to stare at one of the few Japanese taken alive. (NARA)

Colonel Liversedge's 28th Regiment moved up the coast and took up their positions on the cliffs overlooking the Valley, while the remainder of the division attacked from the center and from the east. In a week of attrition the Marines painfully squeezed the Japanese further and further back until, by March 24, the enemy had been reduced to an area of around 50 yards square. Flamethrower tanks had expended over 10,000 gallons of fuel per day burning out caves and crevices. So badly mauled was the 2nd Battalion that they ceased to exist as a fighting force, and the 1st Battalion was on its third commander in nine days. The first was decapitated, the second maimed by a mine, and the third lost his left arm to a burst of machine gun fire.

Again General Erskine tried to persuade the enemy to give up the hopeless struggle, sending Japanese POWs and *Nisei* (Japanese Americans) to contact the defenders but to no avail. In the pre-dawn darkness of March 26, the final act of the tragedy was performed. Between 200 and 300 Japanese troops from Death Valley and

> "The United States is the last country in the world that Japan should fight."
>
> **— LIEUTENANT-GENERAL KURIBAYASHI**

other scattered positions on the west coast silently crept through the ravines of the 5th Division sector heading for a tented area between Airfield No. 2 and the sea occupied by a mixture of Seabees, Air Force personnel, Shore Parties, and anti-aircraft Gunners. Most of them were attacked while they slept. The noise alerted other troops in the area and a desperate battle of shooting, punching, kicking, and stabbing raged on. Dawn revealed the full extent of the carnage: 44 airmen and 9 Marines lay dead with a further 119 wounded; of the attackers 262 were killed and 18 captured. Lieutenant Harry Martin of the 5th Pioneers had hurriedly organized a defense line during the attack and single-handedly killed four enemy machine gunners before dying himself. He was to be Iwo Jima's final Medal of Honor hero, bringing the total to an incredible 27. The circumstances of General Kuribayashi's death have always been shrouded in mystery but most accounts indicate that he asked to be buried by his own soldiers prior to discovery by his erstwhile foe.

AFTERMATH

A total of 2,251 B-29 Superfortress bombers made forced landings on the island during and after the battle. This represented a large number of crewmen who would otherwise have had to ditch in the 1,300-mile expanse of ocean between Japan and the Marianas with a minimal chance of survival.

The capture of the Philippine Islands and the invasion of Okinawa in April accelerated the pace of the war. The 20th Air Force fire-raising raids and the dropping of the atomic bombs on Hiroshima and Nagasaki ended it, and the island of Iwo Jima, secured at a terrible cost in Marine lives, played a major role in these events. The savagery of the fighting and the fanatical defense on Iwo Jima clearly demonstrated the high price the US would have to pay if an invasion of mainland Japan were ever attempted.

A memorial stands near the site of General Kuribayashi's cave in Death Valley. (Taro Kuribayashi)

ORIGINS OF THE CAMPAIGN

The spring of 1945 found Allied fortunes in the Pacific very much in the ascendant. There was no doubt who would be the ultimate victor. The only questions remaining were when the final battle would be fought and how many more men would have to die.

The Japanese knew what was coming next but they did not know exactly where the Americans would strike. The Imperial General Headquarters (IGHQ) narrowed the possible targets to Formosa off the Chinese mainland or Okinawa southwest of the Home Islands and part of the Ryukyus island group. The Japanese began to reinforce both areas as the American 5th Fleet and US 10th Army marshaled at island bases across the Pacific.

OPPOSING PLANS

THE JAPANESE PLAN

In 1945 only scattered remnants of the Imperial Japanese Army (IJA) held out in the Philippines. Much of the Imperial Japanese Navy (IJN) rested on the bottom of the Pacific. Its once feared carrier air arm had virtually ceased to exist. US submarines had cut Japan's sea-lanes while B-29 bombers rained explosives on Japan's cities at will.

Expecting attacks on Formosa and the Ryukyus, Japan prepared to battle the Americans to a stalemate. Hoping that Japanese spirit would endure massed American firepower and limitless material resources, it would strive to inflict unacceptable losses and sue for peace.

The 32nd Army's battle slogan expressed this plan for a "war of attrition" in blunt terms:

One plane for one warship
One boat for one ship
One man for ten of the enemy or one tank

But the 32nd Army under the command of Lieutenant-General Mitsuru Ushijima was not at full strength and could only defend approximately one-third of the region. The 32nd Army's deployment found the 62nd Division covering an area in the south from Naha and Shuri north to a line anchored on the east and west coasts on the second narrowest neck of the island, the three-and-a-half-mile-wide Chatan Isthmus. This north-facing front was dug in on

OPPOSITE
Assault troops of the 1st Marine Division churn ashore aboard a landing vehicle, tracked Mk 3 (LVT[3]) amphibian tractor. This view is toward the amtracs stern and shows a .50cal HB-M2 machine gun. Five-gallon water cans line the amtrac's sides for use ashore and for protection from small-arms fire. The landings on Okinawa were the largest simultaneous amphibious assault in the entire Pacific War and in total over 1,300 ships would take part. (USMC)

some of the first high ground encountered south of the central plains where the Americans would land. A more formidable defense line behind this was centered on the rugged 4,500 yard-long Urasoe–Mura Escarpment, Tanabaru Escarpment, and several ridges running from northwest to southeast across the island. The main defense line, however, was still further south and centered on Shuri Castle and a vast, rugged cross-island ridge and hill complex. The weary advancing Americans would run headlong into well-prepared and formidable defenses.

The 24th Division secured the southern end of the island to prevent landings and act as the 32nd Army reserve. The 44th Independent Mixed Brigade (IMB) was southeast of the 62nd defending the Chinen Peninsula, where it was thought the Americans might land on the island's southeast Minatogawa Beaches (Minatoga in most US documents). The Okinawa Naval Base Force secured the Oroku Peninsula southwest of the 62nd Division and was prepared to fight the Americans at the water's edge as was IJN doctrine. The island's north was not completely abandoned. The 1st Specially Established Regiment (formed from airfield service personnel) screened the Yontan and Kadena Airfields on the central plains. The regimental-size 2nd Infantry Unit, detached from the 44th IMB, was established on the Motobu Peninsula on the island's northwest coast to distract the Americans. One of its battalions was on Ie Shima (island) just west of the Motobu along with other small elements.

The 32nd Army had little faith in promised Japanese air support. In order to survive and slow the Americans to the maximum extent, the Army would dig. Thousands of pillboxes, bunkers, weapons emplacements, and fighting positions were dug. Terrain features were

LEFT
Troops of the 1st Marine Division board a landing craft, vehicle and personnel (LCVP) alongside an assault transport on the morning of L-Day. (USMC)

OPPOSITE TOP TO BOTTOM
The embrasure of a concrete and limestone 10.5cm Model 14 (1925) gun emplacement dug into the side of a hill. Despite having a limited field of fire, it and other widely dispersed guns were able to concentrate their fires on specific areas through which it was predicted the enemy would advance. Similar positions were constructed of logs rather than concrete. (USMC)

This 100ft-long, log-reinforced tunnel had five rooms branching off it. The tunnel was found on Ie Shima, and would have served as a troop shelter, command post, aid station, ammunition and supply store. (USMC)

A heavily constructed concrete, limestone, and log bunker line on Mezado Ridge 500–600 yards southwest of Kunishi and 1,200 yards south of Itoman. Only a direct hit by a large-caliber projectile or a heavy bomb would breach such bunkers. (US Army)

incorporated into the defense and weapons were well-sited with excellent overlapping fields of fire. Multiple defense lines were established across the island anchored on dominating terrain. Extensive tunnel systems were dug, over 60 miles, enough to protect the Army's 100,000 troops. The construction and improvement of these repeating lines would continue through the battle as the Japanese were painfully pushed south. Supplies and munitions were protected in dugouts and caves.

THE US PLAN

The main landing would begin at 0830hrs, April 1, 1945, H-Hour, L-Day. The largest simultaneous amphibious assault in the Pacific War would see the landing of two Marine and two Army divisions abreast on eight miles of beach. III Amphibious Corps (IIIAC) would land opposite Yontan Airfield with its 6th Marine Division on the left. The Division would move rapidly inland, seize the airfield and protect the 10th Army's north flank by severing the island at the narrow Ishikawa Isthmus. Its 22nd Marines would land on the left flank. The 4th Marines would land on the right and would focus on the airfield. The Division's 29th Marines was in IIIAC Reserve to land to order. On the IIIAC's right, the 1st Marine Division would storm ashore south of the airfield and maintain contact with XXIV Corps on its right. The 7th Marines would land on the Division's left and the 5th on the right. The 1st Marines would be in Division Reserve and follow the 7th ashore while the Eastern Islands would be secured as required to further protect the 10th Army's seaward eastern flank.

The Bishi Gawa (stream) served as the initial physical boundary between IIIAC and XXIV Corps. The veteran 7th Infantry Division

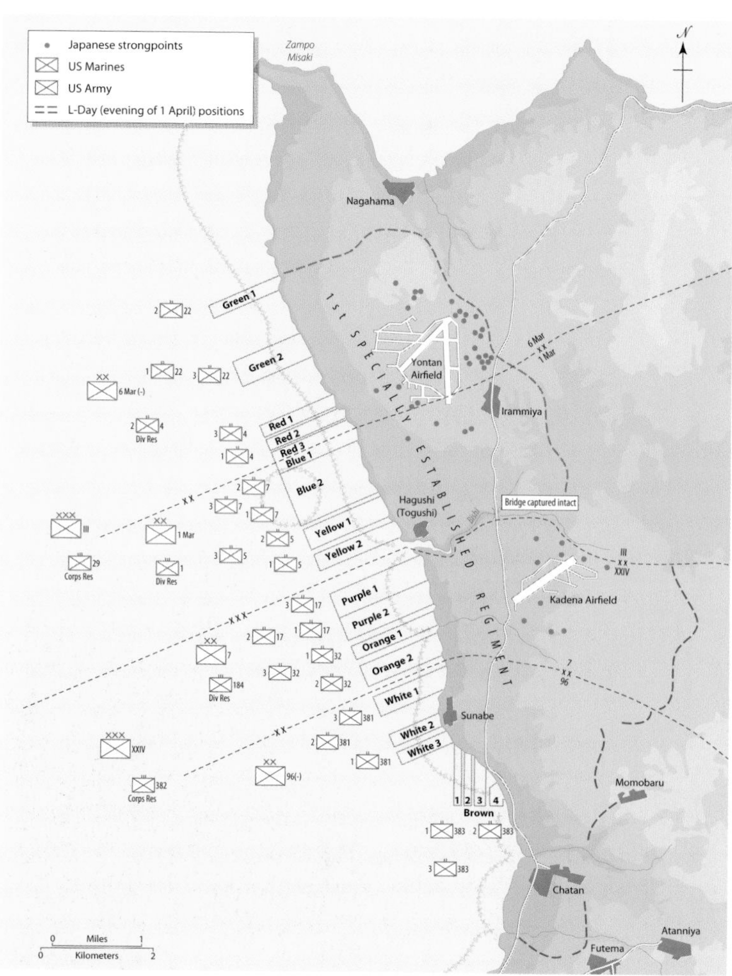

Map depicting the landing beaches at Okinawa. (Osprey Publishing Ltd.)

would land on the corps' left, maintain contact with IIIAC, and seize Kadena Airfield. Its 17th Infantry would be on the left and the 32nd on the right. The 184th Infantry was the division reserve. The 96th Infantry Division would land south of the airfield with its 381st Infantry on the left and the 383rd Infantry on the right. Its 382nd Infantry was the corps reserve. There was no division reserve, but the 382nd would land behind the 381st and be prepared to respond to a Japanese counterattack from the south. XXIV Artillery would land as necessary to support the corps attack. The corps' main mission, after capturing Kadena Airfield, was to swing south and secure an east–west line through Kuba Saki and seal off the Japanese in the south.

The 2nd Marine Division would remain as the 10th Army Floating Reserve along with the 27th Infantry Division as the Expeditionary Troops Floating Reserve.

Once the island was severed and the Japanese forces divided and isolated, with the central portion of the island secured XXIV Corps would advance south with the 7th Infantry Division on the left (east) and the 96th on the right (west) to seize the main objective area: the island's southern end. IIIAC would back up XXIV Corps, securing the occupied sector across the island with its 1st Marine Division while the 6th advanced to clear the north end of the island. The 77th Infantry Division would then seize Ie Shima. The 27th Infantry Division would land as necessary as XXIV Corps' frontline lengthened as the advance pressed south to where the island widened.

Initial air support for the landing forces would be provided by 14 escort carriers. Task Force 51 (TF-51) would transport and deliver the landing forces, sustain them ashore, provide close air support, and deliver naval gunfire support. The 5th Fleet's Fast Carrier Striking Force (TF-58) and British Carrier Force (TF-57) would attack Japanese air bases in the Home Islands and the Ryukyus and any remnants of the Imperial Fleet.

OPPOSING COMMANDERS

THE US COMMANDERS

Rear-Admiral Raymond A. Spruance, as Commander Task Force 50 (TF-50), 5th Fleet and Central Pacific Task Forces, was ultimately responsible for both the Iwo Jima and Okinawa campaigns.

Rear-Admiral Richmond Kelly Turner, as the Joint Expeditionary Force Commander, directed all amphibious landings as he had done at Iwo Jima. Lieutenant-General Simon B. Buckner Jr, the son of a Confederate general, was Commanding General, Expeditionary Troops and 10th Army (TF-56). Three days before the island was declared secure, Buckner would be killed observing his troops' advance on the final organized resistance.

Major-General John R. Hodge had led XXIV Corps during the bitter campaign for Leyte before returning to Hawaii with the rest of his corps to join the new 10th Army and prepare for the Okinawa assault. Major-General Roy S. Geiger had worked with Hodge on Bougainville and Peleliu as Commander of III Amphibious Corps. With the death of Lieutenant-General Buckner on June 18, 1945, Geiger assumed command of 10th Army for a short while, the only Marine officer to command a field army, while retaining command of IIIAC.

THE JAPANESE COMMANDERS

The Imperial Headquarters appointed Lieutenant-General Ushijima as commander of the Japanese 32nd Army on August 8, 1944. The steady and reserved Ushijima selected a very different individual as his chief-of-staff. Major-General Isamu Cho was known for his strong emotions, enthusiasm, and boldness. Cho was the main advocate of the underground defense of Okinawa, but he was also responsible for the disastrous May offensive.

While of comparatively junior rank, an equally important, and unique, member of the 32nd Army staff was Colonel Hiromichi Yahara, the senior operations officer. His higher military education included the Japanese War College. He spent two years as an exchange officer in the United States and was widely recognized as an expert in his field.

OPPOSING FORCES

THE US FORCES – TASK FORCE 51

As a joint command, TF-51 contained elements from the US Army, Navy, Marine Corps, and the three services' air arms. TF-51 was itself a

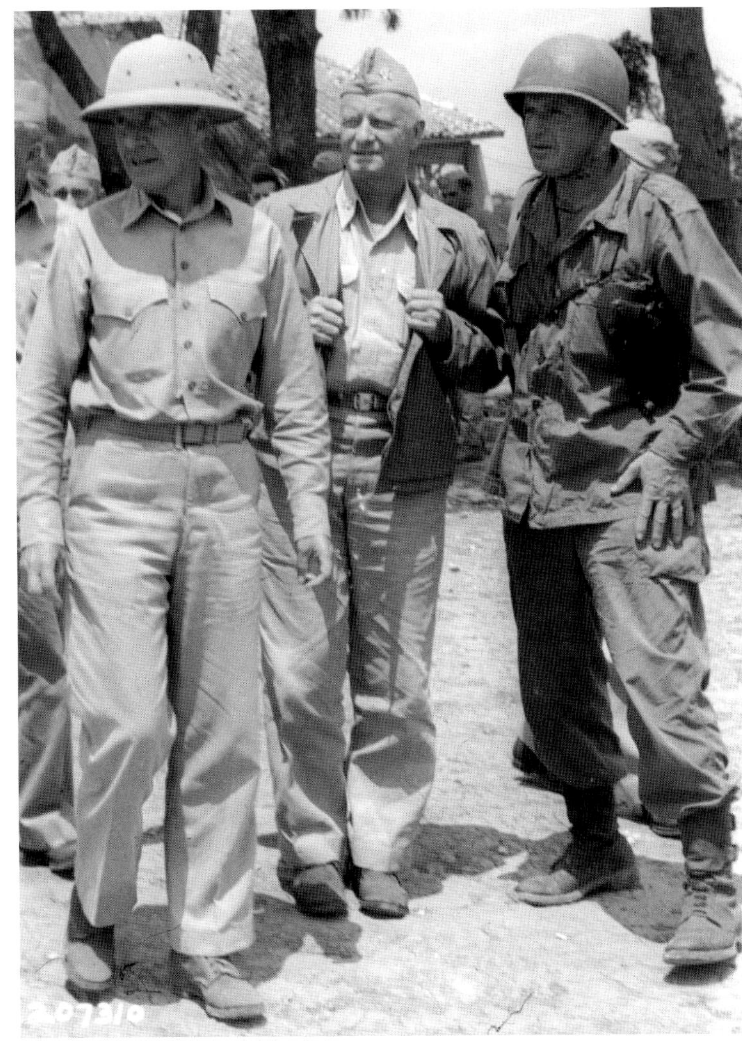

From left to right: Admiral Spruance, Commander, Central Pacific Task Forces and 5th Fleet; Fleet Admiral Nimitz, Commander-in-Chief, Pacific Ocean Areas; and Lieutenant-General Simon B. Buckner Jr, Commanding General, 10th Army. (USMC)

component of another task force, TF-50, the 5th Fleet and Central Pacific Forces under Admiral Spruance. Spruance, as the commander tasked with carrying out the invasion, also directly controlled two other task forces participating in the campaign.

The Fast Carrier Force (TF-58), under Vice-Admiral Marc A. Mitscher, had 88 ships including 11 fleet carriers and six light carriers with almost 1,400 aircraft backed by seven battleships, 18 cruisers, scores of destroyers and escorts, and a massive logistics support group. Vice-Admiral Sir Bernard Rawlings' British Carrier Force (TF-57) contributed four carriers, two battleships, five cruisers, and 14 destroyers plus a fleet train. Most of its 260 aircraft were American-built. Task Force 50 could also depend on support from other commands to include Submarine Force, Pacific Fleet; US Army Air Forces in China, and B-29s of the 20th Air Force flying out of the Marianas.

TF-51, the Joint Expeditionary Force, consisted of five smaller task forces and three task groups under Rear-Admiral Turner. Many of the task force's Navy units had little respite after the Iwo Jima operation. However, Iwo Jima had allowed the Americans to battle-test their command and communications systems, which put them at the advantage.

US Army

The 10th Army was composed of two corps, one Army and the other Marine, and, uniquely, its own tactical air force. It comprized over 102,000 Army troops of which over 38,000 were non-divisional artillery, combat support, and headquarters troops as well as some 9,000 service troops. Over 88,000 Marines were assigned along with 18,000 Navy (mainly Seabees and medical) personnel. 10th Army assault troops, those landing in the initial assault, totaled 182,821 men.

A D-18 bulldozer disembarks from a landing craft, tank Mk 6 (LCT[6]). Other engineer equipment would follow. The 119.5ft long craft could carry four medium tanks or 150 tons of cargo. It was armed with two 20mm guns. The stern could be opened and several LCTs could be anchored end-to-end to serve as a floating causeway between shore and an LST, as vehicles could simply drive through the connected craft. (US Army)

Directly under 10th Army was the 53rd Anti-aircraft Artillery Brigade with five anti-aircraft artillery groups, six 90mm, and three 40mm anti-aircraft artillery battalions as well as military police, signal, and medical groups.

XXIV Corps (Southern Landing Force) was under the command of Lieutenant-General Hodge, and already had valuable experience working with Marines V Amphibious Corps (VAC). XXIV Corps Artillery, under Brigadier-General Josef R. Sheetz, had three artillery groups with 14 battalions of various calibers. Four infantry divisions were assigned to XXIV Corps. The reinforced 7th, 77th, and 96th averaged almost 22,000 troops, but each was some 1,000 infantrymen under strength.

The Regular Army 7th Infantry Division which had fought at Leyte also prepared for service on Okinawa. The "Bayonet Division" was commanded by Major-General Archibald V. Arnold.

The 96th Infantry Division, known as the "Deadeye Division" was under the command of Major-General James L. Bradley for its entire World War II service including Okinawa.

The 27th Infantry Division, the floating reserve, would be the next to arrive on Okinawa. It fielded only just over 16,000 troops and was commanded by Major-General George W. Griner Jr.

The last division to land on Okinawa was the 77th Infantry Division, an Army Reserve division. Under the command of Major-General Andrew B. Bruce, the "Statue of Liberty Division" served as the Western Landing Force to first seize islands west of Okinawa.

US Marine Corps

The Marine Corps' contribution to 10th Army was III Amphibious Corps under Major-General Geiger. III Amphibious Corps Artillery, under Brigadier-General David R. Nimmer, consisted of two three-battalion provisional groups to support the corps' two divisions.

Only two Marine divisions were to fight on Okinawa, although a third was to play an important role. Unlike Army divisions, the Marine divisions deployed with 100 percent infantry strength plus 2,500 replacements.

As discussed previously, the 1st Marine Division, the "Old Breed," was formed February 1, 1942. The division's more than 24,000 troops were commanded by Major-General Lemuel C. Shepherd Jr. The 2nd Marine Division was formed from the 2nd Marine Brigade on February 1, 1941 at San Diego. Most of the division fought on Guadalcanal in 1942–43 as well as on Saipan and Tinian in the summer of 1944. The 22,000-man division was under the command of Major-General Thomas E. Watson.

THE JAPANESE FORCES

The 32nd Army was organized on April 1, 1944, to defend Okinawa, one year to the day before the Americans landed. It was augmented by the 44th IMB although it never achieved full strength.

The 62nd Division, under the command of Lieutenant-General Takeo Fujioka, was also deployed to Okinawa. Roughly 300-man engineer, signal, and transport units completed the 62nd Division along with a field hospital.

The strongest formation on Okinawa was the 24th Division under Lieutenant-General Tatsumi Amamiya. Raised in December 1939, it had seen no combat, but was well trained. Several thousand Okinawan civilians were conscripted into Civil Defense Units and labor units as well as augmenting regular units.

In total, IJA troops numbered 67,000. Of these about 5,000 were Okinawan conscripts assigned to regular Japanese units and about

Each Marine division had a detachment of 12 1-ton truck-mounted 4.5in rocket launchers organized into two six-truck sections. The crewmen were called "Buck Rogers Men" after a contemporary science fiction hero. Each truck, nicknamed a "Sandy Andy" after a popular toy, mounted three Mk 7 launcher racks with each holding 12 rockets. They could fire 36 high explosive and white phosphorus rockets in four seconds to a range of 1,100 yards. (USMC)

29,000 32nd Army troops belonged to labor, service, and specialized support units.

Some 3,825 IJN personnel and over 6,000 civilian combatant employees were also assigned.

INITIAL OPERATIONS

INITIAL LANDINGS

Kerama Retto is a group of eight rugged islands 15 miles west of Okinawa. The Keramas would become the fleet's refueling, rearming, and repair base. The need for such a base was realized during the Iwo Jima assault. Only four of the islands were defended by 975 IJN troops and the islands were easily seized.

Keise Shima, 11 miles southwest of the Hagushi Beaches, was also secured unopposed on March 31. Marine scouts had previously confirmed the islets were unoccupied. The 420th Field Artillery Group came ashore with the 531st and 532nd Battalions to support the main landing and cover southern Okinawa with their 155mm guns.

On March 29 spotter aircraft over Okinawa reported that the entire island appeared deserted. At 1000hrs, March 30, frogmen swam in to demolish anti-boat obstacles. The main assault could now take place.

The amphibious force assembled just west of Okinawa. The Carrier Force took up station some 50 miles to the east. On March 31, the Demonstration Group, 2nd Marine Division, embarked, arriving off the southeast Minatogawa Beaches, which the Japanese considered the most likely site for the main landing. This landing was a diversionary feint. The deception was reinforced by underwater demolition team (UDT) scouts and minesweepers operating offshore since March 29.

THE MAIN LANDING

April 1, 1945 – L-Day – dawned with only a light swell on the landing beaches. Transports and LSTs dropped anchor three–seven miles offshore. At 0530hrs the pre-landing barrage smothered a zone 1,000 yards inland with some 25 rounds per 100 square yards. As the sun rose behind the hilly island, seasick soldiers and Marines saw smoke-shrouded Okinawa for the first time. At 0800hrs, dozens of LCI(G) gunboats cruised toward the beaches with 3in and 40mm guns blazing. At 0815hrs hundreds of circling Amtracs formed into assault waves.

Control craft pennants came down five minutes later and an eight-mile line of churning Amtracs began their 4,000-yard run to the beaches. Sixty-four carrier planes strafed and bombed the beaches as naval gunfire shifted inland. As four American divisions ran in toward the shore, the 2nd Marine Division at the Minatogawa Beaches executed its feint. Ironically, the first troop casualties were suffered by this force as Kamikazes crashed into a transport and LST. Other than attracting air attacks, the demonstration failed to draw Japanese reinforcements.

The first assault waves landed at 0830hrs – H-Hour – as only sporadic Japanese mortar and artillery fire fell short. Resistance ashore was virtually nil as the untrained 3,473 airfield service troops dissolved. Only half of the unit was armed and there were virtually no heavy weapons. Okinawa was not the feared repeat of Peleliu and Iwo Jima with troops slaughtered on the beaches. Instead, in the first hour 50,000 troops landed. Blasted suicide boats and small craft were found choking the Bishi Gawa separating IIIAC and XXIV Corps zones. As soldiers and marines pressed inland, larger landing craft and ships began delivering divisional artillery and support troops at 1400hrs. The receding tide exposed the reef and the unloading of heavy equipment slowed. Late morning found the 4th Marines on the edge of Yontan Airfield and the 17th Infantry at Kadena. The two airfields were not expected to be captured until L+3.

By nightfall a 15,000-yard beachhead was firmly established and another 10,000 troops had landed. The four assault divisions reported only 28 dead, 27 missing, and 104 wounded this first day on Okinawa.

SPLITING THE ISLAND

On the morning of L+1 the 2nd Marine Division conducted another demonstration off the southeast beaches to no avail, other than allowing Ushijima to claim he had forced their withdrawal. The two airfields were securely in American hands as were the surrounding hills. The defenders failed to place demolitions on the airfields, and by the afternoon of L+1 Kadena was usable for emergency landings

Troops of the 32nd Infantry, 7th Infantry Division, rest during the push inland toward Kadena Airfield from the "Orange" Beaches, April 1. The man in the foreground carries an M2 tripod for a .30cal M1919A4 machine gun and a 250-round M1 ammunition can. A gas mask case and M1910 pick-mattock are on his left hip. The flame gunner behind him carries an M2-2 flamethrower. (US Army)

Troops marching across Okinawa. The American landings were virtually unopposed, allowing the attackers to gain a 1,500 yard beachhead by the end of the first day. (NARA)

with Yontan usable the following day. Meanwhile the main bridge over the Bishi Gawa was captured intact. The question in every one's mind was, "Where is the enemy?"

The weather remained favorable for the next two days and the Americans continued their rapid advance. The 6th Marine Division moved north and by April 4 had secured the narrow Ishikawa Isthmus. The 1st Marine and 7th Infantry Divisions reached the east coast on the afternoon of the 3rd and the Marines secured the Katchin Peninsula on the 5th. The 96th Infantry Division wheeled to its right and began moving south as did elements of the 7th on the east coast. By L+3 they were established on a line across the Chatan Isthmus facing south. All units were in positions they had expected to reach after two weeks of hard fighting.

The supply build-up continued and more support units landed. Empty transports departed and each night the fleet dispersed, some fell victim to increasing air attacks, but a picture emerged of a general Japanese withdrawal to the south prior to L-Day.

The weather turned for the worse on April 4 but the American command could only guess at Japanese intentions while air reconnaissance revealed nothing in the south as the Japanese remained underground.

THE OFFENSIVE CONTINUES

THE 10TH ARMY ADVANCES

On April 4 General Hodge ordered the 7th and 96th Infantry divisions to attack south. The Japanese plan was to use the 62nd Division to hold the main northern defense line while the 24th Division and 44th IMB were held in reserve to destroy any new American landings on the southern coasts. The 62nd Division and its supporting artillery were in excellent positions on commanding terrain and had clear line of sight across XXIV Corps' area on the plain below. The 62nd Division's defense was echeloned with its 63rd Brigade dug in across the island and the 64th defending the west coast on its flank.

The 63rd Brigade put up a stiff enough resistance to halt XXIV Corps elements from April 6–8. The covering force had held the Americans off for eight days inflicting over 1,500 casualties on the corps but at a cost of almost 4,500 dead. The outer Shuri defenses were now uncovered and the corps would continue its advance against even tougher resistance.

The 383rd Infantry, 96th Infantry Division, attacked the 1,000 yard Kakuzu Ridge on April 9 and was repulsed. It was not until April 12, after repeated attacks, that the ridge was finally taken. The defending 63rd Brigade lost 5,750 men, the US 96th Division lost 451. During the battle the 7th Infantry Division had made slow progress in rugged terrain against stiff resistance to the east. The 7th Division's sector was only one-third of XXIV

> "While on Okinawa, the marines and soldiers were going through their crucible of hell brought on by rain, heat, poison snakes, mosquitoes ... the stench of human feces and rotting human flesh filled with maggots..."
>
> **— AN UNKNOWN OKINAWA VETERAN**

Corps' front, but the terrain forced narrow frontages and the almost nonexistent road system hampered logistics.

Chafing at their defensive strategy, the more aggressive Japanese officers clamored for a counterattack. Colonel Yahara held them at bay reasoning that even if a counterattack was successful, the troops would be exposed to massive American firepower on the plains. However, General Ushijima gave in when the Americans became stalled in the outer Shuri defenses.

The counterattack was launched at 1900hrs, April 12 with a 30-minute barrage to cover the infiltration. The attack was far too weak and uncoordinated as many commanders, realizing its folly, held back their troops.

In contrast, the US 96th Infantry Division faced a well-organized and sustained attack. The Japanese 272nd IIB's attack was well conducted and gave the US 381st Infantry a difficult night on Kakazu Ridge. The battle lasted into the night of April 13/14. But by dawn it was all over. It delayed the American

US Marines with a .30cal M1917 move up on Okinawa Sugar Loaf ridge. (Tom Laemlein)

An Army tank company prepares to advance from behind a ridge line. These M4A3 Shermans have had their large white stars painted over in black to prevent them from being used as targets for anti-tank guns. The Japanese 47mm Model 1 (1941) anti-tank gun, while of moderate performance when compared to similar contemporary weapons, was effective against Shermans. (US Army)

push a couple of days, but the Japanese lost hundreds of men and the Americans less than 100. The Americans continued to inch south and then prepared to assault the main Shuri defenses on even more rugged terrain.

THE PUSH NORTH

While XXIV Corps fought slowly toward Shuri, IIIAC was engaged in a different kind of war. The 1st Marine Division defended Yontan Airfield and the landing beaches, and secured the zone behind XXIV Corps across the island. The 6th Marine Division had secured the Ishikawa Isthmus with the 22nd Marines to the north where the isthmus began to widen. On the morning of April 6 the 29th Marines launched a tank-supported push up the west coast while the 4th Marines moved up the east. The Japanese had blown bridges and laid mines, but resistance was very light. Finally, on April 8, after combing the hills, it was determined the enemy had concentrated on the Motobu Peninsula on the island's upper west coast. The 29th Marines now moved across the base of the peninsula and westward. Contacts increased over the next few days, but no decisive engagements were fought and enemy resistance, exacerbated by worsening terrain, increased as the Marines moved west.

The enemy was positioned in a redoubt around the 1,200ft-high Yae Take (Mount). The broken ground precluded the use of armor and was ideal for the defenders, the heavily armed 1,500-man "Udo Force" detached from the 44th IMB. Initial skirmishing and maneuvering lasted for days, but on April 14 the attack was begun in earnest by the 29th and 4th Marines. Numerous hills and ridges had to be taken during the approach to Yae Take. The 17th saw the final assault on the Take, but it was not cleared until the next day. Some 700 Japanese dead were counted; although enough managed to escape to conduct a lengthy guerrilla war in the wild north with countless small skirmishes, hit-and-run attacks and sniping taking a heavy toll.

On May 4, the under-strength 27th Infantry Division relieved the 6th Marine Division in the north. The 6th had lost 236 dead and 1,601 wounded. On August 4, the whole of the north was finally declared secure, although small pockets remained. Over 1,000 Japanese had been killed and some 500 prisoners taken.

IE SHIMA LANDINGS

Ie Shima (frequently called Ie Jima) was codenamed *Indispensable*. It lies three and a half miles off the west end of the Motobu Peninsula and 20 miles north of the Hagushi Beaches. The north and northwest coasts are faced with cliffs up to 100ft high, pockmarked with hundreds of caves while the south coast is lined with beaches which range in width from 9–35 yards and are broken into sections of between 125 and 900 yards long separated by low cliffs. Thrusting abruptly upward from the east portion of the island is Iegusugu Pinnacle. This is a conical limestone peak 600ft high, honeycombed with caves and ravines reinforced by tunnels and pillboxes. On the Pinnacle's south side is the sprawling Ie Town of stone buildings. On the island's center were three 6,000–7,000ft long airfields in the pattern of an "XI." The island had a population of 8,000, but about 3,000 had been evacuated to Okinawa. Ie Shima was defended by 3,000 troops of the Igawa Unit, augmented by 1,500 armed civilians including women. Substantial defenses were built around the Pinnacle and within Ie Town.

A flame gunner pictured on his advance across Okinawa as the Americans sought to drive the Japanese from the area. (Tom Laemlein)

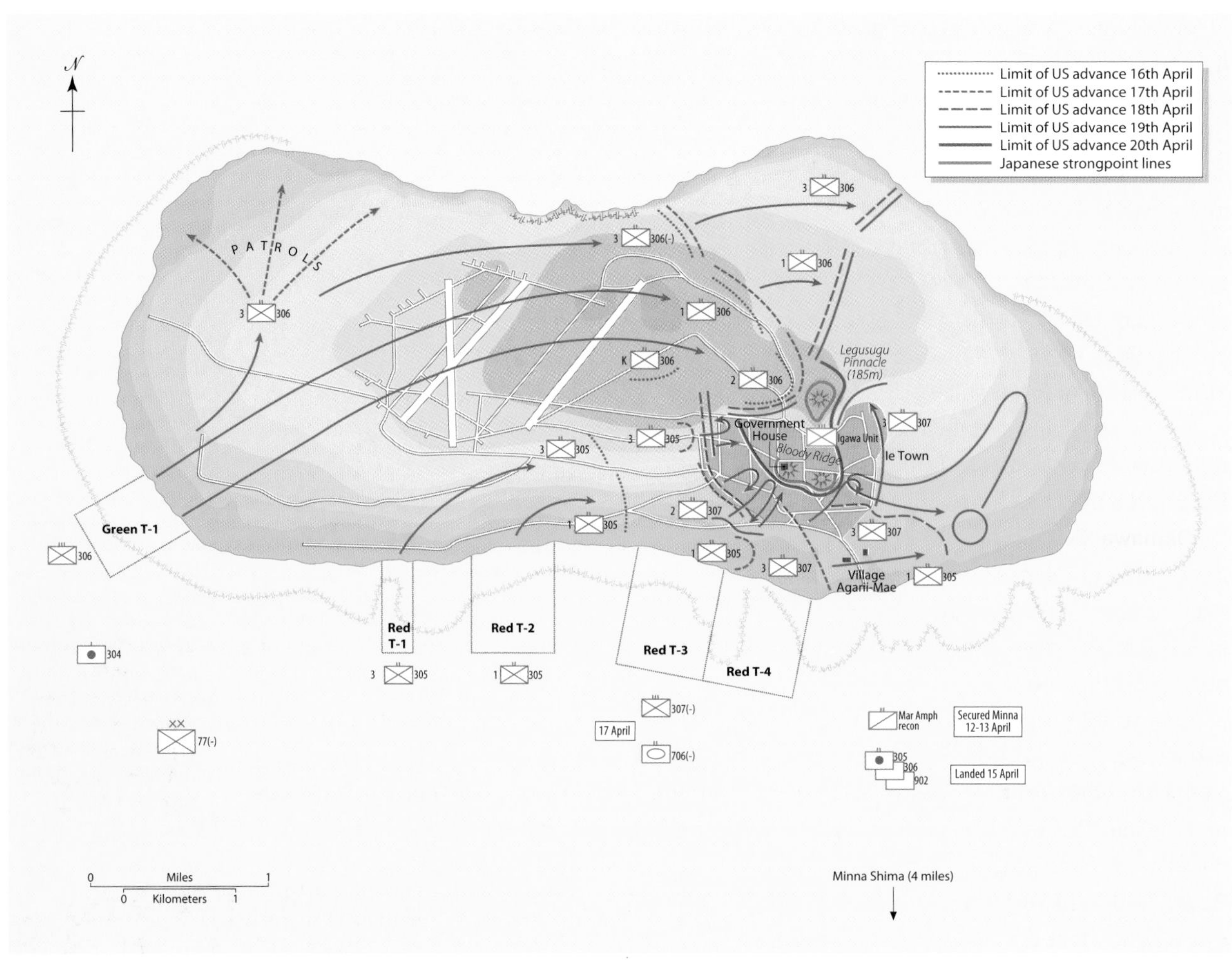

This map shows the US assault on Ie Shima. (Osprey Publishing Ltd.)

Minna Shima, an islet four miles south of Ie, was secured by Fleet Marine Force, Pacific Reconnaissance Battalion troops on April 12/13 and occupied by the three artillery battalions on the 15th. The 77th Infantry Division was moved from its station 300 miles southeast of Okinawa and assaulted Ie Shima on the morning of April 16 (W-Day) with full naval gunfire support. The 306th Infantry landed on Beach "Green T-1" at 0758hrs (S-Hour) on the southwest end while the 305th Infantry (less 2nd Battalion) hit "Red T-1" and "T-2" on the south-central coast. Initially, as on Okinawa, there was virtually no resistance with the airfields soon overrun as the regiments swept east across the island. Resistance increased the next day as Ie Town was approached. The 307th Infantry (less 1st Battalion) was landed on the morning of April 17 with part of the 706th Tank Battalion on "Red T-3." By April 18 the troops had closed in on the north, west, and south sides of the town and Pinnacle amid accusations of taking too long to accomplish the mission. The repeated attacks bogged down against fierce resistance, especially in the town's center around the administrative building, called Government House Hill, and the surrounding high ground known as

"Bloody Ridge." Most of the town was cleared on April 20 but the Pinnacle was not taken until the next day, and resistance continued on its slopes until April 23. Ie Shima was finally declared secure at 1730hrs on April 21, but mopping-up continued until the 26th. The Japanese lost 4,700, including most of the 1,500 armed civilians, and 409 prisoners were taken. About a third of the civilians remaining on the island died. American losses were 218 dead and missing and 900 wounded.

ASSAULT ON THE SHURI DEFENSES

On Okinawa XXIV Corps' Army divisions were now facing the Japanese main cross-island defense line – the Shuri defenses – built on a series of steep ridges and escarpments to the north of Shuri. The 7th Infantry Division was to the east, the 96th in the center, and the 27th to the west. They had not moved since April 14 as preparations for the April 19 assault were undertaken. The entire Japanese front was still defended by the 62nd Division with its 64th Brigade defending the west and center and the 63rd Brigade the east, well dug in on the hills and ridges with the 44th IMB in the rear.

A preliminary attack was launched by the 27th Infantry Division on the night of April 18 when bridges were secretly built across the Machinato Inlet separating Uchitomari and Machinato on the west coast. The 106th Infantry secured a valuable foothold on the northwest end of the Urasoe-Mura Escarpment and cleared Machinato Village during a bold night infiltration attack.

The main attack was launched at 0640hrs, April 19, after a massive 27-battalion artillery barrage while naval gunfire and aircraft pounded the Japanese rear area. The 7th Infantry Division attacked toward Skyline Ridge, the anchor at the east end of the Japanese line, but was thrown back in most sectors by withering fire. The 96th Infantry Division in the center made little headway against the strongly defended Tombstone and Nishibaru Ridges, barely gaining any ground beyond its start line. The 27th Infantry Division on the west flank merely held its ground on the south side of the Machinato Inlet, but made further gains on the Urasoe-Mura Escarpment. Its attack on the Kakazu Ridge failed, however, when the 193rd Tank Battalion was separated from 1st Battalion, 105th Infantry as they crossed a saddle between Kakazu and Nishibaru Ridges, resulting in the loss of 22 tanks.

For the next week the three divisions continued the effort to push south against well dug-in resistance with no unit gaining more than 1,300 yards. The Bradford Task Force, assembled from reserve battalions of all three divisions in the line, and heavily supported by armor, finally overran the Kakazu Pocket on April 24, but by then the Japanese had

1st Marine Division troops on the approaches to Shuri Castle view the carnage and devastation of this hotly contested portion of the battlefield, May 25. (USMC)

abandoned it. The Japanese also lost their one opportunity for a successful counterattack as there were no US reserves; everything had been committed to the line. By the end of the month most units had progressed comparatively well, gaining 1,000–2,000 yards in many areas. The 96th Infantry Division was still held up on its west flank by the Urasoe-Mura Escarpment defended by the Japanese 32nd Infantry. The US 7th Infantry Division had made significant headway on its inland flank, but was held up there on Kochi Ridge by the Japanese 22nd Infantry. Clearly, the divisions were exhausted and their strength low.

It was during this period that it was proposed to execute a flanking landing using the 77th Infantry Division on the southwest coast north of Minatogawa in an effort to force the Japanese to pull troops out of the Shuri defenses. It was rejected by Buckner from April 17–22 as it was too much of a risk to land a single division so far behind Japanese lines, particularly when taking into account the additional logistics burden and the ships required to protect the supporting anchorage.

The 1st Marine Division was attached to XXIV Corps on April 30, relieving the 27th Infantry Division on the east flank. The 77th

What looks to be a Japanese civilian emerges from the devastation on Okinawa, surrendering to US Marines. One soldier holds a .45cal pistol. (Tom Laemlein)

Infantry Division, although short by three battalions, was on occupation duty on outlying islands, and relieved the much battered 96th. The assault continued southward through the main Shuri defenses, an effort continued until May 3, when the Japanese attempted their most determined counteroffensive.

THE JAPANESE COUNTEROFFENSIVE

Frustrated at the prolonged defensive battle, many Japanese commanders desired a counteroffensive to halt the American advance. Colonel Yahara, 32nd Army operations officer, warned of the folly of such an attack, but Major-General Cho, chief-of-staff, prevailed. The Japanese attacked on the night of May 3 with their main effort made in the center and the east by the 24th Division. The attack was supported by raids conducted by forces landed in the American rear on both coasts. Shallow penetrations were accomplished in some areas, but the attack was repulsed. Japanese losses, some 7,000 of the 76,000-man force, only served to further weaken their front. American units had suffered fewer than 700 casualties and they continued to push south. The counteroffensive was nothing short of a blunder.

The Japanese now rebuilt their units, largely with rear service troops, and prepared for a battle of attrition. The 62nd Division, with only a quarter of its strength surviving, defended the western third of the line while the 24th Division, reduced to two-thirds, defended from north of Shuri to the east coast. The 44th IMB, at four-fifths strength, supported the 62nd Division. Japanese artillery had been cut by half and its daily ammunition allotment drastically reduced.

The Japanese Kamikaze or suicide boats were cheaply constructed plywood boats, which carried a 551lb explosive charge inside the bow. Some had a rack on either side of the cockpit for a 264lb depth charge. The boats were hidden in caves or other camouflaged shelters and moved to launching ramps on a two-wheel cart. The 16–17-year-old volunteers were 2nd and 3rd year officer cadets in the five-year officer academy. If one failed to return from his mission, he was presumed successful and posthumously promoted to lieutenant. The hoped for "blasting to pieces" of the American fleet by "whirlwind" Q-boat attacks never materialized. (Tom Laemlein)

OPPOSITE
A gunner of the 22nd Marines, 6th Marine Division, turns a 7.7mm Model 92 (1932) machine gun against its former owners. This was a copy of the British World War I-vintage Lewis machine gun used by the IJN. Its 47-round drum magazines and extra cartons of ammunition lie on the ground. (USMC)

ACTION AT SEA

Throughout the campaign TF-51 provided close air support to the troops ashore, combat air patrols to protect from air attacks, interception of Kamikazes, reconnaissance and anti-submarine patrols, logistical support, floating hospitals, continuous gun fire support, and other indispensable services.

The first two weeks of the campaign saw TF-57 (British Carrier Force) operating off Saishima Gunto to neutralize airfields there. Prior to and during the campaign, the 5th and 3rd Fleets' fast carriers executed attacks throughout the Ryukyus, on Formosa, mainland China, and Kyushu to neutralize Japanese airfields.

KAMIKAZE ATTACKS

Limited Kamikaze attacks were launched during the initial Okinawa landings, but the full fury of the Kamikaze was not felt until a massive 355-plane raid on April 6–7 was unleashed. In 19 hours the Navy suffered six ships sunk and 21 damaged with over 500 casualties. The Japanese lost almost 400 aircraft; Kamikaze and conventional covering fighters. The attacks continued unabated through April with a total of 14 US ships sunk and 90 damaged by Kamikazes, while conventional air attacks sank one and damaged 47. The Japanese paid a price of over 1,100 aircraft. The month of May saw more air attacks, which concentrated on the picket ships, transports, and carriers as well as the American airfields. Especially heavy attacks occurred in late May.

Attacks continued to the end of the campaign, with the last launched on June 21–22. In all there were ten main attacks, Sho-Go 1–10, with 1,465 aircraft interspersed with smaller attacks to total about 1,900 aircraft. The result was 26 US ships sunk and 225 damaged by Kamikazes as well as two sunk and 61 damaged by conventional air attack. These attacks on the fleet caused the highest US Navy casualty rate in the war.

THE SINKING OF THE *YAMATO*

In a desperate effort the Japanese sortied the *Yamato* on April 6 on a suicide mission. The super battleship was to beach itself on Okinawa to the south of the American landing beaches and turn its 18.1in guns on American forces ashore and the transports. There was only enough fuel available for the *Yamato* and its accompanying ships to make a one-way trip. The *Ten-Ichi* Operation ("Heaven Number One") saw the *Yamato*, the light cruiser *Yahagi*, and eight destroyers sortie from Tokuyama Naval Base on southwest Honshu. The force was detected by US submarines soon after it entered the open sea but contact was lost during the night as the force turned west. American carrier planes found the *Yamato* on the morning of April 7 after it had turned southwest toward its target. TF-58 aircraft struck the force at noon, sinking the

BELOW
Dark blue-painted F4U-1 Corsair fighters of Marine Fighting Squadron 232 (VMF-232) roll in over southern Okinawa to hit ground targets. Close air support of ground troops was one of the main missions of Marine aviation. (US Army)

"If you die there will be no one left who knows the truth about the battle of Okinawa. Bear the temporary shame but endure it. This is an order from your Army Commander."

— **LIEUTENANT GENERAL USHIJIMA**, IN RESPONSE TO MAJOR YAHARA WHO HAD ASKED FOR PERMISSION TO COMMIT SUICIDE

Yamato, the *Yahagi*, and four destroyers in two hours at a cost of ten US aircraft. Without air cover the battleship did not even make it halfway to Okinawa and went down with 2,487 crew. Four damaged escort destroyers escaped back to Japan.

SEIZING THE SOUTH

SHURI FALLS

On May 7, IIIAC resumed control of the 1st Marine Division on the west flank. As the Americans pushed south the island widened and it would be necessary to place a fourth division into the line. The 6th Marine Division was soon assigned a sector on the 1st Marine Division's right and inserted a single regiment, the 22nd, into the line. The 77th Infantry Division was strengthened by the arrival of its under-strength 305th Infantry, relieved from garrisoning Ie Shima. The rested 96th Infantry Division relieved the 7th Infantry Division in the line on May 8 (the surrender of Germany was announced that day). The 10th Army's renewed offensive began on May 11 with, from east to west, 96th Infantry, 77th Infantry, 1st Marine, and 6th Marine divisions in the line.

On May 22 heavy rains began. After ten days low ground, gullies, and ravines turned into thigh-deep seas of mud. Small streams and rivers overflowed their banks and the already overburdened roads became impassable in many areas.

The primary objective was Shuri. Progress was slow but steady, although the two center divisions had not driven as deeply into the Shuri defenses as those on the flanks. The 6th Marine Division was held up by furious fighting around Sugar Loaf Hill west of Shuri as the other divisions battled for stoutly defended ridges and hills. No complete Japanese unit remained in the lines, only remnants. On May 29 the 22nd Marines took Naha while an element of the 5th Marines, seizing the opportunity, crossed into the 77th Infantry Division's sector and captured Shuri Castle, much to the Army's exasperation. On the same date Army units broke through on the east coast as Japanese units were routed creating a melee of intermingled US and Japanese units, with many units at times being attacked from both sides.

THE PUSH SOUTH

On May 25, the Japanese 62nd Division withdrew through a defensive line of the 44th IMB southeast of Naha and then attacked XXIV Corps elements to the east. The Japanese 24th Division then withdrew from that sector on May 29 as the 62nd Division established a new line to the rear. The 24th Division established a new line south of Itoman on the west coast as the 44th IMB withdrew on May 31 to establish a line linked to the 24th Division's and running to the east coast. The 62nd Division then conducted a fighting withdrawal through the new lines between May 30 and June 4. The 10,000-man Naval Base Force on Oroku Peninsula, misinterpreting the order, withdrew to the south too early on May 28. Dissatisfied with the positions there, they immediately returned to their base, preferring to die defending it rather than to flee alongside the IJA.

The Japanese 32nd Army successfully withdrew to the south, but of the 50,000 troops at the beginning of the operation, only 30,000 remained. Those wounded but capable of action had been left behind to fight to the death with the rearguards, and the severely wounded were killed. The 32nd Army Headquarters left its tunnel command post beneath Shuri Castle on May 27. It established a temporary command post at Tsukazan the next day before moving to a small ridge (Hill 89) near Mabuni on the south coast the day after that. Heavy spring rains began at this time, arriving two weeks later than normal. Rains hindered both sides' operations, but the vehicle-dependent Americans were hampered most.

On May 24 paratroopers of the Japanese 1st Raiding Brigade attempted an airlanded raid on Yontan Airfield staged from Japan, but only one of the five transports managed to land. A number of US aircraft were destroyed on the ground, but the raiders were quickly killed.

IJN forces still held the Oroku Peninsula on the southwest coast, south of Naha, where the 6th Marine Division was blocked by Naha Harbor. Not to be halted by a mere body of water, the division did what was natural and executed a shore-to-shore amphibious assault launched from the west coast north of Naha and into Naha Harbor to flank enemy forces on the peninsula on June 4 (K-Day).

The 4th Marines landed on Beaches "Red 1" and "Red 2," south of Naha, at 0600hrs to be followed by the 29th Marines. While not given much attention, the two-regiment subsidiary operation was larger than some earlier amphibious assaults. It was also the last opposed amphibious assault in World War II.

The situation was stabilized by May 31 with most Japanese rear guards positioned in the central portion of the crumbling lines as US forces continued to push south into early June.

THE LAST STAND

After hard fighting, the Japanese remnants were driven to the south end of the island, Kiyan Peninsula, by June 11. There were still substantial pockets in the American rear areas. The Japanese intent now was to hold a line running from south of Itoman on the west coast through the hill masses in the center to a point on the east coast south of Minatogawa, an area approximately five miles across and three deep. The 8th Marines landed at Naha on June 15 and was attached to

Marines surround a possible Japanese hideout. Knowing the ground the Japanese had the advantage over the Americans, but, as seen here, the Marines had both firepower and numbers. (NARA)

the 1st Marine Division to assist with the final operations ashore. The 10th Army commander, Lieutenant-General Buckner, was killed observing his troops' advance against the final organized resistance on June 18. Major-General Roy Geiger assumed command of 10th Army.

The assaulting divisions' sectors had narrowed to the point that only three to five of the freshest battalions were required in the line. The 7th Infantry Division overran the Japanese 44th IMB's pocket on Hill 115 southwest of Nakaza on June 17. The US 96th Infantry Division was taken out of the line on June 20 to deal with a large pocket of Japanese 24th Division in the peninsula's center at Medeera and Makabe. It was not reduced until June 22. As the 6th Marine Division cleared the west coast of the peninsula, the 1st Marine Division wiped out the remaining Japanese 62nd Division pocket just inland of the island's south end on the Kiyamu-Gusuku Ridge. The 7th Infantry Division closed in on the Japanese 32nd Army's Headquarters, defended by 24th Division survivors, on a coastal ridge (Hill 89) south of Mabuni. These pockets were largely wiped out on June 21 and Okinawa was declared secure at 1700hrs. Small pockets of resistance remained and the American mopping-up continued for days. At 0340hrs on June 22, Lieutenant-General Ushijima and Major-General Cho committed ritual suicide outside their cave on the south side of Hill 89. The other division and brigade commanders and staffs died during "honorable death attacks" between June 21 and 30.

Kume Shima, 55 miles west of Okinawa, was secured by the Fleet Marine Force, Pacific Amphibious Reconnaissance Battalion, between June 26 and 30 to establish a radar site and fighter direction center. Landing on the island's southeast coast, the force met no opposition from the estimated 50-man garrison, which was later engaged. This was the final amphibious assault of World War II.

AFTERMATH

The armed forces of America and Japan had met in an 82-day, no-quarter battle, proving what was already known by both sides: the victor would have to utterly destroy his opponent. Both sides used their resources, whether limited or abundant, to the utmost of their ability to achieve their goals and gain the tactical advantage. Okinawa provided a glimpse of what would have happened if the United States had been forced to invade the Japanese Home Islands.

Only the much larger and longer Philippine Campaign saw higher casualties in the Pacific Theater than Okinawa. Marine ground and air losses were 2,938 dead and missing and 16,017 wounded. The Army lost 4,675 dead and missing and 18,099 wounded. There were over 26,200 US casualties due to combat fatigue, illness, and non-battle injuries. The joint US air services lost 763 aircraft, 458 in combat. US Navy losses were inordinately high with 36 ships sunk and 368 damaged, of which 43 were so badly damaged they were scrapped. These high rates were largely due to the suicide attacks on the fleet. These attacks were also the cause of the Navy's high casualty rate of the war – 4,900 dead and missing and 4,800 wounded. The British Carrier Force (TF-57) suffered four ships damaged, 98 aircraft lost, 62 killed, and 82 wounded in action.

Over 100,000 Japanese troops and Okinawan Boeitai fought on Okinawa and other islands in the Ryukyus. Estimates of casualties are difficult to determine due to the duration of the action, numbers of enemy forces, inflated reporting of enemy dead, and the nature of combat on Okinawa. The US assessment of Japanese casualties came to over 142,000, more than were on the island. A more realistic assessment is that approximately 66,000 combatants died and half of the survivors were wounded. A total of 7,400 combatants were taken prisoner during the campaign. Some 3,400 unarmed laborers were captured. Large numbers of troops turned themselves in after Japan surrendered. Approximately 10,000 IJA and IJN personnel and 8,000 Okinawan Boeitai and conscripts survived the battle. The Japanese lost 7,830 aircraft; 4,155 in combat, 2,655 operationally, and 1,020 destroyed on the ground on Kyushu and Formosa. Over 4,600 Kamikaze crews died along with hundreds of other pilots. Over 3,650 IJN sailors were lost during the *Yamato*'s sortie and Japan lost a total of 16 warships during the campaign with four damaged.

At the conclusion of the operation, 42,000–50,000 Okinawan civilians were estimated to have died due to Japanese or American combat action or suicide, or were murdered by the Japanese (to prevent their surrender or to steal their food). Postwar studies found that over 122,000 civilians were killed (almost one-third of the indigenous population and a figure rivaling the combined death toll of over 120,000 at Hiroshima and Nagasaki) and a culture was shattered.

Large numbers of Japanese troops were killed in post-operation mopping-up and additional prisoners were taken, ultimately growing to 16,350 by the end of November 1945. It was the first time that large numbers of Japanese troops willingly surrendered. On August 16, Japan announced its intention to surrender. On August 29, those IJN troops still holding out in the Kerama Retto were among the first Japanese troops to surrender after the announcement. On September 7, five days after the official surrender, the Ryukyu Islands were formerly surrendered at Kadena Airfield to Lieutenant-General Stilwell by Vice-Admiral Tadao Kato and Lieutenant-General Toshiro Nomi (both had been stationed in Sakishima Gunto). There were still approximately 105,000 IJA and IJN personnel on the other Ryukyus islands. Small numbers of Japanese renegades and Okinawan rebels conducted a low-level guerrilla war against US occupation forces into 1947 when the last surrendered.

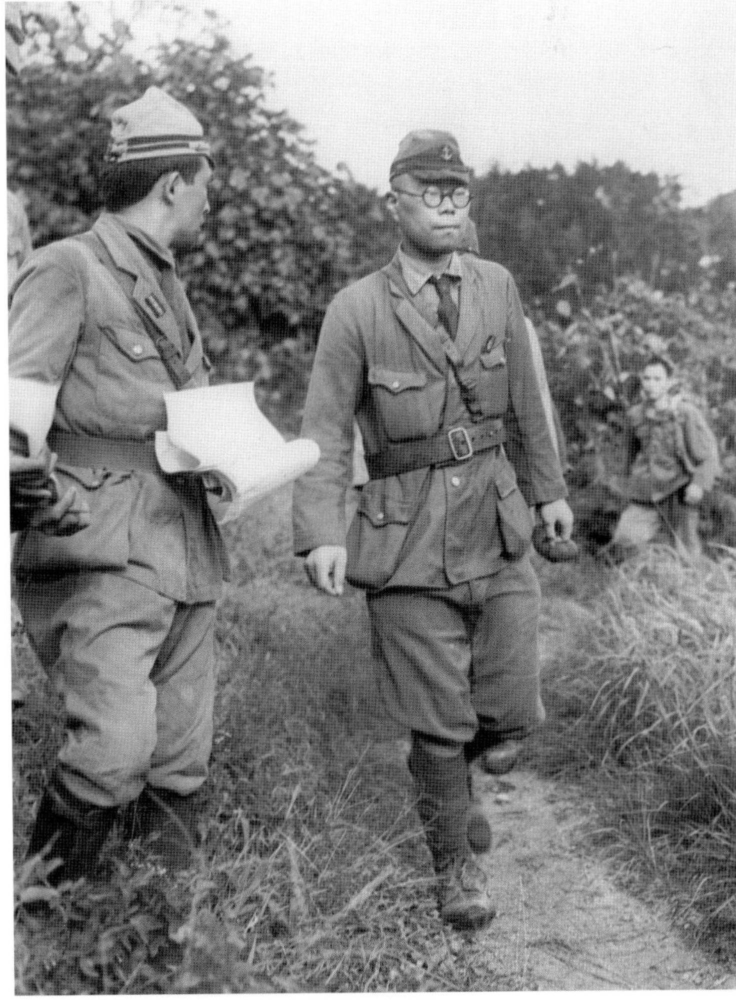

An IJN lieutenant, commander of the 183rd Naval Attack Force Rifle Battalion, surrenders to the 7th Marines, 1st Marine Division, on Motobu Peninsula, September 3. Japanese Navy field uniforms were a darker green than the olive drab worn by the Army. They were further identified by the yellow anchor insignia on their field caps. (USMC)

INDEX

Page numbers in **bold** refer to illustration captions

Abukuma 211
Aichi E131A Type II ("Jake") aircraft 27
Aichi Type 99 carrier bombers ("Val") **8, 27,** 34, 35–36, 60–61, 98
aircraft, Japanese **177**
  Aichi E131A Type II ("Jake") aircraft 27
  Aichi Type 99 carrier bombers ("Val") **8, 27,** 34, 35–36, 60–61, 98
  H8K "Emily" flying boats 164
  Nakajima B5N2 Type 97 "Kate" aircraft 15, **23,** 36, **47,** 56, 60–61, 98
  Nakajima E8N "Dave" float-planes **78**
  Zeke 52 fighters **71**
  Zero aircraft 32, **40,** 51, 53–54, 60–61, 74, 78, 80, 95
aircraft, US
  B-17 bombers 30, 31, 36, 73, **89,** 114
  B-24 bombers 31, 188, 215
  B-25 bombers **79, 213**
  B-26 bombers 74
  B-29 bombers 217, 230, 238, **238,** 243, 245, 250
  Brewster F2A Buffalo aircraft 74
  Dauntless dive bombers **49,** 56, 73, **76,** 79, **201**
  Douglas Devastator aircraft **54, 73,** 74, 78, 79, 80, 81
  Grumman F4F Wildcats 59, 61, 74, 79, 80, 84–85, **95,** 102, **105,** 185
  Grumman F6F Hellcats 193
  Grumman FM-2 Wildcats **205**
  Kingfisher aircraft 125, 128
  P-36 aircraft 32
  P-38 aircraft 114
  P-40 aircraft 32
  P-51 aircraft 217, 230
  P-400 aircraft 102
  PBY Catalina flying boats 72, 73, 76
  SB2C Helldivers 193, **207, 208**
  TBF/TBM Avenger aircraft 193, **195**
  Vought F4U-1 Corsair fighters **262**
Akagi
  battle of Midway (1942) 67, **69,** 74, 78–79, 81, 83, **83**
  Pearl Harbor (1941) 17, 18, 23, 34, 36
Akiguma 23
Aleutian Islands 71, 72, 86, 88, 144
Alwyn, USS 32
amtracs 122, 124, 125, 151, 152, 154, 158, 174, **175, 245**
Anderson, USS 122
Angaur Island 167, 168, 170, 173, 183–185, **184,** 188
Antares, USS 26
anti-aircraft guns **31,** 125
anti-tank weapons 110, 229, **256**
Arizona , USS 29–30, **33,** 34, **34,** 35, 37
Asagumo 213
Astoria, USS **51,** 85, 99
Atago 200
Auburn, USS 228
Australia, HMAS 99, **213**

B-17 bombers 30, 31, 36, 73, **89,** 114
B-24 bombers 31, 188, 215
B-25 bombers **79, 213**
B-26 bombers 74
B-29 bombers 217, 230, 238, **238,** 243, 245, 250
Babelthuap Island 168, 170
Bagley, USS 99
Bailey, USS 122
"banzai" charge 137
bazookas 173, **231**
Birmingham, USS 122
"Bloody Ridge," battle of (1942) 106–107
Blue, USS 34, 99
Bogan, Rear-Admiral Gerald 200, 201, 202, 208
Brewster F2A Buffalo aircraft 74
Browning automatic rifles (BAR) **95,** 122
Buckner Jr., Lieutenant-General Simon B. 249, **249,** 260
Bunker Hill, USS 122

Calalin Island 149–151
California, USS 34, 40
campaign origins
  the Coral Sea (1942) 43–44
  Guadalcanal (1942) 91
  Iwo Jima (1945) 217
  Leyte Gulf (1944) 191
  Marshall Islands (1944) 141
  Midway (1942) 65
  Okinawa (1945) 145
  Pearl Harbor (1941) 15
  Peleliu (1944) 167–168
  Tarawa (1943) 117
Canberra, HMAS 99
Cape Esperance, battle of (1942) 109
Cassin, USS 32, **35, 36,** 40–41
casualties
  the Coral Sea (1942) 58, 59, 60
  Guadalcanal (1942) 94, **103,** 104, 107, 108, 114, 115
  Iwo Jima (1945) 223, 224, 228, 229, 236, **236,** 237, 239, **240, 241,** 243
  Marshall Islands (1944) **153,** 156, 158, 160, 164
  Midway (1942) **64,** 74, 80, 81, 82, 83, 85, **86,** 88, **88,** 89
  Okinawa (1945) 257, 259, 266–267
  Pearl Harbor (1941) 28, 32
  Peleliu (1944) 182, 185, **186,** 187
  Tarawa (1943) 130, 134, **136,** 137
Chicago, USS 99
Chikuma 80, **206**
Chitose 207
Chiyoda 207, 215
Cho, Major-General Isamu 249, 261, 266
Chokai 206
Colorado, USS 122
combat air patrols (CAP) 49, 78, 79, 80, 84–85, 207
commanders
  the Coral Sea (1942) 44–46
  Guadalcanal (1942) 93–94
  Iwo Jima (1945) 218–219
  Leyte Gulf (1944) 191–192
  Marshall Islands (1944) 144
  Midway (1942) 65–67
  Okinawa (1945) 248–249
  Pearl Harbor (1941) 15–18
  Tarawa (1943) 117–120
Condor, USS 23
Coral Sea, battle of the (1942)
  aftermath 62–63
  casualties 58, 59, 60
  clashes of May 7 55–59
  Japanese strike 60–62
  movement to contact (May 5–6) 54–55
  opening moves 52–54
  opposing commanders 44–46
  opposing fleets 46–49
  opposing plans 49–52
  origins of the campaign 43–44
  pre-battle preparations (May 8) 59
  US Carrier Raid (May 4) 54
  US strike 60
Corlett, Major-General Charles H. 144, 159
Crace, Rear-Admiral J. G. 56, 58, 59
Crossbill, USS 23
Crowe, Major Henry 125, 131, 135, 137
Curtiss, USS 41
"Cushman's Pocket" 238, 240, 241

D-18 bulldozers **250**
Dace, USS 200, **200**
Darter, USS 200
Dashiel, USS 122, 128, 131, 134
Dauntless dive bombers **49,** 56, 73, **76,** 79, **201**
Davison, Rear-Admiral Ralph 200, 201, 202, 208, 209
"Death Valley," Iwo Jima 240, 241
Douglas Devastator aircraft **54, 73,** 74, 78, 79, 80, 81
Downes, USS 32, **36,** 41
"Dugout Sunday," Guadalcanal 110
DUKW amphibious vehicles **170**

Eastern Solomons, battle of the (1942) 104–105
Ebeye Island 142, 146, 160
Edson, Colonel Merrit A. 96, 106, 107, 136, 137
Elliott, Private 26, 27
Engebi Island 162
Eniwetok Atoll, battle of (1944) 140–143, 144, 147, **148, 154,** 160–161, 162–163, **164**

Enterprise, USS
  the Coral Sea (1942) 48, **54**
  Guadalcanal (1942) 96, 104, 105
  Leyte Gulf (1944) 192
  Midway (1942) 72, **73**, 76, 78, 79, 80, 81–82
  Pearl Harbor (1941) 22, **22**, 26, 27, 30–31, 41
Erskine, Major-General Graves B. 218, 238, 241, 242
Essex, USS 122

Fiji Islands 43
flamethrowers 122, 173, 185, **230**, **253**, **257**
fleets
  the Coral Sea (1942) 46–49
  Midway (1942) 67–69
Fletcher, Rear-Admiral Frank Jack
  the Coral Sea (1942) 46, **46**, 52, 54, 55, 56, 57, 58, 60, 62
  Guadalcanal (1942) 94, 99, 104
  Midway (1942) 66, 72, 73, 74, 78
Florida Island 96, 97
forces, organization and strength
  Guadalcanal (1942) 94–96
  Iwo Jima (1945) 219
  Leyte Gulf (1944) 192–195
  Marshall Islands (1944) 144–148
  Okinawa (1945) 249–252
  Peleliu (1944) 173–174
  Tarawa (1943) 120–123
"foreign legion," the 124
Frazer, USS 122
Fuchida, Commander Mitsuo 15, 17, 22, 26, 27–28, 36
Fuso 198, 211, 213

Gambier Bay, USS 206
Gansevoort, USS 122
Garand M-1 semi-automatic rifles 122
Geiger, Brigadier-General Roy S.
  Guadalcanal (1942) 105
  Okinawa (1945) 249, 251, 266
  Peleliu (1944) 171, 182, **182**, 183, 187
Genda, Commander Minoru 17, 22, 66
Ghormley, Admiral Robert 93, 94
Gilbert Islands, the 20, 43
  see also Tarawa, battle of (1943)
Goto, Major Ushio 174, 183–184, 185
"Great All-Out War" theory, Japanese 19
grenades 185
Grumman F4F Wildcats 59, 61, 74, 79, 80, 84–85, **95**, 102, **105**, 185
Grumman F6F Hellcats 193
Grumman FM-2 Wildcats **205**
Guadalcanal (1942)
  aftermath 115
  the army takes over 114–115
  August 98–105
  casualties 94, **103**, 104, 107, 108, 114, 115
  commanders 93–94
  the final phase 115
  the landings 96–98
  November 111–114
  October 108–111
  opposing forces 94–96
  opposing plans 91–93
  origins of the campaign 91
  September 105–108

H8K "Emily" flying boats 164
HA-19 (midget submarine) **18**
"Ha-Go" tanks 122, **133**
Halsey, Vice-Admiral William F.
  the Coral Sea (1942) 46
  Leyte Gulf (1944) 190, 192, 199, 200–201, 202–203, 207–208, 209, 215
  Midway (1942) 67, 111, 114
  Peleliu (1944) 167–168
Hammann, USS 89
Hanneken, Colonel Herman H. "Hard Headed" **171**, 172
Hara, Rear-Admiral Chuichi 44, 56, 57, 59
Harris, Colonel Harold "Bucky" D. **171**, 172, 186–187
Haruna **78**, 198
Hatsuzuki 215
Hawaii Operation 20
Hays, Major Lawrence 132, 137
HB-M2 machine guns **245**
Heermann, USS 205
Helena, USS **36**, 40
Helm, USS 31, 41, 99
Henderson Field, the battle for (1942) 109–110
Henry A. Wiley, USS 224
Hiei 112
Higgins boats 124, 135
Hill, Rear-Admiral Harry
  Iwo Jima (1945) 222
  Marshall Islands (1944) 144–146
  Tarawa (1943) 122, 129, **131**
Hiryu 23, 34, **66**, 74, 80, 81, 83, 84–86, **89**
Hodge, Lieutenant-General John R. 249, 250, 255
Hoel, USS 205
Honolulu, USS 40
Hornet, USS
  Guadalcanal (1942) 105
  Midway (1942) 72, 73, 76, 78, 79, 81–82
howitzers 125, 174, 222
Hyakutake, Lieutenant-General Harukichi 93–94, 102, 109, 110
Hyuga 202, 207

I-17 23
I-21 23
I-23 23
Ichiki, Colonel Kiyono **102**, 102–103, 104
Ie Shima 257–259
Independence, USS 122
Indianapolis, USS 122, 132, 221
Inoue, Lieutenant-General Sadao 168, 170, 172, 173
intelligence, US 97, 104, 105–106, 168
  MAGIC code 16, 19
Intrepid, USS 200
"Iron Bottom Sound," Guadalcanal 91
Ise 202, 207
Iwo Jima, battle of (1945) **11**
  casualties 223, 224, 228, 229, 236, **236**, 237, 239, **240**, **241**, 243
  D-Day 221–224
  D+1 to D+5 224–230
  D+6 to D+11 230–236
  D+12 to D+19 237–240
  D+20-D+36 240–243
  opposing commanders 218–219
  opposing plans 219–220
  origins of the campaign 217

Jaluit Atoll 147, 164
Japanese Forces 43
  see also aircraft, Japanese; ships, Japanese; weapons, Japanese
  "banzai" charge 137
  commanders 16–18, 44, 65–66, 93–94, 120, 144, 172, 192, 219, 249
  conscription 251–252
  the Coral Sea (1942) 43–44, 46–48, 49–51, 52–63
  Guadalcanal (1942) 91–92, 93–95, 96–115
  the Hawaii Operation 20
  Iwo Jima (1945) 217, 219, 220–243
  Kamikaze units 208, **211**, 252–253, 262
  Leyte Gulf (1944) 191, 192, 195–215
  Marshall Islands **6**, 43, 140, 143, 144, 146–165
  Midway (1942) 65–66, 67, 69–71, 73–88
  Okinawa (1945) 245–247, 249, 251–267
  Pearl Harbor (1941) 14, 19–41
  Peleliu (1944) 167–168, 170–171, 172, 173–189
  surrender 267
  tactics 103, 170–171
  Tarawa (1943) 116, 120, 122–123, 125–139
Jarvis, USS 99
Java Sea, battle of the (1942) 44
Johnston, USS 205
Jordan, Colonel Walter 130, 131, 135, 229

Kaga 23, 34, 36, 67, 74, 78–79, 81, 82–83
Kakuichi, Lieutenant-Commander Takahashi 56, 61, 62
Kamikaze units 208, **211**, 252–253, 262
Keise Shima 252
Kenyo Maru 23
Kerama Retto 252, 267
Kikuzuki 54
Kimmel, Admiral Husband "Hubby" E. 15, **16**, 19, 30–31
King, Admiral Ernest J. 44, **46**, 51–52, 72, 93
Kingfisher aircraft 125, 128
Kinkaid, Rear-Admiral Thomas C.
  Guadacanal (1942) 111, 112
  Leyte Gulf (1944) 191–192, 201, 203, 204, 205, 208, 209–210
Kirishima 112
Kiska Island 144
Kitkun Bay, USS 206
Kokumbona offensive (1942) 115
Kokuyo Maru 23
Kondo, Vice-Admiral Nobutake 86, 120
Kongo 198
Koror Island 168, 170
Kume Shima 266
Kuribayashi, Lieutenant-General Tadamichi 217, 219, **219**, 220, 237, 239, 240, **243**
Kurita, Vice-Admiral Takeo 192, **192**, 197, 198, 199, 200, 203–206, **207**, 209, 210–211, 213, 215
Kusaie Island 141, 143, 147, 164

Kwajalein Atoll 140, **141,** 142, **142, 143,** 144, 146, 148–149, 156–160, **159**
Kyokuto Maru 23

Landing Craft Vehicle Personnel (LCVPs) 124, 135, 151, 152, 154, 158, 174, **175, 247**
Landing Vehicle Tracked (LVT) **97, 120,** 122, 124, 125, **125, 166,** 173, 174, **175, 245**
LCVPs *see* Landing Craft Vehicle Personnel
Lexington, USS
- the Coral Sea (1942) 46, 48, **48,** 52, 54, 57, 58, 60, 61, **61,** 62, **63**
- Pearl Harbor (1941) 19, 22, **22**

Leyte Gulf, battle of (1944)
- aftermath 215
- ambush in the Palawan Passage (October 21-23) 199–200
- battle of Surigao Strait (October 24–25) 210–213
- battle of the Sibuyan Sea (October 24) 200–201
- the battle off Cape Engaño (October 25) 206–208
- the battle off Samar (October 25) 203–206
- the closing phases (October 25–27) 213–215
- Halsey's 3rd Fleet 202–203, 208
- Kinkaid's 7th Fleet 209–210
- Kurita's Center Group 203–206, 208–209
- opening moves (October 17–22) 197–199
- opposing commanders 191–192
- opposing forces 192–195
- opposing plans 195–197
- origins of the campaign 191
- Ozawa's Northern Force 202, 206–208
- the Southern Force 209, 210–213

Lockard, Private 26, 27
LVTs *see* Landing Vehicle Tracked

M3A1 light tanks *see* Stuart light tanks
M4A2 tanks *see* Sherman tanks
M10 tank destroyers 173
M1917 Browning machine guns **99, 255**
M1919A4 machine guns **253**
MacArthur, General Douglas
- the Coral Sea (1942) 52
- Guadacanal (1942) 92
- Leyte Gulf (1944) 190, **191,** 192, 195, 201
- Peleliu (1944) 167

machine guns **102,** 125, **157,** 222, **226, 236, 262**
- HB-M2 machine guns **245**
- M1917 Browning machine guns **99, 255**
- M1919A4 machine guns **253**

MAGIC code *see* intelligence
Majuro Atoll 140, 146, 149–151
Maloelap Atoll 140, 147, 164
Marshall, General George C. 16, 92
Marshall Islands **6,** 43
- aftermath 164–165
- casualties **153,** 156, 158, 160, 164
- Ebeye Island assault 160
- Engebi Island 162
- Eniwetok Atoll, battle of (1944) 142, 143, 144, 147, **148, 154,** 160–161, 162–163
- Japanese defenses 147–148
- Kwajalein assault 156–160
- occupation of Majuro 149–151
- Operation *Flintlock* begins 148–149
- opposing commanders 144
- opposing forces 144–148
- opposing plans 141–143
- origins of the campaign 141
- Parry Island 163–164
- Roi-Namur assault 151–155

Maryland, USS
- Pearl Harbor (1941) **34,** 34–35, 40
- Tarawa (1943) 122, 128, **131**

Matanikau area 102, 105, 107–109, 112
Meade, USS 122
"Meatgrinder," Iwo Jima 231, 237
Michishio 213
midget submarines, Japanese **18, 41**
Midway, battle of (1942) 44, **54**
- aftermath 88–89
- battle of the carriers (June 4) 74–76
- casualties **64,** 74, 80, 81, 82, 83, 85, **86,** 88, **88,** 89
- commanders 65–67
- the decisive phase 78–82
- the fleets 67–69
- *Hiryu* retaliates 84–85
- the Japanese response 82–84
- the Japanese strike 74
- Nagumo's dilemma 76–78
- opening moves 73
- opposing plans 69–73
- origins of the campaign 65
- sinking of *Hiryu* 85–86
- Yamamoto's decision 86–88
- *Yorktown* attacked 85

Mikawa, Vice-Admiral Gunichi 94, **94,** 98, 99, 104
Mikuma 88
Mille Atoll 142, 147, 164
Minna Shima 258
Mitscher, Vice-Admiral Marc A.
- Iwo Jima (1945) 221
- Leyte Gulf (1944) 191, 207
- Okinawa (1945) 250

Mitsubishi A6M aircraft *see* Zero aircraft
Mobile, USS 122
Mogami 88, 210, 213, 215
Morotai Island 166
Musashi 198, 204, 210
Myoko **50**

Nagara 23
Nagato 198
Nagumo, Vice-Admiral Chuichi 18, 23, 37, 66, **66,** 69, 74, 76–78, 83, 86
Nakagawa, Colonel Kunio 170, 172, **172,** 187
Nakajima B5N2 Type 97 "Kate" aircraft 15, **23,** 36, **47,** 56, 60–61, 98
Nakajima E8N "Dave" float-planes **78**
Nambo machine guns **236**
Namur Island **144,** 146, **146,** 147, **149, 151,** 151–152, **153,** 154–155, **155, 157**
Nauru Island 164
Neosho, USS **55**
Nevada, USS 22, 29, **31,** 32, 34, **34,** 40
New Guinea 20, 43, 49, 50–51, 52, 91, 92, 117, 141
New Orleans, USS 32
Ngesebus Island 173
Nimitz, Admiral Chester W. **218, 249**
- the Coral Sea (1942) 44–46, **46,** 52
- Guadalcanal (1942) 93, 94
- Iwo Jima (1945) 218
- Leyte Gulf (1944) 191, 192, 193, 208
- Marshall Islands (1944) 141
- Midway (1942) 65, 66, 72–73
- Peleliu (1944) 167–168
- Tarawa (1943) 117, 123

Nippon Maru 23
Nishimura, Vice-Admiral Shojo 192, 197, 209, 210, 213
Nomura Admiral Kichisaburo 18, 19–20
North Carolina, USS 96
Nowake 215

Oglala, USS 41
Okinawa (1945)
- the 10th Army advances 254–256
- action at sea 262–264
- aftermath 266–267
- assault on the Shuri defenses 259–261
- casualties 257, 259, 266–267
- Ie Shima landings 257–259
- initial operations 252–254
- the Japanese counteroffensive 261
- the last stand 265–266
- opposing commanders 248–249
- opposing plans 245–248
- origins of the campaign 145
- the push North 256–257
- the push South 264–265
- Shuri falls 264

Oklahoma, USS 22, 29, 30, **34,** 35, 40
Oldendorf, Rear-Admiral Jesse B.
- Leyte Gulf (1944) 192, 209, 210, 213, 214
- Peleliu (1944) 169, **175**

Operation *Catchpole* (1944) 140–143, 144, 147, **148, 154,** 160–161, 162–163, **164**
Operation *Detachment* (1945) 217–243
Operation *Flintlock* (1944) 140–143, 148–165
Operation *Galvanic* (1943) 117–139
Operation *Hailstone* (1944) 160
Operation *Stalemate II* (1944) 167–189
Ozawa, Vice-Admiral Jisaburo 192, 196, 198, 202, 203, 207–208, 213, 215

P-36 aircraft 32
P-38 aircraft 114
P-40 aircraft 32
P-51 aircraft 217, 230
P-400 aircraft 102
Papua New Guinea *see* New Guinea
Parry Island 163–164
Patterson, USS 99
PBY Catalina flying boats 72, 73, 76
Pearl Harbor (1941) 15–41
- aftermath 37–41
- casualties 28, 32, 37–41
- the first wave 23–31
- opening moves 19–20
- opposing commanders 15–18
- origins of the campaign 15

plans 19
preparations 20–23
the second wave 32–37
Peleliu (1944)
aftermath 187–189
Angaur Island 167, 168, 170, 173, 183–185, **184**, 188
casualties 182, 185, **186**, 187
D-Day 174–180
D+1 to D+7 180–183
D+11 to D+14 185
opposing commanders 171–172
opposing forces 173–174
opposing plans 168–171
origins of the campaign 167–168
Ulithi Island 183–185
the Umurbrogol Pocket 185–187
Pennsylvania, USS 32, **36**, 40, **46**
Philippines, the 20, 167, 188
see also Leyte Gulf, battle of (1944)
Portland, USS 122
Prince of Wales, HMS 11
Puller, Lieutenant-Colonel "Chesty"
Guadalcanal (1942) 107, 108, 110
Peleliu (1944) **171**, 171–172, 182
Pursuit, USS 128

Quincy, USS 99

Rabaul 43, 52, 99, 123–124
Raleigh, USS 29, 30, 34, 40
Ralph Talbot, USS 99
Reising submachine guns **95**
Repulse, HMS 11
Requisite, USS 128
rifles
Browning automatic rifles **95**, 122
Garand M-1 semi-automatic rifles 122
Springfield rifles **30**
Ringgold, USS 122, 128, 131, 134
rocket launchers **252**
Roi Island 142, **142**, **144**, 146, 147, **149**, 151–153, 164
Roosevelt, President Franklin D. 16, **136**, 166
Rupertus, Brigadier-General William H.
Guadalcanal (1942) 96
Peleliu (1944) 170, 171, 177, 179, 180, 181, 182, 185, 186
Russell, USS 122
Russo-Japanese War (1904–05) 19, 173
Ryan, Major Michael 119, 131, 132, 134, 136, 139
Ryujo 105

Saipan 168, 172
Santa Cruz, battle of (1942) **66**, 111
Santa Fe, USS 122
Saratoga, USS **22**, 96, 104, 105
Savo Island, battle of (1942) 94, **94**, 95, 99
Sazanami 20
SB2C Helldivers 193, **207**, **208**
Schmidt, Major-General Harry 144, 218, 219, 221, 225, 229, 230, 235, 241
Schoettel, Major John 119, 125, 131
Schroeder, USS 122
"Seahorse," the 115
Shaw, USS **15**, 41
Sherman, Rear-Admiral Frederick "Ted" 46, **46**, 200, 201, 202, 208
Sherman tanks **120**, 122, **124**, 132–133, 135–136, 139, **159**, 173, 175, 224, 226, 230, **256**
Shibasaki, Rear-Admiral Keiji 120, 122, 125, 128, 133, **133**, 134
Shigeyoshi, Vice-Admiral Inoue 44, 51, 58, 62
Shigure 210, 213
Shikoku Maru 23
Shima, Vice-Admiral Kiyohide 197, 198–199, 209, 213, 214, 215
ships, Japanese **203**
Abukuma 211
Akagi 17, 18, 23, 34, 36, 67, **69**, 74, 78–79, 81, 83, **83**
Akiguma 23
Asagumo 213
Atago 200
Chikuma **206**
Chitose 207
Chiyoda 207, 215
Chokai 206
Fuso 198, 211, 213
Haruna **78**, 198
Hatsuzuki 215
Hiei 112
Hiryu 23, 34, **66**, 80, 81, 83, 84–86
Hyuga 202, 207
Ise 202, 207
Kaga 23, 34, 36, 37, 67, 74, 78–79, 81, 82–83
Kenyo Maru 23
Kikuzuki 54
Kirishima 112
Kokuyo Maru 23
Kongo 198
Kyokuto Maru 23
Michishio 213
Mikuma 88
Mogami 88, 210, 213, 215
Musashi 198, 204, 210
Myoko **50**
Nagara 23
Nagato 198
Nippon Maru 23
Nowake 215
Ryujo 105
Sazanami 20
Shigure 210, 213
Shikoku Maru 23
Shoho 47, 54, **54**, 55, **57**, 57–58
Shokaku **20**, 23, **23**, **43**, 47, **58**, 60
Soryu **8**, 23, 74, 78, 79, 81, 82
Sotoyomo 41
Takao 200
Tama 215
Toei Maru 23
Tohu Maru 23
Ushio 20
Yahagi 262, 264
Yamashiro 198, 211–213
Yamato 198, 200, **202**, 210, 262–264
Zuiho 207, **209**
Zuikaku 23, **23**, 47, 59, 60, 198, 207, **209**
ships, US
Alwyn 32
Anderson 122
Antares 26
Arizona 29–30, 32, 34, **34**, 35, 37
Astoria **51**, 85, 99
Auburn 228
Bagley 99
Bailey 122
Birmingham 122
Blue 34, 99
Bunker Hill 122
California 34, 40
Cassin 32, **35**, **36**, 40–41
Chicago 99
Colorado 122
Condor 23
Crossbill 23
Curtiss 41
Dashiel 122, 128, 131, 134
Downes 32, **36**, 41
Enterprise 22, **22**, 26, 27, 30–31, 41, 48, **54**, 72, **73**, 76, 78, 79, 80, 81–82, 96, 104, 105, 192
Essex 122
Frazer 122
Gambier Bay 206
Gansevoort 122
Hammann 89
Heermann 205
Helena **36**, 40
Helm 31, 41, 99
Henry A. Wiley 224
Hoel 205
Honolulu 40
Hornet 72, 73, 76, 78, 79, 81–82, 105
Independence 122
Indianapolis 122, 132, 221
Intrepid 200
Jarvis 99
Johnston 205
Kitkun Bay 206
Lexington 19, 22, **22**, 46, 48, **48**, 52, 54, 57, 58, 60, 61, **61**, 62, **63**
Maryland **34**, 34–35, 40, 122, 128, **131**
Meade 122
Mobile 122
Neosho **55**
Nevada 22, 29, **31**, 32, 34, **34**, 40
New Orleans 32
North Carolina 96
Oglala 41
Oklahoma 22, 29, 30, **34**, 35, 40
Patterson 99
Pennsylvania 32, **36**, 40, **46**
Portland 122
Pursuit 128
Quincy 99
Raleigh 29, 30, 34, 40
Ralph Talbot 99
Requisite 128
Ringgold 122, 128, 131, 134
Russell 122
Santa Fe 122
Saratoga **22**, 96, 104, 105

Schroeder 122
Shaw **15,** 41
Sotoyomo 41
St Louis 35
Tennessee **34, 37,** 40, 122, 152
Utah 22, 29, 30, 41
Vestal 29–30, **34,** 41
Vincennes 99
Ward 23, 26
Washington 224
Wasp 96, 104, 105
West Virginia 31, **34, 37,** 40
Yorktown 46, 48, **49,** 54, **55,** 56, 57, 58, 59, 60, 61, 62, 63, 68, **68,** 69, 72, 73, 76, 78, 80, 84–85, **86, 88**
Shoho 47, 54, **54,** 55, **57,** 57–58
Shokaku **20,** 23, **23, 43,** 47, **58,** 60
Short, Lieutenant-General Walter C. 15, **16,** 19, 37
Shoup, Colonel David M. 119, **119,** 124, 131, 132, 135, 137
Shropshire, HMAS **213**
"Slot," the, Guadalcanal 102
Smith, Lieutenant-General Holland M. **218**
Iwo Jima (1945) 216, 218, 224, 228
Tarawa (1943) 118–119, 124, 139
Smith, Major-General Julian C. 119, 124, 132, 136, 137, 139
Solomon Islands, the 20, 52, **90,** 91
see also Guadalcanal
Soryu **8,** 23, 74, 78, 79, 81, 82
Sotoyomo, USS 41
Spearfish, USS 220
Springfield rifles **30**
Spruance, Rear-Admiral Raymond A. **218**
Iwo Jima (1945) 218, 221
Leyte Gulf (1944) 193
Marshall Islands (1944) 144
Midway (1942) 67, **67,** 72, 76, 85, 88
Okinawa (1945) 248–249, **249,** 250
Tarawa (1943) 117, 118, 132
St Louis, USS 35
Stuart light tanks 95, **99,** 137, 139
submachine guns **95**
submarines, Japanese **18**
I-17 23
I-21 23
I-23 23
midget submarines **18, 41**
submarines, US
Dace, USS 200, **200**
Darter, USS 200
Spearfish, USS 220

tactics
Japanese 103, 170–171
US 95, **124**
Takao 200
Takeo, Rear-Admiral Takagi 44, **44,** 55
Tama 215
Tanambogo 97
tanks, Japanese **180**
"Ha-Go" tanks 122, **133**
tanks, US
M10 tank destroyers 173
Sherman tanks **120,** 122, **124,** 132–133, 135–136, 139, **159,** 173, 175, 224, 226, 230, **256**
Stuart light tanks 95, **99,** 137, 139
Tarawa, battle of (1943)
aftermath 139
casualties 130, 134, **136,** 137
commanders 117–120
D-Day 125–134
D-Day +1 134–137
D-Day +2 137
D-Day +3 137–139
the defenders 133–134
opposing forces 120–123
opposing plans 123–125
origins of the campaign 117
Red Beach 1 129, 132
Red Beach 2 129–130, 132–133
Red Beach 3 131, 132–133
Tasimboko raid 105–106
Taylor, 2nd Lieutenant Kenneth 32, 34, 36
TBF/TBM Avenger aircraft 193, **195**
Tenaru, battle of the (1942) 102–104
Tennessee, USS
battle of Tarawa (1943) 122
Marshall Islands (1944) 152
Pearl Harbor (1941) **34, 37,** 40
Toei Maru 23
Tohu Maru 23
"Tojo Line" 143
"Tokyo Express" 102, 108, 114
Tomonaga, Lieutenant Joichi 74, 77, 85
torpedoes 20, **47**
Truk Island 104, 160
Tsingtao, battle of (1914) 12
Tsushima, battle of (1905) 12
Tulagi 91, **92,** 93, 96–97
Turner, Rear-Admiral Richmond Kelly **218**
Guadalcanal (1942) 94, 99, 112
Iwo Jima (1945) 218
Marshall Islands (1944) 144
Okinawa (1945) 249, 250
Tarawa (1943) 119, 122

Ulithi Island 169, 183–185, 188
Underwater Demolition Team (UDT) 168, 252
US Forces
see also aircraft, US; ships, US; weapons, US
commanders 15–18, 44–46, 66–67, 94, 117–119, 144, 171–172, 191–192, 218–219, 248–249
communications 95, 128
the Coral Sea (1942) 43–46, 48–49, 51–63
the fleet 48–49, 68–69
Guadalcanal (1942) 91, 92–93, 94, 95–115
intelligence 16, 19, 97, 104, 105–106, 168
Iwo Jima (1945) **11,** 217–243
Leyte Gulf (1944) 191–195, 195, 197–215
Marshall Islands **6,** 43, 140–143, 144–146, 148–165
Midway (1942) 65, 66–67, 68–69, 72–88
Okinawa (1945) 245, 247–267
Pearl Harbor (1941) 14–16, 19–41
Peleliu (1944) 167–170, 171–172, 173, 174–189
tactics 95, **124**
Tarawa (1943) 116–139
Ushijima, Lieutenant-General Mitsuru 245, 249, 253, 255, 263, 266
Ushio 20
Utah, USS 22, 29, 30, 41

Vandegrift, Major-General Alexander A. 93, 94, 96, 98, 107, 108
Vestal, USS 29–30, **34,** 41
Vincennes, USS 99
Vought F4U-1 Corsair fighters **262**

Wake Island 20, **54,** 140, 147, 164
Ward, USS 23, 26
Washington, USS 224
Washington Naval Treaty (1922) **69**
Wasp, USS 96, 104, 105
Watson, Major-General Thomas E. 144, 160, 163, 251
weapons, Japanese
anti-aircraft guns 125
anti-tank weapons 229, **256**
flamethrowers 173
howitzers 125
machine guns **102,** 125, **236, 262**
weapons, US
anti-aircraft guns **31**
anti-tank weapons 110
bazookas 173, **231**
Browning automatic rifles **95,** 122
flamethrowers 122, 173, 185, **230, 253, 257**
Garand M-1 semi-automatic rifles 122
grenades 185
HB-M2 machine guns **245**
howitzers 174, 222
M1917 Browning machine guns **99, 255**
M1919A4 machine guns **253**
Reising submachine guns **95**
rocket launchers **252**
Springfield rifles **30**
Wei Haiwei, battle of (1895) 11
Welch, 2nd Lieutenant George 32, 34, 36
West Virginia, USS 31, **34, 37,** 40
Weyler, Rear-Admiral George L. 210, 211
Wotje Atoll 140, 147, 148, 164

Yahagi 262, 264
Yahara, Colonel Hiromichi 249, 255, 261
Yalu River, battle of (1894) 11
Yamaguchi, Rear-Admiral Tamon 66, **66,** 77, 83, 85, 86, 168, 174
Yamamoto, Admiral Isoroku 16–17, 18, 19, 23, 41, 44, **44,** 50, 51, 56, 62, 63, 66, 71, 83
Yamashiro 198, 211–213
Yamato 198, 200, **202,** 210, 262–264
Yap Island 169
Yorktown, USS
the Coral Sea (1942) 46, 48, **49,** 52, 54, **55,** 56, 57, 58, 59, 60, 61, 62, 63
Midway (1942) 68, **68,** 69, 72, 73, 76, 78, 80, 84–85, **86, 88**

Z Operation (1944) 143
Zeke 52 fighters **71**
Zero aircraft 32, **40,** 51, 53–54, 60–61, 74, 78, 80, 95
Zuiho 207, **209**
Zuikaku 23, **23,** 47, 59, 60, 198, 207, **209**